HENRY SALT

Artist, Traveller, Diplomat, Egyptologist

Deborah Manley and Peta Rée

HENRY SALT

Artist, Traveller, Diplomat, Egyptologist

First published in Great Britain 2001 by Libri Publications Limited
Suite 296, 37 Store Street
Bloomsbury
London, WC1E 7QF

ISBN 1-901965-03-1 (Hardback)
ISBN 1-901965-04-x (Paperback)

Cover: The Pyramids and the Giza plateau by Henry Salt; Henry Salt, aged about 20, by John Hoppner, c. 1800.

To Roy, who was with us when we began, and to our children.

Exclusive distribution outside North America by
I. B. Tauris and Co. Ltd, 6 Salem Road, London W2 4BU.

Designed and typeset by Libri Publications Limited
Printed and bound in Great Britain by Biddles Limited of Guildford

Contents

List of Illustrations

1. Henry Salt, aged about 20, by John Hoppner, c. 1800.

2. Henry Salt, by John James Halls, c. 1815.

3. Henry Salt in 1815 by an unknown female artist in Geneva.

4. View at Trinchinum, India, by Henry Salt.

5. The manner of crossing a river between Point de Galle and Colombo, Ceylon, by Henry Salt.

6. William Coffin in the war dress of Abyssinia, by John James Halls, c. 1830.

7. Nathaniel Pearce in Abyssinian dress, by Henry Salt, 1806.

8. View of the stela at Axum, by Henry Salt.

9. The residence of the Ras at Antalo, Abyssinia, by Henry Salt.

10. Mehemet Ali, Viceroy of Egypt, from John Madox's *Excursions*, 1826.

11. Sir Joseph Banks, Chairman of the Trustees of the British Museum, by T. Phillips, 1810.

12. John Lewis Burckhardt disguised as Sheik Ibrahim, by Henry Salt.

13. Giovanni Battista Belzoni by Gauci, from Belzoni's *Narrative*, published in 1820.

14. William John Bankes MP, by Sir George Hayter, c. 1832.

15. The Sphinx uncovered by Captain Caviglia and recorded by Henry Salt, 1818.

16. Dr Madden attending a lady of the harem, by Henry Salt, 1826.

17. Reproduction of a scene in Seti's tomb in the Valley of the Kings, by Henry Salt, 1818.

18. The sarcophagus of Seti I in the Sir John Soane Museum, from J. Britton's *The Union of architecture, sculpture and painting exemplified by...the house and galleries of John Soane*, published in 1827.

Acknowledgements: Bodleian Library, Oxford: 4, 5, 6, 7, 8, 9, 10, 12, 13, 15, 16, 18; National Trust: 14; The British Museum: 17; Private collections: cover, 1, 2, 11.

Acknowledgements

We would like to acknowledge the help given to us by the following people (and many others) and to thank them.

Reginald Alton, Professor Emeritus, St Edmund's Hall, Oxford; the Earl of Belmore; Mrs Betti; Sarah Bridges, formerly of the Dorsetshire Record Office; Peter Clayton; Neil Cooke; Harry James, formerly of the Department of Egyptology at the British Museum; Roger Keersmacher, of Graffito Graffiti, Belgium; Jill Lever, formerly Curator of the Royal Institute of British Architects print collection; Dr Jaromir Malek, of the Griffith Institute, Oxford University; Virginia Murray of John Murray Ltd; Professor Richard Pankhurst, of Addis Ababa University, Ethiopia; Professor John Rodenbeck, of the American University Cairo; Sir Michael Salt; Dr Jason Thompson, of the American University Cairo; Dr Patricia Usick; Dr Hugh Vernon Jackson of Cairo; and the staffs of the British Library Manuscript Room, the Public Record Office, the National Library of Malta, and, above all, the understanding staff of the Upper Reading Room of the Bodleian Library, Oxford.

Mirza Mumbarack

Duphonet I.

Surtsullie I.

Harrarat I.

Emallie I.

Bernadee I.
Dudhbaret I.
Dohul I.

Dubarut I.

Myzartuban or Zeteban I.

Daza I.
Delfeida I.
Dalcoos I.

Saiel Arabie

Irwee I.
Agerbeschid

DHALAC

A l a l a o u

Arkeeko

Arkeko
B.

Aduli
Illerbeh
Six Wells
Leberee
B.

Shillokee

Coast Line of Br.

Shillokee
We'ah
B.

Hamhama

Saiel Malie

Chummah

MISRAS I.

Dry
Arkeeley Bay

Taranta
Orine

Hurter
Hurter S.E. Point

Arenah
Sarbo Zeghir I.
Gebel
Buchah

Howakel I.

Opsian Bay

Markelah

HAZORTE TRIBE

Dixan
B.
Saddon
B.
Lila

Taranta
B.

Geble Morch

Geble Sarbo

Ras Ratta

Sister Hills

Hamhammo

Hadawi

RUSAMO TRIBE

Ras Amphila

Ras

Sadoo

Hadhadhid
B.

Burying Ground

Thuddo

Assoobah
Bur.g Ground

Illtilah
the Pass

Fremona
B.

TARANTA
Mt.

Dixan

Zerai Plain

Hadogwe

Hade-shad

Daroo Tree

Bakanka
Maybo
Barraddo Wells

Mandoba

Sewarré or Serawe Plain

Abha
Market

Hade-kowe

Asceriah

Gurgubbo
Pass

Geshen

Village

Stream of Nuzeranch

Recaito

Negote

Pass
Springs

Ruinous
Villages

Adowa
B.

Axum
B.

Awarledo

Pass

Shihah

R. Degai

Angwil

Gunduftchi

Debra Muttai V.s

Calaut

Afharshen

Gullimuckida
Ersubha

AGOWMA DISTRICT

Mumsai

Genater

Fremona

Adowa

Axum

Abba Garama

Abussama

Calam Negus

Bashaw Guebra Eyat's Man.
Fit Ays

Plain of Ayaddah
with 12 Villages.

Fit Aurai Yasous
Man.

Pass

Takota

Ayto Guebras Vill.e

Stream

Riv.r Werie

Ayto Guebras
Residence

Vill.e

Rocky

Gallybudda

Mansion of Debib

Abukasubha Church

Akbara M.t
Pass

Admara

Hasemko

Vill.e

Derhah

Gibbeh

Plain
or
Sambela

Rocky Hills

Muccullah

Lahaina

ANTALOW

Pass

Chelicut

R

I

Map of the Nile and the Red Sea, from Narrative of the Life and Adventures of Giovanni Finati, etc, dictated by himself and edited by Wm. John Bankes Esq.

MEDITERRANEAN SEA

CYPRUS

Aleppo
Antioch
Latichea
Kalaat el Medyk
Hamah
Tripoli
Baalbec
Hems
Beirout
Damascus
Missemie
Sayda / Saida
Sidon
Tyrus / Tyre
SYRIA
Hauran
L. Houle
Acre
Mt Carmel
L. Taberias
Oomkais
Nazareth
Dierash
Bostra
Jaffa
Bisart
Assalt
Ascalon
Jerusalem
Gaza
Hebron
Wady Mojeb
Dead Sea
El Arish
Karack
Alexandria
Bay of Aboukir
Damietta
Menouf
Lake Menzaleh
Tineh
Mansourah
Matarieh
Pyramids
Geezeh
CAIRO
Suez
DESERT
Shobeck
Memphis
Wady Mousa (Petra)
Meddoon
Palmyra
Benysouef
Minieh
EGYPT
Ashmouneim
Ben y Hassan
Melawi
Sheik Abbadi
Akaba
Mt Sinai
Tor
Monfalloot
Ras Mahomet
Moyleh
Siout
Gau
Tahta
Echmim
Girgeh
Gheneh
Dendera
Guft
Herment
Coseir
Thebes
Esne
Edfou
Medina
Redesia
Jedeed Bogaz
Koum Omba
Bedrionin
Great Oasis
The Cataracts
Assouan
Yambo
Beriss
Phile I.
Tayfa
Kalapshe
Girshe
Dakke
Maharraka
NUBIA
Amada W. Sebouch
Derr
Taraba
Bisce
Abousombul
Ibrim
Gulla
Basille
Barusce
Wady Halfa
Second Cataract
MECCA
Taif
Djidda
Semneh
M. Arafat
Succeot
Say I. Amara
Matluas
Tinareh
Mograt
Dongola
Argo
DONGOLA
SHAGEJAH
Ruins & Pyramids Merowi
Old Dongola
Corti
Berber
Mogram R.
Souakin
Lid
Confitta
DARFUR
Damer
Messorat
RED SEA
ARABIA
HEDJAZ
Shendy
Alfayha
Alefoan
Arkeeko
Loheya
KORDOVAN
Fasuolo
Sennaar
Bahr el Abiad
Mokha

Euphrates R.
Tigris R.

Dareia

Prologue

N Pearce 1819
Five months from Addwar
in Abyssinia, after being
in that Country 14 years
in the service of the EARL
of Mountnorris and H SALT Esq
March XXXI MDCCCXIX

The temple island of Philae is one of the earth's magical places. From a jetty on the dam-formed lake above the First Cataract of the Nile, we embarked in one of the old wooden motor launches with canvas awnings, and, leaving the dusty shore and the insistence of the vendors of tourist junk behind, puttered across the pale water, among rocky islands like bathing elephants. At last, round the heft of one grey-brown flank, the honey-gold pillars and pylons of Philae appeared, rising from the still water. No tourist party cluttered the hot afternoon, and we wandered almost alone among the columns and porticos and into the cool secret gloom of the inner chambers.

Among the gods and hieroglyphs of the Ptolemies incised upon the walls, we began to notice later inscriptions, themselves also history, and seeming, in the numinous light, as remote as, but even more evocative than, the carvings of the Pharaohs.

Here was recorded, in March 1799, the arrival of Napoleon's army under General Desaix; there, with less martial elation, the deaths in 1884-5 of "9 Officers and 92 NCOs and Men of the Heavy Camel Regiment", during the unsuccessful attempt to rescue General Gordon from Khartoum. Everywhere were the roughly-scratched names of those who wanted to record "I was here", but said no more. N. Pearce, with his so detailed, so enigmatic message, caught at our imagination.

The first inscription was carved on a wall of the small, square, sky-open building called the Kiosk, or Pharaoh's Bedstead. At the back of the 'Birth House' behind the first pylon of the temple, we met N. Pearce again:

March XXXI MDCCCXIX
N Pearce
de la BRETAGNE
est de retour de L'Abyssinie

ou il reste XIIII ans au service de
L'EARL de Mountnorris et H SALT Esq
25 Years from his native Country 40 yrs old
Born at Acton near LONDON
March XXXI MDCCCXIX

Who was N. Pearce? How had he come from Abyssinia to Philae, and why had he been in that country in the first place? In what way had he served the Earl of Mountnorris and H. Salt Esq.? Across 170 years, the man seemed to challenge us — there is a story here, if you can find it. We could not resist.

From *Burke's Peerage* we learnt that George Annesley, Viscount Valentia, later Earl of Mountnorris (1770-1844), travelled to Abyssinia in 1805, to survey the coast and investigate the possibilities of opening up trade with the country. At least a connection with Abyssinia was there. The *Dictionary of National Biography* yielded up Henry Salt Esq., (1780-1827)... traveller and collector of antiquities...went on an eastern tour, to India, Ceylon and Abyssinia, with Viscount Valentia...was British Consul-General in Egypt, 1816-1827.

But Pearce himself must surely elude us; the servants even of the famous seldom leave so much as their names to posterity. But no — with an admirable eccentricity, the editors of the *DNB* had decided that Nathaniel Pearce (1779-1820) was worthy of inclusion. Even from the brief account of his life, one could see why they found him irresistible. Traveller and scapegrace, his adventures read like the scenario for a Hollywood swashbuckler.

Here was undoubtedly a story — our curiosity was whetted rather than satisfied. One source led to another, enticing us into a world of amazing events and fascinating characters — so many speaking in their own voices, in books, diaries and letters, not only of their travels in Egypt, but of each other. And one man was connected to them all, as friend, employer, patron or mediator with the Egyptian authorities — the British Consul-General, Henry Salt.

In the long history of European interest in the antiquities of Egypt, the period of Salt's consulship is peculiarly significant, for at its beginning the emphasis was still almost entirely on the exploitation of Egyptian antiquities as a source of exotica for public or private collections, but by its end, as the hieroglyphs began to yield up their secrets, the era of scholarly interest in Egypt's tremendous past was well begun.

To us today, the wholesale removal of the treasures of antiquity from their countries of origin seems disgraceful. However, it was against the background of an undisturbed conviction of the right of European nations to take away all they admired of the culture of less 'civilised' lands, that Henry Salt arrived in Egypt in 1816, to take up the post of His Britannic Majesty's Consul-General. One of his duties was to learn about the history of Egypt; he had also been urged by Sir Joseph Banks, President of the Trustees of the British Museum, to seek antiquities to enhance the collections of the Museum.

It was an activity which mirrored Anglo-French political rivalry in Egypt: as Richard Burton observed, "the archaeological field became a battle-plain for armies of Dragomans and Fellah-navvies. One was headed by the redoubtable Salt; the other owned the command of Drovetti [the French Consul], whose sharp Italian brain had done much to promote the great Pasha's interests."[1] And he, Mehemet Ali, the "great Pasha", sat between. He placed no historic value on the spoils of a country with which he had no ancestral ties — but he judged shrewdly the political value of 'permissions to dig' as a lever in his machinations to keep England and France in a co-operative rather than a coercive attitude towards his rule.

However, this book is not intended as a critique of early nineteenth-century approaches to Egyptology, but is primarily a biography of Henry Salt. Apart from his antiquarian activities, it deals with less well-known aspects of Salt's life. For example, his Consular work is often dismissed as merely light duties of no importance, because his frequently delicate diplomatic negotiations with the Pasha were unknown to his contemporaries and have been largely ignored by subsequent researchers. The importance of his two missions to Abyssinia, also, have been underrated by those whose interests lie in Egyptology, although in Ethiopia today it is for these that he is remembered, while his Egyptian career is little known.

Posterity has treated Henry Salt with less than the kindness and liberality which characterised his own behaviour towards his acquaintance. In secondary sources, books written in many cases more than a century after Salt's death, a picture is presented of a vacillating, procrastinating, insensitive man, eager to aggrandise himself at the expense of a more deserving colleague, greedy to make a fortune from the spoils of Egypt; sad, lonely and frustrated; even (according to E. M. Forster), "rather shady".[2] Did we really want to spend the years necessary to research this book in the company of such an unattractive character?

But, from the original sources, the testimony of Salt's life and writings, and those of his friends, a very different person soon emerged — not faultless, but by and large a courageous, honourable, generous and kindly man, held in esteem by his employers and affection by his friends. Though his health and the circumstances of his life were often to leave him sad, lonely or frustrated, he seems seldom to have lost his dry sense of humour nor his forbearance under provocation. So, this book, besides being an account of extraordinary people in an exciting era, is a long overdue appreciation of Henry Salt.

1

A Lichfield Man

" SURELY you will nowhere find a better society, or truer friends than at Lichfield." Far from England, beneath the unforgiving sun of Egypt, Henry Salt often yearned to be with the friends of his youth, to see the "beautiful spires" of his native city and to wander the cool green fields of his childhood.[1]

Even today, despite the demolitions and accretions of the last 200 years, Lichfield in the county of Stafford retains at its heart, around the cathedral close, much of its charm. Henry Salt now seems almost forgotten in his native place, but in his own time and in his own sphere, he was almost as well-known as the great Dr Johnson, Lichfield's most famous son.

The youngest of the eight children of Thomas and Alice Salt, Henry was born on 14 June 1780 and baptised ten days later in the nearby parish church of St Mary. Thomas Salt, the only son of a well-to-do tradesman, had served as a surgeon in a militia regiment for a number of years before he settled in Lichfield. In 1766 he married Alice, the daughter of Cary Butt, also a surgeon, who in due course relinquished his practice to his son-in-law. Thomas was a sensible, well-educated man, with a "no inconsiderable share of original humour." Through temperate habits, hard work, and an almost parsimonious frugality, he was able to to raise and educate his numerous family with credit.[2]

Henry's sisters remembered him as a sweet-natured child who, though volatile and quick-tempered, was always amenable to correction. Even in childhood, his kindness reached beyond his family circle and, visiting Lichfield in later years, he would always call on "all the old washerwomen, &c, &c", whom he had then known.

Educated first at the free school in Lichfield, Henry, aged ten or eleven, was sent to a boarding school at Market Bosworth, Leicestershire. A former schoolfellow remembered him as clever but very idle, "full of spirits and fun, and the ringleader in every frolic and probably in every mischievous prank"; he was kind-hearted and very popular with the other boys. Another fellow pupil never forgot that he owed his life to Henry's quick wits and courage in rescuing him from a deep pond into which he had fallen. Though disinclined to lessons, Henry was always a voracious reader, and his sister Bessy Morgan recalled that when he had money given to him, he spent most of it on books, and in fine weather would lie reading for hours in the garden.

While at Market Bosworth, he suffered a severe illness, which damaged his spleen. Disease of the spleen was the eventual cause of his death, and probably accounted for many of the illnesses he suffered throughout his life, and also for some of the languor of manner remarked upon by many people in his last few years.

When he was fourteen, Henry was sent to Birmingham to study classics under his eldest brother, Dr John Butt Salt, and other subjects with various tutors. He met Thomas Bingham Richards, who was to remain a lifelong friend, in his drawing classes. After a year or so, Henry returned to Lichfield to complete his education, and having decided to become an artist, took drawing lessons from John Glover, the watercolour landscape painter.[3] Then his father was persuaded to place him with another landscape painter, the Royal Academician, Joseph Farington, in London.[4] The choice of both masters indicates that Mr Salt and his advisers were somewhat ignorant about art, for Henry's ambition was to be a portrait painter, and neither artist, though talented in his own field, had much knowledge of portraiture.

On 14 August 1797, Farington, an indefatigable diarist, noted that he had found lodgings for his new pupil with a Mr Young. On 24 September, Henry moved in, joined a few days later by Samuel Lane from Norfolk. Also aged 17, Samuel had been deaf since a childhood accident, but apparently not completely so, for Farington arranged for the two boys to learn French, at one guinea for eight lessons.[5]

On 25 September, Farington recorded that "Salt began to draw". He was a conscientious teacher, unlike many other artists, whose pupils were expected to learn by dogsbodying, with little formal instruction. Samuel Lane told Farington that Henry was "convinced that our manner of studying under you occasioned our going on so fast afterwards. The attention & correctness which you required from us laid the best foundation for our future progress."[6]

On 6 January 1799 Farington had a "long conversation" with Salt about his future, because he had received a letter from a Mr White of Lichfield, whose interest is unexplained, proposing that Henry should return home and teach drawing, "at which He expressed surprise, and declared How disagreeable such an employment wd. be to him. I then told him it was time to determine what department of art He wd. fix in which to practise. He said portrait painting. I told him I had endeavoured to avoid byassing his mind to any particular pursuit, to Landscape painting, for instance, by setting before Him my works or tempting him by my practise. That Portrait painting undoubtedly offers more certain employ than any other branch, of Course there is less risk. That Landscape painting is not so much encouraged as it has not the advantage of being supported by self love, while portraits from that motive will always be had at from the highest to the lowest prices." Henry said he feared his father expected him to be able to support himself at the end of three years, and would be very unwilling to help him any further, "but that He wd. rather run any risk of difficulties than devote himself to the employ of a drawing master."[7]

Henry's appalled response may have aroused Farington's pity for he read him a letter from his brother John, who "seemed to have a much more liberal Idea of what his future employment shd. be...and on his saying that His Brother will soon be in town — we agreed to refer this conversation to him." John said he was "fully of opinion that He shd. proceed in the portrait line". Now aware how poorly the boys were being prepared for their projected profession, Farington set Henry and Samuel to drawing studies of figures taken from great artists; later they drew plaster casts, and began oil painting, and finally he entered them in the Royal Academy Antique School.

A few months after Henry came to London, he heard of the arrival from Colchester of John James Halls. Robert Halls, younger half-brother of John's father, had married Henry's eldest sister Jane in 1795. Henry lost no time in calling upon his "half-nephew", who was also an artist, and the two soon became inseparable. John Halls, who was eventually to be his friend's biographer, described Henry when they first met as "a tall, thin, and somewhat ungain-looking young man, of insinuating address, and of frank and pleasing manners."[8] Four years the elder, Halls confesses he was at this time the naive boy from the provinces compared to Henry; on the other hand, he was far more advanced in artistic skills and could help Henry in the difficulties with which he was struggling, recognising that due to his so-far inappropriate training, he had "a sad up-hill game to play."

Attending the Royal Academy Antique School was an experience Henry would have gladly missed. At that time, said Halls, the school's standards were low. The students were almost totally unsupervised, and there was "a lamentable display of idleness, vulgarity, and indecorum...very repugnant to a young man of Salt's natural good taste and acquired habits, for, thoughtless and eccentric as he occasionally appeared, he never was low-minded or ungentlemanlike."[9] Years later, passing Somerset House with Halls, Henry would point to the building with an involuntary shudder at the recollection of the disgust and discomfort he had experienced. It was not surprising that the volatile Henry made little progress there.

Often desperately frustrated and depressed, he struggled on, only too often sinking beneath the weight of his own artistic shortcomings, as his lively imagination seethed with ideas which he was without the technical mastery to realise. When his spirits were low, he appeared "the very image of inertness and misery." Halls would try to cheer him by pointing out that the attainment of skill was a very slow but progressive process, and that his very consciousness of his own deficiencies gave the best hope for his ultimate success. Gradually and painfully his innate sensibility, allied to an accurate eye and the ability to persevere when he really set himself to, began to over-come many of his difficulties. Even so, at the end of his time with Farington, he was still in no position to support himself.

It was clear that years of drudgery, disappointment and poverty lay before him and that, even then, success was not guaranteed. The thought of such prolonged, dreary and possibly unrewarded effort was almost unbear-able to one of Henry's temperament. Halls considered that his mind was of "too versatile and excursive a nature" for him to absorb himself in the often boring grind necessary to attain the skills he needed. He had talent, taste and critical judgement, and a real love of art, but more in the manner of a con-noisseur than of a working painter. Or, as Farington put it, "I was only apprehensive that He might devote rather more of his time to visiting his acquaintance and to talking about art than to practising it."[10]

There were distractions, too, in the temptations of the metropolis. Eager for experience, he was continually falling into indiscretions, for which his better feelings would then reproach him. Inevitably, given his warm and affectionate nature, some of these indiscretions involved women, but, though condemning his "irregular and wild conduct", Halls admitted he could scarcely recall anyone "more capable than he was of the most tender and durable attachment, or who displayed a greater degree of generosity and disinterested kindness to the more amiable portion of human nature". Convivial and charming, he had a large and lively circle of friends, but he was content to live frugally, and good sense kept him from serious trouble, "so that it may truly be said of him," claims Halls in a splendid phrase, "that not many men have escaped with greater impunity from the dangerous vortex of London dissipation."[11]

One of Henry's most amiable (and unusual) characteristics was his ability to accept criticism. He did not always act on good advice, but he did not forget it, and remembered warmly those who had "warned him from the paths of destruction". On one occasion, Henry's advisers tried to detach him from a girl with whom he had fallen in love. There was nothing disreputable about the affair; pretty and pleasant, Kate came of a respectable family — but she was only sixteen, Henry scarcely older, and neither had financial prospects that would enable them to marry. His friends, having no idea of the depth of his feelings, dealt out advice and ridicule "in no very measured terms", but he bore it all with good-humoured forbearance.

They might have spared him their teasing, for Kate died of a 'decline' early in 1800. Heartbroken, Henry shut himself up in his rooms, for several days refusing to eat or drink or be consoled. His first act as he began to emerge from despair was to paint a portrait of Kate from memory. Halls had never seen the girl, but he realised that it was an extraordinary likeness when he met her brother over thirty years later and recognised him from his resemblance to his sister's picture. For many years, Henry would speak sadly to Halls of his lost first love; even as late as 1819, when Halls' sister, Julia Hanson, asked him to stand godfather to her expected child, he asked that, if a girl, she be called Katherine, "a name on several accounts very dear to me from recollections of a sister, and another person long dead."[12]

Henry had one bad fault, that of putting off till tomorrow what should have been done yesterday. Halls said that he carried this practice of procrastination "in early life to a greater excess than I have ever observed it". He often scolded Henry, who accepted his rebukes meekly, once writing to him, "most of the difficulties I have met with have taken their source from it, and though I have often reasoned with myself on my folly in giving way to it, yet hitherto, I fear, it has increased with my years. It is time to rouse myself from this infantile slumber, so disgraceful to my age, and exert the energy of my mind, the strength of which has not yet been tried. It will be kind in you to lend an assisting hand. Hints on this subject cannot be thrown away, and be assured I shall consider them proofs of a friendship which becomes dearer to me daily, as I grow more sensible of its value."[13]

Halls suspected that the childhood disease that had damaged Henry's spleen was at the root of his "general indolence". His frequent physical lethargy would oppress his intellectual capacity, while his often depressed spirits would react unfavourably on his health. In no other way could Halls account for the extraordinary contradictions he could evince in his mental and physical efforts, for, "like the wild Indian, he slumbered away existence till the calls of necessity, or ambition, awoke him from his trance, and compelled him to bring into action those powers of body and mind with which he was so highly gifted...with his game in view, the eagle itself pounces not on its prey with more velocity and certainty than he displayed whenever occasion called for exertion."[14]

Thomas Salt had expected the almost three years his son had spent with Farington to fit him to support himself and naturally became impatient when he heard this was not so. Halls, himself by now established, fully realised the desperate situation of his friend. With no practical knowledge of portrait painting, without adequate financial resources, and with "the feelings and high spirit of a gentleman", Henry, he believed, was headed for disaster, and he strongly advised him to confess all frankly to his father (including, it is hinted, some debt), and to persuade him to allow further instruction from some leading portrait painter. Henry's father agreed to support him during a further period of tuition. At Halls' suggestion, John Hoppner RA, the most eminent portraitist of the day, was the master decided upon. Hoppner offered to take Henry as a pupil for twelve months, for 100 guineas, and at the end of that time, possibly keep him on as an assistant at three guineas a week.[15]

Salt's professional relationship with Farington was at an end, but they had one more long conversation when Henry called to settle his final account in July, and Farington "gave him such advice as I thought might be of service to Him". Henry continued to call on his old master from time to time.

With his efforts at last properly directed, Henry worked hard. Within a few months Hoppner wrote to Halls that he was pleased with his friend's progress, and behaviour — "but how can he fail in either under such a master? By the time I have licked him into shape he will be as great a bear as any of us. Don't be jealous!"[16]

This warm and kindly style seems to have been typical of Hoppner and his family. Henry and Halls were always welcome to drop in uninvited, and Henry was treated more as a member of the family than a pupil. Hoppner painted an affectionate and perceptive portrait of him at this time. In likenesses made in his mid-thirties, the boy depicted here has learned to guard his evidently vulnerable and emotional nature from the public eye.

The pleasant tutelage was brought to a sudden halt in March 1801. Through a chance meeting with an acquaintance from Lichfield, Henry heard that his mother was dying. Her illness had been concealed from him by his father. Deeply attached to his mother, Henry was distraught at the thought of her dying while he was far away. He must go to Lichfield at once — but, as not infrequently, he was penniless. Hoppner unhesitatingly said he must go and provided the necessary funds. Though Henry repaid the money, he felt the kindness beyond repayment, and was always to remember it with tears in his eyes.

When he first arrived, his mother was barely conscious, but a little later she recognised him with great pleasure, "called me her dear lad, and entreated that I would not go back again," he wrote to Halls. A few days later she was much worse, and all hope seemed gone. He asked Halls to send him some painting materials, as his father wished him to make a portrait of her. But the next day, 25 March, Alice Salt died; "My brother, the doctor, and my eldest sister, did not arrive until it was too late. My own sufferings are almost lost in the poignancy of theirs. How grateful do I feel to Mr Hoppner, by whose means I enjoy the only consolation that now supports me. I would not have given up the satisfaction I feel in having seen my dearest mother for anything on earth."[17]

This was the last letter Halls received from Lichfield for many weeks, for Henry himself fell seriously ill. At first he suffered only an extreme lethargy, but in a week or two more violent symptoms in the stomach and bowels heralded an attack of malignant typhus fever. A doctor was sent for, and found Henry in such a state that he warned Mr Salt that even if "by almost a miracle", his son should recover, he would probably be an idiot for life. Happily, when the fever passed, though he remained for many weeks "in the most lamentable state of imbecility", he very slowly recovered his faculties.

When he heard of his friend's illness from Henry's brother Charles, Halls wrote at once, but it was 19 May before he received a few almost illegible lines and almost another three weeks before Henry was able to write at greater length.

"Everything since my illness has gone on with me by fits and starts. First I was seized with an eating fit (no bad sign, you will say). This still continues. Next, a writing fit, during which paroxysm, poetry, French, Latin, and English, by turns employed my pen...I have lately been tormented by a fidgety fit, therefore thank your stars for so long a letter, as I have not sat so long for this week past; and yet, my dear Halls, I am far from well. I fear I shall be an invalid for the summer. Weakness still oppresses me, and I am plagued with painful boils, some as large as pigeons' eggs; my mind, too, is not quite at ease; anxiety to get to town, and the wish to pursue my profession, hang as weights upon me..."[18]

During his illness, his father guessed he was in financial difficulties and without an angry word undertook to settle everything. Eased of these worries, and much sooner than he had feared, by July Henry was back in London, eager to take up his studies with Hoppner. He was now, says Halls, "exceedingly stout and strong". He seemed to have acquired an increased vigour and energy and had grown into a "fine, personable-looking young man", with a somewhat commanding air. Had it not been for the wig he was obliged to wear while his hair recovered from its shaving while he was ill, it would have been difficult to believe that only a few months before he had been near to death.

Henry's skills had improved considerably under Hoppner's tuition, and towards the end of 1801 he took some "very humble" rooms in Panton Street, Haymarket, and set out on his professional career. Hoppner gave him picture-copying work when he could, and various friends commissioned their portraits — at bargain prices. He had a knack for catching a resemblance, "for he had a remarkably quick perception of character", but he still lacked that knowledge of the "management and conduct" of a picture only to be acquired by the years of practice and experience his early training had denied him. These failings almost guaranteed that he could not succeed in a profession which Halls frankly admits depended "greatly upon caprice and fashion", so that not only talent but also luck was necessary to be certain of even a modest income and reputation.

Henry, so eager for the world's recognition, yet so easily reduced to depression and apathy by difficulties, was only too aware that fame and fortune as an artist were probably beyond his grasp, and he could not tolerate the idea of existence as a mere hack. He determined to escape his dismal situation at the first opportunity that might arise.

It is not often that a chance encounter leads to the complete alteration of one's apparent destiny, but so it was for Henry Salt. On 4 June 1799, Henry's maternal uncle, the Reverend Thomas Simon Butt, accompanied his friend, George Annesley, Viscount Valentia (1770-1844), to Fuseli's gallery in Pall Mall. Only one other person was there, a young man who immediately came over and spoke to Mr Butt "in a very cordial manner, but was received with so much coolness that he directly retired." Thinking this odd, Valentia asked who the young man was. Butt replied he did not know, but had supposed him an acquaintance of the Viscount. When Valentia assured him he was not, but that it appeared from his manner he was some one who knew Butt well, he went back to the stranger, and was soon in friendly conversation. He brought him to Valentia, exclaiming, "Why it is my nephew, Henry Salt!" Not having seen Henry since boyhood, Butt had failed to recognise him, while Henry, shocked and hurt that his uncle should, as he supposed, be ashamed to acknowledge him when in the company of one who "bore the appearance of a man of rank and fashion", had turned away without giving his name.[19]

This account was taken by Halls from Valentia's own diary, using "as nearly as possible" the original words. The source is important, for one of the slurs that has been cast on Salt is that he scraped acquaintance with a lord, in the hope of furthering his own interests. But it is perfectly clear from Valentia's account that he, who was not unconscious of his own status, had no sense that this was so, and it is certain that Henry would have felt himself lacking in courtesy, let alone family duty, had he not approached his uncle, no matter whom he was with.

In fact, had Henry recognised Valentia, he had excellent grounds for introducing himself, since the Viscount already had strong connections with his family. Thomas Butt's elder brother George, Rector of Kidderminster and King's Chaplain, had tutored Valentia for three years, and it was under his roof that the Viscount became a close friend of a fellow pupil, Henry's brother John. From then on, whenever he was in London, he saw a great deal of Henry, and introduced him to his family and friends.

It was nearly three years later that this friendship suddenly offered Henry a chance of escape from his hated life as an unsuccessful portrait painter. Valentia announced that he was planning a voyage to India; instantly, Henry seized his opportunity: he begged Valentia to take him along, as combined draftsman and secretary. It was not uncommon, before the camera, for wealthy travellers to be accompanied by an artist. Valentia, somewhat reluctantly, agreed to take him, moved, one suspects, more by affection for both Salt brothers than by any real belief that Henry would prove useful.

Samuel Lane, calling on Farington in April 1802, told him that Henry was to go to India in June with Valentia, and that "He means to paint portraits and make views, — that Lord Valentia is to bear His expences, and in case of His Lordships death to leave an allowance to bring him home, and in case He wishes to remain in India to get him an appointment."[20]

And so Henry Salt, through a chance meeting and an opportunity determinedly grasped, was set on a course which would shape his whole future life and career.

2

Voyage to the East

" ON THE 3rd of June, 1802, I left London, accompanied by Mr Henry Salt, as my Secretary and Draftsman, in order to embark on board the *Minerva,* extra East Indiaman..." So begins Viscount Valentia's account of his voyage to the East. It reveals him as a man capable of shrewd observation, who, securely confident of his own judgement, was always ready to point out ways of improving social and economic situations in the countries he visited. The impression that he would have loved to interfere, had he not been but passing through, is borne out by his activities when he did have an opportunity to institute reforms.

Although the three fat volumes of Valentia's *Travels* mainly recount events from his own viewpoint, Salt shared in those experiences. These years of travelling were to be formative, giving him a breadth of experience in dealing with all manner of situations and people; he was being better fitted to be a Consul in an Eastern land than most diplomats. At the same time, he was meeting influential people on terms impossible to him without Valentia's patronage, for the Viscount treated his young secretary, if not precisely as an equal, at least more as protegé than employee.

Once it was settled that he should accompany Valentia, Salt was in his element: "full of life, activity and hope, he was no longer the depressed and dejected being he had previously appeared for many months. The world seemed opened before him, and his sanguine spirit had already, in imagination, subdued every anticipated difficulty that might be opposed to his progress."[1]

But, as departure drew near, his spirits were inevitably affected by the thought of leaving family and friends. A parting of several years' duration was then a more emotionally-fraught affair than it is today. Letters would take weeks, if they arrived at all, and, as well as danger for the voyagers themselves, it was inevitable that one or more loved ones were parted with forever. But the bustle of preparation, and then the excitement of new scenes and experiences could alleviate Salt's feelings, while Halls felt for some months afterwards "like one who had suddenly been bereft of some important member of his body."[2]

Though Valentia and Salt left London on 3 June, due to contrary winds it was not until the 20th that the *Minerva* left England behind. Nine days brought them to Madeira, where they stayed a few days. On 25 July, they crossed the equator. As it was a Sunday, those on board crossing 'the line' for the first time were spared the "immemorial custom" of being shaved and ducked. This rite of passage took place later; even then, the Captain's passengers were exempted, while "the midshipmen and my servant were most mercifully dealt with". Like most servants who accompanied travelling gentlemen, sharing their adventures while almost certainly suffering far more discomfort, this young servant of Valentia is never named, but Halls identifies him as William Coffin, a man who was to play an important part in Salt's life.

When they reached St Helena on 20 August, Valentia and Salt received kindness and hospitality from the local gentry. A stay of five weeks enabled the energetic Viscount to study and comment upon the island's flora and fauna, social life and economy, while Salt began to prove his usefulness by drawing botanical specimens and sketching local views. They set sail again on 23 September, delayed two weeks beyond expectation by the late arrival of their travelling companion, the East Indiaman *Lord Eldon*, a ship of inferior sailing capacity.

Salt wrote to Halls, painting a vivid picture of life on board: "We are now about two hundred miles from the Cape; the weather is remarkably fine...We had, indeed, one or two severe squalls this morning, but it is nothing when one is used to it...I have at last got rid of the sea-sickness, with which I suffered very much until some time after my leaving St. Helena...

"The manner in which we live aboard ship, is, upon the whole, not so bad as one might reasonably expect, yet, God knows, it is bad enough.

"Imprimis: — It is very much like being hung up in a cage, and swung from one side of the room to the other; but what is this but necessary exercise? and though, as I often think, the motion very much resembles that which a crow must experience when perched on the end of an ash bough, which shakes to and fro with the wind, yet this only assists our animal frame in its necessary operations, and serves to digest the quantity of excellent provisions which we daily consume. We are, indeed, stowed away at night like so many malefactors dangling in chains, where we are continually awakened by the creaking of ropes, the harsh grating of the rudder, the piping of the boatswain, and a few other equally amusing sounds; but this will only teach us, on our return, how to relish a peaceful home, though in small lodgings, and moreover affords ample time for reflection.

"The *Minerva,* being an extra ship, is not of course so large as the regular East Indiamen; but on this account we have no reason to complain. Lord Valentia has one half of the roundhouse, which is about as large as your small closet, and I have a cabin below, about six feet by five. The cuddy, in which we assemble together at dinner, &c. is an excellent room, where we get very handsome 'feeds'."[3]

Salt described their meals: meat both salt and fresh (these great ships

11

carried live sheep, pigs and poultry), and puddings and pies, and praised the pleasantness of the company. Captain Weltden "has been accustomed to very good company, and has little of the sailor's character about him, except it be in an openness of heart and a little desire of 'cutting a dash', peculiar to these sons of the ocean." One of the mates had once been master of a slave-ship, "which has given him a slight tinge of the barbarian; yet at bottom he is, I believe, humane, and a man of strict integrity", while the surgeon was "a complete gentleman; but, what is better, he has a well-inclined heart, and a spirit of honour, which shines resplendent amidst the foibles which he shares in common with us all." It is an interesting insight into the qualities of character that Salt admired.

Valentia, "as you may imagine, gives the whole spirit to the party". Salt was very impressed with his "uncommon attention" in gathering information, while "as to his continued kindness to me, I am sure had I been his brother he could not have been more assiduously anxious for his welfare than he appears to be about everything that can tend to my advantage. There has not been even unpleasant words between us more than once; but though I must regret the occasion, from knowing that I was myself in the wrong, yet, as it gave me reason to be more than ever satisfied with his good intentions towards me, I cannot but feel pleased with the cause."

The letter came enclosed in a short one from Valentia, in which he remarked kindly if patronisingly, "I have the pleasure to inform you that he gets on better than I expected, and I have no doubt that when he becomes acquainted again with water-colours, his drawings will be superior to my hopes...I have little doubt that he will make money in India, which, I think, he would never have done in London."[4]

At two in the morning of 20 October, Captain Weltden roused them to "take a peep at the celebrated Table Mountain, which by the light of the moon had a fine effect, and in grandeur by no means disappointed my expectations." During the next ten days, Valentia and Salt, with an old friend of his lordship's, Brigadier General Hall, made a round trip of 300 miles into the interior, receiving hospitality from British and "boor" landowners alike.

Back at the Cape, they found their sailing delayed, as the *Minerva* was boarding extra provisions to cope with a large increase in passengers — General Vandeleur and a regiment of the 8th Light Dragoons. One wonders how the officers were accommodated, let alone the rankers and their families.

Travellers today complain bitterly of a few hours' delay to their plans; then, days or weeks could be added to a voyage under sail by a wind from the wrong direction. The *Minerva* departed the Cape on 5 November, but, driven from their course several times by contrary winds, it was Christmas Day before she again crossed the line. "In the evening it was perfectly calm...we placed lanterns in the rigging, and, with the soldiers' wives for partners, joined in a merry dance. The scene was very gay, for the soldiers covered the sides of the vessel, the poop and the rigging."

It was 17 January before India at last came into view. The coast was only about 12 miles away but, as the breeze was light, it was another three days before the *Minerva* dropped anchor at the mouth of the Hoogly River. The sounds and scents of India drifted across the water. The purser went ashore with public dispatches and letters from Valentia to the Governor-General, Marquess Wellesley, while the *Minerva* crept slowly upriver, able to navigate the intricate sandbanks and sudden bends only when the tide was high.

From this snail-like progress, the Viscount's party was released when Lord Wellesley sent down the state barge to convey them the last few miles to Calcutta. The barge was magnificent: "very long in proportion to its width, richly ornamented with green and gold; its head, a spread eagle gilt; its stern, a tiger's head and body. The centre would contain twenty people with ease, and was covered with an awning and side curtains; forward were seated twenty natives dressed in scarlet habits, with rose-coloured turbans, who paddled away with great velocity."

In Calcutta, the East India Company's capital, Salt and Valentia were accommodated in apartments in the house of a Mr Graham, and with him, on 26 January 1803, attended a fête to celebrate the peace of Amiens at Government House, an imposing mansion of great rooms, high-ceilinged and marble-floored, its form capturing whatever grateful breath of air there was. It had cost £167,359 to build, a sum "considered as extravagant by those who carry European ideas and European economy into Asia," defended Valentia, "but they ought to remember, that India is a country of splendor, of extravagance, and of outward appearances: that the Head of a mighty empire ought to conform himself to the prejudices of the country he rules over; and that the British, in particular, ought to emulate the splendid works of the Princes of the House of Timour, lest it should be supposed that we merit the reproach which our great rivals, the French, have ever cast upon us, of being alone influenced by a sordid, mercantile spirit. In short, I wish India to be ruled from a palace, not from a counting-house; with the ideas of a Prince, not with those of a retail dealer in muslins and indigo."[5] Such an assessment by his mentor of the image necessary to uphold the honour of Britain abroad, must have influenced Salt when he himself became a representative of his country, albeit at a humbler level.

The party was certainly on a princely scale. About 800 Europeans, Indian princes and their representatives, and Armenian merchants, were received by Wellesley at around ten in the evening. The rich dress of the guests was like a masquerade, but one where nobody stepped out of character. To Salt, to whom the magnificence of even the British court was unknown, it must have seemed like an exotic dream. There was dancing until a supper served in a marble hall, whence the guests were summoned about one o'clock to various verandahs to watch the fireworks and illuminations. The citadel, facing the mansion, was covered with a blaze of light, and all the approaches were lined with lamps suspended from bamboos. The rockets were spectacular, and the colours of the set pieces excellent, while "the merit of singularity, at least, might be attributed to a battle between two elephants of fire, which by rollers were driven against each other."

A few days later, Valentia and Salt visited Wellesley at his less grandiose country residence upriver at Barrackpore. At the Governor-General's special request, Salt stayed on for four days, to make sketches. He returned to Calcutta, "much gratified by his visit, as he had not only been treated with an attention highly flattering to a young man, from a person of Lord Wellesley's elevated rank, and acknowledged talents, but had also received the warmest applause from His Excellency and others, on the rapidity and fidelity with which he sketched the scenes from the river."[6] Two days later, Valentia took to Barrackpore a nearly finished watercolour drawing of the house and grounds, together with views of the Cape.

"This admiration is not surprising, for Salt's drawings were of a quality rarely seen in India," comments the art historian Mildred Archer. "He inevitably saw the countryside with the eye of his age. His compositions follow a conventional pattern with a dark and rocky foreground, the middle-distance holding the interest. Boldly massed trees often frame the subject, and small dark-skinned forms add that touch of wildness so valued at the time. His palette too was the favourite one of his day — grey and brown washes, dull blue and green colours which were considered to give 'harmony'. Indeed in choice of subject, composition and colour, his drawings are very similar to those of Thomas and William Daniell, who had visited India a few years before. Yet at their best his sketches show a vigour, energy and sensitivity to atmospheric effects which drawings by the former often lack."[7] The party shared this opinion; Salt's pictures were "all highly admired and the palm was unanimously given to them in preference to the works of Daniell or Hodges."[8] The engravings Salt later published, as well as his sketches, are, says Archer, "something more than 'the tame delineation of a given spot'. They reveal India as seen by the intelligent traveller engaged in a novel grand tour, and make an authentic contribution to the English Romantic tradition."

They were off on their travels again, with Lucknow the ultimate goal. Since none of them could speak a word of the language, they were "bold at least in venturing to set forward on a journey of 800 miles without an interpreter."

This tour of India, mainly to pursue 'botanical researches', being without precedent, had exercised Wellesley as to how "a person of Lord Valentia's Rank, unconnected with any official station," was to be treated, and he "found it necessary to establish Rules for the guidance of the British Resident at Lucknow, and of the Civil and Military officers at a distance from the Presidency, with regard to the degree of attention, precedence and respect, which I deemed proper to be shown..."[9] Where there was no convenient East India Company officer to put them up, the party travelled by night as well as day. This was made possible by the 'dawk' or post system, with men to relieve each other every few miles in carrying the three palanquins bearing Valentia, Salt and Coffin. The palanquins were long enough to lie in at full length, and furnished with pillows, shawls, and venetian blinds for privacy so that sleep was perfectly possible. Salt sketched picturesque views tirelessly, sometimes remaining behind the others to finish a drawing.

On 21 March, a month after leaving Calcutta, they reached Lucknow, where they found the first letters they had received in the nine months since leaving England. They remained there four months. The Viscount engaged a full *suwarry* or state equipage, consisting of two *soontaburdars* or servants of state carrying short silver sticks, six *hircarrahs* or running footmen, one *jemmadar* to command the lower servants and six *kijmutgars,* who waited at table, and were "always Mussulmans".

Now properly equipped to pay visits of state, they called on the Nawaub Vizier of Oude. The *suwarry* going before, the Viscount and a Colonel Scott on elephants, with Salt and Scott's secretary following, and palanquins in attendance, they made their impressive way to the palace. In the first courtyard they were greeted by the upraised trunks of state elephants, ornately howdahed, by camels, and by led horses, richly caparisoned; in the second court, soldiers presented arms. Disembarking from their elephants, the party entered the palanquins, to be carried to a verandah of the palace, where the Nawaub greeted them and embraced Valentia "as his equal".

On departure, the Viscount was presented with 20 trays of shawls, muslins, gold stuffs, etc., and a tray of jewels. A fully caparisoned elephant was also pressed upon him. All was politely refused, in accordance with Company policy. When the Nawaub protested that Valentia was not bound by Company regulations, he agreed, but said he considered the presents offered "on such a public occasion, not as a free gift, but a kind of tribute required from a man of his rank, when visited by a person in my situation", and took only a pair of shawls. Scott and Salt followed his example. When the Nawaub returned the visit, he did not feel at all constrained by Company regulations, and he and his sons accepted the ritual 20 trays of shawls and one of jewels "with little difficulty".

15

Throughout their stay in Lucknow, the Nawaub and his family treated them with the utmost attention, and apparently genuine friendship, and less lavish presents, offered informally, they sometimes accepted. Once a large sum of money was sent for Valentia's servants and, following the custom of the country, Coffin, as 'head domestic', might have taken about a third for himself, "but to his credit he declined any part, saying, he supposed it was meant only for the native servants."

Salt fell very ill of a bilious fever, during which he had a vivid dream that, his mind being in a turmoil of anxiety about his future, his mother appeared to him, telling him not to concern himself, as he was declining with a slow fever which "would soon lead me to the grave. I awoke with a strong impression that I shall never more reach England."[10]

They left Lucknow on 26 July, and struggled for ten weeks through monsoon weather, arriving at last, by boat down the Ganges and Hoogly, at Calcutta, where they settled down to enjoy the lively winter society of the city: "the fêtes given by the Governor-General are frequent, splendid, and well-arranged." Valentia felt he was received most properly, and noted in his journal, "Salt also has reason to be vain of His Excellency's attentions."[11] Several large dinner parties did not please so well — "a small and quiet party seems unknown in Calcutta."

Valentia conceived a new outlet for his energies — an expedition to map the African coast of the Red Sea. It seemed extraordinary, he declared, that if this coast was really as dangerous as now represented, "the ancients should invariably have navigated it in preference to the eastern coast." The British fleet was having difficulties provisioning in the Red Sea, and it would be a great thing if fuel, food and water were found to be available on the islands the ancient Egyptians and Romans had settled so as to trade with Abyssinia and the African interior. Trade was another consideration; it was a favourable time to open communcations with Abyssinia, as normal trade routes to the interior had been disrupted, first by Napoleon's invasion of Egypt, and then by the civil war between the Ottoman government at Constantinople and the Egyptian Beys. The British navy had never been so strong in the area. To Valentia, it reflected badly on England that less was known of this coast of Africa than had been familiar to the ancient Greeks. Wellesley agreed, and when Valentia offered his "gratuitous services" to make a survey, he gladly accepted and provided a cruiser for the purpose.

But first there was a tour to Ceylon (Sri Lanka). They sailed on the *Olive* on 6 December, disembarking at Pointe de Galle to go on by land. With an escort of seven *sepoys* (native soldiers) and 50 bearers, Valentia and Salt travelled in palanquins, each borne by eight bearers, while Coffin rode in a *doolie,* a lightweight bamboo carrying chair. The road wound along the shore through luxuriant jungle, "the richest field for a botanist that I ever beheld, except the Cape of Good Hope." About sunset, they crossed a river in a boat formed of three canoes fastened together by a platform with an awning of white cloth and a chair "covered with the same", a mark of distinction usually reserved for the King of Candy or the Governor, the Hon. Frederick North.

They were the guests of the Governor. This "amiable, learned and excellent man" showed great kindness to Salt, and their friendship was to last for the rest of their lives. Valentia was not at all well, which was one reason for preferring the society of Ceylon to the showiness of Calcutta: "No splendour is attempted; but every thing is neat, and the reception is most hospitable. The hours are early, which to me was a pleasant circumstance; we were generally in bed by nine o'clock." Whether this sober society was quite so pleasant to Salt he did not record. North, "though he loved good things, could never scold, and consequently his dinners were the worst in Colombo; at which he would often laugh himself, and express his satisfaction when he was to dine out, where, as he said, we should have something eatable."[12]

As the cruiser for the Red Sea expedition was to be ready at Mangalore by early February, somewhat reluctantly they started towards India in mid-January 1804. It was already 9 February when they reached Madras, where Coffin fell very ill with fever. Though the season for an easy passage up the Red Sea was slipping away, "I could not possibly think of leaving him behind me, after he had so faithfully followed me through all my travels; besides," Valentia added practically, "I knew I should stand much in need of his services both there and in crossing the Desert." He planned to survey his way up the Red Sea to Suez, then go overland to Cairo.

Twice during the journey Salt was sent off on his own, once because there was a scarcity of bearers, once because Valentia would not leave Coffin. On 6 February, from Pondicherry, Salt set off by an unfrequented road among the hills, rejoining Valentia four days later with drawings of the 'Seven Pagodas' of Trinchicunum. The second excursion was more ambitious. He was dispatched to the falls of Cauveri, with a peon who could speak a little English and 16 palanquin bearers so that he could travel about twenty miles a day and yet have time to draw as he wanted.

It was intensely hot and he travelled mainly by night, making his way through "a very wild and romantic country, which by the clear light of the moon was perhaps rendered more beautiful than it would have appeared by day." He found many pagodas to draw and describe, some, as at Malabar, utterly deserted, one, at Narsipore, on an island "filled with monkeys, that are constantly fed and reverenced". At Ossour he came upon a festival, with a god being processed on a highly ornate vehicle; "I took a view of his chariot". Two days later, his peons killed a tiger measuring upwards of eight feet from nose to tail.

On 29 February he arrived at Talicut early in the morning into a thick and unpleasant fog. Salt presumed the natives believed the miasma to be noxious, as they were "all wrapped up in coarse black mantles, with their mouths cautiously covered, and looked more like spirits of the infernal regions than human beings" — one of his not infrequent word-pictures as vivid as a drawing. He prudently shut himself up in his palanquin until the sun had partly dispersed the vapour. He had often travelled not 20 but 40 miles a day and "my bearers were nearly worn out, notwithstanding I had eight additional to assist them for the last stage."

At Saligut, the nearest station to Cauveri, on 1 March, Salt explored the nearby ruins before proceeding about a mile to the falls. They were rather a disappointment as the water was too low to make even a 150-foot waterfall 'grand' in the romantic manner. After viewing it from various places, he descended into one of the deepest chasms and made several drawings, "undisturbed by the tigers, which are reported to be very numerous in the neighbourhood". He wanted to explore the other fall, but his guide insisted there was nothing more worth seeing.[13] On the evening of the next day he rejoined the others at Seringapatam, finding them installed in a palace of Tippoo Sahib, described by Valentia as the "late haughty tyrant of Mysore".

On 8 March they reached Mangalore and five days later boarded the *Antelope* and immediately set sail for the Red Sea. In order to ensure that the Viscount's word should be paramount in any difference of opinion during the voyage, Wellesley had placed the ship's captain under his command. Captain Keys appeared "perfectly gentlemanly" and inclined to do all he could to make Valentia's voyage comfortable. The cabin was of a "tolerable size"; rather more than a third was partitioned off for Valentia, while the rest served as a dining room, in which Keys and Salt swung their cots at night.

It was 17 April before they again felt land beneath their feet, when they went ashore on the Arabian coast to collect shells, while Coffin and Hall, the mate, took guns and dogs to try to bag some game. Salt and the ship's doctor, James M'Ghee, bathed, and everyone got sunburnt; those who had exposed their bodies suffered severely, the more prudent "escaped with losing the skin off our noses".

The next day the *Antelope* anchored off Mocha, and Pringle, the manager of the British Factory, invited Valentia to stay while the ship reprovisioned. It was now that Captain Keys began to cause anxiety. He was so averse to the plan of surveying the African coast that he wanted to stay at the Factory until he could get a passage back to Bombay, as "ill health" had decided him to give up his command to his first officer. Whether it was entirely the perils of navigating an unknown shore, or whether resentment at being under another's command in his own ship also swayed him, when the serious consequences to his career if he persisted in this course were pointed out to him, Keys gave in — for the moment.

A local *dhow* was hired, to guide the *Antelope* through any straits they might encounter, and to enable them to visit islands which the *Antelope* was unable to approach. On 10 May they reached across the Red Sea, and worked their way slowly up the African shore, landing frequently. While Valentia's servants collected shells and other specimens, Salt and Keys made observations and took soundings; Salt was adding chart-making to his skills. About 19 May, near Amphila, they anchored off a particularly picturesque small island which had never before been described; as they were probably the first Europeans to visit it, they named it Valentia.

A few days later, Captain Keys began to give real trouble, the immediate cause being Valentia's calling into question some statements made by the explorer James Bruce. One of the few Europeans before this time to have visited Abyssinia, Bruce was there between 1769 and 1771. When he returned to England, he was at first made much of for his undoubted intrepidity and enterprise, but soon aroused disgust with his stories of life in Abyssinia. This deterred him from writing up his travels for many years, and when he finally did, he dictated them to an amanuensis, with little reference to his original journals, resulting in perhaps a livelier, but certainly a less accurate account. "Vanity and the passion for the picturesque led him to embellish minor particulars and perhaps in some instances to invent them."[14] Oddly, the same kind of people who had pooh-poohed Bruce's tales in his lifetime waxed indignant when Valentia and Salt claimed to have proved that, in some instances, minor embellishment was putting it mildly, and both were attacked for their presumption.

It seemed to Valentia that statements made by Bruce were so often at variance with his own observations, that it would be "of the greatest public advantage" to find out the real situation and shape of the islands. But his request for one of the ship's boats to make a two-day exploratory trip was refused by Keys: it was contrary to ship's regulations that any of the boats should be out all night, he said. This was quite unacceptable to Valentia, who considered that Wellesley's instructions that Keys give him every assistance must supersede any mere Company rule.

Salt now had the invaluable experience of being involved in the confrontation of two self-willed and obstinate men. He was sent to Keys to threaten that if he continued to thwart him, Valentia would report him to Government, and consider whether he must abandon his plans altogether. Keys indignantly denied being obstructive, asserting that he was Captain, so that discretion to comply with his lordship's requests lay with him, and accusing Valentia of intending to take all the credit for discoveries and observations made by himself and his officers. Keys' behaviour seems extraordinary, considering the effect that thwarting the Governor-General's friend must have on his career.

The Viscount gave not an inch, responding spiritedly that he was acting for the public good and that the credit for the plan "of viewing these doubtful countries, of ascertaining the real manners of their inhabitants, and of facilitating the sailing along their coast, would be mine in defiance of him and his observations." The dispute ended, but Keys "continued very gloomy", and Valentia believed "we should never cordially agree."

Salt, with second lieutenant Maxfield, was sent in the *dhow* to explore the island of Dhalac-el-Kibeer, where they were well received by the Dola, or governor, and his people, as the first Europeans to visit in living memory; indeed, the Dola came aboard the *Antelope* to bring a letter for the Nayib of Massowah, praising their good behaviour while at his island. As he asked to hear one of the "great guns", the Captain fired a one-gun salute as his catamaran left the ship.

The approach of the *Antelope* to Massowah caused great alarm, as the inhabitants, taking them for their enemies the Wahabis (a fundamentalist Muslim sect), summoned their chief, the Nayib, and spent the night under arms. Maxfield went ashore to reassure them, telling them a great man was on board, going to Suez, and that the ship would salute the fort with three, five or seven guns, whichever the Nayib would return. He, at the head of his troops, said that he would be happy to receive the great man, and would return five guns, but did not wish for more, as it would alarm the Bedowees of the hinterland, who would hasten down to protect him.

The *Antelope* fired its salute; of the returning shots, the first two guns fired were loaded with ball, "the whizzing of which, though the guns were pointed wide of us, we could plainly hear, and from such bad marksmen was by no means pleasant." It would have been a pity indeed to be sunk by the misaimed enthusiasm of their hosts.

Donning plain muslin Indian dresses, with a shawl round their middles, Valentia, Salt and Coffin made a formal call upon the Nayib, who received them civilly. At a later, private, audience, Valentia explained the purpose of their voyage, pointing out the advantages to the Nayib of having British ships provisioning along his coast. The Nayib promised assistance, with the cautious caveat that he could not answer for the behaviour of all his people.

This was all very promising for the success of one part of Valentia's plans — but Keys now first refused to tell him their longitude, and next, claimed his timekeeper was out of order, so he would take Bruce's longitude and start a new rate. Valentia connived with Maxfield to take his own bearings. Keys refused to accept them: "Mr Bruce is a very accurate observer and

I shall take his latitude and longitude" — this though Maxfield had "certainly proved him otherwise in his survey of the Bay."

Keys claimed it was now too late to complete the projected survey if the ship was to be sure of her return passage down the Red Sea. Valentia worked out there was not even time, by abandoning all plans of discovery, at least to reach Suez and cross the desert to Cairo while still having the protection of the ship behind them. They would have to return to India. Furious, Valentia made it very clear that he would report Keys for breach of orders. He was even angrier when he discovered the Captain had bought two Abyssinian slave boys, in defiance of the Nayib's orders, "a gross violation...which may have an unpleasant effect on those who come after us."

At Mocha, Valentia and Salt stayed in the Factory, until the *Fox,* another East Indiaman, returned from up the Red Sea, when Valentia requested a passage for himself to Bombay, then formally resigned his command of the *Antelope,* which sailed on 9 July. Salt sailed with her, to ensure Valentia's letter of complaint was delivered safely; it must have been a most uncomfortable voyage for him. In Bombay, the wretched Keys was put under arrest.

Reaching Bombay in mid-September, Valentia decided to return to England via the Persian Gulf and the desert. While awaiting the necessary permissions from the Pasha of Baghdad, Salt and he made a journey to Poonah, during which they observed with distress many scenes of devastation and famine caused by the Mahratta wars. Then, towards the end of November, Valentia received dispatches from Wellesley suggesting that the survey of the Red Sea could usefully be continued, and "delicately hinting, that I might possibly be induced to make an attempt to complete what I had so well begun." So complimentary a hint was irresistible.

The cruiser *Panther* was made ready, and Charles Court chosen Captain for his very high reputation both as a seaman and a man of science.[15] Maxfield, so cooperative when second lieutenant on the *Antelope,* was given command of a small schooner, the *Assaye,* to be used in the tricky navigation expected above Massowah, and, impressed by him on the first voyage, Valentia also took the surgeon, M'Ghee. Captain Henry Rudland of the East India Company army, going home on leave, asked to accompany them. Setting sail on 4 December, they spent Christmas Day of 1804 at Mocha; 14 Europeans were present at the Factory, "a large party of white faces for so distant a part of the globe."

* *

When Valentia sent Keys back to India as soon as possible, he had another motive besides wishing the tiresome fellow out of his sight; he was concerned by the number of the *Antelope*'s crew deserting almost daily, lured by promises of reward from the local rulers, who supposed the sailors to understand the working of 'great guns'. Once ashore, they were forced by their new masters to become Muslims, to learn the prayers and undergo circumcision, and forbidden access to European medicine if they fell ill. Many did not survive.

One deserter had his own pressing reasons for escaping from the *Antelope* before she returned to India — he feared he was wanted there for murder. Though officially turned 'Mussulman', this sailor sent a message to Valentia to beg a Bible. Complying, Valentia wrote warning him of the criminality of his conduct. In a long reply, the man claimed saucily that he could "now be as good a Christian as before, and indeed that he had more time to pay his respects to God Almighty." But a few days later he came down without leave, "to beg some medicine from me...the man looked wretchedly, and told me he was afraid I was right in saying he should soon repent."

When the *Panther* arrived at Mocha, the sailor met Coffin in the town and sent Valentia a message "declaring his sincere repentance, and beseeching me to permit him to attend me, even as a slave, to Europe." Touched, Court and the Viscount arranged that on the night before the *Panther* sailed for Massowah a boat be sent to a secluded place to take aboard all the English 'renegadoes' who wished to leave. But only two appeared, the rest were too afraid of being caught.

This young sailor became the protegé of both Valentia and Salt for the rest of his life. Here assembled for a few short months in one place are the three men whose names inscribed on a temple wall in far-off Egypt so intrigued us that we set out to discover who they were: George Annesley, Viscount Valentia, later Earl of Mountnorris; Henry Salt, later his Britannic Majesty's Consul-General in Egypt; Nathaniel Pearce, a renegade seaman.

Pearce's life before this time had been no less adventurous than it was to be in Valentia's 'service'. Of all the characters in this book, it is he who can be read most clearly; he carried no sophisticated shield to conceal his inner self; what others say of him, what his own actions and writings tell of him, is all of a piece. He was open, rash, impudent, fearless, had a lively though uncultivated intelligence and was loyal beyond the call of duty to those to whom he considered himself bound. Salt's portrait shows him, aged about 26, with the curly hair and wide eyes which must have made him look misleadingly cherubic as a small boy.

Born on 14 February 1779 at East Acton, Middlesex, by the age of seven he was so unruly that his father sent him away to boarding school, where his "wild tricks... fairly tired out" his teachers. Home again, his wild ways continued. His father twice apprenticed him in London and each time he soon ran away to sea.

22

He joined a naval sloop of war which, in May 1794, was captured by a French frigate in the Channel. Pearce twice escaped from prison but was recaptured and eventually incarcerated at Vannes. The gaoler's family became attached to him and when the English prisoners were to be moved, the wife made him so ill with a decoction of boiled tobacco that he was put into hospital with a supposed fever. The hospital director decided to keep him, put him in charge of weighing and serving out rations, and made rather a pet of him, giving him pocket money and taking him out riding — "however all this did not satisfy me: I rather wished to ride on board of one of my own country's ships than the director's pony."

Hearing the English fleet was in Quiberon bay, Nathaniel escaped with five young French aristocrats. Soon retaken, they were marched to a hill overlooking the town, where despite the pleas of some of the officers in pity of their youth, the five boys were shot. Laughing, the major told Nathaniel that if he escaped again with emigré prisoners, he would be shot with them. Undeterred, he was soon over the hospital wall again with another young aristocrat, and found a small boat to take them out to the English fleet.

He joined the *Bellerophon,* but deserted six months later. Working his passage on trading brigs, he reached London, where his father, who had connections in India House, found him a berth in an East Indiaman, bound for China. He essayed desertion in both Malay and China, but was caught and flogged with special care by the first mate, Mr Hall, who had "been persuaded by my father to tame me if possible". He had more success at the Cape of Good Hope by giving himself up to Captain Edwards of HMS *Sceptre* as a naval deserter. He was soon a favourite with the captain, who offered to make him a midshipman, "but I always refused, saying I was not fit for the office."

Later, in India, the *Sceptre* was put into dock for repairs, and her crew sent ashore, where they heard that Englishmen who deserted to the service of the Mahrattas were made "officers, generals, colonels, captains, &c., &c." This was irresistible and soon Pearce and six messmates were on their way to Poonah. But when they met several Englishmen in a wretched condition, Pearce realised the stories of becoming officers were stories only and persuaded his companions to make for Goa in hopes of getting aboard a Portuguese ship. They were captured by the British Resident, who, however, treated them kindly and wrote to Captain Edwards recommending mercy. The men were merely flogged and ordered back to their duty.

Again at the Cape, the *Sceptre* was wrecked in a storm; Pearce was one of the few saved of her crew of 400. The survivors remained in hospital until Admiral Sir Roger Curtis arrived, in command of the *Lancaster,* in which ship Pearce served and saw action all over the world for several years.

About 1803, now aged 24, he was in hospital in Bombay, suffering from the effects of old wounds. When he began to feel better he tried to leave the hospital without permission. The sentry hit him with his musket-butt and in the ensuing struggle, Pearce felled him to the ground. Under arrest, Pearce "pretended to have occasion to step out" — the door was guarded but the window was not and he successfully passed a sleeping sentry at the hospital gate.

Hearing the soldier he had struck was likely to die, Pearce for once was frightened. He met an officer of the East India Company marine, Mr Hall, and told him all. Mr Hall, now first mate on the *Antelope,* took him aboard, and they sailed to Mangalore to await Viscount Valentia.

"Dear sir," Pearce ended the account he later wrote for Salt, "you know as well as I do every particular after that time...believe me, I shall always consider you as my master and only friend in this world...so I conclude, remaining until death, Your very affectionate and humble servant, Nathaniel Pearce."[16]

* *

The *Panther* sailed for Massowah on 2 January 1805. On board were the two Abyssinian boys illegally bought by Captain Keys, and re-purchased by the Government in Bombay to be returned to the Nayib of Massowah in earnest that the British would not violate his laws while in his dominions. In the event, the boys asked to join the ship's crew. They were re-christened — instead of the "slavish names of Sidi and Pompey", they were henceforth to be George Habesh (Abyssinia) and Harry Gondar. Christians these name-sakes of Valentia and Salt had been born, "but of the doctrines of Christianity, or indeed those of any other religion, they had no idea." Pearce was set "to teach them to read and pray."

Captain Court and Salt made the complete survey of Dhalac that Keys' intransigence had prevented, an expedition which proved that James Bruce's account was wrong in so many particulars that it seemed probable he had never visited the island. Salt acquired two monumental stones from a mosque on Dhalac, "and wrapping them up very carefully, proceeded back to our lodgings, not quite satisfied, I own, with the propriety of what I was about." The locals considered his action to be very *im*proper and gathered in front of his lodging to tell him so; but when Salt assured them he would return the stones if the Nayib wished it, and distributed somewhat generous presents, their scruples were "completely removed...and they immediately assisted most cordially in repacking the sacred spoils, and in fastening them to the back of a camel."[17]

Having renewed friendly relations with the Nayib at Massowah (and obtained permission to keep the stones), they hoped to complete the survey of the coast, but adverse weather, and a shortage of water and provisions, forced their return to Mocha. However disappointed, Valentia comforted himself that at least, by their conduct towards the local population, "we have done the best we could to leave behind us a good impression of the British character, and, so far as we can judge, have succeeded", so that there was much hope for future connections between these people and England, "if cultivated by those who follow us, and not violated by caprice or tyranny, as has too often been the case."[18] Such admirable sentiments may well have come naturally to Salt, who always gives the impression of having an unprejudiced sense of other men's worth, but the principle must have gained in its effect on him by its being so clearly important to Valentia.

They reprovisioned at Valentia Island, landing to collect shells and plants. Valentia named a hill Mount Norris, "out of respect for my father, as being the highest place in the island". The Dola was delighted to see them again and his wife cooked them a dinner. At Mocha, they found the Factory in disarray. Unable to bear his isolation, Pringle the manager, had so taken to drink that he was no longer capable of running the Factory nor of maintaining the prudent and conciliating relations with the locals necessary to give "respectability to the British character". During Pringle's absence on business, Valentia took it upon himself to reform the Factory, and enforce a stricter control over the Arab servants. Unable in the circumstances to rebuild the place or improve its environs, he expressed plenty of thoughts on the subject. What Pringle thought is not recorded.

Forced to abandon his plan of reaching Suez that season, Valentia turned his mind to opening up communications with Abyssinia, if possible sending a party into the country. Informed that the Ras of Tigre, the most powerful chief in the land, was anxious to hear from him he had sent him a message from Massowah, "expressive of my wishes". On 3 June, the Ras's answer reached Mocha — he hoped that Valentia would come, or send someone, to see him. Valentia considered it of the greatest importance to seize this opportunity — however, it was not an opportunity he was prepared to take in his own person. Salt later told Joseph Farington that "His Lordship had too great a stake in life & was of too much importance to have his life risqued by it" — Salt's life being "comparatively of no consequence", it was he who was to be the envoy.[19] It says something for the young man whom Valentia had been somewhat reluctant to take with him on the voyage to the East three years earlier, that he by now felt able to place so much confidence in him, both for discretion and valour. Salt was to need an abundance of both.

3

The Ras of Tigre and the Pasha of Egypt

CARRYING what presents could be procured at Mocha, on 20 June 1805 Salt was dispatched to Massowah, in the *Panther* rather than a *dhow*, both to give him "more importance in the eyes of the natives", and to provide protection. After the ship had departed, a message arrived from the Nayib of Massowah that he did not yet give his consent to Salt's passing through his lands; and who could enter Habesh (Abyssinia) without his permission, for "was not he the gates of it?" Though fairly confident that when his emissary appeared in an armed cruiser all would be well, Valentia quickly sent a letter after Salt, recommending that he tell the Nayib that "if he were the gates of Habesh, I was the gates of Massowah; and that if he shut the one against me, I could shut the other, by not letting a single dow enter the place." It was an inauspicious start to a journey that, even with the Nayib's cooperation, would be both difficult and dangerous.

Salt was at Massowah by 28 June, but it was almost a month before he could successfully conclude negotiations, a month in which any lessons he had learnt on how to be authoratative without being uncivil, firm but sensibly flexible, were tested to the limit. When the Nayib was first told of the party's requirements in the way of attendants, mules, asses and camels, the hour of prayer was conveniently announced. "The moral effects, however, of this religious service were not very apparent," commented Salt drily, "though the highest sum previously demanded had never exceeded eight hundred dollars, a message was now brought from the Nayib that he expected a thousand."[1] This wryly ironic remark is typical of Salt's writing, which is more lively and humorous than Valentia's often didactic style.

Salt beat down the Nayib's demands by a shrewd combination of firmness, reminders of the Nayib's 'friendship' with Valentia, and suggestions that his present conduct might bring adverse treatment upon him from the British — an exercise in the kind of diplomacy he would often have to use as Consul-General of Egypt. The bargain struck, Captain Court sweetened it by sending as much rice as he could spare to the Nayib, as it was understood there was a scarcity in his dominions.

On 18 July Salt's party with their baggage disembarked from the *Panther* and sailed from the island of Massowah to the mainland town of Arkeko, where there were further delays and efforts at extortion, even after the party had started on its way. Just then, the *Panther* was accidently blown from her anchorage towards the town, and Salt quick-wittedly told the

Nayib that Court was coming to check that he was safe, and if he found all well, would return in ten days for the message Salt was to send him from Dixan in the dominions of the Ras of Tigre. Within a very few minutes, without further argument, all was miraculously ready.

The company which set out on 20 July consisted of Salt; Captain Rudland; a Mr Carter, perhaps one of the *Panther*'s officers; Hamed Chamie, "a respectable Arab...in the service of Mr Pringle", as interpreter; Andrew, a renegade boy allowed by the Dola of Mocha to attend Salt as a servant, who spoke a litle Arabic; Nathaniel Pearce, who had some Arabic; two Arab servants; a boy from Massowah who spoke Arabic and the language of the country; and an old man who carried the pedometer; about two dozen *askari,* soldiers of the Nayib, ten camel drivers and a guide from a local tribe. An aged sheik, with his little boy, on a trading expedition, also prudently attached himself to the company.

On the second day out, 18 miles from Arkeko and the *Panther,* the *askari,* putative guards of the party, thinking it now at their mercy, began to display "insatiable rapacity and insolence", and were joined in this unpleasing behaviour by the camel drivers. They threatened, unless they were given money, to leave, taking all the beasts with them. Salt told them sturdily that they "might themselves depart as soon as they pleased; but that I would certainly shoot the first person whom I should see meddling with the camels."

Next morning, the attendants would not move, saying they awaited more mules from the Nayib. Fortunately, at this moment, an Abyssinian, Guebra Michael, arrived from Dixan, with ten mules sent by the Ras to convey them with all possible speed to his presence, and with his "strictest orders" to ensure the party's safety. With the Ras's protective hand reached out to him, Salt tried to dismiss the *askari,* but as they promised to reform their conduct, they were allowed to remain.

That night a great storm raged for four hours, in the midst of which the *askari* cried out that strangers were approaching. Out rushed the party "into so drenching a rain as would presently have rendered our fire-arms entirely useless." The alarm proved false, set up, Salt was convinced, by the *askari,* who, "if we had not shown ourselves ready to repel aggression, would in all probability have taken the opportunity of at least plundering us." He was amused to observe in the morning how completely the tent was filled, not only with themselves and their servants, but also *askari,* cameldrivers, and three asses, all having crept in during the night for shelter.

Guebra Michael advised that, as provisions were short, Salt should dismiss the *askari,* and this time he succeeded, by bribing each with two dollars. With his 'protectors' gone, Salt felt much safer, and the night watch, so far kept by himself, Rudland, Carter and Pearce, was handed over to Pearce, Hamed Chamie and Guebra Michael, with muskets fired at set intervals.

Five days out of Arkeko, as the ground became too uneven for camels, they were replaced by a bullock and several porters. Next day they began to ascend Taranta. Realising that once this mountain was passed, they could no longer safely impose on the party, the few remaining of the Nayib's men made a flurry of attempts to obstruct further progress. First they deserted, but when Salt found a local sheik to guide them, the Nayib's guide returned hastily, seized the bridle of Rudland's mule and tried to force them to make camp. He next laid hold of Salt, who drew his sword and threatened to cut him down. After one more attempt, he accepted defeat, and "the exaggerated perils and toils of the passage of Taranta" were overcome in only three hours. They came down quietly into the tranquillity of a little green valley, shaded by trees and "adorned by a pool of water".

In the afternoon of the following day, a week from Arkeko, they came to Dixan through a relentless rain, soaked through and without any of their baggage, which was scattered upon the road "in proportion to the strength or willingness of those who carried it". Shivering in their wet clothes, they miserably endured a cold night. Salt sat till nearly morning with his feet in the embers of the fire. All the next day the rain fell remorselessly as the baggage trickled in piece by piece, mostly drenched.

The governor, or Baharnegash, of Dixan treated Salt politely on hearing his mission and advised writing to the Secretary of the Governor of Adowa to ask that 25 mules be sent down as soon as possible. Salt, writing to Valentia of his safe arrival at Dixan, mentioned that the locals had doubted the party's being Christian, until they were convinced by seeing on Pearce's arm a tattoo of Christ crucified. Pearce proved useful again, and displayed an unexpected accomplishment: the Baharnegash was very anxious to have a picture for his church, and Pearce "painted the Virgin Mary and the infant Christ in most flaming colours, which gave great satisfaction". This tall, elderly, mild-faced Baharnegash was to become well known to Salt, who was very attached to him for his humane and Christian character — "I can truly say, that I have seldom felt more respect for an individual than I did for this worthy man."[2]

After almost two weeks a large retinue arrived with mules and provisions and messages that everything in future would be provided free at the command of the Ras; furthermore "if any man should dare to molest us, his head must answer for it." Even under the protection of their Abyssinian escort, they were not always treated with civility on their journey, and once nearly found themselves in the midst of a battle. Two young chiefs, the brothers Aggoos and Subagadis, intended to attack some villages, but when the party met Aggoos a few days later, he told them that hearing they were passing that way, he had considerately deferred the action. When they came to Genater, Subagadis' village, they were received by him with great kindness and hospitality; he was "in his manners by far the most polished Abyssinian we had yet seen...for the first time we found ourselves among people who were above begging." Salt was soon able to repay his hospitality; coming up with the party later at a village where he could find no accommodation, but Salt and his people had a house, he was pressed to share it with them. Subagadis, little more than 20 years old, but famed for his courage and ability, years later himself became Ras of Tigre.

On 28 August the party reached the residence of the Ras at Antalow. As they approached they were pressed about by a shouting crowd, eventually numbering about three thousand. They could scarcely make a way through the throng, and were not allowed to dismount from their mules until they reached the entrance to the great hall. At the far end, Ras Welled Selasse was seated on rich satin pillows, while on each side his chiefs sat on the carpet. Salt saw a small, slender man of about seventy, with a shrewd expression and considerable dignity. He and his companions kissed the back of the Ras's hand, and he did the same to each of them, thus placing them on an equality with himself. In the evening, the Ras sent for the firearms of the party — if Salt felt mistrustful, he does not admit it. Pearce, who took the guns to the Ras, was seated beside him on his couch and given *maize* to drink while he examined the arms with admiration.

Having been woken both at midnight and at 4 a.m. by civil messages from the Ras, Salt and his friends were invited in the morning to take breakfast with him, when he again treated them as equals, to the extent of feeding them by hand, "somewhat in the same way as boys in England feed young magpies." Later Salt delivered Valentia's presents and letter, all of which delighted the Ras, and gave, through the interpreter Hadjee Hamed, a full account of his mission, while the Ras laid before Salt the uneasy state of public affairs in Abyssinia, and the reasons why he must refuse to let him visit the Emperor in Gondar, for fear of his falling victim to one of the many disturbances in the country. Though Welled Selasse was probably the most powerful man in Abyssinia at this time, while the Emperor was a puppet, his position could never be called unassailable, and he spent a good deal of his time at war with one or other of his rivals. Matters had changed little since Bruce's visit, when Ras Michael Suhul of Tigre occupied much the same position in the country's affairs as his successor.

In a few days, however, the atmosphere changed: though still perfectly polite, the Ras became cool and avoided any private meeting. Salt suspected he was being intrigued against, and eventually, having been repeatedly refused an audience, boldly invaded the Ras's presence uninvited, accompanied only by Rudland. The old man, who was playing chess, gave them his hand and seated them by his side, but did not speak. At length the interminable game was over, and Salt put his case. At first the Ras remained reserved, but gradually his former warmth returned, and they parted good friends. Though not the end of all trouble, there it rested for the moment.

Salt had already asked permission to visit Adowa and Axum; the latter, the ancient capital of the country, was then almost ruinous but for a church. He was now allowed to go. At Axum, Salt, with Pearce's assistance, surveyed and made a plan of the site, descended into two curious excavated caves, one containing tombs, and braved nettles to examine a small square enclosure with a pillar at each corner, on a seat within which the emperors were once crowned. He sketched the one great stele, about 80 feet high, which still stood upright and was very excited by a smaller monument, about eight feet tall, covered with Greek characters, which he spent hours carefully copying. These several days of intensive study of the ruins of Axum were an important introduction to the archaeological activities in which Salt was to engage with such enthusiasm in Egypt.[3]

On 26 September, Rudland in his British uniform and Salt in Abyssinian garb, joined the Ras on his couch to watch a review of his troops, which took place in a circular enclosure about 300 yards in circumference. Each chief came in with his followers, and rode round the enclosure several times, then presented himself before the Ras, "in a menacing attitude, recited in pompous language the actions which he had performed, and concluded by throwing down before him the indubitable trophies of his valour, which had before been hanging above the bracelets on his right arm" — the private parts of those he had slain. Not only the chiefs but "every ragged rascal among the foot soldiers...had the same privilege." Salt, horrified and disgusted to observe in some cases the "unquestionable evidence that boys, not men, had been the victims of their fury", expressed himself so strongly to the Ras that, "actuated by the same feelings", he refused these men the approval he had shown to others. Salt and Rudland were both very impressed by the horsemanship of the Abyssinian warriors, and how they handled their spears; "they are particularly expert, and they have a peculiar method of vibrating it in the hand, which has a very warlike and classical appearance."

A grand feast followed the review, at which only the Ras, and behind him Salt and Rudland, sat upon couches, while the chiefs ranged themselves two and three deep round the table on their haunches. While curries and *teff* bread were served, "the cattle were killed on the outside of the hall." A large piece of flesh, in which the fibres were "yet quivering", was distributed to each chief, who cut it into strips and ate it with his left hand. Contrary to Bruce's assertion of 30 years earlier that "no man in Abyssinia of any fashion whatever, feeds himself, or touches his own meat", Salt observed that the highest chiefs quite often helped their neighbours and even their women.

Over the next few days the Ras's lingering mistrust of his visitors was dispelled when he appointed a new interpreter. As the Ras heard Salt's account through him, he was frequently moved by admiration or surprise. He, as well as Salt, he declared, had been "much imposed upon"; he had been warned by many different persons that the Europeans meant him harm, and only now fully understood the motives for Salt's visit. He protested, however, that he had not believed all he had been told against them, having found their conduct quite different from that reported, and was, indeed, "much attached" to them. Much of the mischief was to be traced to the former interpreter, Hadjee Hamed, who was also in the pay of the Sheriff of Mecca; the Muslim interest was naturally opposed to any kind of alliance between England and the Christian country of Abyssinia.

The party was now on such familiar terms with the Ras that they went in and out of his room as they pleased, and were allowed free communication with the town. Salt, at the Ras's particular request, painted him a picture of the Virgin and Child. But, sadly, just as real rapprochement was reached, it was time to return to Massowah, for the ship would be awaiting them.

There is no doubt that the Ras would have dearly liked to keep his new friends with him — indeed, the Abyssinians had a reputation for welcoming Europeans to their land, but never letting them depart. It may have been only his desire to establish relations with England that persuaded the Ras to let Salt and his companions go. There was one he had set his heart on keeping with him — Nathaniel Pearce, who himself wanted to stay. Salt thought hard before consenting, worried lest Pearce find himself "deceived in his expectations". But he realised that his presence in Abyssinia might prove very useful for several reasons; his quickness in acquiring languages would enable him to act as interpreter for any future British mission, he wrote well and lucidly, and he should be able to collect much interesting information. "He is, so far as I have seen, well inclined, and a deserving man, and will not, I think, disgrace his country by cowardice or meanness."[4]

In his first interview with his new man, the Ras questioned Pearce closely about his "capacity as a soldier, his ability in painting, and his knowledge of physic; to which Pearce replied that he was only slightly acquainted with the two latter arts, but would do his best for him; that as to the other, it had been the employment of his life." The Ras was pleased that he could read and write in English and promised him every help in learning the language of Tigre, so that he could act as his interpreter in any future dealings with the British. He was also promised protection: the Ras would keep him "always near his own person", and if he ever wanted to leave, provide him with the means of reaching Massowah. Pearce told the Ras that "being an Englishman, he never knew what fear was; with which the Ras was much gratified; and answered, that, though very old, his own feelings were the same."[5] Reasonably happy that he had done all he could to secure Pearce's safety, Salt left him everything he could spare and made him some drawings of St George and the dragon and other heads to aid his role as an artist.

The Ras produced letters to George III, purportedly from the Emperor of Abyssinia, but actually from himself, for the puppet Emperor had been placed on the throne by Guxo, chief of the Edjow Galla and arch rival of the Ras. As he left on 10 October, Salt again recommended Pearce to the Ras's protection, "as his own guest, and our countryman", which he "most feelingly promised". The Ras was so affected by the parting that he could not speak as he took their hands.

Accompanied on their way by their old friend, Baharnegash Yasous of Dixan, the party made their way to the coast — even under the protection of the Ras, not without incident. As they neared Arkeko, they became anxious, as it was reported that the *Panther* had not yet arrived, which was only too likely to result in trouble and danger. Salt tried to raise his companions' spirits by assuring them the ship would be there in time, and fortunately so it was. This considerably impressed the retinue, particularly old Yasous, who kissed Salt's hand, exclaiming "You know everything!" Even with the ship in sight, the party were stoned by some of the townsfolk. Salt sent for the Nayib's son, loaded all the muskets before him and told him he would shoot the next man to attack his people. This menace had the desired effect, but everyone was thankful when the *Panther*'s cutter came to carry them aboard.

The Baharnagash, received with great kindness by Valentia, was astonished and delighted by the ship and by the working of the cannons, though he had been greatly alarmed by the 11-gun salute fired in honour of Salt's return, which he at first imagined to be an attack upon the town. With all the expenses of his stay paid, he departed full of gratitude, promising to befriend Pearce and protect him with his life.

Valentia sent Pearce some supplies and money, two muskets, so that with his own gun, he would be "the best-armed man in Habesh", and promises that he should have money to leave the country whenever he wished.

A letter from Pearce to Valentia on 28 February the following year shows him fully conscious of what was expected of him:

> ...I shall look into every thing particular and visit as many particular places as possible as I am through your Letters to the Ras Greatly in favour with him and he will not deny me any thing of that kind I ask him in your Name...My Lord I most heartily thank you for your Goodness and am determined to Follow Your Advise and Stop with the Ras and every thing particular I can learn or find out I will send to Your Lordship Instantly but at Present I have

had no Opportunity as the Ras as Been...preparing to get reddy to go against Guxer...

    I am my Lord Your most Humble Slave until Death.[6]

Valentia was altogether well pleased with what Salt had achieved: "The direct communication between Abyssinia and other Christian nations may be considered as again opened...after having been closed since the year 1558, when Soolimaun Basha conquered Massowah, Dhalac, and Suakin, and deprived the Abyssinians of all access to the Red Sea." He detailed the advantages which might accrue to both England and Abyssinia if trade were opened between them, and expressed gratification that Salt's conduct had been such as not only to "conciliate the esteem" of the Ras, but to leave a favourable impression of the English character throughout the country.

Now at last, on 14 November 1805, Valentia and Salt turned towards England, planning to sail up the African coast to Suez and cross the desert to Cairo.

The fourth day of the voyage was almost their last. A violent storm arose, and all the anchors parted as they tossed helplessly in a small bay bounded by two reefs and a sandy island. Captain Court took Valentia's hand, saying, "Alas! poor *Panther!* nothing can save you — we must now all be broken together, and do the best we can for each other." But then he observed that the wind had shifted a point and instantly decided to try to cross the eastern reef. In a tempest wind, gunwale under water, the ship passed barely two cable's length from the point of the reef. An attempt to return to Massowah to reprovision was aborted by the hostility of the inhabitants. After a slow and hazardous voyage up the Red Sea, the *Panther* dropped anchor off Suez in the afternoon of 26 January 1806.

Valentia wrote to Cairo to arrange his journey across the desert. A week later, letters arrived from Mr Aziz, the British Consular representative in Cairo, and a message from Mehemet Ali, Pasha of Egypt, that Valentia was to be treated with every mark of respect, and his baggage admitted free of duty. Major Missett, the British Consul, then based in Alexandria, wrote to congratulate Valentia on his arrival, and gave him the "agreeable news" of Nelson's victory at Trafalgar.

The imposing caravan returning from Mecca, commanded by Sheik Chedid, escorted them across the desert. Besides Valentia, Salt, Coffin, Rudland and the surgeon M'Ghee (who went to Cairo to bring back dispatches for India), there were 1,500 camels, 300 armed Arabs, some 30 Turkish soldiers with two officers, to guard the *mahmal,* or sacred covering for the Kaaba of Mecca, and Mr Thomaso, a Christian turned Muslim, as interpreter. Valentia travelled in a *takterouane,* a box-like conveyance, only five feet long and very uncomfortable, slung on shafts between two camels.

The others travelled in *mohaffas,* little seats slung each side of a camel, with an awning to keep off the sun. The Viscount found the motion of his box unpleasant enough; as the others jerked about they enjoyed themselves still less. Coffin enterprisingly bribed a young Arab to lend him his horse, sword and musket, on the promise he would fight if the caravan were attacked.

In the evening of the third day from Suez, all but Valentia by now on horseback, they came to the Nile. Early on 6 February 1806 Salt entered for the first time the city which was to be his home for so many years. Mr Aziz escorted them to quarters in the British Factory, where they dined quietly and went to bed early, "highly pleased to find ourselves in an excellent house and in civilized society". Even excellent Egyptian houses were found, however, to be ill adapted for wet weather, when later Valentia's room was deluged and M'Ghee driven from his bed by the rain descending upon him.

Valentia received complimentary calls from the most prominent Europeans, from the consulates and the monasteries. The Pasha sent his interpreter with messages of welcome, offering every assistance for them to visit all the sights, and regretting that "the situation of the country was such as to render it uncomfortable to strangers." He averred that he was "attached" to the English, and, being so lately raised to his high office, was eager to cultivate the friendship of those nations who were friendly with the Porte, his masters in Constantinople; he wished to show every attention; if anything were neglected "which ought to be done, he hoped I would attribute it to his being a rough soldier, little accustomed to the formalities of peace."

Who was this 'rough soldier' whom Salt was later to know so well? There are many accounts of his early life. Mehemet Ali was born in 1769 (the same year as Wellington and Napoleon, as he liked to point out) in Cavallo in Macedonia of a family originally from Anatolia. Orphaned early, he was protected by a wealthy Aga, became a successful tobacco dealer and married a widow in his protector's family, to whom he remained devoted. In 1798, when the Porte called up troops from the Ottoman provinces to repel Napoleon's invasion of Egypt, Mehemet Ali was put in command of 300 Albanians. After the battle of Aboukir he was promoted to lead a thousand men, and soon became second-in-command under Tahir Pasha.

He showed himself a "brave and ready soldier" of judgement and sagacity. For a time his corps was attached to the British army and, according to Consul-General Murray, "he evinced such high courage and conduct" that he earned the personal approval of the Commander-in-Chief, General Hutchinson. "Like most successful captains he was the darling of his soldiers. His rough manners, his ready jests, his daring courage" brought him their entire devotion. He was the chosen spokesman, the sole mediator, between them and authority.[7]

Once both French and British troops had left Egypt, chaos ruled. Both Turks and Mamelukes were divided amongst themselves. In May 1803 the Albanian soldiers in Cairo, angry at not being paid, mutinied and attacked the Citadel. When their leader, Tahir, was murdered, Mehemet Ali took his place. Joining with the Mamelukes, the Albanians defeated the Turks, and the Ottoman Governor of Egypt, Khusrau Pasha, fled to Damietta, was captured and for a time held in the Citadel at Cairo.

The Albanians still wanted their pay and ultimately it was the hard-pressed local people who had to pay them. When the Mamelukes cut off the grain supplies to Cairo, famine was imminent. In this chaotic situation, both the French Consul, M. Lesseps, and the British Consul, Major Missett, decided to back the Mamelukes. In the event, it proved the wrong decision.

While Mehemet Ali discreetly befriended the local sheiks, the Porte sent to Kurschid Pasha, the new Ottoman Governor of Egypt, reinforcements who were even more rapacious than the Albanians. Mehemet Ali was away from Cairo when this rabble arrived, but soon returned with 4,000 troops — still looking for their pay. After an unruly conflict, the populace proclaimed him Governor of Cairo, from which position of power, he cleverly played off one side against the other.

Colonel Drovetti, who had replaced Lesseps as French Consul, wrote to Paris that the measures of the "enterprising Albanian leader" made him think that Mehemet Ali planned to become Pasha. The time was ripe. The Sultan sent an emissary empowered to confer the pashaliq on whosoever appeared able to sustain the role. Mehemet Ali mounted a battery on the Moqattan Heights that rise above Cairo's Citadel to the south, and compelled Kurschid Pasha to surrender. On 7 August 1803, Kurschid departed, and Mehemet Ali became Pasha of Egypt.

This might have meant little. Pashas had come and gone rapidly. In Mehemet Ali's hands it resulted in the establishment of a dynasty which lasted nearly 150 years in a country which for centuries had known no continuous leadership. "I came to this country," he told John Barker in 1827, "an obscure adventurer...but soon...I was served first; and I advanced step by step, as it pleased God to ordain; and now here I am."[8]

Valentia's first audience with the Pasha was on the afternoon of 18 February. Five wonderfully caparisoned horses had been sent for the party, and an escort of several of the Pasha's *Chaous*, servants with silver sticks to keep off the crowds. They were ushered into a room crowded with soldiers. When Mehemet Ali entered by a side door, Valentia rose and paid his compliments after the European fashion, but Mr Aziz, as a native subject of the Porte, kissed the hem of the Pasha's garment and remained standing throughout the audience.

It was Salt's first sight of the man who was to play such a central role

in his life. Valentia described him: "He is a little man, of an intelligent countenance, with a reddish brown beard of moderate dimensions, but of which
he seemed to be proud, as he was continually stroking it." Plainly dressed,
he wore no jewels. He addressed Valentia then and always as 'General'.
When Valentia praised the care that Sheik Chedid had taken in bringing him
across the desert,"His Highness gravely answered, that if he had behaved
otherwise, his head should have answered for it."[9]

Coffee was served, the Pasha's cup set with diamonds, those of the
guests embossed with gold. The Pasha once more assured Valentia of his
great regard for the English, and his wish to do all he could for them, "and
particularly for a person of my consequence". Sherbet was served, a hint to
depart; as they left the house, a salute was fired.

Over the next few days, Valentia returned the visits that had been made
upon him, and in the evenings the party played cards. With escorts provided by the Pasha, they went sightseeing. Valentia so admired the view of
Cairo from the Citadel that he instructed Salt to make a series of drawings
"which would answer as a Panorama". Salt spent several days at this task
without trouble, but on the last one had to leave rather hurriedly, "as they
began to celebrate the festival of Beiram, by firing musquetry with balls; an
amusement by no means safe for the by-standers."[10]

Disturbances had made it too dangerous for the past three years for
individuals to visit the Pyramids, so that when it became known that
Valentia was to travel under the Pasha's protection, many people applied to
accompany him, and a party of about 40 set out, attended by two of the
Pasha's *Chaous*. They also had the services of Mehemet Ali's interpreter. He
had already been invited by the French Consul to be present as he celebrated Napoleon's victory over the Russians, but the Pasha ordered him instead
"to go and dine with the General and accompany him to the Pyramids".

This was but one of the incidents of special favour shown to Valentia
in Egypt, which, he was patriotically pleased to observe, "extremely mortified the French Agents...M Drovetti, their Consul, could not contain his
vexation. He exclaimed, 'how very ridiculous, to make such an uproar
about a private individual!' but he well knew," added the Viscount, "that,
although in fact his observations were just, yet I was on this occasion a public pageant, as no one believed that I had come without political motives."
Major Missett, the British Consul, actively fostered this notion, to counter-
act the intrigues of the French Agents, who "had for some time unblushing-
ly asserted, that England considered Egypt as of no consequence, and did
not wish to keep up any connection with it." This supposed political moti-
vation, however useful to Missett, cost the Viscount the chance to go to
Upper Egypt, as he found it impossible to persuade the Pasha that his
"objects were not political". The British had always been on friendly terms

with the Mameluke Beys in that region, and the Mamelukes were by no means resigned to losing their former power to the Pasha — " the most distant hint of visiting Upper Egypt therefore excited alarm and I was oblig-ed to abandon the idea."[11]

An outing to the Pyramids gave the Pasha no such anxiety. Having spent the night of 2 March at the convent of St George in Old Cairo, the company rose at five, but rumours of a planned Mameluke attack delayed the outing for two days. At the Pasha's order, the party was augmented by no fewer than 2,000 infantrymen and two pieces of curricle artillery, com-manded by his nephew.

Valentia professed himself not immediately impressed by the size of the Pyramids: "The idea of a Pyramid is easily conceived, and consequently sur-prise cannot enter the feelings of a person when he first beholds them. When, however, reason points out the prodigious labour, with which they must have been erected, and the incomprehensible motives, which could have led to such vast exertions, astonishment gradually increases, and the mind is lost in conjecture and admiration." His view of the purpose of the Great Pyramid is interesting — not a tomb, he considered, but intended for the celebration of sacred mysteries, and the empty sarcophagus in the King's Chamber "destined for the supposed body of Osiris during the annual lamentation for his loss".[12]

Arabs cleared the passage to the sepulchral chamber in the Great Pyramid and guided the party with lighted flambeaux. They were unable to take all the time they would have liked, as the commander kept sending in nervous messages urging them to hurry back. Once he had assembled his charges he prepared to attack the Mamelukes, who were lurking in the date groves, "but his Albanians thought it safest to proceed so slowly, that the enemy had sufficient time to retire before they were within reach." So 'our' cavalry attended the tourists peaceably under the blazing sun to Giza. They reached Cairo "heartily fatigued...having been in motion for twelve hours."

Next day Valentia paid his farewell call upon the Pasha, and was received with even more than the usual attention. "He presented me a sabre with his own hand, requesting I would keep it for his sake." Salt, Rudland, M'Ghee and even Coffin were each presented with a sabre by an attendant. Next, the Viscount was given a rich sable pelisse into which "I immediately put my right arm...and again sat down." He asked Mehemet Ali if he had any commands for England, and promised to procure him, as requested, "a good pair of pistols". The audience ended with the most marked gesture of all: "On my taking leave, he rose up and spoke to me [i.e. not through the interpreter] — a most pointed compliment, and contrary to his religion, as well as his dignity."

The Viscount sent the Pasha a diamond ring, which he rather ungraciously remarks was "more than equal in value to his presents". Nor was this the only expense he had been put to — he complained that the rank which the Pasha "had been pleased to bestow upon me", and the importance he attached to the visit, had involved him in heavy expenses. "The journey to the Pyramids cost me above four hundred dollars, and the visits to the Pasha three hundred more, in presents to his servants."

M'Ghee bade farewell to his companions of the past three years and returned to the *Panther*. The others sailed down the Nile to Alexandria, via Rosetta. At Alexandria on 23 March, Valentia was greeted by an 11-gun salute from the fort of the Pharos, "a compliment which is only paid to Pashas of three tails", and was met on the beach by Major Missett, the British Consul, and the dragomans of all the consuls whose countries were not at war with England at the time and 40 *Chaous* belonging to the Governor of Alexandria. Even Consul Drovetti mastered his chagrin long enough to express his regret that "political circumstances put it out of his power to wait on me".

They stayed with Samuel Briggs, merchant and at various times acting British Consul in Alexandria, a man who was to become a trusted friend of Salt. It was Briggs who suggested the construction of a canal between the Nile and Alexandria, and who told the Pasha that one of the obelisks known in Europe as Cleopatra's Needles might be acceptable to George III "as unique of its kind in England". Although the offer was accepted, it was another 60 years before the obelisk was raised from the sand near Alexandria, to find a new home on London's Embankment.

Valentia was anxious to be on his way to England. As it was considered important he should run no risk of falling into the hands of the French with all his papers, Missett wrote to Malta to request an armed ship to be sent for him. During the six weeks which must elapse before their ship could come in, Valentia, Salt and Rudland went to view the ruins of antiquity around Damietta. Salt's pencil was kept busy recording standing monuments and some of the antiquities Valentia bought, in case any accident should befall them. "Whoever discovers an antique," commented Valentia, "has a right to dispose of it; they say it is God's property, and he gives it to whom he pleases."[13]

On 20 May, they found their ship, the *Queen,* awaiting them at Alexandria. As Missett had received a report that war was imminent between Russia and the Porte, in which England would be involved, Valentia was anxious to be off, but the wind was against him. Salt filled in the time by making a survey of Alexandria, which it was hoped would enable them to pinpoint the position of "most of the great edifices mentioned by the ancient geographers."[14]

It was 11 June before they took leave of Alexandria. The ship was crowded with "Turks, horses, ostriches, antelopes, monkeys, jerboas and parrots", which rendered it "very uncomfortable, though the Captain was a good creature, and would have kept them in better order if he could." At Malta some six weeks later they were housed first in the Lazaretto, in statutory quarantine for the plague. But occupying an apartment looking across the strait to the ramparts of Valletta, and well supplied with books, newspapers and "the luxuries of ice and fruit, to which we had long been strangers", the time passed pleasantly enough.

Released early, Valentia and Salt explored the island until the Governor, Sir Alexander Ball, obtained them a passage on the *Diana,* one of a fleet of transports returning from landing troops on Sicily. They landed at Portsmouth on Sunday, 26 October 1806, four years and four months after leaving England.

Salt, calling on Joseph Farington, observed rather wistfully that, after his long absence from home, and from news of home, he had found many changes among his friends and family. "He saw in an English newspaper an acct. of the death of His Brother Dr Salt...He met a person in the street who told Him His Father had again married. He also had learnt that His Sister widow of Dr Halls was married to Col De Visme & has two children — He said that He found in London that in four years and a half Lads whom He knew had become men, & young girls Women."[15]

4

The Government Mission

HENRY Salt was now in his mid-twenties. Six feet tall, attractive, articulate and amusing, with the glamour of daring exploits in distant lands about him, he was a 'lion' in London society. If he had tales to tell of Abyssinia almost as strange as those of James Bruce a generation earlier, he also had a witness to his veracity. Bruce's companion, the artist Luigi Balugani, had died in Gondar; but Captain Rudland was alive and in London, to confirm Salt and ever ready to declare that, on more than one occasion, it had only been Salt's "vigilance, judgement and intrepidity" that had saved the whole party from death at the hands of the *askari*.

Many of his new friends were prominent and influential men, but old friends were never forgotten. Halls found him changed and matured by his adventures; his courage, resource and diplomacy had been challenged and he had proved equal to the challenge. He had gained a new steadiness and independence of character though he could still on occasion be "frolicsome and eccentric". Indeed, despite the later years of disappointments, tragedy and ill health, his wry sense of humour was never to be wholly quenched, but, beneath the "habitual gaiety and apparent levity" of Salt's social persona there lay an ambitious man, hungry for a name in the world and prepared to work for it. At this time it seemed well within his grasp – his star was in the ascendant.

He spent the greater part of 1807-9 preparing his drawings and the journals of the travels he had made apart from Valentia for the Viscount's monumental three-volume *Voyages and Travels to India, Ceylon, the Red Sea, Abyssinia and Egypt*.

When it was published to acclaim in 1809, Salt's contributions did not go unnoticed. The *Gentleman's Magazine* remarked, "It is in the knowledge of all our Readers that not the least interesting part of Lord Valentia's *Travels*...is the narrative of Mr Salt's expedition to the Ras..."[1] Besides his several contributions to the *Travels*, Salt worked up a selection of his sketches which were published in 1809 in a large format with coloured plates, as *Twenty-four Views taken in St Helena, the Cape, India, Ceylon, Abyssinia, and Egypt*.

Meanwhile, as well as arranging his own journals, antiquities and specimens of exotic flora, fauna and shells, Valentia was busily pushing his idea of opening up trade with Abyssinia and Arabia. In September 1808, he presented to George Canning, the Foreign Minister, a lengthy and detailed account of the state of trade in the Red Sea, suggesting how Britain could seize a part in it. Arabia appeared to present the best immediate opportunities, but Abyssinia, though offering less prospect of immediate profit, might ultimately be of greater advantage to Britain by "affording an extensive market for every kind of European manufacture".

The Viscount brought forward another reason to pursue his suggestions: the ever-present desire in every patriotic English breast to foil the French. An alliance formed with the fundamentalist Wahabi in Arabia, and "the friendship of Abyssinia cultivated" would acquire for Britain the influence "which the French are now grasping at" and by monopolising the Red Sea trade, "one great resource of our mischievous enemy [Napoleon] would be cut off, and an insuperable bar...put to his future progress", should he ever again be at liberty "to meditate on the destruction of the East." Besides Abyssinia, "a Christian country would be liberated from a most dreadful state of anarchy, and a large extent of country would be snatched from the Mussulman's control." And, he concluded complacently, "I have only to add that this may be done without the violation of one principle of right, and not only without loss, but with an incalculable profit."[2]

But the Foreign Office and the Court of Directors of the East India Company remained unmoved. A merchant, William Jacob, was more favourably impressed and when his firm applied for a licence to trade direct with Abyssinia, the Court of Directors could scarcely refuse, though it imposed many restrictions.

Valentia was nothing if not a sticker. He suggested to Canning that the voyage of Messrs Jacob would be a good opportunity for the Government to respond to the friendly letters and the presents supposedly from the Emperor of Abyssinia, but probably solely from the Ras of Tigre, which he had presented to George III. Perhaps realising it was as cheap a way of doing it as could possibly be managed, Canning agreed and asked Valentia to select suitable presents. The Viscount also urged the unique qualifications of Henry Salt as the emissary to the Emperor. This was not his opinion alone: according to the *Gentleman's Magazine,* "no more suitable person could possibly have been found, as he possessed a mind well stored with general knowledge, a personal acquaintance with the place and its inhabitants, experience of dangerous enterprise, and the greatest firmness and intrepidity of character."[3] Salt was accepted for the mission.

On 6 January 1809, Canning wrote to Valentia requesting him to deliver to Salt the Royal letter and selected presents, and to advise him on "the regulation of his conduct". Valentia accordingly wrote to Salt on 16 January, with a formal memorandum for his guidance. This detailed closely how Salt was to present himself, and the Government's case, in Abyssinia: "Mr Salt will follow the example of Lord Valentia in endeavouring, by every means in his power, to cultivate the friendship of the different tribes on the coast of the Red Sea."[4]

Salt had another commission. The African Association (The Society for Promoting the Discovery of the Interior Parts of Africa) had been founded in 1788, to encourage exploration of "the mysterious dark continent". Salt was invited to a meeting on 26 December 1808, and he told the committee he was anxious to do all in his power to be useful to them, also that he thought Nathaniel Pearce might be engaged to explore into the Abyssinian interior, or otherwise to gather information.

The committee resolved to place £500 at Salt's disposal, to employ Pearce or some other person, "in procuring usefull & curious information, relative to the interior of Africa". He was asked to keep a separate journal not only of his expenses, but also of the information procured, and the character of the person who procured it, to assist the Association "in Weighing the probabilities of truth which really belong to every extraordinary assertion by coupling it with the name of the person from whom it has been obtained & others comparing it with the tenor of his character & the rest of his details. In matters where Men only half civilized are to be dealt with it is lamentable to observe how little they scruple to assert falsities & how little shame they feel on detection, of this Mr Salte [sic] will necessarily be aware at every Step he takes & in every inquiry he institutes."[5] The merchant William Jacob, a member of the Association, offered to defray Salt's expenses incurred on its behalf.

It was probably through the Association that Salt met W. G. Browne, traveller in Egypt and the Middle East; John Lewis Burckhardt, at this time preparing himself for his travels as an Arab among the Arabs, on the Association's behalf; Sir Joseph Banks, who had sailed around the world with Captain Cook as official botanist and was now President of the Royal Society and a trustee of the British Museum, as well as a founder member of the African Association; and William Richard Hamilton, who, as Lord Elgin's secretary, had overseen the transport of the Elgin Marbles from Athens to England. Charles Yorke, another member, who held in his time several high government offices, was to prove on many occasions a generous-hearted patron to Salt.

In the event Salt had very little time to make his final preparations for Abyssinia. Only four days after Valentia's official letter, on 20 January 1809, Salt embarked on Messrs Jacob's ship, the *Marian*. On his last evening in London he dined with Halls at the house of a mutual friend and saw him afterwards to his door. "At this moment of trial, my fortitude deserted me. He said everything he could to console me; but his efforts proving fruitless he knocked at the door, and holding his hands over me, and ejaculating some words, the sense of which escaped me, he rushed from my presence."

It was not, however, their final farewell. The *Marian,* in company with the East India fleet, ran into heavy gales only half a day out of Portsmouth and after five days of being beaten about, managed to struggle back to land. Many of the Indiamen were badly damaged, but the *Marian* suffered only "the loss of sundry ducks, fowls, &c. and the fracture of one arm, which, however, did not occasion much pain to the sufferer, nor any great trouble to the doctor", as the accident was to *Marian*, the ship's figurehead, wrote Salt to Valentia from Portsmouth, adding that he had been seasick, "only in a trifling degree...Coffin, as usual, is quite well."[6]

And here Valentia's 'English servant' of Salt's first voyage at last emerges from his anonymity. Presumably chosen by Salt for his proven qualities, William Coffin was acting on the mission as supercargo, the person in charge of the cargo — or, at least, of the presents for the Emperor of Abyssinia, quite a considerable freight. There were arms after the fashion of the country but ornamented with gold and jewels, satins, cut glass, painted glass, jewellery and fine British muslins, all amounting to about £1,400. There were also two pieces of curricle artillery, with the harness complete, 150 rounds of ball and a quantity of powder; the first cannon to be seen in Abyssinia since the Portuguese left the country in the seventeenth century, and, since "the sound alone would terrify a race of people who have never heard a louder explosion than that of a matchlock", the Ras would be able to march from one end of the country to the other without ever actually meeting an enemy. Unlisted here was a marble table, and some religious pictures by John Halls.[7]

Halls was sitting at breakfast, imagining his friend far on his way, when there was a quick loud step on the stairs, and Salt burst in, exclaiming, "It is not my ghost yet, Halls!", a reference to a half-joking pact they had made to try to appear to the other at the moment of death. (In fact, Halls did 'see' Salt years later, at a time when he almost died.) "There are moments of unalloyed happiness in this life, that seem, at the time, to outweigh years of discomfort and sorrow, and this was one of them," says Halls.

For the moment, the friends put aside all thoughts of the future, and when, towards the end of February, Captain Weatherhead of the *Marian* summoned Salt to Portsmouth, Halls went with him. As they entered the town, they were deeply distressed to observe a division of Sir John Moore's army, straggling through the bitterly cold streets, without shoes or stockings, barely clad, the officers in as bad a case as the men. Due to bureaucratic inefficiency ashore in arranging quarters for their reception, the wretched men had been left for six weeks aboard the transports that had brought them from the war in Spain. Many died miserably, within sight of their homeland.

The *Marian* set sail, with a Brazilian convoy, on 2 March 1809. The ship was nearly wrecked in a sudden storm off the Cape, where the Captain had called to deliver some cargo, noting in his journal that it was dangerously late in the season, and he had "an unpleasant impression that some accident might occur". He was not mistaken; on 29 May, a tremendous gale rolled a huge swell into Table Bay, forcing the ship aground, tearing away her rudder and stoving in her stern.

Salt had introductions to Admiral Bertie and the Governor of the Cape, Lord Caledon, and to many "agreeable English families", and also met several Dutch families, "which added greatly to the pleasure of my stay at the settlement and enabled me to form a tolerably fair estimate of its society." The Dutch seemed to wish to associate with the English, and "when they find a person willing to do justice to their character and to conform to their manners, they seldom fail to cherish his acquaintance, and to treat him with distinguished attention...their habits of life, to a person with unprejudiced feelings for any particular system, are neither disagreeable nor to a certain degree difficult of adoption."[8]

The delay also enabled him, by mentioning the dangers from French privateers along the east coast to Admiral Bertie, to obtain an escort of two brigs of war for the *Marian* as far as Mozambique. Salt accepted its captain's offer of a passage aboard the brig *Racehorse* for this leg of the voyage.

For several days they were among whales — "At times we had twenty or thirty in sight; some of them passing close by the vessel, others darting away, making a snorting noise, and throwing up water like a fountain. At different times they seemed to be pursuing each other, wildly rolling and tumbling about, occasionally rising erect out of the water, shining like bright pillars of silver, then falling on their backs and flapping their enormous fins violently on the surface, with a noise somewhat resembling the report of a cannon."[9]

They came on 25 August to Mozambique, where they were received in a friendly manner by the Portuguese governor. There, Salt saw the slave trade in operation. He watched more than once, with distress, the captives dancing — considered good exercise by the slavers; "it appeared to me that the slaves were *compelled* to dance. I shall never forget the expression of one woman's countenance...when constrained to move in the circle, the solemn gloom that pervaded her features spoke more forcibly than any language the misery of her forlorn condition." Despite official government disapproval, views on slavery in Britain were still divided. Salt was decidedly in the anti-slavery camp: "If there be still a sceptic who hesitates to approve of the abolition of the slave trade, let him visit one of these African slave-yards a short time before a cargo of these wretched beings is exported, and if he have a spark of humanity left it will surely strike conviction to his mind." He felt "happy in thinking that so nefarious a traffic has in this quarter already received a check from British interference..."[10]

During his weeks in Mozambique, Salt closely observed the Portuguese colony, often with some distaste. All his admiration was for the toughness of the Africans in struggling against their would-be colonisers. "To follow any European settlers through the scenes of bloodshed and injustice by which they have established their foreign possessions is an ungrateful and disgusting task...in the atrocity of the means which the Portuguese used to attain their purposes in the East, they were not behind-hand with the Spaniards in the West. Their success, however, was by no means parallel; the natives of Africa were not tame enough, like the feeble inhabitants of South America, to crouch at the feet of an invader, or to yield their country without a struggle. On the contrary, they from the first undertook, and maintained a kind of warfare, which, if not always successful, at least deserves to be so." He took an unsympathetic view of the Portuguese missionaries' efforts to convert the natives, which were "as abortive as their schemes of conquest...their motives proceeded rather from an idle vanity of extending the list of their proselytes, than from any actual desire to benefit the individuals whom they pretended to convert."

Again and again, Salt demonstrates the rather uncommon ability to regard people of other cultures as fellow human beings, whose ways of life, however alien to himself, they had every right to defend. An incident later in the voyage underlines his attitude. One of the sailors having 'wantonly' rubbed a piece of pork fat on the head and neck of an Arab, a most terrible insult, there was considerable trouble, which Salt had to settle. He details the occurrence, he remarks, because of the many fatalities which had followed similar examples of misconduct, in excuse for which natives had been quickly blamed as barbarians, whose behaviour, "were the facts impartially examined, might not only prove justifiable, but possibly meritorious, from the due chastisement they had inflicted on the rude invaders of their rights."[11]

The *Marian* dropped anchor near Aden in the first week of October. Salt had heard there were ancient inscriptions in some old Turkish towers atop the crags behind the port, and set out to climb the steep and difficult path. When they reached the highest ridges, so narrow and with so deep an abyss on either side that the rest of the party firmly sat down and refused to go further, Salt, intent on attaining his goal, struggled on. He managed to climb into a tower by clinging round an angle of the wall, where, supported only by one loose stone, "I had to pass, over a perpendicular precipice of many hundred feet, down which it was impossible to look without shuddering...I...found nothing to reward me for the danger I had encountered, except the view...at this moment, I confess, I could not help looking round with a feeling of gratification, somewhat bordering on pride, at beholding my less adventurous companions, and the inhabitants of the town gazing up from beneath together with the lofty hills and the broad expanse of ocean extended at my feet." His pleasure was considerably allayed by having to retrace his steps, "which required a much stronger effort" than the climb in had done. It was only utter necessity which enabled him "with a sort of desperation" to force himself back the way he had come.[12]

At Mocha on 13 October, Salt took up residence in the Factory, where the new manager was none other than his old friend Captain Henry Rudland, now accompanied by his wife. As agent for the East India Company, with orders from Bombay to open up trade with Abyssinia (which seems at variance with Valentia's reception from the Court of Directors in London), Rudland had already been in touch with Ras Welled Selasse of Tigre through Nathaniel Pearce, who in his reply had stressed the Ras's disappointment at not hearing from England. Pearce suggested various articles which would sell in Abyssinia, and Rudland had accordingly sent trade goods and presents to Pearce at the Bay of Amphila. The expedition was nearly fatal for Pearce. Protecting the goods from the continuous extortions of people along the way, orchestrated by his supposed protector, a young Abyssinian chief called Alli Manda, he finally discharged his blunderbuss injudiciously near the chief and one of his relations as they were preparing to loot the bales of velvets, fatally wounding the kinsman. The Ras, astonished and delighted that Pearce had managed to bring all the goods safely through, said merely that he wished Pearce had killed a dozen more. Alli Manda and his people took a different view.

Salt dispatched letters to the Ras asking that Pearce be sent down to whatever part of the coast thought best, with enough people and mules to convey the presents for the Emperor. As October and November passed with no reply, he became alarmed and decided to sail over to Amphila rather than Massowah, where the disinclination of the Nayib to let trade pass through his domain had been strengthened by an equally hostile Turkish Aga now in command of Massowah.

At Amphila, Salt was horrified to find that the Somali boatman sent with his message was dead, probably poisoned. The Nayib was attempting to bar any English contact with Abyssinia by the Amphila route. He and the Aga had sent a letter to the local chief, Alli Goveta, and all the Bedowee chiefs which instructed bluntly: "If any property belonging to the English (Feringi) should again be brought into your districts or towns, seize it and *kill the persons in charge of it*, and all the property you may thus obtain divide equally among yourselves."[13]

Despite such a temptation, Alli Goveta was friendly. Salt wrote new dispatches, to be delivered by his nephew, Alli Manda. Ignorant of Pearce's troubles, Salt thought rather well of him — he had "a strong and lively expression…his manners were completely Abyssinian; he displayed the same affectation in holding his garment over the mouth, customary among the higher orders in that country, the same kind of stately reserve which on a first interview they assume, and, on being satisfied with his reception, discovered the same open and unrestrained love of conviviality which characterises that singular people." Staking his life on the safe delivery of the letters, he refused payment until his return, which inclined Salt to trust him. One of Salt's people who went with him soon returned, utterly exhausted by the pace set by the young chief, who had travelled night and day "like a dromedary", he complained.

Salt began negotiations to pass through Alli Goveta's district. Though ultimately willing to cooperate, the chief mentioned the Nayib's letter, the bad behaviour of Pearce in not sending down the presents he had promised, with sundry other matters — all of which Salt managed to smooth over; "the subject of presents was next discussed, on which point it requires an uncommon share of patience to listen even with seeming attention to this people… at length I had the good fortune to satisfy him with regard to these *important* matters", and a bargain was struck, bound by the customary ceremony of laying their hands respectively on the Bible and the Koran and promising friendship.

On Christmas Eve, Salt visited the chief at his house. After proper compliments had been exchanged, a silence fell. Alli Goveta fell asleep and the Dola "busied himself in sewing up a new garment, while the natives of the place, gaping with astonishment, crowded in to catch a sight of us." Salt managed to stifle his amusement at the scene, "which was as complete a burlesque on court-ceremony as can well be conceived". On departure, he was presented with a bullock. Christmas was celebrated by dressing out the ship with every flag she possessed and feasting on roast bullock and plum pudding.

Alli Manda appeared on 6 January with letters from Pearce, for which the Dola tried to extract money. It took nearly an hour before Salt "by raising my voice, and affecting great irritation" (which cannot have tried his acting abilities severely), could obtain possession of them. Pearce argued against travelling to Tigre via Bure, the route through Goveta's domain; the Massowah road was the best and safest. He added, "The Ras says, that every day seems like a year until he shall meet you." In a second letter, Pearce said plainly that he himself would be in danger on the Bure road, but "P.S. In case *you are determined* to come this road beware Alli Manda and his friends, as we are at great variance, and blood lies upon me in their country. Should you make friends with him, I will come down at his return, but whatever will happen," he ended with typical insouciance.[14]

A few days later Salt's acquaintance from his last voyage, the Dola of Dhalac, arrived with the welcome news that the hostile Aga had been removed from office and the new Aga wished to promote friendship with the English. With this route now open, Salt dispatched Coffin to Pearce, arranging to meet him at Massowah in two weeks' time. Once Salt heard that Coffin was safely in the Ras's domains, he told Alli Goveta he would be taking the Massowah route.

When the *Marian* dropped anchor at Massowah on 10 February, to Salt's relief he saw Coffin and a party of Abyssinians on the pier, including a young chief, Ayto Debib, sent by the Ras to attend on Salt during his visit.[15] As for Pearce, Salt found it "truly gratifying to witness his raptures at finding himself once more among Englishmen, and in an English ship. In the fullness of his heart he seemed to consider every countryman on board as a brother, and it was interesting to observe, with what respect and astonishment our sailors looked up to him in return, from the various accounts they had previously heard of the intrepidity with which he had surmounted so many dangers." He sped about the ship and climbed aloft so fast that none of the sailors could keep up with him.

He had written to Salt, "You said you hoped you should not have occasion to employ an Interpreter. I can assure you Sir if I had been that great dunce as not to know both Tigre and Amharic I should be greatly ashamed, I knew them both two years after you left me, also greatly amended myself in the Arabic."[16] Salt himself acquired at least a smattering of Amharic, for he is said to have spoken it in the delirium of his last illness, but he comments that Tigre "is reckoned by the natives very difficult to acquire", adding that Pearce now had "so perfect an insight into the manners and feelings of the Abyssinians", that he was invaluable as an interpreter.

The party, with mules and bearers from Abyssinia, was perhaps the largest that had ever left the coast since the time of the Portuguese. Besides Salt, Coffin, Pearce, Smith the surgeon, and a servant named Thomas Ingram, there were three Arabs, three Hazorta chiefs, a dozen "rascally" camel-drivers and about a hundred Abyssinians, many of them "wild and desperate young men", accustomed to accompany the Ras on his warfaring forays. Fourteen carried firearms and spears, the rest merely slings, knives and short heavy sticks. With this mob about them, the journey to the pass of Taranta, while not without incident, was at no time so dangerous as Salt's first expedition.

Salt's literary style, while clear and unaffected, is often prosaic, but now and again the artist's eye is turned upon a scene, bringing it to vivid life. Arrived in their own country, the Hazorta guides celebrated by dancing; "the reader must fancy himself stationed on a clear night amidst a grove of lofty trees, standing in a lonely valley and skirted by abrupt mountains, bordered by a winding stream...the dance had a peculiarly wild and fantastic effect, greatly heightened as it was by the gleaming dashes of light thrown on the different objects from a number of scattered fires, round which the natives were clustered in irregular groups."

Six days out from Arkeko, Salt was greeted "with the hearty welcome of an old acquaintance" by Barharnagash Yasous of Dixan. His venerable aspect, his mild manners and Salt's memory of his previous good services "added a peculiar gratification to our meeting". Salt woke at dawn next day to the well-remembered sound of the Barharnagash calling his family to prayer. When he joined them, "the interval of four years...appeared like a mere dream."

Salt had a high and affectionate opinion of Barharnagash Yasous. "Among all the men with whom I have ever been intimately acquainted, I consider this old man as one of the most perfect and blameless characters. His mind seemed formed upon the purest principles of Christian religion; his every thought and action appearing to be the result of its dictates. He would often, to ease his mule, walk more than half the day...if a man were weary, he would assist him in carrying his burthen, if he perceived any of the mules' backs to be hurt, he would beg me to have them relieved; and constantly, when he saw me engaged in shooting partridges or other birds, he would call out to them to fly out of the way; shaking his head and begging me in a mournful accent not to kill them."[17]

Resting one day, they observed armed bands appearing one after the other from different parts of the hills, as if meaning to encircle them. They took up defensive positions, with Coffin in charge of the guns upon some rising ground, while Pearce and Debib told Salt to sit down with them and pretend, with seeming unconcern, to smoke a hookah. "It became a picturesque, though somewhat alarming sight, to see the parties winding down from among the hills", all armed with spears and matchlocks. Their chief approached, backed by some 150 "desperate and rascally-looking fellows", and accosted Salt and his companions brusquely. Recognising Pearce and Debib, he became more civil, and looked disconcerted when told by Debib, "assuming all the consequence which his station conferred", that these were the Ras's strangers, and moreover that Salt was the envoy of a sovereign whom the Ras considered his own equal. Soon the chief rose and made off, muttering under his breath, "It won't do, we had better let them alone." His men followed reluctantly, regarding the packages, Salt thought, "with a wistful eye, that very evidently spoke of their regret at being compelled to leave them unexamined."

On 15 March the party came to the hill above Chelicut appointed for the first reception of the mission. Salt, riding a richly caparisoned mule sent him by the Ras, had considered what to wear for this occasion before leaving England, and prepared a "suitable dress", most importantly a dark red velvet pelisse trimed with fur, which concealed the clothes beneath, presenting an appearance the Abyssinians could respect: for he had observed last time that European costume "tended to excite a species of contempt and ridicule that occasionally became very unpleasant in its effects". The other Europeans dressed as neatly as possible. To the hill came two chiefs to escort them, honouring them by dismounting and baring themselves to the waist. During the descent into Chelicut the crowd around them increased by the moment, until "with a great bustle and confused clamour, reckoned honorable to the guests", they were led into the presence of the Ras.

As all the chiefs stood and bared themselves, the Ras rose "with eagerness to receive me, like a man suddenly meeting with a long lost friend, and, when I made my salutations, joy seemed to glisten in his eyes, while he welcomed me with an honest warmth and cordiality that nothing but genuine and undisguised feeling could inspire." Salt was seated at his left hand, the second place of honour — in the first already sat a brother of the Emperor. Asking after Salt's health, the Ras declared he had always had a premonition he should see him once again before he died.

After a meal, Salt and his companions were led to Pearce's house, more comfortably arranged for Europeans than the usual Abyssinian dwelling. In its large garden, Pearce had sown seeds sent him by Rudland and the party could enjoy eating familiar vegetables, such as cabbages. Still attended by Debib to make sure all Salt's wishes were met and that he received the same attentions as if he were the Ras himself, the party settled in. Salt thought Pearce's wife, daughter of a Greek called Sidee Paulus, fairer-skinned than most Abyssinians, "very amiable...and extremely agreeable in her manners." Her name was Thuringa, but Pearce called her Tringo.

Salt spent much of each day with the Ras, going to him at will through a private door between Pearce's garden and that of the palace. One day Pearce arrived breathless to announce that the Ras was on his way to do Salt the greatest honour in his power by visiting him in his own house. Salt found him in the garden, supported only by Pearce and Debib, and accompanied by one slave, who carried his sword. He smiled and pointed to the cabbages, asking "Are they good?" then laid his hand on Salt's shoulder and walked with him into the house. He stayed more than an hour, looking at drawings of English buildings, ships, carriages and other things, and conversing on English customs "in the most familiar manner". Pearce was immensely pleased by this visit, which made a great noise throughout the country, for it was many years since the Ras had paid such a compliment to any but the high priest and his own nearest relatives.

Only one thing marred the real happiness to both of this reunion; such was the state of affairs between the Ras and the Galla chief Guxo, who stood between Tigre and Gondar, that, for fear of his life, Salt could not be allowed to go there without an army to protect him. The Ras intended a foray on Gondar and was willing to take Salt with him, but this was impossible until after the rainy season in October, and, unfortunately, having strict orders to return to England in the *Marian,* Salt could not hold her in Africa for eight or nine extra months. Not at all sure how his actions would be received in England, Salt was "under the disagreeable necessity" of delivering King George's letter and the presents designed for the Emperor to the Ras. An entire week was spent in arranging the offerings and presenting them at court. Salt accompanied the Ras to the church at Chelicut to see how various articles had been "advantageously arranged". The marble table became a communion table, Halls' picture of the Virgin was suspended above it as an altarpiece, and the painted glass window placed where it gave a "remarkably pleasing effect". The multi-talented Pearce, at the Ras's desire, played on a hand organ, presented some time before by Captain Rudland. "Notwithstanding the instrument was considerably out of tune, yet, I confess, that, from an association of ideas, I never listened to any thing like music with more delight."

The Ras and his chiefs were overcome with admiration at the effect. "Etzub, etzub" (wonderful, wonderful), exclaimed the Ras. He ordered that a prayer be offered up weekly for the health of the King of Great Britain. Everyone was deeply impressed by the presents. "The purity of our religion ceased to be questioned, our motives for visiting the country were no longer doubted." Salt's consequent importance led the Emperor's brother to try to secure his interest if the government should change, but Salt rejected any idea of interfering in the internal politics of the country, and, as seemed to him proper, "consulted on all such occasions confidentially with the Ras".

Although he would not let Salt go to Gondar, the Ras allowed him to make a tour to the Tacazze River with Coffin, protected by Pearce, Debib and a chief of one of the districts they would pass. Salt kept a meticulous record of bearings and distances, to map his journey, made careful observations of the flora and fauna and sketched a hippopotamus, wallowing in a stream. After a tour of some 120 miles, they were back at Chelicut by 13 April. The Ras had evidently missed them; his visit to Pearce's house was made next day. But soon Salt would have to leave.

The Ras asked Salt to permit one of his men to stay behind with Pearce, to manage the precious new cannons, for though his enemies were much alarmed, they knew he was ignorant of their use, and would soon lose their fear; but "leave me only another *jagonah* [warrior] like Mr Pearce, and they will never dare to meet me in the field." As Coffin had already spoken of his wish to stay, Salt told the Ras that he should dissuade no one of his people from remaining if he wanted to — "the personal freedom which British subjects enjoy, left every man perfectly at liberty to act as he might think proper on such occasions."

On 25 April, the last day of Lent, the Ras moved to Antalo, inviting Salt to join him. With the rule of no food until sunset at an end, several days of feasting began, "and so large a quantity of *brind* [raw beef] was consumed by both priests and laity, as clearly evinced that they were determined to make up as speedily as possible for the restraint which had so long been laid upon their appetites." In the highest spirits, the Ras invited Salt to drink from his own drinking vessel, an honour so unprecedented that all the chiefs were astounded. Some of them had been expressly sent for by the Ras to ensure their good behaviour to Salt on his return journey.

During one feast, there was an event which nearly had the most serious consequences. Among the presents from England were some fireworks, mostly serpents, small wheels and crackers, with which Salt had frequently amused the Ras and his court; the Ras delighted to light them himself and throw them among his attendants. Several strange chiefs and their followers were present when the Ras one day requested that some fireworks should be let off. Salt told Pearce to set up one of the largest, labelled 'a flower pot', in the middle of the great hall, which was about 30 feet by 60, and crowded with guests in flowing cotton garments; "eager expectation sat on the countenance of all". But when the fuse was lit, "such a deluge of sparks and fireballs were almost instantaneously showered upon us", that there was an uproar. Some chiefs cried that this was the destruction they had expected from the Europeans, some squeezed under the couches, and some ran screaming into the corners of the room. Salt instantly jumped up and stood before the Ras with spread arms to keep the sparks from him, assuring him there was no danger. He sat, perfectly cool and collected, smiling at the alarm of his guests. He was one of the few whose garments were not singed, and when the sparks died away, was soon laughing at the terrified chiefs, though he said afterwards to Salt that in future firework displays had better take place when they were by themselves. Salt and his companions also laughed heartily later in private, and the court jester, a talented mimic, worked the incident up into a farcical act, but had the Ras been hurt, the Europeans would probably have been instantly cut to pieces.

On 27 April, Salt had a public audience with the Ras, who formally handed over a letter for the King of England, at the same time presenting Salt with a medallion engraved with the armorial bearings of the Abyssinian emperors, on a gold chain, "as the highest compliment it was in his power to confer". He wanted to send Debib as his envoy to England, but Salt felt he must decline, having no authority "to adopt a measure to which so much importance and responsibility were attached".[18] Two small lions were also declined, as he did not think they would survive the journey.

At midnight on 2 May, the Ras made a solemn declaration before four of the priests of Antalo of his intentions towards Pearce and Coffin, promising always to treat them with kindness, to supply them with stated rations, and to do all in his power, if ever they wished it, to enable them to return to England. The agreement was sanctified by a prayer. Salt had done all he could to protect his countrymen from any change in the Ras toward them, but it must have occurred to him that he had safeguarded them only during the lifetime, or the secure power, of the Ras.

All the next day, as final preparations for departure were made, the Ras was very depressed. He kept Salt by his side, often fixing him with a sorrowful look, and asking again and again if he should ever return. Reluctantly, Salt had to reply that he did not believe it likely.

At 2 a.m. on 4 May, the party said their farewells. The Ras spoke of his gratitude to the English King for "regarding the welfare of so remote a country", and, while acknowledging the difficulties, promised to do all he could to promote trade with Great Britain while Salt assured him that he would never lose sight of the interests of Abyssinia. Both were deeply moved. When, at daybreak, Salt and his people rose to leave, the Ras went with them to the door of the hall, "where he stood watching us, with tears running down his face," until they were out of sight.

The journey to the coast was broken at Axum, so that Salt could check his observations of four years earlier. At Adowa, Richard Stuart appeared, a man who had joined the *Marian* at Cape Town, and whom Salt had used the African Association's money to send into Ifat and Hurrar, an expedition which had largely failed. At Adowa, too, Salt met Pearce's Greek father-in-law; Sidee Paulus had been 50 years in Abyssinia and had met James Bruce, and asked if Salt was his kinsman.

From Adowa the party was accompanied only for a few miles by Pearce and Coffin, whom both the Ras and Salt feared to risk among the dwellers on the borders of Abyssinia, many of whom were hostile to their remaining in the country. Their parting was most melancholy for they could not expect ever to meet again.

Debib, however, continued with the party to the coast. At Massowah on 24 May, due to the miscarriage of Salt's letters, the *Marian* had not yet arrived, placing them in a perilous situation. Salt almost at once fell ill with a violent fever, brought on, he thought, by a combination of the change of climate to the foetid humidity of the coast, and his anxiety at their position. He considered that his life was only saved by the care of Mr Smith, the surgeon, and the timely arrival of a *dhow* prepared to transport them to Mocha.

Salt had to be carried aboard, but feeble as he was, took pleasure in presenting Debib with something he knew, through Pearce, the young chief longed for, an English gun, indeed his own. Debib, who scorned to beg, was overjoyed.

Captain Weatherhead intended to sail direct for the Cape but the winds directed otherwise. With the vessel increasingly unseaworthy, it was necessary to make for Bombay. It was 4 October before the *Marian* was fit to put to sea again, and not until 11 January 1811 that she made landfall at Penzance.

Salt took a deep pleasure in his mission to Abyssinia. He wrote to Captain Court on his voyage out, "You, my dear friend, who know how much my heart has been bent on benefiting this country, will easily conceive the delight which I feel in being thus employed. May I only prove the instrument of recovering the consequence of this ancient and neglected country, or even of stemming for a season the tide of barbarism that surrounds it, and I shall be completely happy."[19] He never forgot his feeling for Abyssinia, as he was years later to prove; but knowing how little the English King was concerned and how little was to come of Salt's mission, the Ras's gratitude seems peculiarly poignant.

5

The 'Lion' of Abyssinia

ONE JANUARY evening, John Halls and the lawyer Henry Broughton, sitting in their lodgings, talking as so often of their absent friend, heard a loud knock on the door. The servant announced a gentleman of the name of Salt; an instant later a tall figure, muffled in a rough seaman's coat, strode into the room and seized Halls by the hand, crying, "I always told you, Halls, that 'The Bad Shilling' would come back again in safety!"

When they tried to help him off with his 'wrap-rascal' coat, Salt, laughing, held it open to convince them that he had better, for decency's sake, keep it on. All the clothes left to him after his prolonged journey were a waistcoat and a pair of black silk breeches, which hung about him in ribbons. Great was the amusement as he recounted how, in this "sorry trim", he had had to report himself first to Marquess Wellesley, now successor to Canning as Foreign Secretary, and then to Mr Jacob, the owner of the *Marian*, in his drawing room — where to increase his discomfiture, the ladies of the house strenuously urged him to remove his coat, lest he take cold on going out into the night air. To these exhortations, he "judiciously turned a deaf ear". Halls summoned a tailor forthwith, and invited Salt to stay until he found other quarters, which he soon did near by, at 17 Great Marlborough Street.

For some time Salt was occupied in settling his affairs and attending at the Foreign Office. Somewhat anxious about having given the King's letter and presents to the Ras rather than the Emperor, he apologised to the Foreign Office, saying that the Ras had understood they were for the Emperor, and as such had received them. "But even," he wrote rather desperately, "if I had entertained doubts of his sincerity I beg leave to ask what other mode of proceeding could I have adopted?"[1]

As he understood the letter from the Ras to confirm he had accepted the presents in trust for the Emperor, and to set out his reasons for preventing Salt's going into Gondar, it was important to have it translated. Salt suggested that the best person would be the Reverend Alexander Murray, a Scottish clergyman, who had taught himself all it was possible to know about Abyssinia without actually going there, edited the second, 1805, edition of Bruce's *Travels*, and published a life of the traveller in 1808. The letter proved not very satisfactory from Salt's point of view, as it merely said that the Ras did not accept the Emperor made by Guxo, as he was "not orthodox in the faith". But Murray said firmly that the Treasury should regard the Ras as king in Tigre, and the probable future king-maker of Abyssinia, if supported by Britain. Presents given to the Emperor would be "absolutely thrown away", while presents to the Ras "will open his province and probably fix his ascendant".[2] This knowledgeable support satisfied the Government and Salt's standing with the Foreign Office was high. Wellesley gave him his "unqualified approbation".[3] This approbation did not cause the Foreign Office to hasten to reward him for his valuable services. On 18 September 1811, when delivering a map for Lord Wellesley, Salt took the opportunity to mention "a circumstance of the utmost importance to me", that Wellesley might not know, as he was not in office when Salt was employed; "I will feel obliged to you to communicate it to his Lordship, that *I have not hitherto received any salary* during the time I have had charge of the Mission or in any other way been remunerated for my services, having merely been paid the expenses actually incurred the whole amount of which in two years and a half did not exceed £2,000 and I have to add that Mr Canning expressly stated in a letter dated Foreign Office January 14, 1809 to Lord Valentia that *'the question of remuneration will have to be settled on Mr. Salt's return.'"[4]

Four months later he wrote anxiously of "being at this time pressed for very considerable debt." On 18 February, Wellesley at last sent an official note to Canning asking what remuneration should be given Salt for his Mission, "in which he appears to have acted with great Diligence and Zeal". With amazing speed, Canning replied the next day that as far as he could recollect no precise sum had been stipulated but "on account of the uncertain duration and unascertained nature of the service", it was left to be settled when a judgement could be made upon "Mr Salt's merits". As Canning had no knowledge of what had occurred, he could not possibly conjecture what might be the just amount. By 9 April, £1,000 was being mentioned, but Charles Yorke, when consulted, recommended £2,000, to include the expenses. These came to £573.8s.11d, including 46 guineas to Halls for pictures. On 11 April, Salt addressed the new Minister, Lord Castlereagh, hoping at least for the reimbursement of the expenses account, exclusively of whatever sum he might "judge adequate to the actual remuneration of upwards of two years' arduous service". £2,000 was at last recommended, including the expenses. Halls thought Salt only received £1,000 — and this at least 16 months after his return from the mission.

Infinitely more agreeable and satisfactory was his reception by the African Association. At the General Meeting of 25 May 1811, a brief account was read of the information Salt had brought them. Though unable to obtain answers to any of the Association's specific questions and though Richard Stuart's tour into Ifat and the Hurrar had been aborted (but he had kept a journal of his experiences), the information Salt had gathered at Mozambique, Aden and Mocha, together with the vocabularies he had pro-cured of the Makuana, the Monyou, the Sawali, the Samauli and the Hurrar Languages, were judged likely to be of great use to the Association.[5] As well as considerable information about the peoples, places and customs he had observed or been told of, Salt compiled vocabularies for more than a dozen languages spoken in Abyssinia. He brought back and presented, mainly to Sir Joseph Banks, 146 plant specimens, many previously unknown genera, of which *Saltia abyssinica* and *cotalaria Saltiana* were named for him. He presented to Lord Stanley more than 70 specimens of bird, several never before described. There was also an unknown number of such things as ani-mal hides and horns. A previously unknown dik-dik, "little bigger than a hare", called *madoqua* in Tigre, became *madoqua Saltiana*.[6]

On 30 May 1812, Salt himself gave the General Meeting of the African Association a fuller account of his travels, and said he did not wish to receive any pecuniary compensation but "would consider himself amply repaid by being elected an Honorary Member".[7] Not only did the meeting unanimously resolve to do so (the only other men ever being so honoured, both in 1792, were Perkins Magra, Consul in Tunis 1789-1804, and James Rennell, the eminent geographer), but also insisted he accept £100 "as an additional mark of the approbation of the Association". The following year, on 17 February, Salt was also elected to the far more exclusive African Club, a dining club which met periodically at the Thatched House Tavern in St James's. These informal meetings were not profusely attended and the min-utes show that on 21 March 1814 Salt's only dinner companions were two rather elderly gentlemen, the Reverend Dr Luttrel Wynne and the Duke of Norfolk.

* *

When Valentia's *Travels* were published, a clamour arose from the contem-porary equivalents of the men who had earlier mocked James Bruce into a resentful seclusion, highly indignant at Valentia and Salt for presuming to criticise the now dead, and newly revered, hero of Abyssinian travel. Knowing that he would be making more criticisms of Bruce in his own book, Salt may have expected some coldness from Bruce's biographer. But instead Reverend Alexander Murray wrote frankly that Bruce was "old and indolent" when he finally composed his work, and his notes made upon the spot were often at variance with the final tale. However, though admitting the justice, Murray criticised the tone of Valentia's comments: "Lord Valentia has rather displayed a kind of ostentatious and triumphant pride in conquering Bruce, which resembles that species of glory which the

Abyssinian soldiers show when they brandish their spears over the head of the Ras, and throw down the trophies taken from the enemy. Now this is not good. It makes ignorant people think that Bruce had no merit." But, Murray continued, "I look with much more pleasure to your own mode of confuting Mr Bruce. You put down hard facts and proclaim no victory...I have that opinion of your candour to believe that a refutation of Bruce's narrative...would not lead you to parade your own discoveries, so much as it would prompt you to enlarge, by native industry and adventure, the bounds of true knowledge. You have already extended them. I wish to see your merit warmly patronised."[8]

Salt replied, "You certainly go full as far as I do in your strictures on him, though you do not perhaps feel so strongly the consequence of his defects", which, with an apparently unvindictive desire for the truth, did worry Salt. He had taken considerable trouble while in Tigre to question people who had known Bruce, who had confirmed many of his accounts, but denied the truth of others.

The tales that had aroused most disgust and disbelief had been those of 'living feasts'. There were two separate stories: the first, that when on a march, soldiers would cut a steak from a living cow, then, plastering over the wound with clay, drive it on; the second, that at banquets in Gondar a live cow, lowing in agony, would be hacked to pieces at the door of the hall, and brought bit by quivering bit to the table. It was in fact only the tale of the feast that the Ras, the Emperor's brother and many others denied, while Pearce had witnessed what might be called a 'living picnic', on a marauding expedition. Pearce, despite his hunger, had been too disgusted to eat the meat; the animal walked afterwards rather lame, but managed to reach the evening camp, where it was slaughtered. But "so commodious a manner of carrying provisions along the road", in Bruce's jovial phrase, was declared by Pearce and others to be a very rare occurrence.

In his book, Salt apologised for his criticisms, saying he had "selected only a small portion of the contradictions", being "anxious to enter only so far into the question, as might tend to justify the observations I felt myself compelled to make...for, had I altogether evaded the question, I might, with some justice, have been supposed to have compromised my own opinions from the dread of his numerous advocates, or from a culpable desire of sheltering myself under his acquired reputation. I am perfectly aware how much Mr Bruce has accomplished; and no man can more truly admire his courage, his perseverance, his sagacity, or his genius than myself...I shall never cease to regret that any weakness of character or unfortunate vanity should have induced him in a single instance to have swerved from the plain and manly path of sincerity and truth...since the ground which he occupied was far too elevated for him to stand in need of any such unworthy and adventitious aid."[9] What most upset Salt in Bruce's account was his denial to Balugani, his young employee, of any part in the glory he attached to reaching the source of the Nile, by dating the man's death to the previous year, although both his own notes and those of Balugani showed he was still alive. Salt felt "there was something of cruelty so perfectly inexcusable in his whole conduct towards this young man, who very materially assisted him in his researches, that it can admit of no apology...it may, perhaps, be asked, what motives Mr Bruce could have had for such wilful deviations from the truth? The answer is plain: that he was impelled to it by an anxious and vehement desire of obtaining the sole credit of having first visited the sources of the Nile, and an aversion from his being known to have had any partner in his researches on this occasion; motives which however unworthy of an enlightened mind, are known to have operated so strongly on our author's feelings, that he has made them the ruling features in his work..."[10]

If it seems too much has been made of Salt's criticisms of Bruce, it must be realised that they were to have far-reaching effects upon his own reputation. It is a pity that the critics could not read two letters from Pearce which are far less charitable than anything Salt had said. Pearce commented on Bruce's tales, "I think they ought to be Burnt and so dose all who knew him espicily the old Ras...all the lies Mr Bruce has told that I have Proved I have wrote down Lord what a man must that be to invent such lies. He is gone poor fellow God forgive him"; and again, "every body who knew him says he turned Mad after he got home and Wrote all lies".[11] Unfortunately, Pearce gave no details of these 'lies'.

Is it too much to conjecture that when, years later, an ex-employee did his best to tarnish Salt's reputation, by accusing him of taking to himself all the glory of their joint enterprise, a recollection that Salt could be thought to have behaved rather shabbily to a man who was not alive to defend himself made it easier for people to believe what they were now hearing? And is it too much to conjecture that the man so vehement in his disgust with Bruce's self-seeking treatment of Balugani was unlikely to have changed so much in only a few years?[12]

* *

Some time in 1812, Salt obtained for Halls from the Dean of Lichfield a commission to design a stained glass window for the Cathedral, and Halls was able at last to meet his friend's father, which from all he had heard of his eccentricity, he had long wished to do — nor were his expectations disappointed. He and Salt found the old man walking in his garden. After a short conversation, Salt remarked that he should soon bring Halls again, to dine.

"No, no, Master Henry," Mr Salt replied, "that will never do; I prepared an excellent dinner for your friend yesterday, and it was his own fault if he did not choose to come in time to partake of it."

"But, sir, the mail was full, and Mr Halls could not get a place till last night."

"Very well, I can only say, he lost a good fillet of veal and some fine mackerel, which I had provided for him, and I am not going to be served so again."

However, Thomas Salt called on him every day at the house of Henry's sister, Bessy Morgan, where he was staying, and entertained him very much with his amusing and original conversation.

Later that year Salt and Halls took lodgings together in London, at 10 Argyll Street.[13] Salt was invited on a party touring Wales, but on 20 October he wrote to Halls from Arley Castle, Valentia's seat in Staffordshire, that he would shortly be with him and was looking forward to spending "a most agreeable winter in the bosom of friendship and the *arts*." He spoke too soon, for on 2 November he had to report that he was very unwell with a swelling on his right leg, and did not feel he could move without his doctor's permission.

When he did reach London the swelling became so much worse that it had to be operated upon. With no anaesthetics, Salt's suffering must have been horrible, though he went to his bed afterwards, seemingly in excellent spirits. Very early the next morning, Halls was called by his servant — Mr Salt appeared to be dying. "I was exceedingly alarmed, as I beheld him, for the first time, labouring under one of those terrible spasmodic affections to which he was occasionally liable throughout nearly his whole life...all the muscles of his body were distorted and drawn into knots, and the writhings of his whole person presented to the view a species of terrible sublimity which, even in that moment of anxiety, put me forcibly in mind of the statue of Laocoön." (What it is, in moments of stress, to have had a classical and artistic education.) Halls feared tetanus, but as the spasms subsided a little, Salt was able to whisper "Ether", which Halls recollected was the medicine he always used in "what he called his hysteric attacks". The cause of this attack proved to be the swelling of the lint inserted in the incision to prevent it closing, which had thus pressed on the adjacent nerves. Confined to his couch for several months, Salt alleviated his boredom by writing "squibs" and "saucy messages" to his friends both male and female.

At about this time he applied to become a Fellow of the Royal Society. He was elected on 26 November 1812, recommended from their "personal knowledge" by 11 distinguished Fellows as "a gentleman well versed in several branches of science" who had explored much of Abyssinia.[14]

At the end of May 1813 Halls went to Shrewsbury to work at the glassworks on his window for Lichfield Cathedral. Salt wrote to him there on 4 June, "I am at this moment in such a humour that I do not know whether to laugh or to cry. I have had a slight relapse of my leg, and I am advised to go to the sea-side."

In mid-July he wrote from Southend, "I have been...witnessing scenes of such a very distressing nature that I am, for once in my life, disposed to be serious." An acquaintance visiting Southend, Mrs Gambier, in the absence of any male member of her family, had begged Salt to support her in caring for her 11-year-old son, who had typhus. As it had nearly killed Salt in 1801, it must have taken some courage to expose himself to the risk of catching the highly infectious disease again. Mrs Gambier and he alternately relieved each other, until the child died.

He returned to London, much improved in health, though his leg still sometimes troubled him and did not completely recover for another few months. Halls considered his confinement no bad thing, for he had previously been enjoying such a gay social round, "not only among the middling, but the higher classes of life", that he had made little progress on his book about his journey to Abyssinia. Writing came easily to him and his retentive memory and "clear intellect" enabled him to make rapid progress.

In late summer, the two had to make new living arrangements. Halls' father had died, and on his rapid re-marriage his daughters decided to join their brother in London. However, Salt, in lodgings at 106 Great Russell Street, spent many happy evenings with Mary, Elizabeth and Julia Halls and their brothers, which he evoked forlornly in a letter to Mary some years later. "I am often present with you, as St Paul says, in spirit, and delight in imagining myself a member of your fireside coteries...with John just descending from his painting-room to humanise, Elizabeth brightening into a smile, and you yourself, though rather grave before dinner, gradually taking an interest in the conversation, and enlightening it with your keen remarks; while Brother Tom, as the cloth is just taken away, comes in rather warm, and protesting he did not think it had been so late...and I cannot help fancying I hear you sometimes say, 'Now we want nothing but the Bad Shilling to make our party complete.'"[15]

By October Salt had come to an arrangement with the publishers Messrs Rivington, as he told Valentia, "...upon terms which appear to me to be very fair...they are to pay me £800 certain, and I am to have two-thirds of all additional profits on the first edition...the printing is to begin in about a fortnight." Matters did not proceed as fast as he hoped; he was still revising in May 1814 and it was July before the book was published.

He could be certain it would be noticed, for Lady Eliot, a sister of Charles Yorke, had introduced him to Lord de Dunstanville, through whom he had obtained permission to dedicate his work to the Prince Regent. Salt took the opportunity in his dedication to advance the interests of Abyssinia with the Prince: "Should [the book] succeed in attracting to your notice the present forlorn and distracted state of Abyssinia, so far as to induce YOUR ROYAL HIGHNESS to promote the welfare of that country...I shall feel that my exertions in this cause have not been in vain..."[16] Probably the Regent gave not a moment's thought to Salt's plea, but he did invite him more than once to one of his "splendid entertainments". Salt probably never met the Prince's estranged wife, Caroline, Princess of Wales. She, who had "a system of seeing all remarkable persons", had written to George Canning in February 1810 to learn where Salt "lodged". The Foreign Secretary replied: "My dear Madam, Mr Salt lodges at the Raas's (I do not know the name nor the number), somewhere in Abyssinia."[17]

Travels in Abyssinia was well received by both reviewers and the public, and read with avidity, says Halls, by those "best qualified to form a correct judgement of its merits." The charts — the coastal ones made mostly by the Captain of the *Marian*, but that of mainland Abyssinia by Salt — were considered to be the most accurate then existing; while, though Halls thought the engravers not up to the standard of those employed on Valentia's book, the plates were "nevertheless full of character and nature, and may be relied on for their striking resemblance to the scenery and individuals" represented. The bibliophile T. F. Dibdin, advised "of recent authors, few stand more deservedly high than Mr Salt...his researches... rank him high in the class of Abyssinian travellers. If I am asked, by the economical Collector, to give up Bruce, or Mr Salt? I shall unhesitatingly say forgo the former, and secure the latter."[18]

Charles Yorke's reception of the copy Salt presented to him was music to an author's ears: "I have read, or rather devoured, your most entertaining book, and am highly pleased with the whole of it; with the simplicity, clearness and modesty, as well of the arrangement and matter, as of the style. It only makes me desirous of more..."[19]

With his book off his hands, Salt went to Lichfield, to see his father and sister Bessy, then, in early September, in his gig, made a leisurely tour through Wales to Holyhead, and sailed, gig and all, on the packet to Dublin. Of the "city of the Pats" he had mixed views — admiration for many of the public buildings, shock at the little attention paid to the upkeep of the churches and distress at "the raggedness of the beggars hovering round every corner of the streets", presenting "a hopeless and despairing picture of the inhabitants."

Leaving Dublin, Salt visited several acquaintances, eventually reached Camolin Park, Co. Wexford, Valentia's Irish home, at the end of September, and joined in the lavish celebrations of the coming of age of his son. "It would have given you great pleasure to have seen Lord Valentia acting in his proper station," Salt wrote to Halls, adding, "Pray tell your sisters that they may expect to find me, on my return, a perfect Irishman, as I have already acquired a very tolerable share of the brogue." After several weeks with Valentia, Salt set out for Dublin, detained by the hospitality of more than one friend along his way. Dublin provided a daily round of parties, at which "I have enjoyed the company of most of those who are esteemed eminent in the society of the capital," he wrote to Valentia, "so that, in fact, I have been quite spoiled by the manner in which I have been fêted." The day before, he had dined with some of these eminences, and "upon the whole, I never spent a pleasanter evening, as they were all in high spirits and anxious...to turn the conversation upon Abyssinia." Lord Caledon, whom Salt had liked and admired when he had met him as Governor at the Cape, was back in Ireland, and called upon Salt with a pressing invitation to his seat in County Tyrone, "and as I conceive this may tend to strengthen my interest with the Yorke family I accepted his invitation." Caledon had married, in 1812, Catherine Yorke, daughter of the Earl of Hardwicke and niece to Charles Yorke, and 'interest' was more necessary than merit in those days for one who had his way to make in the world.[20]

Salt crossed to Port Patrick, and thence to Edinburgh. His visit was most satisfactory. He met, among "all the principal people of the place", Walter Scott, the poet and author, John Playfair, professor of natural philosophy at Edinburgh University, and Francis Jeffrey, lawyer and editor of the prestigious and outspoken *Edinburgh Review*.

'Lionised' in society everywhere with flattering respect and attention, Salt may have felt, with some justification, that his reputation was assured; his financial position, unfortunately, was not. He was now 34 years old, still had no settled career and had been put to the necessity of borrowing from his father.

On 13 April 1815, Salt wrote in some excitement to Valentia in Ireland, "I have now to communicate an event which is of much consequence to me. Yesterday I received intelligence that Major Missett, the Consul-General in Egypt, had resigned...in consequence I waited directly on Mr Hamilton...and he promised immediately to write, in my favour, to Lord Castlereagh, urging my claims, which he admitted 'were undoubtedly such as would entitle me to the situation, if no private patronage interfered'." Indeed, it is almost inconceivable that there was a more suitably qualified person or one with a more considerable reputation likely to apply for the consulship. But, with patronage so important in both civil and military appointments, Salt could not be sure merit alone would win him the post and begged that Valentia would do what he could, "as my mind is most earnestly bent on obtaining the situation."[21]

Although Valentia did send Salt a letter for the Foreign Office, it seems to have been unnecessary. When Salt applied to him, Charles Yorke instantly wrote a "very strong letter", as did Sir Joseph Banks. Sir Joseph wrote that hearing that "my friend Mr Salt who has done himself so much credit and the Public so much service in the Abyssinian journeys" had applied for this post, "from an intimate acquaintance with Mr Salt I consider him as more capable than any other person I know to execute with ability and integrity the Duties of that office and able as well to promote the interests of Science wheresoever it may be his privilege to be stationed."[22] Yorke's reply was even more unreservedly warm: "I have seen a good deal of him and lived in a degree of intimacy with him for some years...I have found the more reason to esteem him the more I have known him..."[23] Salt thought Yorke's letter the chief cause of his winning the post. He was probably right, for in 1820, replying to Yorke's request to grant Salt a leave of absence, Castlereagh wrote: "I shall be most happy to give Mr Salt the leave his health requires, which he has so well merited by his zealous endeavours to be useful in all ways to his country, and I thank you very much, both for pointing him out originally to me, and now for suggesting the manner in which I can contribute either to his personal convenience or to the restoration of his health."[24] Salt was told privately by 2 May that Castlereagh had agreed to his appointment, but owing to the crisis of Napoleon's escape from Elba engaging the Minister's attention, it was 13 June 1815 before it was formally gazetted. Joseph Farington, his old teacher, met "Salt, the new Consul to Egypt" a week later, at the British Institute Evening Exhibition, clearly in a state of elation. He told Farington that "Lord Castlereagh sd. though many applications had been made to Him He thought Mr Salt best entitled to the situation." Salt added that his salary would be "towards £2,000 per annum" and that the office would secure to him "a provision from Government for life"; Missett, who had been Consul *Eleven years only*", had been allotted a pension. Whoever so informed Salt misinformed him; Government was not disposed to be so generous on either count. He had dined that day with the East India Company directors and hoped to be given an appointment by the Company to transact business for them during his consulship; it would have been useful financially, but seems not to have materialised. Of one piece of financial good fortune he was secure: "His father...was so much pleased with the good reception of His publication of 'His acct of Abyssinia' that He gave Him £200."

The new Consul was told to proceed without delay to Malta, and thence to Egypt. He should make his "permanent residence at the place where the officer invested with the Government of Egypt [Mehemet Ali] resides...You will not however consider yourself as precluded by this instruction from making temporary incursions to any other parts of that Province which from any motives you may deem it expedient to visit."[25] Such "temporary incursions" were in part to enable Salt, as was expected of

British consuls, to further British knowledge of the culture of the country. Both Halls and Salt himself said that Sir Joseph Banks strongly encouraged Salt to collect for the British Museum, but only, it seems probable, in conversation. However, the Society of Antiquaries, at the instance of the eminent student of hieroglyphs, Dr Thomas Young, formally requested him to search for fragments broken from the Rosetta Stone, as well as any other inscribed stones, and make drawings and casts of them. His expenses would be met; "there is no doubt that whatever might be the expense of the undertaking, whether successful or otherwise, it would be most cheerfully supported by an enlightened nation, eager to anticipate its Rivals in the prosecution of the best interests of literature...and science," wrote William Richard Hamilton, Salt's superior at the Foreign Office.[26]

At last in a position to marry, of a strongly affectionate nature, and knowing the want of "reputable female society" in Egypt, Salt may have deliberately set out to look for a wife. However it was, he fell seriously in love with Mary, a pretty and accomplished lady, the only daughter of a wealthy inhabitant of Birmingham, and was extremely upset when, after showing definite signs of liking, she eventually turned him down. "I told her, too frankly for my own interest, the actual state of things in this country," he wrote ruefully to his friend Bingham Richards, "and, by the advice of her friends, she has thought it right to break off the proposed connexion." The letter was written from Cairo in 1817, so it seems Salt had still not been without hope when he left England. His will made in her favour was not revoked until the time of his eventual marriage.

There were now but a few weeks left for Salt to make all his arrangements and to bid final farewells to family and friends — more final on this occasion than ever before, for it would be many years before he could return, even on leave. His 80-year-old father he could not hope to see again.

Valentia travelled from Ireland, it seems expressly to see Salt before his departure. Their letters, which crossed, show clearly that their relationship had grown into a warm and genuine friendship. He wrote "My dear Henry...I should be very sorry that you left England without my again seeing you...I do most earnestly request you will pay me a visit at Arley. Consider how long we may now be separated, and the possibility, not to say probability, that we may never again meet in this world...I will be at peace with you if you stay only one day. If you do not do this, I shall be really hurt," and signed himself "Yours most affectionately".[27] Salt wrote he felt "most anxious to see you, for the purpose of hearing all your wishes, respecting the antiquities, &c. &c. that you are desirous of my procuring for you in Egypt. At the same time I am desirous of having a few days even of your company before our long separation takes place." That he should also sign himself "Believe me most affectionately yours" says even more for the ease existing between the two men.[28] Salt was at Arley Castle from 29 to 31 July, and again from 3 to 8 August, when he bade his friend of more than 16 years a final farewell.

He was not to travel alone. "One of Sir William Beechey's sons is to go out with me on my simply paying all his expences. This will, for a year or two be very pleasant to both, I conceive, and to him singularly useful as at present he is losing his time in England and hanging a heavy burthen on his Father. He draws well, and understands both French and Italian."[29] Sir William Beechey RA had a numerous family, by two marriages, and Henry William, the eldest son of the first family, was at this time about 26 years old. Did Salt see himself, by giving this opportunity to the young man, as performing the same service as Valentia had to him, when he took him to the East? The outcome was certainly not as successful: Henry Beechey was an agreeable young man, but he was no Henry Salt.

As he parted from him the night before Salt went down to Brighton to embark for France, Halls had a bitter presentiment that this was the last time he should ever see his friend. On 28 August Salt was joined in Brighton by Halls' brother Tom, then living nearby. Due to sail on the evening packet for Dieppe, he dined in a seafront hotel with Tom and another friend. Though he put on a cheerful face, Tom knew him well enough to recognise it for a brave front, and noted how ever and again his eye glanced towards the sea. A gun was fired. After a moment's pause, not looking seaward, Salt said, "It's only the first gun, we have yet a quarter of an hour good", and ordered another bottle of claret. "You know our familiar phraseology: — 'It's a very fine world, Tom?' said he — 'Yes,' I replied, 'and it's a very fine scene! But we must not make too much of a scene of it.' — 'Right!' said he, with one of his particular looks; and then he asked Littledale for one of his stories."

But soon they must walk down to the Custom House, where lay the boat to carry the passengers out to the packet anchored further off shore. Tom could not afterwards remember if he took any formal leave of his friend at all; "I let go his arm, and he was in the boat in an instant." Standing up in the stern, Salt turned to Tom, laughing, to point out a large wave approaching, which just as they were afloat, broke over them, to the screams of the lady passengers, and "a general laugh, which for the moment broke in opportunely enough upon our feelings".

As the boat slipped away, Salt still stood, waving to Tom. On the calm, hot summer evening, his tall figure was reflected distinctly in the glass-smooth sea in a way Tom Halls was never to forget. He turned and walked slowly away. At the rise of a hill, he looked back: the packet was still just visible, a mere speck in the shining sea. A little further on, he turned again. The speck was gone.[30]

6

Mr Consul Salt and the Pasha of Egypt

B Y 7 OCTOBER 1815 Salt was in Geneva, writing to Valentia about the disturbed state of France. From Paris he had travelled with Sir Sydney Smith (defender of St Jean d'Acre against Napoleon) to the review of Russian troops at Vertus in Champagne. It was an occasion "grand in the extreme": 150,000 men supported by 500 pieces of artillery moving by signal and firing together. Watching the review were the Emperors of Austria and Russia, the King of Prussia and "half a hundred other princes". Salt was admitted into the royal circle and overheard Lord Wellington observe that it was the finest sight he had ever witnessed and that it gave him a much higher opinion of the Russians than he had ever before entertained. Some dozen years later Salt would recall this occasion when he attended another military review, and he may, too, have cast his mind back to the great gathering of Ras Welled Selasse's warriors in Tigre.

He was relieved to leave Paris where "all was tumult, dissipation, show, wretchedness and vanity", for Geneva where he found "a quiet and agreeable society linked together by the best ties of the heart." The experience made him feel "all earthly grandeur is futile".[1] He had the time to have his portrait painted by a female artist.

From Geneva he travelled over the Simplon Pass, where the scenery far exceeded all he had "ever conceived of picturesque beauty", and, in spite of himself, his sketchbook was continually in his hand.[2] This sense that now he was a diplomat rather than an artist deprived the world of much. The few completed views and the occasional surviving sketched portrait remind one of what could have been during the years in which Salt was probably the most accomplished European artist living in Egypt.

In Venice, Hoppner's son Richard was Consul and Salt enjoyed a pleasant visit with him and his pretty and amiable Swiss bride, although he found Venice sullied by stagnant waters and presenting "a melancholy picture of... the faded splendour of former magnificence."[3]

Despite the urging of the Foreign Office to make haste to Egypt, he made a leisurely journey south. In Rome he met the Swedish diplomat, orientalist and linguist Johann Akerblad, who had made "some successful efforts in deciphering the hieroglyphics", and who promised to help in any researches Salt made in Egypt.[4] There is no evidence that Salt followed up this offer, and Akerblad died, somewhat unexpectedly, three years later.

In Naples by the end of the year, he took great pains to examine the remains of Pompeii and climbed Vesuvius to look down into the fiery furnace. From Naples he sailed to Malta to pick up a ship for Alexandria. He was almost at his destination — so he thought. But no suitable ship was available for three weeks. Salt used his time well, getting to know Sir Thomas Maitland, the Governor, who took a very proper view of affairs in Egypt. He wished to have "a more intimate connexion" between Malta and Alexandria and agreed that Egypt should be visited at least twice a year by a British frigate. This would make Salt's own situation more agreeable and enable him to keep up a regular intercourse with friends in England.

In his letters to his male acquaintance, he gave no indication of any longing for home, but to his sister Bessy (Mrs Morgan) he wrote differently. After a brief solicitous query about their father, he asked her to tell him "all you know on another subject, upon which I feel scarcely less at ease. Has she been to Lichfield? How does she look? Does she sometimes mention me? Do pray let me hear all that you know respecting her situation. Where is she? What is she engaged in? And a thousand other questions, which I need not put upon paper." He sent Bessy the Geneva portrait, hoping perhaps that 'she' would see it and be reminded of him.[5]

In Malta the news from Egypt gave him reason for optimism. He wrote to Halls on 22 January 1816: "The Pasha of Egypt...has gotten the better of his mutinous troops, and, which is very extraordinary for an Eastern prince, has actually reimbursed all the merchants and others who suffered during the rebellion." (The previous May Missett had written to the Foreign Office about this uprising against Mehemet Ali and the Europeans in Cairo who were thought to be influencing him too much. "Unless the insurgents are punished, they will ultimately oblige all Europeans to abandon that city."[6]) "The trade in corn," Salt continued, "which he [Mehemet Ali] monopolizes, appears to be enormous. No less than six vessels laden with that and beans, have arrived in this port [Malta] within the last fortnight. He has several fine vessels of his own, both in this sea and the Red Sea. With such a man, I should think that a great deal may be done."[7]

* *

At the end of March 1816, Salt arrived at last in Egypt, having touched at the island of Melos where the inhabitants had recently unearthed the white marble theatre overlooking the bay. He was warmly welcomed by Colonel Missett. Salt found him "dreadfully reduced by the severe attack of disease under which he has laboured, but still retaining extraordinary vigour of mind", despite his partially paralysed body. Missett's secretary, Robert Thurburn (who had aspired to become Consul-General) had arranged all the affairs of the Consulate "in as able and regular a manner" as to leave Salt

"but few difficulties to encounter in entering upon the duties of my Office."
Salt foresaw that most of his problems would arise from the Pasha, who was
"daily becoming more difficult to treat with and less inclined to pay attention to the rights of European Nations," — a situation readily explained
when the British Consul-General was in decline and the Pasha's friend,
Colonel Drovetti, had been replaced as French Consul.

All the foreign consuls vied with each other in paying the new Consul-
General every attention, and Peter Lee, Consul to the Levant Company,
which represented British commercial interests in Alexandria, was delighted
that Salt was at last there to take responsibility.

It was ten years since Salt was last in Egypt, and he was impressed by
the changes he saw. He wrote to William Hamilton at the Foreign Office of
the flourishing trade of Egypt, "or rather the Pasha's monopoly". There
were no fewer than a hundred ships in the harbour, more than a third of
them under English colours, waiting mainly for cargoes of grain. Salt's survey of Alexandria in 1806 and his resulting plan had given him a unique
appreciation of the city and its quarters.[8] Now he found "the Pasha, has
made so many alterations that it is scarcely to be recognised as the same
place. He has, very absurdly in my opinion, repaired or rebuilt, the whole
line of the old walls, which in consequence have become, instead of picturesque ruins, a regular and ugly mass of fortifications...too weak, and far
too extensive, to prove the slightest use in case of a siege. The same misfor-
tune has likewise befallen the old Pharos, which is now completely modern-
ized, and would make a becoming object only for the bottom of a citizen's
garden." The Pasha was now levelling the hills outside the walls. "Some
hundreds of poor devils of Arabs and buffaloes are engaged in this wise
undertaking, which are watched in their labours by a pretty large detachment of troops; yet still, as might be expected, they advance very slowly in
their operations, removing heaps of rubbish from place to place without any
system, and thus reducing one hill only to form another." Salt had hoped
that any antiquities revealed below these masses of ruins might be laid bare.
But he was disappointed. The manner in which the work was carried out
made it likely that only something "very hard indeed would resist being broken to pieces by their clumsiness."[9]

These works of 'modernisation' by Mehemet Ali are important when
considering ancient Egypt through early nineteenth-century eyes. The Pasha
often acted like the worst sort of modern developer, eager to tear down in
the name of progress without care or concern for the value of what was
destroyed; happy to find a cheap source of building materials in the quarry
of ancient temples.

Salt, whose month in the Delta with Valentia 'archaeologising', with
his own natural interest and a brief that extended to ancient as well as

modern Egypt, would have liked to investigate further, but the plague season was approaching and he hurried up to Cairo while he could. His haste did not prevent a stop at Sais el Haggar to investigate the ruins seen by Hamilton in 1801, and he reported to Hamilton that a superb, immensely heavy, dark-coloured granite sarcophagus had recently been unearthed there by the locals. He drew the hieroglyphs inscribed on it, confirming Thomas Young's idea that, in reading them, you should start on the side to which the figures look or "as it may be expressed, head to tail".

Near Rosetta, Tousson Pasha, Mehemet Ali's youngest son, was encamped and, wishing "to do honour to the British Nation", invited him to visit. Tousson had drawn up his troops in a double line from the water's edge to his tent, and when Salt stepped off his boat and entered the lines a salute of cannons was fired.[9] To the incoming Consul-General this was a moment to savour.[10]

Arrived at last in Cairo, Salt found the Pasha and all the Europeans shut up in quarantine from the plague, and he too was incarcerated in a small tower at the Cairene port of Bulac belonging to Yousuf Boghos.[11] Salt found Boghos, the Armenian dragoman or chief interpreter of the Pasha, "a very gentlemanlike and agreeable man", but the house was a perfect oven and there were daily funeral processions of the plague-dead past the windows on the way to a nearby mosque. The days dragged. He had engaged Mr Aziz, who had acted as Missett's emissary in 1806, to remain as his chief interpreter. "He is not a very active man, but has the character…which is much more rare, of being an honest interpreter." Through Aziz, Salt forwarded complaints from Peter Lee to the Pasha. These mainly concerned the behaviour of the Pasha's agents who appeared "to entertain a constant desire to encroach on the privileged interests enjoyed by British subjects", by witholding provisions from a merchant ship, levying illegal duties and even forcing European inhabitants to pay for their daily supply of water. Salt wrote a long letter to Pearce in Abyssinia, having heard in England that he had died and now, happily, learning that he was alive. He urged him to keep in contact through Jedda. He also wrote to William Coffin, sending a box of gifts and some money to be delivered to named acquaintances.

At last in June the plague ceased and Salt was able to make first a private and then a public visit to Mehemet Ali and to renew his acquaintance with Burckhardt, "just returned, black as a negro, from Mount Sinai". At his public reception on 10 June, Salt was presented with "notable gifts": a capital horse and a pelisse lined with sables — "an honour never before bestowed on a Consul here". In return he gave cut glassware on silver stands to the Pasha and pistols and guns to his sons. Mehemet Ali received him most graciously and Salt wrote to Halls that he was "in reality much delighted that a person had been sent with whom he was in some degree acquainted, and not, as he observed, 'a stiff, unaccomodating Englishman'." Salt, on his side, at this reunion must have had in mind the assessment Valentia made in his *Travels*, and probably developed between the two men at the time.

Mehemet Ali, Valentia had recorded, only ruled Egypt in 1806 from a little above Cairo to the Delta. The Mamelukes ruled Upper Egypt and, even in the Delta, Elfi Bey had held great sway. The Pasha was, Valentia had considered, "decidedly a man of talent, but necessarily the slave of the undisciplined freebooters whom he ostensibly commands, and is obliged to plunder the defenceless natives to gratify their rapacity, for his revenue is in no way equal to his expenditure, even with all the additions which requisitions from the Arabs, and exactions from the merchants, can bring." At that time the trade with the interior of Africa was "at an end" and even the commerce with Jedda was "greatly diminished from the dread of the immoderate extortion under which the merchant labours."[12]

According to George Gliddon, a great admirer of Salt, who was then a boy living in Egypt with his merchant father and who later became American Vice-Consul, "There is in Egypt a traditionary legend to the effect that, when Lord Bathurst dismissed Salt, on the departure for the seat of his Consular magistracy, he gave him this parting advice as a rule for his observance: 'Salt, keep things quiet.' Never was an injunction more scrupulously obeyed," said Gliddon. Salt, as Gliddon saw him, was more concerned with "literary studies, poetry and pictorial sketches" or fighting with the French Consul Drovetti over "a mummy pit or an idol than with Mehemet Ali's Monopolies"[13] Other people too overlooked Salt's very real duties as Consul-General, and even Halls' account hardly touches on them, reporting mainly on antiquarian and social activities, necessarily ignorant of the details of his professional life which are to be found in the Consul-General's letters to the Foreign Office. Certainly on this occasion the Pasha gave every indication that he was anxious to "stand on good terms with the British Nation" and that "all subjects liable to dispute" should be arranged in such a manner to "prevent if possible, for the future, all kinds of unpleasant discussion between them." Over the years there were to be times when 'unpleasant discussions' did occur, but it is clear that the two men had a calm and friendly relationship in most matters, and Salt told Valentia that he got on "uncommonly well" with the Pasha, who in December even invited him to dinner; afterwards they walked together for a couple of hours in the garden.

On this first formal occasion, they talked on all manner of subjects. The first and dominant, was the Pasha's business with India, carried on in conjunction with Briggs and Co. Mehemet Ali was talking in terms of a million dollars' worth of trade — a figure which led naturally to the question of Egypt's interests in the Red Sea. The Pasha spoke of the threats in that area from the fundamentalist Wahabis who had lately attacked and captured one of the smaller vessels of his private merchant fleet. To protect his interests he wanted to keep some kind of naval force there. Without this it would no longer — or so he said — be safe for his people even to go and come from the Hadj to Mecca. He hoped the British Government would give up their opposition to his sending ships around the Cape of Good Hope to the Red Sea. He was obviously testing the ground to see whether Salt would yield where Missett had stood firm. Salt spoke, diplomatically, of the dangers the ships would have to encounter on the way.

The Pasha smiled. "My captains are anxious to brave them. My own concern," he added, "is for the honour such a voyage would confer on myself — for no Mussulman ships have before accomplished this."

Salt advised the Foreign Office that the time might in fact be ripe to grant this favour — in order to get concessions from the Pasha. It might be better that Mehemet Ali should have "a preponderating influence" in the Red Sea than "such pirates as the Wahabis", and, because of his dependence for power on trade, the Mediterranean fleet could "bring him to our terms, in the event of a rupture, without any additional force." A couple of frigates in the Red Sea would look after British interests. Salt's knowledge of the area had influence at the Foreign Office — and at the Porte — and in due course it was agreed to allow the Pasha to have a small naval force in the Red Sea.[14]

It was, by this time, probably no longer necessary for Salt to take the views of the Sheiks about the 'Albanians' into consideration, as Missett had had to do earlier. The Beys were decimated and powerless above the Cataract in Nubia; Mehemet Ali was squarely on the throne of both Lower and Upper Egypt. Trade, which in 1806 had been in the doldrums, whether to the interior of Africa, within the country or with the rest of the world, was now not only restored but increased.

* *

Mr Consul-General Salt was now formally accredited to Mehemet Ali's court. Colonel Missett had not lived in Cairo since September 1814 and the consular house had been sold. A new one was soon found, by order of the Pasha, in a very good position in the Frankish quarter. Edward Lane, the great contemporary scholar of modern Egyptian life, described the area: "The motley population of this part of the metropolis gives it the appearance of a quarter in a sea-port town, like Alexandria...The chief thoroughfare-street... is the soo'ck called the Moo'ski, where there are a few shops filled in the European style, with glass fronts...and various European commodities."

Nearby, down a short street, was the Frank inn, the only one in Cairo in the late 1820s. The great Ezbekiah Square was close: an open space for part of the year and a lake at the time of the inundation of the Nile. "The

British Consul resided in a large commodious house, at the end of a narrow street. Behind it is a small garden, communicating with one of considerable extent, which has wide, raised walks, and is stocked with a variety of plants; (but by 1828 was in a very neglected state). To this garden the principal Franks of the neighbourhood used to resort in the cool evening-time; and dancing girls, conjurors, or musicians might often be seen there on occasions..."[15]

The house had a terraced roof, which commanded an extensive view of the city. John Carne, a traveller staying there in Salt's absence in 1821, found it "delightful to rise by night, and walk there in the brilliant moonlight, which has the appearance of a tranquil and beautiful day: you can see to read with perfect ease." Carne looked down onto the terraces of other dwellings all around "on which numbers of the inhabitants lie buried in sleep...The lonely palm-trees scattered at intervals around, and rising high above the houses, are the only objects which break the view."[16]

Its situation was clearly very pleasant, but Salt did not regard the interior as suitable for European habitation until a great deal of work was done on it.

He wrote enthusiastically about the house to Valentia, having decided it would suit him exceedingly well. "It is irregular but has two large salles and my own bedroom, or rather library, looking on really a respectably-sized garden, and plenty of other rooms for my secretary and the strangers who occasionally visit us." (Later there would be visitors almost constantly.) "The halls are all paved with variously coloured marbles, and the ceilings of the rooms painted in the Constantinopolitan style." The work was still not completed, had already cost him £250 and would cost half as much again before it was finished. He had paid Colonel Missett £400 for furniture and the same amount to others for further furnishings. His salary was three quarters (nine months) in arrears and he would have been "greatly distressed for money" if Messrs Briggs and Co. had not been able to advance him funds. Looking into the future, Salt realised that his salary alone would hardly meet the expenses of the "establishment necessary to keep up Consular respectability". He listed some of the essential expenses of his position. "I have three horses to keep with their grooms, two janissaries, a steward, cook, two footmen and a gardener; a camel to fetch water from the Nile; a *sackia* or water-carrier; a *Bourique* or jackass, for odd jobs; a bullock, for the garden and mill, and a washerwoman." He does not include in this list the dragoman, an essential employee in this polyglot society (for whom he had an allowance of £150 a year), nor the clerks at the Chancellery. In addition he had to provide everything for Beechey, his secretary. His plaint ends, "All these expenses are absolutely indispensable, and, as you may well believe, cannot be defrayed for much less than the whole amount of my salary" — which amounted, because he did not pay the newly introduced income tax, to £1,500 a year.

The next spring Salt wrote anxiously to Hamilton about his extraordinary expenses. He was finding his salary "barely equal to the establishment requisite to support the British character and consequence in this country" — a sense of what was appropriate for an English official abroad which he had learned from Valentia. At much the same time, he wrote to Bingham Richards, his friend and agent, who had recently married, saying that he was beginning at last to get everything tolerably in order, and in the garden the roses, jasmines and pomegranates were in flower — "it wanted only one thing to render it a delicious retreat — a *wife*."[17]

John Carne found the way of life of the Consulate very pleasant: "...a cup of coffee and a piece of bread are ready at an early hour for whoever chooses; at midday comes a luxurious dinner, of foreign cookery, with the wines of Europe and the fruits of the East; and seven in the evening introduces supper — another substantial meal, though less profuse than the dinner; and by ten o'clock most of the family retire." It was not, thought Carne, a life-style best adapted to the climate.

At the start of 1818 Salt wrote again about his financial problems, this time to Joseph Planta, Under Secretary of State for Foreign Affairs, saying he had had to meet "many extra expenses not chargeable to government, and from which all other consulates were free, owing to the peculiar customs of the country." These included annual presents of dresses on the King's birthday to all his servants and dependants, and affording accommodation to strangers visiting the Country "whom it would be disgraceful to the National Character to leave in the miserable auberges of Cairo". There were indeed many people who thought it their right to stay with their Consul and would not have even considered staying in one of these 'miserable auberges'.

Salt's complaints about the expectations of his role and the monies provided for them were not unusual. The Foreign Office correspondence from Consulates around the Mediterranean is full of requests, from Albania, the Ionian islands and other posts, for increases in salaries and money to keep up the position of the British. The Foreign Office were extremely reluctant to respond.

Despite his financial difficulties, Henry Salt, by the summer of 1816, after his official presentations, was "sustaining the rights of our Merchants and others, and in acting as mediator on all occasions with the Pasha". His relations with Mehemet Ali were central to all he was to do.

Everyone who came to Egypt talked about the Pasha; many wrote about him. From the lordly traveller to the most humble fellah, everyone had his view of Mehemet Ali. Who was this man — 'the Pasha' — who ruled

Egypt with so tight a grip that every traveller had to have his leave to travel and permission to employ workmen to excavate in the ancient sites of Egypt?

Mehemet Ali, Viceroy of Egypt under the Ottoman Sultan, had attributes common to many outstanding leaders: he was ruthless, shrewd, charming and vain. He had been Viceroy since 1805 and would remain so until the year before his death when in 1848, his son, Ibrahim, toppled him on grounds of insanity. The dynasty he founded would run its course until his great-great-grandson, King Faruq, was removed in 1952 after a reign of 16 years — and left accompanied by his 'Albanian' bodyguard.

Opinions about Mehemet Ali were often contradictory. Undoubtedly he was ruthless, possibly cruel even by the standards of his time, and most certainly callous. The bloodthirsty way in which he rid Egypt of the Mamelukes is still spoken of with horror today. Like most contemporary rulers he showed very little concern for the lowly people he ruled. He was vain and reputed to enjoy his own celebrity, but there are few, even elected rulers, particularly when they have been long in power, who are not vain and vainglorious. He was said to have 95 harem girls and yet was loyal only to the offspring of his first wife and, until she died in 1824, lived, to outward appearances, in a comparatively simple way. As he grew older, he liked to be thought younger than he was, and the trappings of his power became more elaborate. He was certainly shrewd — even wily — but whether he did his country of adoption ultimate service or not, is still a matter for debate. As a despotic ruler who tried to drag Egypt into the nineteenth century and out of its near-medieval past, he achieved much: making Egypt a country of comparative order and stability in contrast to the turmoil in Greece and the Holy Lands. Mehemet Ali improved the irrigation systems upon which Nile life depended and, using near-slave labour, constructed the Mahmoudiyah Canal between Alexandria and the main flow of the Nile, bringing Cairo closer, in travelling time, to the Mediterranean. By many Egyptians he is regarded as the father of modern Egypt. Foreigners, some reluctantly, admired his achievements, and European governments and their consuls sought his favour. Egypt has a pivotal position in that corner of the world, and Europe preferred to deal with Mehemet Ali rather than the ever-changing line of Mamelukes. Salt, who had seen the misery into which the Mamelukes and the French invasion had forced Egypt, may have deplored Mehemet Ali's oppressions but he certainly admired his improvements in trade, industry and security.

When Salt and Valentia rode into Cairo on 6 February 1806, Mehemet Ali was still insecurely on the vice-regal throne, glad of the British support provided by their appearance. But it was not long before this appearance of support abruptly disappeared.

Later that same year, when the Sultan at Constantinople recognised

Napoleon as Emperor of France, the British believed this could mean the re-opening of Egypt to the French. Valentia and Salt, who did not reach Britain until late October, can have had little influence on the government's reaction to this turn of events: to step in first. On the night of 20 March 1807 British troops occupied Alexandria and Missett called the Elfi Mamelukes to their aid. Drovetti fled to Cairo and Mehemet Ali.

Elfi Bey had continued to be a formidable opponent of Mehemet Ali. Valentia had reported in his *Travels* that Elfi Bey occupied the Faiume (sic) "over which he tyrannises", but "many Albanians had deserted to him and he had a large Arab force, whom he assured of his close connection with England" and told of his expectation of a large British army "to place him at the head of government". Here, apparently, was that 'large army'.[18]

On 21 April a column of British troops set out to capture the port of Rosetta. The expedition was badly planned and ill-led. There were disastrous encounters. Many British soldiers were killed; many were taken prisoner (including one William Thomson whom Salt was to know as Osman). Mehemet Ali behaved with unusual grace for an Ottoman victor. He allowed the heads of the fallen to be paraded through the streets — having been carried to Cairo by their comrades — but treated the prisoners comparatively well. Although prisoners of war traditionally became the slaves of their individual captors, he offered to return them to the British, to protect British trade and to oppose any force (which was only likely to be the French) which sought to enter Egypt. In September the British surrendered Alexandria. Most of the prisoners were duly freed and all those who had assisted the British were pardoned. According to Dr Madden the British reverse was in great measure due to plans drawn up for the Pasha by Colonel Drovetti: "he it is whose prudence and dexterity seated Mehemet Ali on the throne."[19] Mehemet Ali owed him much. But the British, too, owed a debt to Drovetti. He had intervened on behalf of the British prisoners, suggesting to the Pasha it would be more humane to offer his men double the sum for a live man than for his head. Major-General Fraser, Commander of the British army, wrote to thank him on 7 May 1807: "Not only this army but the British Nation will ever be indebted to you."[20]

Bernardino Drovetti was, at that time, in his early 30s, a tall, dark-visaged man with the appearance traditionally associated with a brigand. Born in Barbania in Piedmont, he had served in Egypt in Napoleon's campaign and remained as French Consul-General until 1814, when he fell from grace with the new French government because he would not relinquish his Piedmontese citizenship. He stayed on, advising Mehemet Ali and taking an increasing interest in antiquities, until he was re-appointed in 1820. When Salt arrived in Egypt, Drovetti was no longer his opposite number, but still a powerful figure in Cairo.

By the end of 1807 Mehemet Ali was recognised as ruler of Egypt and the representative of the Porte; the British had been ousted but on friendly terms; the French could not enter but were his allies. Both in his *Travels* and presumably in conversation, Valentia deplored the way Britain had "in their late fatal expedition to that country...handed over our friends the Arabs to the Albanians." But by then Mehemet Ali's only real rivals were the Mamelukes.

The behaviour of the Mamelukes had become intolerable. Consul-General Sir Charles Murray would gather a shocking catalogue of their iniquities: their concubines were displayed with reckless spendour; their sexual proclivities included unmentionable activities. The people were ground to dust; the peasants allowed nothing but what was barely sufficient to sustain life. Persons were bastinadoed and executed without the least form of trial; neither age nor sex was safe. Elfi Bey himself was reputed to have passed hooks through the chins of some Arabs and hung them up in rows on trees. Strangers and ladies could not walk the streets in safety. Commerce was interrupted; Egypt's renowned silk trade abandoned. Notorious robbers were famed for their audacity and adroitness — along the Nile "even the common wants of nature could not be satisfied with safety". Every 'species' of learning had decayed. Such, wrote Murray, was the appalling state of affairs from which Mehemet Ali rescued Egypt.[21]

By 1811 the Pasha felt sufficiently strong "to put his grand project of exterminating the Mamelukes into execution". To celebrate the investiture of his son Tousson when he took command of an expedition to Arabia against the Wahabis, he ordered a banquet in Cairo's Citadel on 1 March. Between 400 and 500 Mameluke guests rode into the Citadel, and they all, with the exception of one man, were slaughtered in cold blood in the sight of, and at the bidding of, Mehemet Ali, "whose memorable words, *Vras! Vras!* (Kill! Kill!), are not," wrote Madden, "likely to be forgotten."[22] If Salt thought of these events when he was received by Tousson and Mehemet Ali five years later, he remained silent; but he had, of course, been made very aware of the Mameluke threat and the chaos into which Egypt had fallen, and his knowledge may have made him more tolerant of the Pasha's method of ridding Egypt of his rivals.

A contemporary, and horrible, report of the events of 1811 was written by one Gally Knight to Stratford Canning, George Canning's cousin, a youthful but senior diplomat in Constantinople. Knight was in Cairo on the day of the massacre and wrote a few days later.

"On the appointed day all assembled in the citadel. The Pasha clothed his son with his pelisse in the great hall, after which the word was given for the procession to begin to move. In the meantime a secret order had been given for the citadel gates to be shut. The Beys, under the pretence of giving them the most honourable post, were placed in the centre of the Pasha's troops. The procession moved on a little way, till they got the Memloucs into a long narrow passage, where it was impossible for them to defend themselves. The two officers then who alone were in the secret…suddenly ordered their troops, the Albanians and Osmanlis, to fire upon the Memloucs." The troops hestitated, doubting whether they had heard the order right.

The order was repeated and they fired. "The butchery went on the whole day, and not a Memlouc who had entered the citadel came out of it alive." Then the soldiers went out to find the "Memloucs" who had not come with the Beys. "Cairo was like a city taken by storm. Firing was heard all the day." The soldiers even ransacked the Harem, seized the women's jewellery and even the women themselves, particularly the white slaves. "These scenes were going on for six days. At length the slaughter ceased, because there were no more to slaughter…About a thousand were computed to have been put to death…and the Pasha was obliged to put several of his own men to death before he could stop the evil." "The Pasha," wrote Knight, "to justify himself, says that he only anticipated the Beys, who had formed a conspiracy against himself; but this is not believed."[23]

After the massacre the few surviving Mamelukes were hunted down throughout Egypt; a small number fled beyond the Cataract into Nubia. Whatever his excuse, Mehemet Ali's action was excessive and suited his own purposes. The massacre was still a bloody stain on his reputation when Salt took up his post — and so it has remained.

* *

There are many contemporary descriptions of Mehemet Ali. Portraits are surprisingly consistent. According to Madden, who had many opportunities to observe him in 1826, he was "about five foot six inches in height, of a ruddy fair complexion with light hazel eyes, deeply set in their sockets, and overshadowed by prominent eyebrows. His lips are thin, his features regular, extremely changeful, yet altogether agreeable in their expression when he is in good humour. At such times his countenance is that of a frank, amiable and highly intelligent person. The motion of his hands and his gestures in conversation are those of a well-bred person, and his manners are easy and even dignified. He perambulates his rooms a great deal when he is at all disturbed, with his hands behind his back, and thinks aloud on these occasions. He sleeps but little and seldom soundly."[24]

Dr Richardson, who accompanied the Earl of Belmore up the Nile in the winter of 1817-18, spent much time in Salt's company, making his comments especially interesting. At 40, he noted, Mehemet Ali could neither read nor write: he learned then to do both "though as might well have been expected, is no great proficient in either." (He never learned to speak Arabic, the language of the ordinary people of Egypt and his army.) However, in the Turkish empire a knowledge of letters was not necessary to govern men. More important were, "a certain dexterity in managing the horse and arms of a soldier, in firing with precision at a mark, throwing the djerid, playing skilfully with the sword, joined to address and shrewdness in conversation, with a prompt, decisive character in action" — with these talents and skills Mehemet Ali was well endowed.[25]

Once established, Mehemet Ali set about ruling Egypt to his own advantage, assuming "all the men, women and children, all the land, everything it produces are his property; that his subjects have no rights that they can call their own" and that they were bound to serve him in return for a scanty allowance of food and clothing "which he graciously concedes to them". From this position he taxed and taxed...and taxed. The peasants had been ground down by the Mamelukes, and continued to be ground down by Mehemet Ali, his descendants and their 'Turkish' officers. The serfs or fellahs were watched by the Pasha's agents to ensure that "not one grain of produce is converted to the use of the grower".

Much of this plunder was used increasingly to build up armaments and armed forces. In Salt's time the pressure on the people was rather less — though 25,000 Egyptians were said to have died constructing the Mahmoudiyah Canal. The Pasha began to send young men abroad for training, but before that he was dependent on foreigners to run the factories and businesses he founded and to train his army. Most of these were Italian, a few were French (particularly the army officers), one at least was American and one, Mr Brine who managed the sugar factory at Manafalout for many years, acted as host to passing travellers, and died in Cairo in 1823, was English — recruited from overseeing a sugar plantation in the West Indies. Moyle Sherer, an army officer who travelled the Nile in 1823, commented that "the protection given to European travellers [was] based on Mehemet Ali's desire to employ Franks, so he must accustom his subjects to their presence. In keeping his independence with the Porte," Sherer added, "his relations with Europe were very significant."[26]

Mehemet Ali, Richardson concluded, "may be a good soldier, but he is a wretched governor — one who can never make a great or happy people" and one who can never "reign in the hearts of his subjects, nor bless the land with joyful abundance. But," he added, "all happiness is relative, and Egypt enjoys more advantages under its present ruler than it has experienced for many years under his predecessors."[27] Nevertheless, Moyle Sherer could remark "Men grow tired of shedding blood as of other pleasures, but if the cutting off of a head would drop gold into his coffers he would not be slow to give the signal...His laugh has nothing of nature in it now — a hard, sharp laugh, such as [that of] strong heartless men who would divide booty from the feeble...However, one thing I heartily rejoice. It is said that our Consul-General has great influence with him and it is known that it is always exerted freely and amiably for Franks of all nations in distress or difficulty and often for natives also."

Some foreigners may have admired the Pasha, but the ordinary people of Egypt loathed him. One man told Madden quite openly that he would "die happy if he could cut the throat of Mehemet Ali and drink his blood."[28]

****

Salt was able to report to Valentia at the end of 1816 that he was managing to get on uncommonly well with the Pasha. He acknowledged that the Pasha's revenue was enormously increased, but also noted that "though the merchants cry out, they are all making money, and fresh European adventurers are daily flocking into the country."

Salt's main role was political and commercial, but he was also concerned with Egypt's history. His explorations in the Delta with Valentia had given him a taste of the riches easily discovered. Within days of landing in Egypt he was engaged — as he had been urged by William Hamilton and Sir Joseph Banks — in searching for, and learning about, the antiquities of Egypt.

In December 1816 Salt told Valentia that he had "taken every possible means to collect" and had been very successful and was "now so bit with the prospect of what may still be found in Upper Egypt, as to be unable to abstain from forming a collection myself."[29] Valentia had evidently sent his friend a 'shopping list' which included an entire mummy, a good head, seeds from ancient Egypt and coins for his son. Salt was also proud to report that the French Institute had done him the honour of making him one of their foreign correspondents.

It is easy today to criticise Henry Salt, and many other Europeans and later Americans, for carrying away the splendours of the Egyptian past, but it is important to record also how that other 'foreigner', the Pasha, was treating this heritage.

In 1844 the former American Vice-Consul, George R. Gliddon, published *An Appeal to the Antiquaries of Europe on the Destruction of the Monuments of Egypt*. Emotional and ill-constructed though it is, his record of the destruction of Egypt's ancient past by its rulers is a devastating indictment. Voices were raised against this careless plundering. Salt strongly opposed the removal of integral parts of buildings, such as the Zodiac of Dendera, and protected the tomb of Pharaoh Seti at Luxor with a door.

Gliddon's message was clear: "Words cannot express our rage, nor are we able to find scope for our anathemas, about all the demolition which has here [at Karnak] taken place since 1836...In a very few years travellers may save themselves the trouble of a journey beyond the precincts of the British and Continental museums..." He takes his readers down the Nile from Aswan pointing out the destruction by the Pasha's agents, using as his marker the French *Description de l'Egypte*, Hamilton's *Aegyptica* and Colonel Martin Leake's "admirable map". Above Aswan the cataract made it difficult and expensive to take away large objects. Yet William Bankes transported an obelisk from Philae to his garden in Dorset; Waddington and Hanbury carried away a granite sarcophagus to the Fitzwilliam Museum in Cambridge; Lord Prudhoe's Nubian lions welcome us to the Egyptian Galleries in the British Museum.

Until about 1820, according to Gliddon, Mehemet Ali was too busy establishing his dominance "to attend to the antiquities of Egypt, for or against them" and left them to European antiquity-hunters or their agents, or, in the case of obelisks, used them as gifts to other rulers. After 1820 he felt more able to do as he wished, having learnt that talk of ideals was enough, he need not actually look after his people, abolish slave-hunts, reduce armaments, protect the monuments — it was enough to promise these things to satisfy the European governments he wanted to impress. Though he started in about 1823 to quarry in the monuments at Aswan, it was another decade before the destruction was fully under way. Yet, by then, of course, what was being destroyed was understood, appreciated and valued — and deserved the government's protection more than ever.

Gliddon ended his 'journey' on a crescendo of anger against the Pasha who destroyed "more Monuments of Antiquity than the sacrilegious violence of the remote Hykshosh — the conquest of the infuriated Cambyses — the wrath of Ptolemy Lathyrus — the spoliations of the Romans — the bigoted hatred of the early Christians — the overwhelming threat of Saracenic invasion — the earthquake mentioned, I believe, by Eusebius — the misrule of the Memlooks — the mutilations of the Fellahs — the indifference of the Turks — the cupidity of the Antiquity-traders — and the carelessness of wanton European travellers."[30]

Of course this is not the whole story, but it does, at the very least, put the 'antiquity-seekers' into context and gives the more honour to those who took from the great sites of Egypt little more than immensely detailed records of all they saw.

7

The Sheik and the Giant

TWO MEN who were to play very important roles in Salt's life preceded him to Egypt. The first to arrive, in 1812, he had met several
times in London, almost certainly at the house of Sir Joseph Banks.

John Lewis Burckhardt was born in Lausanne, Switzerland, on 25
November 1784, into a wealthy family in the silk manufacturing industry.
In 1806, he went to England, carrying an introduction to Sir Joseph Banks.
The African Association were looking to replace the latest explorer they had
sent to find the source of the River Niger, and in March 1808, Burckhardt
offered his services and was accepted. "To a mind equally characterised by
courage, a love of science and a spirit of enterprise, such an undertaking
afforded peculiar attractions."[1] He was not to go via Tripoli, like his lost
predecessors, Ledyard, Hornemann and Mungo Park, but to try a more east-
erly route, with a pilgrim caravan from Mecca returning into Africa through
Cairo.

As it was considered he would travel most safely as an Arab, he was to
spend two years in Aleppo in Syria to perfect his knowledge of the language
and manners of the people, having already spent several months in
Cambridge intensively studying Arabic, medicine and mineralogy. Salt
repeatedly invited him to join his second expedition to Abyssinia, to take a
westward route from Gondar, "yet I have declined it,"[2] apparently unwilling to relinquish his careful plans to travel as an Arab.

From the moment he left England in March 1809, Burckhardt assumed
the persona of Sheik Ibrahim Ibn Abdullah. At Aleppo, he and the British
Consul, John Barker, decided he should live in the Consulate as an English
merchant while he perfected his Arabic. During his two and a half years in
Syria, Burckhardt made expeditions to Palmyra, Damascus, Baalbek, and
into the wild and dangerous country of the Harouan. Once confident he
could pass unremarked in a pilgrim caravan, he made his way to Cairo, not,
however, by a direct route. Little was known about the countries on the eastern border of the Jordan River and the Dead Sea, and he was eager to find
out what he could for the African Association. On 22 August 1812, he
became the first European for six centuries to pass through the narrow defile
called the Siq into the ancient Nabatean city of Petra. He spent less than a
day and a half there, under the extremely suspicious eye of his guide, but
described it more accurately than many later and less harassed travellers.

Only four months after he arrived in Cairo, in January 1813, he set out for Nubia, which he penetrated nearly to the Third Cataract of the Nile. On his way he explored Thebes, especially remarking the colossal head of 'Memnon' (actually Rameses II); on his way back, he came upon the great buried temple at Abu Simbel and noted a fallen obelisk at Philae.

At Esne, in April, learning there would be no pilgrim caravan that year, he determined to make the pilgrimage or Haj to Mecca, having observed that to be a Haji afforded the greatest respect and safety a traveller could hope for in a Muslim country. The journey across the desert and the Red Sea to Jedda took four months in which there was scarcely a moment of any day when he was not in danger, even as a Muslim, either from desert raiders or lack of water, like all his companions, or from the suspicions or bullying of some of them.

It may have been when he was buying "the dress of a reduced Egyptian gentleman" in a tailor's shop in Jedda that he met a man who was to become his faithful servant and friend, and later to be important to Salt. William Thomson, born in Perthshire, Scotland, was serving in the 78th Highland Regiment in Egypt, when he was taken prisoner by the Turks during General Fraser's disastrous defeat at Rosetta on 21 April 1807. Enslaved and forced to become a Muslim, he took the name Osman. Shortly before Salt's arrival in Egypt, Osman asked Consul Missett to obtain his freedom from the Pasha, but was told to wait until Salt was in post and appeal to him. Salt was successful, probably because he told Mehemet Ali that Osman was the only Englishman (sic) still enslaved in Egypt, and as such a stain on the Pasha's honour.[3]

The traveller James Silk Buckingham, who met him in Jedda, wrote of Osman: "Though he preserved all his northern peculiarities of light complexion, sandy hair, and moustaches, freckled face, light-blue eyes, and yellowish eyebrows and eyelashes, his dress, air and manners were completely those of a Turk. He preserved, however, all his veneration for his native country, and his sympathies for all who came from thence."[4] As he did to the end. Alexander Kinglake, who knew him in 1835, shortly before his death, recorded "The strangest feature in Osman's character was his inextinguishable nationality...in vain men called him Effendi; in vain he swept along in eastern robes; in vain the rival wives adorned his harem; the joy of his heart still lay plainly in this, that he had three shelves of books, and that the books were thoroughbred Scotch — the Edinburgh this, the Edinburgh that, and above all, I recollect, he prided himself upon the 'Edinburgh Cabinet Library'."[5]

With insufficient funds to complete his pilgrimage, Burckhardt wrote of his plight to Mehemet Ali, "who knows me well, and when at Cairo had often expressed himself in my favour". The Pasha, who was encamped at Taif, near Mecca, preparing to attack the 'heretic' Wahabi, sent money and clothes and a command to come to him. No rigid follower of the Faith, he gave no indication when told of Sheik Ibrahim's intentions, that he did not believe him to be the Muslim he must be to complete the pilgrimage without committing sacrilege. However, he later told Salt and Peter Lee that he had known perfectly well he was not, "but that his friendship for the English nation made him overlook the circumstances."[6] Ten days later, with no further assistance from the Pasha, Burckhardt rode away with great relief from the intrigue-ridden atmosphere at Taif. Entering Mecca on 9 September, he conscientiously performed all the proper rituals of the pilgrim. In January 1815, he completed his pilgrimage by visiting the tomb of the Prophet Mahomet at Mdina. He fell desperately ill with malaria, which came and went for three months till he was too weak to stand and resigned himself to die in Mdina — a desirable fate for a Moslem, but not for a man whose goal in life lay far south in Africa. He reached Cairo at last on 24 June, after two and a half years away. He became a guest in the house of Boghos, the Pasha's chief interpreter, and it was probably there that he was introduced to the second of the men who were deeply to affect Salt's life.

Giovanni Battista Belzoni claimed, when he arrived in Egypt in early June 1815, to have "devoted the last twelve years...to the study of mechanicks".[7] This was a very partial account of his previous experiences, and one he anxiously promoted. The truth, though less dignified, is far more interesting.

Belzoni was immensely tall, perhaps as much as six feet eight inches, immensely strong, dark-haired with blue eyes and a fresh complexion, both handsome and intelligent, enterprising and persistent. Usually mild-tempered and amiable, he was flawed by a nature suspicious to the point of paranoia, "always inclined to put the very worst construction upon the acts of others if they were in some way foreign to his purpose," according to his biographer, Colin Clair.[8]

Born in Padua, Italy, on 5 November 1778, the son of a barber, Belzoni went to Rome, "where I was preparing myself to become a monk". In 1798, when the victorious army of Napoleon swept into Rome, he fled north, apparently becoming an itinerant pedlar of religious objects in Italy and France. By early April 1803 he was in London, appearing at Sadler Wells Theatre in 'Jack the Giant Killer', playing the Giant to the Dwarf of the famous clown Grimaldi. He also, as the 'Patagonian Samson', performed extraordinary feats of strength.

How Belzoni emerged from his mercantile activities as a Hercules is shrouded beneath the veil he firmly drew over his early life, but given his great size and strength, it was an obvious course to pursue, and pursue it he did, to popular acclaim, at fairs and theatres around the country. The memory of people who saw him made it impossible later, in England at least, to keep his early career the dark secret he so much wanted it to be. "I...contrived to live on my own industry and the little knowledge I had acquired in various branches. I turned my chief attention to hydraulics, a science that I had learned at Rome," is his version of these years. He certainly more than once created stage effects based on waterworks.

In 1812, with his 15-year-old Irish servant, James Curtin, Belzoni spent time in Portugal, Spain and Gibraltar, perhaps sometimes performing for the British troops then engaged in the Peninsular War. He returned only briefly to England and in 1814, with his wife Sarah and James Curtin, was intending to travel to Constantinople, where the Sultan often employed foreign artistes in his extravagant public entertainments. But, like many another traveller, he was detained for several months at Malta, and met there a man who changed his plans and the course of his life.

Captain Ismael Gibralter was one of several agents employed by the Pasha of Egypt to seek out foreign experts in various fields to help him drag Egypt into the nineteenth century. Belzoni so impressed Gibralter with his expertise in hydraulics and his idea for a waterwheel of a strong and easily manufactured design, which could be worked by one ox instead of the usual four, that the Captain arranged for him to go to Cairo to build a prototype for the Pasha. And so, as he boarded ship for Egypt on 19 May 1815, the cloak of the showman slipped from Belzoni's shoulders, to muffle forever, as he hoped, his previous incarnation. Three weeks later, Belzoni the expert in "mechanicks" stepped ashore at Alexandria.

There are a great many accounts of Belzoni's magnificent appearance, but of his wife Sarah's practically none. It seems she was born in Bristol in January 1783 and her maiden name was Banne. J. T. Smith described her as having "a sensible and intrepid cast of features", but when he met her she was in her mid-30s and weather-worn by Eastern suns. Her height has been variously described as that of a dainty midget, perched atop a pyramid of acrobats carried by her husband, dressed as Cupid and waving a small crimson flag, and that of a giantess, forming an enormous Gog and Magog pair with Belzoni. Independent and self-reliant, courageous and shrewd, she "more than equally shared in all his enterprises".[9] Since she married Belzoni about the time he came to England, she may also have been in the theatrical world. The marriage was childless: Belzoni wrote to his parents that he had been married almost 12 years, "and have had no children, nor would want to have any, as they would be a complete hindrance in my travels."[10] Whatever Sarah's views may have been, she herself was never a hindrance, being willing for any adventure, and able to fend for herself when her husband abandoned her for one of his expeditions.

On 1 July the Belzonis set out for Cairo, in the company of William Turner, a young diplomat on leave from Constantinople. On 7 July, from the northern head of the Delta, the Pyramids came into view, the last remaining of the seven wonders of the world, remarked the entranced Turner, but Belzoni says nothing of his first view of these monuments which were to engage him so deeply.

They landed at Bulac, the waterside suburb of Cairo which "consists chiefly of the merchants' stone magazines, dirty bazaars, and some good houses, which the better sort of inhabitants prefer to Cairo, from their proximity to the water and consequent coolness".[11] The Belzonis had been provided with a house by Boghos, to whom Belzoni had an introduction, probably from Drovetti, who had befriended his fellow Italian in Alexandria — an amity which was not to last. Boghos, wrote Belzoni, was well-disposed towards Europeans and had "great acuteness of understanding". His house had less to recommend it, giving every sign of being ready to fall about their heads. They made the best of it — "we had mattresses and linen with us... we sat on the ground; a box and a trunk served as a table."

Sometime in August, Belzoni came to an arrangement with the Pasha to build him a prototype waterwheel. He was to receive a salary of £25 a month and move from the ramshackle abode at Bulac to a small house in the compound of the governor of the palace of Shubra. Set in gardens rich in fruit trees, roses and vines, about three miles from Cairo, on the banks of the Nile, this palace was a favourite with the Pasha.

Many of the Pasha's advisers were opposed to his efforts to reform Egypt's economy, while the officials in charge of waterwheels in particular foresaw their empires diminished disastrously if the number of oxen required were quartered. Delayed permits and substandard materials obstructed Belzoni's efforts. But, where a less determined man might have given up in despair, opposition always stiffened Belzoni's resolve, and in three or four months the machine was completed.

Its demonstration was delayed by the Pasha's absence from Cairo, and it was probably June 1816 before he appeared at Shubra, "accompanied with several connoisseurs in hydraulics". One ox was harnessed in the treadmill and water began to flow into the irrigation canals with an abundance Belzoni judged equal to that normally produced with six or seven beasts. Even the Pasha pronounced it to be as productive as four ordinary wheels, then, "by way of frolic", ordered men to replace the ox. Some 15 crowded into the wheel, including young James Curtin. The wheel began to move, the men leapt out in fear and James, unable alone to counterbalance the weight, was thrown out, breaking his thigh. It was only Belzoni's quick reaction and the exertion of his mighty strength to stop the wheel that saved James from possibly fatal injury.

The Pasha's advisers triumphantly persuaded him the accident was an inauspicious omen, and the machine was abandoned. Burckhardt wrote indignantly that Belzoni, "not being able to contend with the intrigues of a Turkish court, and too honourable to participate in them…was dismissed as unfit for his business, and five months of pay still remain due to him."[12]

The two men had taken a liking to each other. Burckhardt thought Belzoni "as enterprizing as he is intelligent, high-minded and disinterested."[13] Belzoni, whose praise of others was usually faint to the point of invisibility, whole-heartedly admired Burckhardt: "He was the most candid, disinterested, and sincere being I have ever met with; totally free from that invidious and selfish disposition, which is so often to be found in travellers, who wish to be alone in one quarter of the world, to relate their stories agreeable to the suggestions of their own imagination to the people of another. But Burckhardt had none of that littleness of mind: he was a true explorer, and a hardy one, without pride, or ambition to be thought more than he was.'[14]

He was entranced by Burckhardt's tales of the wonders he had seen in Upper Egypt, such as the colossal head known as the 'Young Memnon', which lay separated from its body in a temple at Thebes. Diodorus Siculus, in the first century BC, ascribed the temple correctly to 'Ozymandias', the Greek version of Rameses, and quoted the inscription on one of the statues as: "My name is Ozymandias, king of kings, if any would know how great I am and where I lie, let him surpass me in any of my works", transformed by the poetic genius of Shelley into the memorable "My name is Ozymandias, king of kings: look on my works, ye Mighty, and despair." William Richard Hamilton, travelling up the Nile with William Martin Leake in 1801, had admired the head. The French had tried to remove it, apparently using gunpowder to "blow off its wig"; but the damage had fortunately not marked the face, and Hamilton described it as "certainly the most beautiful and perfect piece of Egyptian sculpture that can be seen throughout the whole country."[15]

Burckhardt tried to persuade the Pasha to present the head to the King of England, but, remarked Belzoni, "it must have appeared to a Turk too trifling an article to send to so great a personage." Burckhardt's tales excited the acquisitive instincts of the wealthy traveller, William John Bankes, who actually took ropes and pulleys up to Thebes to remove it, but he too failed. To Belzoni, the mechanical expert, the challenge was irresistible. But however eager, neither he nor Burckhardt had the necessary funds for the enterprise, and there the matter rested — until the new British Consul-General arrived in Cairo. Henry Salt, encouraged by Sir Joseph Banks to collect antiquities for the glory of his nation, lent a willing ear. But even at this auspicious moment the foundations were laid for the future unpleasantnesses and disagreements in the relationship between himself and Belzoni.

According to Belzoni, having often told Burckhardt that he was prepared to move the head to Alexandria, he said again to Salt, that he "should be happy to undertake the removal of the bust, without the smallest view of interest, as it was to go to the British Museum. The consul seemed inclined to comply, but was indecisive for some time, saying he would think about it. A few days after this, he avoided all communication, keeping himself in strict seclusion, as the plague had begun to show itself in the streets of Cairo."[16]

In truth, Salt would have been only prudent to take very careful thought before embarking on a project bound to involve considerable expense. He had barely arrived to take up his new responsibilities, he did not consider it proper to use his consular salary for anything but consular expenses (which, indeed, he was to find it but inadequately covered), and he had only a small private capital already severely diminished by the expenses of going to Egypt, while the delay in paying his salary was even to oblige him to borrow "considerable sums". The enterprise was just of the kind to appeal to him, but events so far suggested it would fail. However, statements from others than Belzoni show that he did not hesitate long.

When the plague began in Cairo, Mehemet Ali retreated to Alexandria; when Belzoni's wheel was ready for demonstration, the Pasha's verdict must await his return, and until then, Belzoni was still in his employ and presumably expected to remain so. When the plague began in Cairo, Burckhardt, determined not to be shut up in quarantine like the Franks, departed on 20 April for Sinai, did not return until 14 June and on the 16th wrote to William Bankes that Salt was still quarantined.[17] Salt, having seen Missett off at Alexandria, arrived in Cairo about 18 April and was at once quarantined at Bulac.

Salt had brought with him to Cairo a 17-year-old dragoman inherited from Missett's service. Of Greek birth, but brought up in Cairo, Giovanni d'Athanasi, known as Yanni, was the Arabic and Turkish interpreter for the British Consulate for many years. According to him, it was not until the plague abated that "we gave free access to our friends, amongst whom was Mr Burckhardt, who always turned the conversation to the subject of the celebrated edifices of Upper Egypt, and the antiquities which were to be found there…These discourses daily excited increased ardour and curiosity on the part of Mr Salt." One day Burckhardt introduced Belzoni as one lately employed by the Pasha who "had been obliged to give in his resignation". Burckhardt urged Salt to employ Belzoni to go to Upper Egypt, saying it was "a most providential occurrence which had thrown him in the way of such a man…Nothing…was resolved in the course of this interview." But some days later, Belzoni came with his wife, who "with tears in her eyes began a recital of all the hardships which her husband had suffered in the service of the Pasha. Touched at the sight of her tears, and affected at the details of the misfortunes of this family, Mr Salt at length decided to send Mr Belzoni into Upper Egypt."[18]

Yanni spent many months in Belzoni's company and grew to dislike him heartily, but, except for the strong hint that Salt decided to employ Belzoni only reluctantly, out of pity (Salt never suggests this), there are, as we have seen, known dates to support his timing of the event to after the plague season.

When the Pasha rejected the wheel and Belzoni lost not only his job but the pay that was owed him, he says he could not bear the idea of leaving a country "ever...one of the principal points of research among the learned" without making some investigations of his own. Deciding that "in an economical way" he could travel as far as Aswan, he hired a small boat, and betook himself to the British Consulate to apply for a firman, or permit, from the Pasha. As a native of the part of Italy which had lately come under Austrian government, "I might have applied to the Austrian consul...but as I enjoyed the British protection, I applied to the British consul" — implying it was a purely arbitrary decision. But, Salt pointed out, "Mr Belzoni knows that he studiously avoided letting it be known in Egypt that he was from the new Austrian dominions, and that he invariably represented himself to be a 'Roman'. The memorandum in the consular office, left by my predecessor, Colonel Missett, is as follows, 'Mr Belzoni came to Egypt with a British passport, and having no natural protector (being a subject of the Pope), was in consequence admitted to the privileges of a British protegé.'" Nor could the Austrian consul have given Belzoni a firman to excavate, but only to travel, as the former were given only to consuls for persons in their employ.[19]

How fortunate that Burckhardt was with the Consul when Belzoni arrived, and had been busy on his behalf: "It seems he had persuaded the consul to avail himself of the opportunity of my ascending the Nile, by offering to pay half the expense. Accordingly, when I had informed the consul of my intended journey...he expressed his joy by exclaiming, 'This is a godsend indeed!'" He was told that they had determined to offer the colossal head as a present to the British Museum, "if I would kindly undertake the removal of it. I replied that my capacity was little, but that I would use all my efforts to succeed in the enterprise; adding that I should be happy at all times to increase the British Museum with the product of my exertions. To which the British consul answered, 'And I shall be glad to do every thing in my power to promote your wishes.' This was all that passed on either side."[20]

Whether Belzoni at this time saw himself as an employee of the two partners in the enterprise, or even then as a third partner, supplying his labour as his contribution, one cannot tell; later he certainly felt that a subordinate position demeaned his achievements. "It has been erroneously stated," he wrote with massive dignity. "that I was regularly employed by Mr

Salt...for the purpose of bringing the colossal bust from Thebes to Alexandria. I positively deny that I was ever engaged by him in any shape whatsoever, either by words or writing; as I have proofs of the case being on the contrary. When I ascended the Nile, the first and second time, I had no other idea in my mind, but that I was making researches for antiquities, which were to be placed in the British Museum; and it is naturally to be supposed that I would not have made these excursions, had I been previously aware, that all I found was for the benefit of a gentleman, whom I had never had the pleasure to see before in my life."[21]

The 'proof' he quotes is the document, dated 28 June 1816, he received from Burckhardt and Salt, with meticulous instructions which bear the hallmark of the former's attention to detail and knowledge of the country. He was told to obtain the necessary implements to move the head, then go up to Siout and present his firman to whomever was in charge there, and consult with a Dr Scotto on his further proceedings, obtaining through him a soldier as escort, who was to hire the men needed for the work, "as otherwise they are not likely to attend to Mr Belzoni's orders". He was to engage a suitable boat for bringing down the head. He was then to proceed to Thebes.

> He will find the Head referred to on the western side of the river, opposite to Carnak, in the vicinity of a village called Gournu, lying on the southern side of a ruined temple, called by the natives Kossar el Deka'ki. To the head is still attached a portion of the shoulders, so that altogether it is of large dimensions, and will be recognized, — 1st, by the circumstance of its lying on its back with the face uppermost — 2dly, by the face being quite perfect, and very beautiful — 3rdly, by its having, on one of its shoulders, a hole bored artificially, supposed to have been made by the French for separating the fragment of the body — and 4thly, from its being a mixed blackish and reddish granite, and covered with Hieroglyphics on its shoulders. It must not be mistaken for another, lying in that neighbourhood, which is much mutilated.
>
> Mr Belzoni will spare no expense or trouble in getting it as speedily conveyed to the bank of the river as possible; and he will, if it be necessary, let it wait there till the river shall have attained sufficient height, before he attempts to get it into the Boat. But, at the same time, he is requested not to attempt to remove it, on any account, if he should judge there would be any serious risk of either injuring the Head, or burying the face in the sand, or of losing it in the Nile.
>
> If, on arriving at the ground, too, he should perceive that his means are inadequate, or that the difficulties of the undertaking, from the nature of the ground, or other causes, are likely to prove insurmountable, he will, at once, relinquish the enterprise, and not enter into further expense on that account.
>
> Mr Belzoni will have the goodness to keep a separate account of the expenses incurred in this undertaking, which, as well as his other expenses, will gladly be reimbursed; as, from the knowledge of Mr Belzoni's character, it is confidently believed they will be as reasonable as circumstances will allow.

The boat should be hired for long enough to allow the Head to be carried all the way to Alexandria, but Belzoni was to stop at Bulac for further instructions.[22]

As will be seen, had Belzoni been less determined, and obeyed these instructions to the letter, the Head might be lying there still.

Unfortunately, though this document was undoubtedly intended by its two signatories as a brief to an agent or employee, Belzoni could quite correctly "beg leave to observe, that in the whole of these instructions, though written in an assuming style (in his book, he omits Burckhardt's signature, presumably so as not to include him in this accusation of arrogance and pretentiousness), not a word is said about any payment to myself, which would certainly have been the case, had I been employed in the way that has been represented."

It was certainly very unbusinesslike of the two gentlemen not to have made a written stipulation about payment over and above expenses, but this is precisely the sort of document Salt received from the Foreign Office when he went on his mission to Abyssinia. Though the Foreign Office also did not mention a salary, Salt could have no doubt whatever that he was an employee of the Government.

Belzoni continued: "Seeing I undertook the enterprise cheerfully, the consul did me the honour to request something more, which was, to purchase whatever antiquities I could on the road…and for this purpose he supplied me with money, as well as for the removal of the colossal head." Salt can have seen no reason to explain that he was not in a financial position to be continually laying out money for gifts to the British Museum, so that Belzoni could later easily convince himself that he had not known he was collecting for a private individual rather than a national institution. He was supplied with a firman from the Pasha, "for liberty of excavation, etc., [which] expressly states Mr Belzoni to be *a person employed by me* [Salt's italics]; without which he would not have been permitted to have carried on such an undertaking".[23]

Only two days after the signing of the document, on 30 June, the Belzonis set sail from Bulac, with James and a Copt interpreter. Salt had no inkling of the mixed blessings his 'godsend' was to bring upon him. Belzoni was on his way into history.

* *

Burckhardt wrote to Colonel Leake at the African Association, "Mr Salt I believe has already acquainted you with our project of conveying the fine granite head of the Memnonium to Alexandria, with the intention…of offering it in our joint names to the British Museum. You know that beautiful specimen of Egyptian workmanship; the impression which it made upon you and your travelling companions…was the chief incitement to Mr Salt, who had not yet seen it, to engage in the proposed scheme…Mr Salt and myself have made a common purse to defray the expenses…and have given Mr Belzoni the necessary instructions. If we do not succeed, our intentions at least were too good to be laughed at; but should the head reach its destination, and become, as it deserves to be, an object of general admiration, it will afford me infinite satisfaction to have been a promoter of this enterprize."[24]

Five days after leaving Bulac, Belzoni presented his letters at Manfalut to Ibrahim Pasha, son of Mehemet Ali, who requested Belzoni to deliver them to the Deftardar Bey (Mehemet Ali's son-in-law) who commanded at Siout. Drovetti, who was with Ibrahim, kindly warned Belzoni that the Arabs of Thebes would refuse to work for him; yet more kindly, he made him the present of a granite sarcophagus he had been unable to remove from its tomb — "if I could take it out, I was welcome to it."

In the absence of the Bey from Siout, Scotto, physician to Ibrahim Pasha, at first apparently complaisant, soon began to raise difficulties, so that Belzoni in disgust made his own arrangements. Salt says the idea of firmans to excavate was then "altogether new and…excited…considerable jealousy among the Turks". But on his return, the Deftardar Bey received the Pasha's firman politely and provided Belzoni with orders for the Casheff of Erments, who commanded at Thebes.

On 22 July, after a tantalisingly brief view of Luxor and Karnak, Belzoni crossed the Nile to the 'Memnonium'. The temple, now more correctly named the 'Ramesseum', stood a little above the highest level reached by the Nile inundation. Belzoni found the colossal bust he was to take away "near the remains of its body and chair, with its face upwards, and apparently smiling on me at the thought of being taken to England."

Studying the route the head must travel to the Nile, Belzoni realised that when the flood came in a month's time, the land between temple and river would be under water, and the lowest places would be covered even sooner. Time was of the essence. He requested the Casheff of Erments for a work force of 80 fellahs. However, it required a judicious application of presents before, three days later, labourers appeared and the operation could begin.

The implements Belzoni had managed to assemble consisted only of 14 poles, four palm leaf ropes and four rollers. Onto a carriage made with eight of the poles, the head was slowly levered. A roller was inserted at front and back, the head securely tied on, and men stationed at each side with levers in case the load should turn. Some men dragged, while others changed the rollers — and the head moved several yards. The fellahs set up a shout — "Though it was the effect of their own efforts, it was the devil, they said, who did it; and, as they saw me taking notes, they concluded it was done by means of a charm." Triumphantly, Belzoni sent off a courier to Cairo with the news that "the bust had begun its journey to England".

The head made steady progress until, on 5 August, it reached low-lying land which would be under water within the next few days. It was no coincidence that at this moment the labourers were forbidden to work any longer for "the Christian dogs". The local governor, the Caimakan of Gournu, was "an old acquaintance of a certain collector of antiquities in Alexandria" — the first overt example of the rivalry that was to develop between Drovetti and his agents and those of Salt — a rivalry cleverly exploited by the Egyptians to their own advantage. Confronted by Belzoni, the Caimakan claimed his orders came from the Casheff. At Erments, the Casheff at first equivocated, but when Belzoni promised him an even finer pair of pistols than those belonging to Salt which he had lent Belzoni, he put his hands on Belzoni's knees, saying "We shall be friends", and firmans were written forthwith.

On 8 August the head moved out of danger, and four days later, "thank God, the young Memnon arrived on the bank of the Nile." In later years, many large monuments would be moved, but never again would one of such an awkward shape be moved with such primitive implements under circumstances of such interference from the authorities.

No more could be done until the Nile was high enough for the head to be loaded onto a boat, and Belzoni turned his attention to the sarcophagus so kindly given him by Drovetti. He was led into one of the holes in the mountains of Gournu, "so celebrated for the quantities of mummies they contain", and conducted along passages sometimes so low they were obliged "to creep on the ground like crocodiles". After a moment when it seemed he might be entombed forever, Belzoni scraped a way out through a recently concealed entry, to discover that the sarcophagus was only about a hundred yards within. The Arabs had hoped, by leading him astray, to charge a high price for showing him how it might be taken out.

The fellahs bringing the sarcophagus out were soon hauled off to Erments, "bound like thieves". Some agents of "Mr D —— " had just arrived with presents for the Casheff, who now claimed the sarcophagus had been sold to the French consul and no one else should have it. Belzoni said indifferently he would write to Cairo about the matter. He had anyway to apply to Salt for a boat, for there was none strong enough to carry the head at Thebes.

No response could be expected for a few weeks, so Belzoni built a mud wall round the head, and set off up the Nile. Burckhardt had sung him a siren song of other great wonders to the south. He who could move the immovable head of Memnon, could surely disinter the buried temple of Abu Simbel.

When he saw Abu Simbel, Belzoni felt less optimistic: "the amazing accumulation of sand was such that it appeared an impossibility ever to reach the door", which he estimated must be at least 35 feet below the soft and ever-shifting surface. But 'impossible' only challenged Belzoni and "perseverance, stimulated by hope" spurred him at least to make an attempt. Consent to dig was easy to obtain, for the Nubian Casheffs saw the activity as both hopeless and senseless. Paying the labour was more difficult, for everything here was done by barter. Belzoni sent a man with a piastre to the Reis, or captain of his boat, who gave him for it enough millet to feed a man for three days. This graphic illustration of the power of money had its effect — which was more than Drovetti had managed a few months earlier. He had given Daoud Casheff 300 piastres to open the temple, but on his return from Wadi Halfa it was handed back, "as no one cared for such small pieces of metal".

While awaiting his consents, Belzoni sailed on south to the Second Cataract. Caught in an eddy, the boat was driven on a rock and for a moment seemed split in two. "I might have swam on shore; but Mrs Belzoni was no small charge to me on this occasion" — one of the very few occasions that could be claimed.

Sarah was almost certainly the first European woman to penetrate so far up the Nile. Yet her achievements are consistently undervalued or ignored. As much in danger from disease or attack as her husband, Sarah had also to endure, for weeks on end, loneliness and boredom, while Belzoni enjoyed his explorations, usually finding it convenient to leave her to fend for herself among strangers. But whatever she may have on occasion said to her husband — and one can imagine some spirited exchanges — in her own account she made few protests.

The *Monthly Review*, in its notice of Belzoni's book, grunted chauvinistically, "Annexed to this volume is a 'Trifling Account' by Mrs Belzoni... She is herself, we learn, an amiable woman: and the most candid manner in which we can notice her labours is to say nothing about them. She journeyed to the Holy Land and was much incommoded with fleas."[25] Very droll — and very unjust. As an observer of local life, she had the advantage over male travellers of having free access to the women, and made some shrewd and distinctly unvarnished remarks about them.

At Abu Simbel, Sarah visited Daoud Casheff's wife, who "had put herself and palace in order". Once her fair skin and the colour of her hair had been admired, the great curiosity was Sarah's clothes. By now she was dressed "as well as I could", as a man. Her black silk neckerchief was untied, the buttons on her coat closely examined. "Their remarks on my corsets, which I still wore, were extremely sensible. I made them understand they belonged to the female part of my dress, not knowing the custom that is come up since I left Europe." She sounds regretful — if only she had known corsets were out of fashion, how much more comfortable she might have been. Mrs Daoud called women in to dance; "but unfortunately I did not appreciate this mark of respect they thought they were paying me."

Sarah says nothing of one of her adventures, and her husband treats it casually. While Belzoni directed digging at the temple, two men unobtrusively slid away down to the boat, and finding Sarah alone but for a little village girl, "were rather impertinent to her," and tried to get aboard to rob the boat. When neither gesture nor voice availed to stop them, Sarah smartly produced a pistol, at which they fled up the hill. She sprang from the boat and pursued them, but "they mixed with a number of their fellow savages, and it was impossible to find them out; for they were all like so many lumps of chocolate seated on the sand at work, and not to be distinguished the one from the other."

Digging down 20 feet, Belzoni uncovered one of the northern colossi at the front of the temple down to its shoulders, like the one to the south which the diagonal flow of the sand had always exposed. But the time to be in Thebes to embark the Memnon was approaching; even this, he remarks rather irresponsibly, would not have deterred him from continuing, "and no doubt I should have accomplished my undertaking", but for want of that article which, a few days before, was so despised and unknown — money. With a promise from the Casheff that no one would be allowed to touch the temple till he came again, he departed, "with a firm resolution of returning to accomplish its opening".

Above the First Cataract, he explored the island of Philae, marking down trophies to be carried off, including some carved blocks, and an obelisk which he claimed in the name of the British Consul and paid to be guarded. At Aswan, after some difficulty, and at a steep price, he hired a tiny craft, scarcely large enough to hold the Belzonis, the interpreter and the janissary; not the relief poor Sarah had hoped for after being "screwed up" in a small boat for a month in Nubia.

"We at last reached Luxor," Sarah wrote, "Still there was no rest for the soles of our feet." And still no boat to take the head. Belzoni was about to send a courier to Salt when a large boat appeared on its way to Aswan, carrying Jacques Rifaud, a sculptor and artist, who excavated for Drovetti, and Frederic Cailliaud, a mineralogist, who had accompanied them both to Nubia the previous year. In the presence of the Aga of Gournu, Belzoni bespoke the boat on its return.

The boat had been moored close to the head. "I will not waste my time," said Belzoni scornfully, "in describing the remarks made by the two French agents of Mr D, on seeing the head: suffice it to say, they positively declared, in spite of the evident mark it bore on its breast, that the French army did not take it away, because they thought it not worth the taking!" Told of Belzoni's success in collecting other antiquities, their dragoman, "a renegado Frenchman, observed to me, that, if I persevered in my researches, I should have my throat cut, by order of two personages; one was the Casheff of Erments, the other I shall not mention at present."

Lodging Sarah in the house of an Arab at Luxor, Belzoni sailed to Esne with the two Frenchmen to conclude his bargain for the boat — one can imagine the atmosphere aboard. He had, because of the boat owners' reluctance, to promise the huge sum of £75 for the voyage from Thebes to Cairo. Returning to Karnak, he set 20 men to work on the west side of the temple where no one had dug before and was soon rewarded with about 18 statues, six of which were perfect, including a white one "as large as life, supposed to be of Jupiter Ammon." He also had a thorough look at the Valley of the Kings, and with that combination of observation, instinct and good fortune that attended so many of his finds, discovered the tomb now known to be of the priest Ai, briefly pharaoh after the death of Tutankhamun.

> Here, reader, was the beginning of those discoveries, which have caused me so much trouble, not from the exertion and arduous labour required in these researches, but in the atrocious persecution they have drawn on me, from malice, jealousy, and envy…Had I not determined to stand, like a pyramid defying the wind, against all their numerous attacks, which poured on me like a torrent, I should not have been able to proceed…many travellers of various nations…witnessed, that the greatest difficulties I had to encounter were not in the discovery of antiquities…but in controlling the complicated intrigues of my enemies and false friends.[26]

The boat returned from Aswan, but Rifaud and Cailliaud had persuaded its owners that the head would certainly crush the craft and they would receive no recompense. Belzoni's deposit was returned. "My vexation was great"; the Nile was lower daily and would soon be too low to embark the head. But fortune suddenly smiled. A soldier came from the Casheff of Erments with a present of two small bottles of anchovies and two of olives and an invitation to a feast. "Strange as it may appear, it will be seen that the effects of a few salted little fish contributed the greatest share towards the removal of the colossus…which, in all probability but for them, would not have been in the British Museum to this day." For these small jars had been a present to the Casheff from his friend Drovetti, and he was enraged at such an insultingly paltry gift.

At Erments, Belzoni was received by the Casheff with lavish compliments, with offers of all the labour he wanted, with assurances he could embark the great head the next day, and the disputed sarcophagus or anything else he pleased. "Had I requested…the colossi of Thebes, Tommy and

Dummy, as the Arabs call them, he would have had no objection to my putting them on board my little boat that night."

With 130 men, Belzoni began to build a sloping causeway to the Nile, by now 18 feet below the level of the bank. On 17 November the head was embarked. It sank into the fresh earth of the causeway as it descended on its rollers, but this was preferable to its sliding too rapidly, for "if this piece of antiquity should fall into the Nile, my return to Europe would not be very welcome, particularly to the antiquaries." But his arrangements had been careful and competent and all went smoothly. Crossing the river, Belzoni embarked seven of the statues from Karnak and set sail for Cairo.

There, Belzoni found that Salt was in Alexandria, but had left instructions with his secretary, Henry Beechey. Everything but the head was to be landed and lodged at the Consulate: "I could not conceive the reason of this distinction, as I thought that all the articles I collected were to go to the British Museum." But it seems unlikely he could have thought this, for he says himself that he saw Burckhardt "in the first hour of my arrival", who wrote to Salt on 18 December; "Mr Belzoni has succeeded beyond the most sanguine hopes you could entertain, and certainly done his utmost to execute his commission in full. He has brought, besides the head, seven statues, which will be a most valuable ornament to your future gallery. One of them is what he calls 'the young man', a sitting figure, I rather believe a portrait, with the ram's-head on his knees. The others resemble those two statues Mr Bankes carried off, and of which the French have given a drawing. Belzoni...says sixteen others, exact copies, were transported by him to the beach, where they were left for your orders."[27]

Even if Burckhardt did not enthuse to Belzoni about the proposed gallery, the fact that Salt told the Italian that he could select for himself, as a present, two of the best of the statues still at Thebes, surely should have indicated that Salt regarded them as his own property, to be disposed of as he wished. Equally, Belzoni clearly did not feel he was misappropriating British Museum property either then or when he sold these two statues a few months later to the Comte de Forbin, for the Louvre, for the equivalent in English money of the time of £175.

For the next two weeks, swarms of Cairenes, of all classes, constantly crowded the vessel at Bulac to marvel at the head.[28] Then Belzoni superintended its journey to Rosetta, and its removal to a sea-going *djerm* — a comparatively easy operation with proper tackle and workmen. At Alexandria by 14 January 1817, the head was landed with the help of the crew of a British transport, and lodged in the Pasha's magazine to await a ship to England.

A few days later, Salt and the Belzonis returned to Cairo. "There the worthy Burckhardt would insist, that I should receive a present, half of which he obtained from the consul, as an acknowledgement of my success with regard to the colossus." Salt's account is rather different: "We came to a settlement, and I must attest that it was with great reluctance that we could get Mr Belzoni to accept anything for what he had so zealously performed; at length, at my repeated solicitations (which he chooses to forget), and from my stating that if he did not take anything, it would render it impossible for me to give him another commission as I proposed, he consented to receive what we had offered him, about four thousand piastres: of this, two thousand were put down to the account of the head, of which I paid half, and the rest was paid exclusively by me," presumably as an acknowledgement of Belzoni's successful excavations at Karnak; all this beside his two statues. Salt was drawing not on memory for his statement, but on accounts "in my possession, signed by Mr Belzoni, so that," he adds temperately, "he does not act quite fairly in stating that what was given 'was obtained as if reluctantly from me by Mr Burckhardt.'"[29] The whole sum for moving the head down to Alexandria and embarking it was about 14,000 piastres, "somewhat more perhaps", then about £350 in English money.[30]

It was still many long months before the head reached England. It was not until 12 October 1817 that Salt could write to Lord Castlereagh that "the Head of the Young Memnon, a celebrated fragment of Egyptian sculpture" had left Alexandria for Malta on the *Neachus* transport.[31]

As it left its native shore, Rev. Thomas Joliffe witnessed its narrow escape from a watery grave. "I accompanied the English Consul [Peter Lee]...to assist at the embarkation of a colossal head of red granite..." The *Neachus* was too large to tie up at the quay and a smaller boat had to ferry the head to her. As the boat was lower than the pier, the sculpture had to slide down, on nothing so substantial as Belzoni's earth ramp, but over some planks. The 30 Arabs hired to "restrain" the Head's descent "appeared anxious to acquit themselves to the satisfaction of their employers, and seemed to take a strong interest in bestowing the treasure with safety; but from some imperfect adjustment of the cords, and the confusion of so numerous a party engaged in working them, the machinery became unmanageable, and the head rolling forward with irresistible violence, was on the point of being precipitated into the water — when one of the slabs fortunately broke under the pressure, and occasioned it to fall on a large quantity of grain placed in the bottom of the scherm."[32]

At Malta, the head was transferred, at the direction of Admiral Sir Charles Penrose, to HM Storeship *Weymouth*. It had to share the vessel with various architectural bits and pieces from Leptis Magna, gathered up by a Captain William Henry Smyth as a present from the Bey of Tripoli to George III. These were finally disposed artistically at Virginia Water, where they may be seen to this day.

On 14 March 1818 the British Museum trustees were informed by the

Foreign Office and the Admiralty of the arrival of the *Weymouth*, but it was not until 9 May that a sub-committee was appointed to consult with the architect Robert Smirke about the placing of the Memnon Head.[33]

At this time, the British Museum was still in Montagu House, on the site of the Museum's present Smirke building. The Memnon was first housed in the Townley Gallery, which, originally planned in 1803 to receive the Egyptian treasures arriving from Alexandria, had been enlarged to take the sculpture collection of Charles Townley, purchased for the nation after his death. The head's huge size meant that the whole Egyptian Room had to be reorganised, in order to preserve the symmetry of the display. It might even have been sited outdoors. In 1818, Salt wrote to Hamilton, tactfully masking his horror, "Your idea of placing it in the courtyard is good, but has two objections — the difficulty of preserving it from sun, frost, and rain, which will very soon decompose the granite, as I have seen in many instances, and the difficulty of placing it in a proper light, the whole effect of it entirely depending upon this latter circumstance."[34]

The intractable bulk of the head continued to be a nuisance. When it was removed in June 1834 to the new Egyptian Gallery, an entire detachment of Gunners was engaged for the task — a tribute indeed to the skill of Belzoni and his workmen.

Burckhardt said, "Mr Salt and myself have borne the expenses jointly, and the trouble of the undertaking has devolved upon Mr Belzoni, whose name I wish to be mentioned, if ever ours shall…because he was actuated by public spirit, fully as much as ourselves." In the *Quarterly Review*, the reviewer of Belzoni's Narrative, commenting upon his complaints that Salt had misrepresented him as being in his employment, quoted this letter, adding, "We regret to perceive any feeling of irritation on a matter which appears to us as of no importance, and on a point too wherein the merit of our author has never been called in question. The name of Belzoni alone is coupled with the bust of Memnon in the Museum, and this, we think, ought to satisfy him."[35]

If this refers to a label on the sculpture, it is, regrettably, no longer there; at present, credit is given only to the two donors. Here, at least, posterity has done less than justice to Giovanni Battista Belzoni.

8

Captain Caviglia and the Pyramids of Giza

“ AN AMIABLE and enthusiastic devotee at the shrine of antiquarian
learning...who has sacrificed country, home, friends, fortune, for the
refined though eccentric taste of exploring the hidden mysteries of the
Pyramids and Tombs of Egypt."[1] In 1837 *Tait's Magazine* described Captain
Giovanni Baptista Caviglia, who had by then been excavating in Egypt off
and on for 20 years. Born in Genoa in 1770, he was a master mariner and
owner of a Mediterranean trading vessel. Normally based at Malta and sailing under the British flag, he had come to regard himself as an honorary
Englishman. Salt came to know him well and over the years Caviglia often
stayed in his house. He was fond of the kindly seaman, describing him as "a
gentleman with whose amiable character is blended an ardent enthusiasm
for antiquarian research," and one who carried on his researches "with a
disinterested zeal that merits general admiration, and will ensure him the
gratitude of all who take pleasure in the studies of the antiquarian."[2]

A devoutly religious man, Caviglia had long believed that among the
unexplored ruins of ancient Egypt there might be that which would throw
light upon the rites of her peoples. He had become particularly fascinated by
the enigma of the Pyramids of Giza and determined that one day he would
help solve the mysteries which hung over them, and explain the real intention of their numerous passages and interior chambers. Unlike other, more
sophisticated, explorers into Egypt's past, Caviglia's interest was as much
with the mystery as with the history of his discoveries.

At the very end of 1816 Caviglia left his ship at Alexandria and reached
Cairo the day after Christmas. There he quickly entered into an arrangement
with two others: Mr Kabitziek, a young man employed by the Pasha's interpreter, Boghos, and a M. La Fuentes, that they should go together "with
cords and other necessary apparatus" to the Pyramids. They reached them
on 8 January 1817. Caviglia's activities were to be reported by Salt to the
world through the *Quarterly Review* in April 1818. The *Review* applauded
Salt for his own part in the explorations: for his "zeal, personal exertions,
influence with the pashaw [sic], and great pecuniary liberality" which
brought many of the hidden treasures of Egypt to light.[3] Caviglia had read
a fair amount and knew what he was looking for. His first ambition was to
examine the 'well' in the chamber of the Great Pyramid which he believed
to be "an enterprise never yet accomplished".

Caviglia clambered down into the main chamber, fastened a rope around his waist, took a lamp and, with the other end of the rope passed over a cross-bar, got his companions to let him down. When he reached the bottom of the shaft, about 20 feet down, he found that the second shaft, which took a strong turn to the south, was choked with stones. With some understandable difficulty, he persuaded the boldest Arab to go down to help him remove them. A further descent through a mason-worked drop of some 14 feet opened into a grotto — too low for a man to stand up in. The well continued downwards. Caviglia called his two companions down to help him, and was dropped further into the bowels of the pyramid. The heat was excessive, the air impure, and his lamp soon began to burn with "a faint and glimmering light". He was now some 100 feet below the grotto, but the passage still opened below him like "an unfathomable abyss". At last it ended among loose stones and rubbish, and he hastened to return. As he reached his companions all the lamps went out in quick succession — occasioning such alarm that the whole party made "a precipitate retreat".[4]

Back in Cairo, Caviglia and his companions were congratulated on their lucky escape. Salt knew that "those who have visited the pyramids and seen the stoutest men faint in getting up even into the gallery, and have experienced the enervating effect of the foul air in this subterranean channel... and knew of the stories of men who had died which abounded in Cairo... how to appreciate the firmness of nerve, undaunted resolution and admirable presence of mind displayed through this adventure."[5]

Caviglia was neither satisfied nor frightened away. At the bottom of the well the ground below his feet had given off a hollow sound and he believed there had been a concealed outlet. Soon he was back at Giza, determined to excavate to the bottom of the well. Kabitziek found that "his occupations forebade him from engaging actively in the labour"; La Fuentes "ceased to take further interest in the undertaking".

Captain Caviglia set up home in one of the nearby tombs, in two rooms cut into the rock, with just a curtain for a doorway. A later traveller gave a delightful picture of how Caviglia settled in for a dig. Captain Moyle Sherer was at Memphis in March 1823 and met Caviglia, noting that he had "a countenance very foreign, with the deep lines and brown stain of a travelled and weather-beaten man." Caviglia had just discovered at Saccara "a very fine colossal statue of a noble countenance, with a scroll represented in its closed hand, and striped clothing on the thighs", and was erecting his *Maison rustique* close to his treasure: "plans and drawings were hung all around, concealing and ornamenting its walls; his books established on shelves and tables; in fact, it looked the sort of home in which the soldier and the traveller find some comfort in their sojourning."[6]

In 1817, once settled in, Caviglia hired some Arabs to remove the rubbish from the well with baskets and cords. Salt thought it astonishing that

101

Caviglia managed to inspire the men to work alongside him in such a confined space, in which a light would not burn more than half an hour, so that
everything was done by feeling not by sight, while the heat and foul air made
it impossible to work more than half an hour "without suffering the perni-
cious effects". One workman was brought up in a faint; others collapsed on
reaching the surface. The men said they were prepared to work for Caviglia
but not to die for him. He had to give up.

He turned his attention to clearing the main entrance of the Great
Pyramid so that it was no longer necessary for visitors to creep in on their
hands and knees. He was rewarded by the discovery that the passage continued in the same inclined angle downwards and that, although obscured
by masses of stone, was of the same quality of mason-work as the rest of the
passage. As Caviglia and his men burrowed on down they encountered the
familiar impure air and suffocating heat they had found in the well. Only by
"conciliation and increased wages" did he get the workmen to carry on. But
by now his own health was affected and he was attacked by "a spitting of
blood". Even this did not deter him. On 14 February he was about 200 feet
down the passage when he discovered a doorway on the right. From it came
a strong smell of sulphur. Could this be the very sulphur that he had burned
in the well to purify the air? His guess was proved right. The channel beyond
the doorway opened into the bottom of the well — and there lay the baskets, cords and implements he had abandoned weeks before. A complete circulation of air in the bowels of the pyramid was at last possible again, and
all danger from the impurity of air was gone.

A few days later Captain Caviglia proudly led Mr Consul Salt on a tour
of the new passage and up the well shaft of the great gallery "without much
inconvenience".

Salt and the merchant Samuel Briggs, on their return to Cairo from
Alexandria, visited Giza with Belzoni and Beechey to see Caviglia's work.
They were filled with admiration and offered to share in the expenses of
"the indefatigable excavator". Salt also suggested that Belzoni, recently
returned from his triumph with the Young Memnon, should help Caviglia.
Belzoni declined. In his *Narrative,* he explained that he thought it "would
not be right to attempt to share the credit of one, who had already exerted
himself to the utmost of his power....Besides it would have been a poor victory on my part to enter into the field after the battle had been fought, and
conquest gained by another." He did, however, cast his eye at the second
pyramid and "entertained hopes of [his own] success" there. Belzoni, to be
blunt, had no wish to share credit with anyone.[7]

In March Caviglia was visited by two fellow seafaring men: Captains
Charles Irby and James Mangles of the Royal Navy. The two captains, both
in their late 20s, had been friends since early in their careers. In May 1815,

Irby had been forced by ill-health temporarily to resign his commission and, in August 1816 he was joined by Mangles who had seen his last service afloat. They decided to tour Europe together. Europe, however, proved to be but the beginning of their adventures. "Curiosity at first, and an increasing admiration of antiquities as they advanced, carried them at length to Egypt."[8] On the night of 21 March, the trio, all skilled in naval navigation, observed the vernal equinox from the inclined passage of the Great Pyramid, and established that, on that night, the north polar star was visible. Irby and Mangles returned to Cairo to prepare for their journey up the Nile, and further discoveries, but Caviglia's work at the pyramids was far from complete. He returned to the new passage.

A pattern was beginning now to emerge: in all the pyramids opened, and by 1818 this amounted to some half dozen, the entrance sloped at the same angle of 26-27°. The *Quarterly Review* of that year commented that "it is quite impossible that this coincidence could be accidental; it must have been the work of design, executed for some special purpose." It seemed likely, the *Review* concluded, that the priests of the day "connected their sacred duties with their favourite study — combining religion with astronomy."[9]

Caviglia worked on. The passage led into a spacious chamber, which he rightly estimated was immediately under the central point of the pyramid. This large chamber was nearly filled with stones and rubbish. With considerable labour, he and his team cleared it. Salt thought this might be the chamber described by Strabo in 25 BC. They found some Roman characters, so rudely formed as to be almost unintelligible, marked with a candle flame on the rock, but little other evidence. Salt thought this chamber "disfigured by the effects of time and the rude hands of curious inquirers" had once been highly ornamented. It is not clear what gave him this idea, and even Halls queried his friend's reasons for this supposition.[10]

Caviglia went on to explore the chamber discovered by Nathaniel Davison (then British Consul in Algiers) in 1763, climbing down from the great gallery on a rope ladder. He set to work cleaning away the rubble — including the bats' dung which in Davison's day had been about a foot deep and was now nearer 18 inches. To the south and east of this chamber, Caviglia crept along excavated passages on his hands and knees for some 20 yards until they abruptly terminated. This was Caviglia's last labour at the pyramid at this time and Halls regretted that "it did not appear to have been rewarded by very important results."

Caviglia had, however, made two important discoveries: he had shown the purpose of the well and "how far the living rock had been made an auxiliary in the construction of the pyramids."

He turned his attention to the numerous edifices and tumuli scattered around the pyramids "as the graves in a churchyard round a church", and spread out as far as the eye can see. He was probably the first person to examine these lesser monuments carefully. Like the Great Pyramid, the buildings of this necropolis were full of sand and rubbish. Caviglia set to work to clean them out.

The tombs are built in a generally oblong form, facing north and south, and made of masses of stone, with the slight inward incline found in most Egyptian structures, flat-roofed with a parapet around the top. Many bore traces of hieroglyphics; others were quite plain. Some, Salt believed, would be "considered as objects of the greatest curiosity" if they had not been over-shadowed by the pyramids.

In the first tomb he cleared Caviglia found rough wall paintings of the sacred boat and a procession of figures, each carrying a lotus in his hand. There were also "several mouldering mummies". The second tomb had fragments of statues, including two pieces which made the entire body of an almost life-size walking figure. Salt believed these statues were portraits of the deceased person placed in positions where they could be seen by their living friends as they passed. The statues had eyes of glass or transparent stone to give them "an air of living men."[11]

Caviglia also unearthed a separate head, that Salt considered even in its battered state similar to the Sphinx with "the same facial line, the same sweetness of expression and marking in the mouth". In these statues and other fragments, Salt, by now deeply involved with Caviglia and his explo-rations, saw evidence of "a higher idea of Egyptian sculpture...with a close attention...to the markings of joints and muscles." In the fragment of one leg he observed "a fullness of the parts, and strictness of proportion, not unlike the school of Michael Angelo", and the finish of the work, he considered, "not behind the sculptors of Greece". This appreciation of the quality of some Egyptian work he shared with William Hamilton, who had spoken with equal enthusiasm of the temple of Luxor. Salt was to state his belief later in a letter to the British Museum that these works of ancient Egypt were to be as greatly valued as those of classical antiquity.

There were more discoveries: a large stone boat with a square sail "dif-ferent from any now employed on the Nile", and more paintings, in bas relief, of men, oxen, deer and birds. The men were planning and preparing articles of furniture, hewing blocks of wood, and pressing out skins of wine or oil. One scene showed a quarrel between some boatmen and other men at work: ploughing, hoeing, bringing in their corn on asses and stowing it away. On yet another wall, vividly painted, was a band of musicians and a group of dancing women. Caviglia and Salt made another fascinating dis-covery. In all these monuments there was a deep shaft or 'well' leading to a narrow passage and a subterranean chamber, which served as "a receptacle for the dead". In one of these Caviglia found a sarcophagus, lidless and empty. Almost everywhere that the antiquarians of the early nineteenth century went, others had been before, searching not for history but for gold.

Salt frequently visited Giza, to linger, sometimes for hours, in the chambers "contemplating with peculiar delight the effects of the singular combination of bas relief, and of colouring after life, which presents a species of reality that mere painting can with difficulty produce."

Caviglia turned his attention to the catacombs near the pyramids. He and Salt went into a few of them to the west, but found them too 'uninviting'. In those to the south they found traces of painted sculpture, some remarkable hieroglyphics and several mummy pits, well turned over by the local people. In another group of caves they discovered what they thought was a zodiac and some beautiful figures of animals sculpted on the walls. Salt wrote to Halls the fish and birds were so accurately described that their species might be "distinguished at a glance, particularly the hoopoo, paddy bird, and Indian hen; and among the fish, the mullet and the boolty, which last is reckoned by far the best fish of the Nile."

Caviglia was always happy to share his discoveries with others and many people came to look. In August the traveller John Carne gave a charming picture of Caviglia at work. Salt introduced Carne to Caviglia who warmly invited him to his "desert abode". It was dark before they arrived. The Arabs came out of the apartments of the rock on which the Pyramids stand to welcome them. Caviglia led Carne to the tomb he shared with his German assistant, Mr Spinette. They sat on the floor to sup on boiled fowl before retiring. The next day they visited Caviglia's recent excavations: a gateway of fine white stone covered with hieroglyphs, three subterranean apartments, one with two large rock-cut coffins in it, and a curious square room which had been discovered by Salt himself. At this time Caviglia was engaged in what Carne, rightly, considered an almost impossible task: trying to find an underground passage which he was sure linked the Pyramids of Giza with those of Saccara 15 miles away and to the ancient city of Memphis.

Carne listened and looked with admiration. "A man," he said, "must be animated by no slight enthusiasm to live in this desolation, deprived of the joys of civilised life, toiling like a slave, with forty or fifty Arabs, from day break to dusk, amidst rocks, sand and beneath burning heats." Caviglia was a thoughtful host and after work entertained Carne with visits to the local sights. One night they went to the Great Pyramid and into the great chamber; another evening they visited the dervish who lived in a spacious chamber nearby. On the last evening Carne sat with Caviglia "near the door of his rocky abode, as the sun was going down…its red rays lingering on the Pyramids, the desert and its dreary precipices and wastes. Of all the sunsets I ever beheld, none are so beautiful as those of Egypt". It is, indeed, a marvellous place to be as the sun goes down and the locals relax after a long day of tourist-hunting and return, leisurely, to their homes.[12]

* *

In the estimation of the *Quarterly Review* the most brilliant of Caviglia's discoveries was yet to come. That was the uncovering of the great Andro-sphinx — an operation which they had wrongly ascribed to Belzoni in a previous issue. Here Caviglia worked again with "that indefatigable perse-verance that became the astonishment of every person who witnessed his labours."

The work at the Sphinx was made tedious by the fact that each night the wind drove back more than half the sand cleared in the day. For three months Caviglia and his 60 to 100 workmen toiled on, each week the days growing warmer, until they had laid open the whole figure to its base, and cleared an area a 100 feet from its front. The task was remarkable not least because, unless it was done with the very greatest care, mass after mass of the sloping sides came tumbling down "till the whole surface bore no unapt resemblance to a cascade of water". In some places as soon as the men stopped work, the sand poured down "in one continual and regular torrent" and the men could work for days with no discernible effect. But at last it was done.[13]

There was a small temple made of three huge flat stones ("like a sim-ilar shrine in the possession of Mr Salt") with fine specimens of bas relief of a man making an offering to the Sphinx. Beyond the temple was an altar and then steps leading some distance below the paws to the base of the temple. Salt believed this descent was meant to impress the beholder — "who would first have viewed the Sphinx at a level with a more imposing idea of its grandeur when he viewed its full magnitude from below." On one paw of the great creature was cut, in Greek, lines which Thomas Young would turn into English verse. They were by the writer described by Gibbon as "the ele-gant and philosophical poet Arrian":

> Thy form stupendous here the gods have placed,
> Sparing each spot of harvest-bearing land;
> And with this mighty work of art have graced
> A rocky isle, encumber'd once with sand;
> And near the pyramids have bid thee stand:

Salt, although at first thinking commentators like the Dane Frederick Norden and the Frenchman Vivant Denon, over-lavish in their praise of the Sphinx, came to feel differently as he prepared his own portrait of it. His 'portrait' gives not only a vision of the Sphinx as it was when Caviglia uncovered it, but also a sense of the drama of that unveiling. "The more I studied it at different hours of the day, and under different effects of light, and of shade the more I became convinced of their (Norden and Denon) comments have hardly done justice to its merits: it must indeed be allowed, that the drawings by both these gentlemen but faintly accord with their encomiums, but after having repeated the same task myself with little success, I must admit, that the difficulties which attend the undertaking, are sufficient to baffle the efforts of anyone not professionally dedicated to the arts."

Salt's words strengthen the vision of the monument which even 20 years later had been so much defaced that Colonel Vyse would say "these beauties are no longer visible". Salt's repeated and accurate observation while he was drawing had given him "a tolerably complete idea of its original perfection." This Salt saw and reported in the *Quarterly Review*:

"The contemplative turn of the eye, the mild expression of the mouth, and the beautiful disposition of the drapery at the angle of the forehead, sufficiently attest the admirable skill of the artist, by whom it was executed. It is true that no great attention has been paid to those proportions, which we are accustomed to admire nor does the pleasing impression, which it produces, result from any known rule adopted in its execution; but it may be rather attributed to the unstudied simplicity of the conception, to the breadth, yet high finish, of the several parts, and to the stupendous magnitude of the whole."

Salt was looking at this great work of art with the eye of a trained artist. It had been hidden or partly hidden for centuries and, from now on, when uncovered, would deteriorate. Thus he must be one of the few artists who ever had, and took, the opportunity to portray the Sphinx in a near-original state.

By now the work at the Pyramids had cost him and Samuel Briggs, about 18,000 piastres (some £800), yet they had liberally agreed that the disposal of whatever was found at Giza should be left to Captain Caviglia. He, in turn, "generously requested that everything should be sent to the British Museum, as testimony of his attachment to that country." Compared to how many of the other excavators treated their finds, this showed an almost unparalleled spirit of generosity.

In September 1817, Salt took Captains Irby and Mangles to Giza in the company of his house guests, Colonel Straton of the Enniskillen Dragoons and a Mr Fuller, who had recently arrived from Palestine and Greece, using Salt's "elucidative plan of the pyramids, sphinx, and all their interesting environs, and viewed all the work done."[14]

At last, after ten months unremitting labour, Caviglia's health brought him down. Struck by the dreadful and immensely painful opthalmia, even he had to stop work. In October 1817 he returned to his ship at Alexandria, but not before covering over the Sphinx. This act was to be criticised by

Count Forbin, director of the French Royal Museums.[15] He complained that he was unable to profit by the discovery of the temple of the Sphinx "which an unpardonable egotism had caused to be buried up and covered over again." Caviglia was outraged when this accusation reached his ears and wrote on 23 November 1819 to the *Journal des Voyageurs* to refute it: "as this leads to an implication that it was M. Saltalio [sic] discovered that beautiful monument, I think it right to exculpate this gentleman from the above charge of egotism...it was I and not Mr Salt that caused the temple to be covered again." He gave as his reasons that, having, within the Great Pyramid, found nothing all around but "the live and natural rock", he had investigated the base of the Sphinx to see whether a passage led from it to the Pyramid. Once he had cleared out everything around the Sphinx, taken its dimensions and "the most correct designs of all those antiquities", he was concerned to find that Arab women, "allured by superstition" were coming to worship and kiss the images in the temple and then "not content with this proceeding, afterwards to break off fragments or pieces, to serve as amulets or charms" so that already several hieroglyphics had been disfigured. Fearing that the very object that he had laboured to reveal to the world "should come to destruction", he resolved to rebury it "till circumstances more auspicious might authorise the disclosure of to every eye."[16]

Caviglia was far from finished with his researches. He returned to spend months making new discoveries and setting straight new areas. Often he stayed with Salt between bouts of work and travellers who were also guests spent long hours talking with him about his discoveries and his interpretations. In January 1822 Salt would write to William John Bankes from Cairo telling him of a new society they had formed to assist Caviglia "who has returned and making new researches in the neighbourhood of the Pyramids". He had made several interesting discoveries — which Salt promised to report giving more particulars (if he did the letter is missing).[17]

9

Digging Out the Temple

ON 22 MARCH 1813, John Lewis Burckhardt left his camel and his guide at the top of a sand-choked cleft above the Nile in Nubia and made his way down to examine the temple of "Ebsambal, of which I had heard many magnificent descriptions". This was the exquisite small temple of Nefertari, wife of Rameses II, which stood a little aside of the great pitch of sand, about 20 feet above the surface of the river, entirely carved out of the steep side of the rock.

Burckhardt explored and paced out measurements as best he could without proper lights, then turned to climb the sandy height again, somewhat to the south of his line of descent. Then, about 200 yards from Nefertari's temple, he "fell in with what is yet visible of four immense colossal statues cut out of the rock...they stand in a deep recess, excavated in the mountain; but...they are now almost entirely buried beneath the sands, which are blown down here in torrents. The entire head, and part of the breast and arms of one of the statues are yet above the surface; of the one next to it scarcely any part is visible, the head being broken off, and the body covered with sand to above the shoulders; of the other two, the bonnets only appear...They do not front the river...but are turned with their faces due north, towards the more fertile climes of Egypt, so that the line on which they stand, forms an angle with the course of the stream. The head which is above the surface has a most expressive, youthful, countenance, approaching nearer to the Grecian model of beauty, than that of any ancient Egyptian figure I have seen; indeed, were it not for a thin oblong beard, it might well pass for a head of Pallas."[1]

The statue which breasted the angled flow of sand measured 21 feet across the shoulders and its ear was 40 inches in length. On the wall between the four statues was a figure of the hawk-headed Osiris, surmounted by a globe, "beneath which, I suspect, could the sand be cleared away, a vast temple would be discovered".

Could the sand be cleared away...Burckhardt could only marvel, and turn to trudge on up the shifting drift of sand.

* *

In 1816, Belzoni's attempt to open the great temple had been frustrated by running out of time and money. Never disposed to regard a setback as a defeat, as soon, he says, as he had delivered the head of Memnon to Alexandria, he proposed to Salt that he should return to Nubia to complete the task; "nothing could be more pleasing to me, than to find that my proposal was accepted." He requested that if he were successful, Salt would give him an official letter of introduction to the Society of Antiquaries when he returned to England and Salt promised to do so, though he warned Belzoni not to hope for a satisfactory response.

Later, Belzoni suggested that Salt had, at this time, formed no intention of sending him into Nubia, and Salt's own account says merely that he engaged Belzoni in 1817 to undertake a second voyage, "to be carried on at my exclusive expense". Once again, unwisely, but "confiding in the apparent respectability of his character, and from my experience of his talents", Salt did not specifically settle the remuneration, "conceiving he had been satisfied with our first settlement, and not suspecting we should ever have any difference on the subject."

Sarah Belzoni was left with James Curtin in the household of the chief clerk of the British Consulate. Belzoni was accompanied instead by Henry William Beechey, Salt's secretary, who was to study and make drawings of the monuments of Thebes. They were "furnished with a still stronger *firman* by the Pasha, as *being in my employ*." The expedition which departed on 20 February 1817 also included an Arab cook, one of the Pasha's janissaries (soon dismissed for being both useless, and insolent to the 'Christian dogs'), and a young man referred to by Belzoni as Beechey's Greek servant, in fact Yanni d'Athanasi, the consulate interpreter. They went equipped with everything that "could tend to their convenience or comfort" during the expedition.

Which included, according to Sarah, silver knives and forks for the use of Beechey. Belzoni commented a little patronisingly: "Nothing could suit me better than to have a companion in a young gentleman, with the prospect of whose society from what I had seen of him, I had much reason to be pleased. I was fully satisfied that, after having weaned himself from those indulgences to which he was accustomed, he would make a good traveller, though it is not easy, to one who is not accustomed to an arduous life, to pass on a sudden from the accommodation of a comfortable house to that of a rough uneasy boat, and much less to a life that is so irregular. However Mr Beechey soon accustomed himself to the change, and in a few months became quite indifferent to the many inconveniences he had to undergo."

At Minieh, they found two Copts, "dressed as Franks", agents of Drovetti in the purchasing of antiquities. Worse, when they arrived at the sugar factory run for the Pasha by a Mr Brine, they learnt these men were making a forced march to Thebes, to forestall the English by buying up everything available. Worse yet, the site at Karnak Belzoni wished to dig was "so evidently pregnant with objects worthy the risk of excavation" that he had no doubt the agents would take possession of it.

"Mr Belzoni became furious," reports Yanni, "and would have given all he was possessed of in the world to have been able to reach Thebes that very night, and mark out all the ground, in order that M Drovetti's men, when they arrived, might not find a neutral spot to explore, nor even place sufficient to sit down on." At once Belzoni abandoned Beechey and the boat and, on relays of horses, asses or camels, he and Yanni rode "as if we had been carrying the news of the capture of some fortress which had been twenty years besieged."[2] In five and a half days, Belzoni boasted, he slept but 11 hours. He beat the agents to Karnak, but to his disgust, learnt that the Governor of Upper Egypt, the Defterdar Bey, on the pretence of having "taken it into his head to be an antiquary", had set his physician, Maruki, to excavate where Belzoni had discovered the sphinxes. Finding only four good specimens, Maruki crossed the Nile to Thebes to forbid the fellahs to sell anything to the English. His motive became clear to Belzoni when Drovetti's agents arrived, immediately took possession of the 'Bey's sphinxes', and themselves set to work digging on a "very extensive scale". The situation was not easy, for the Defterdar Bey favoured the Drovetti party.

Reunited with Beechey, who had charge of the money, Belzoni worked fast, with the few men he could get, fearing that once the Bey heard of his successes, "he would put a stop to our proceedings by some intrigue or other."

Beechey set up home in a chamber of the temple of Luxor, for the boat had been rendered uninhabitable by the quantities of large rats, which had given them "no peace day or night, and at last...succeeded in fairly dislodging us". They took out the provisions and drowned the boat, the usual method of getting rid of such an infestation, but the rats, being good swimmers, "saved their lives, and hid themselves in the holes of the pier; and when the provision had been put on board again, they all returned cheerfully, a few excepted, and were no doubt grateful to us for having given them a fresh appetite and a good bathing."[3]

Belzoni was indefatigible. At dawn he would set men to work at Karnak, then, leaving Beechey or Yanni to oversee them, before noon would cross the Nile to inspect the work at Gournu. Here he was "researching among the mummies" chiefly for the papyri hidden in the folds of their bandaging. This often involved him in penetrating underground chambers crammed with "heaps of mummies", and with air so suffocating it could bring on faintness. The year before Belzoni had not managed to persuade the people, "who make a trade of antiquities of this sort", to show him the depositories of their stock-in-trade, but this time he was about so constantly that they realised he would inevitably catch them at work — and soon also realised that to be paid a daily wage whether they found anything or not, was to their advantage.

Sometimes Belzoni remained overnight at Gournu, joining local families and their sheep in their tomb dwellings. The conversation turned "wholly on antiquities. Such a one had found such a thing, and another had discovered a tomb. Various articles were brought to sell to me..." Mummies were omnipresent — cases, rags, bones, were used as fuel, "hands, feet or sculls are often in the way".

At Karnak, Beechey was superintending the excavations when a red granite head came to light, even larger than the Memnon, but less bulky, as it was broken off at the neck; an arm of the same colossus lay nearby. There, too, Belzoni collected an altar with six gods in alto relievo. He brought out, with great difficulty, the cover of the sarcophagus which Drovetti had 'given' him the previous year.[4] These things and more, enough to fill a large boat, Belzoni gathered together at Luxor, ready to embark; "it was well that I did so."

Petitioned by the French agents, the Defterdar Bey forbade his subordinates to help the English party in any way. The Sheik of Gournu, who was "rather attached to us", apologised to Belzoni, saying he dared not disobey. Belzoni rushed off to see the Bey and show him the Pasha's *firman*. The Bey countered with various tales against his party, which Belzoni indignantly refuted. He then accompanied Belzoni to Gournu, ordered the Sheik to bring him an unopened mummy, and finding no gold or jewels about it, accused the poor man of having already robbed it, and had him beaten nearly into insensibility. Belzoni tried to stop this brutal injustice and Yanni invoked the names of both the Consul-General and the Pasha himself — but the Pasha's son-in-law merely ordered the man beating the Sheik to "Go on, go on, and hard." However, when Belzoni declared he would report this to Cairo, the Bey apparently took thought of his position, and promised an order for labourers.

Yanni kept it "well secured in his pocket, as the most mighty order that had ever been given: and he often boasted of having it in his possession." One fateful day it was shown to the only Sheik who could read. He perused it silently, then turned a look of astonishment upon Belzoni, inquiring if he wished it read to the others. On Belzoni assenting, he read out: "It is the will and pleasure of Hamed, the Defterdar Bey and present ruler of Upper Egypt, that no Sheiks, Fellahs, or other persons, shall from this moment sell any article of antiquity to the English party, or work for them; on the contrary, it is hereby ordered, that every thing that may be found shall be sold to the party of Mr Drovetti; and whoever disobeys this order will incur the displeasure of the Bey." At such blatant treachery, even Belzoni gave up — but Abu Simbel beckoned.

About 1 May, a courier was despatched to Salt with an account of events and, presumably, a request for permission to excavate Abu Simbel. Far from Belzoni's later claim that he had shown "no interest" in what had happened, Salt wrote that he had spoken very strongly to Mehemet Ali about his son-in-law's conduct towards both Belzoni and the poor bastina-doed Sheik, and demanded action, or he would at once withdraw his people, and "take care how I again trusted any person attached to me" to go into the Bey's districts. The Pasha seemed "much vexed and hurt" and promised to send an express courier with a strong letter to the Bey.

Salt, as Consul-General, could speak to the Pasha with more effect and freedom than any ordinary 'Frank', but his reply to Beechey is an example of how scrupulous he was not to use his official position to further his private pursuits. "You must be aware that neither yourself, nor Mr Belzoni are at present engaged in any official employ; you are simply in the same situation as two travellers forming a collection, and are therefore only entitled to such reparation as any English gentleman would have a right to expect. It is absolutely necessary that this should be explicitly understood, for as you know I have no authority from Government for employing any person in such pursuits, and that I am bearing the whole expense and collecting for myself, you can only be considered as acting in a private capacity...I would rather give up all idea of collecting than be embroiled in continual quarrels on that account." How Belzoni, who must have seen this letter, could later claim he thought he had been collecting for the 'public', as represented by the British Museum, is incomprehensible.

Salt commended Belzoni for accepting the Bey's pretext for beating the wretched Sheik, "for in all cases where you have to deal with such people, it is a necessary act of policy never to take to yourself an insult for which the party concerned deems it prudent to assign another cause." Halls commented with admiration, "I do not know that I have ever met with a shrewder, or more sensible observation...and, as far as my experience goes, it is entirely new."⁵

Salt sent up a janissary to protect them, "and I would wish you, in consequence, to stay at Thebes until his arrival." But by the time they received this letter, his employees were at the island of Philae, above the First Cataract, having left Thebes on 23 May. They camped in and around the temples in searing heat. Despite not yet having heard from Salt, preparations began for ascending the river. Yanni was dispatched down to Esne to purchase provisions.

At this time, long before the dam built in 1908 removed the hazards of the First Cataract, but doomed the lovely temples to semi-drowning for much of the year, the paint still showed brilliant upon them: coral, aqua, verditer. Belzoni noted signs of the whole temple having been "fitted up for

Christian worship." Plastered mud and Christian religious figures hid the original decorations, but where the mud had fallen away, hieroglyphs showed beneath.

Soon there was a welcome increase to the company. The two naval commanders, James Mangles and Charles Irby, their appetite for exploring antiquities whetted by what they had seen of Caviglia's work at Giza, were pressing resolutely on into Nubia, despite advice that travellers to that wild land should be both numerous and well-armed. They were delighted to find Belzoni and Beechey prepared to accept their company. Their cheerful good humour and readiness for a lark made them invaluable additions to the party.

These qualities are abundantly illustrated in the journal written by Mangles but published in both their names. Many times they record, "we could not help laughing", at the foibles or pretensions of the people they encountered (nor, though not publicly, did they find at least one of their companions lacking as a source of amusement). Of Irby, one gathers little, except that he was the less forthcoming. Belzoni later observed of Mangles, rather uneasily, in a letter to William Bankes, that "he certainly [has] a sort of means to extract what he want from the busom of others."[6] The Fourth of June was the birthday of King George III and Belzoni's "jolly companions" proposed it be celebrated in style. They planted a flag atop the highest propylon on the island and at noon fired a salute. As their fire-power amounted to only five guns, for a suitably impressive effect, they had to reload each immediately after firing, and the barrels were soon too hot to touch. The ragged firing and the men's cheerful voices must have echoed strangely among the temples and reached into dark sanctuaries where surely such secular notes had never resounded before. They commemorated the event by carving an inscription on top of the propylon: "British Colours hoisted on this spot and a Royal Salute fired June 4 1817 by G B Belzoni, Jas Mangles, C L Irby, H W Beechey."[7]

The day after these patriotic revels Sarah Belzoni arrived, accompanied by the faithful James Curtin. It was probably a surprise to her husband, who had thought her safely in Cairo, but Sarah had enjoyed Nubia and "my wishes were to go also." Belzoni persuaded her that they could not afford a second boat. By his own account, there was only one boat available, but perhaps he thought his resourceful wife quite capable of conjuring up another one.

So Sarah, to her "great mortification", must remain at Philae, never to see "the inside of that interesting temple which had occasioned us so much anxiety the previous year". She added stoutly, "I was informed by some one who was there, that the boatmen as well as the servants of Mr Salt...had as much merit in assisting the concern as the other gentlemen, but they were not English. Had I been there, I should have helped to remove the sand as well as them, as far as my strength would have allowed me...and claimed as much merit." One feels sure she was, indeed, quite capable of earning her share in the adventure.

When Yanni returned from Esne, the janissary sent by Salt for the expedition's protection was with him. Though referred to by Salt as 'the Albanian', Giovani Finati came from Ferrara in Italy.[8] There can have been few men better qualified to give support to this expedition, but his experience seems to have been little appreciated by the others.

To an extent, this attitude both to Finati and Yanni is explained by Mangles' impatient comment that, "It is a great inconvenience to a traveller in this country, that both servants and interpreters always think themselves wiser than their masters; and therefore when desired to say or do any thing, always act according to the dictates of their own judgement, never letting their employer's wishes have the least influence with them." An inability to be certain that one's remarks are being translated to the letter, let alone in the spirit intended, must inevitably arouse unease and distrust.

Belzoni claims that their project was "deemed nearly imaginary, a castle in the air, as no one supposed that any temple really existed there"; and his gloss on Salt's positive response was, "To my great satisfaction, Mr Salt complied with my wishes of opening the temple of Ybsambul, which I had so often suggested to him; and I must give him much credit for risking the expense of such an undertaking, the uncertainty of which would have deterred most people from doing it, particularly as he himself entertained strong doubts of the existence of a temple there; for he said, in the same letter, that he thought we should find no entrance, but that it would turn out to be like some of the mausoleums round the pyramids."

On 16 June they set sail, after settling a quarrel between two of the crew, in which one was cut through the calf to the bone — a premonitory beginning. Besides the six Europeans and an Arab cook, the expedition included the Nubian crew of five men and three boys. One man, Hassan, who, because he wore a blue shirt, was "nic-named the blue devil...will," said Mangles darkly, "be by and by a conspicuous character in the narrative". The terms agreed were 160 piastres (four pounds sterling) a month, the crew to find their own food, with a baksheesh at the end of the voyage, if the crew's behaviour had been satisfactory, "a stipulation which always forms part of similar bargains in this country."[9]

Sarah took up residence on top of a temple at Philae, with mud walls built to enclose two "comfortable rooms". Belzoni had engaged some Nubians to protect her, but Sarah felt it advisable to guard herself against *them;* she and James kept their arms at the ready, and made sure her protectors were aware she was fully able to defend herself — "it is well known that people fear you when you do not fear them." Much of the luggage was left in her charge, including Beechey's silver tableware, the last vestige of civilised consular life.

On the second afternoon, the mountains closed in upon the river, presenting "some very grand though rude scenery. This, by some travellers, is termed the boundary between Egypt and Nubia." There were frequent piles of stones on the highest places, to indicate the vicinity of the Nile to caravans from the interior. During the voyage eight chameleons were brought aboard. They were useful, for if the annoyance from flies became too much, one had only to place a chameleon nearby, and it would catch them in great numbers with its long tongue.

On 27 June, at Deir, it was a blow to find Hassan Cashef away, for it was he who had promised Belzoni the previous year that none but the English should dig at Abu Simbel, on condition that he was to have "half the gold" that was found; the Nubians could not credit that the Franks were digging only for statues and inscriptions; convinced this was a cover for a search for gold, they were naturally convinced of their right to a share. Belzoni must now treat with Hassan's sons, Daoud and Khalil. Leaving a request for an order for workmen, the party sailed on. At Abu Simbel, when no response awaited them, Belzoni sent a message asking leave to start work when he returned from the Second Cataract.

At the Second Cataract, they took a long hot walk to the Rock of Abu Sir. Impressed by the views of the cataract from the cliff the previous year, Belzoni was now somewhat disappointed, for the river was lower and lacking the "foaming eddies" of white and green he had admired. But the captains were thrilled. They could now number themselves among the handful of Europeans who had penetrated so far up the Nile: William Bankes in 1815; Drovetti, with Rifaud and Cailliaud in 1816; "Sheck Ibrahim, a real friend of ours"; and Mr and Mrs Belzoni.

A few days earlier at Deir, the boatmen had demanded double pay, saying that the addition of the captains made "two parties". Mangles says, perhaps unjustly, "We have no doubt but our janissary and the Greek servant put them up to this request, as the soldier took a poor cowardly part, and urged that we were in a savage country, and had better temporize till we were on our return, thus showing of how little use these fellows are to protect travellers."[10] Those complaints had been rebuffed, but now the "vile" crew gathered an armed group of local men about them and fed them tales of the ungenerous behaviour of their employers. They refused to return to the boat, saying the Franks could buy it if they chose, but that *they* would not navigate it, adding defiantly that they "did not value their lives a pigeon, and for half a one that they would take ours". The Franks used a tactic which was to stand them in good stead on many subsequent occasions.

116

Affecting complete unconcern with the threats and grumbles from the shore, they made ready to get under way. This, Belzoni admits, "was more in appearance than reality, for we never could have got the boat out of that place". Even the crew had the utmost difficulty.

More demands for money came down, with accusations of having been starved. The local men advanced menacingly, demanding baksheesh for allowing the foreigners into their country and for seeing their cataract. "We now told them, that if we had seen the cataract without paying, so they had seen us without giving us any thing as a recompence, though we were as novel a sight to them as their cataract was to us, and therefore we were quits."[11] Eventually, after further parley and promises of baksheesh once the boat was into the middle of the river, the crew embarked, but with little decrease in ill-will and with their daggers fastened to their left arms above the elbow, ready to be drawn in a flash.

On 4 July, at Abu Simbel, there was still no word from the Cashefs, but the crew, fearing their behaviour would be reported, came "to beg a recon-ciliation, saying that they had forgotten and forgiven every thing and hoped that we had: they said they would behave well in future" and excused their conduct by pleading ingenuously that "they were poor, and always made a practice to get all they could from passengers and strangers."[12]

The fine promises were soon broken. When the boatmen threatened to stab Yanni and Finati, they were sternly told that the first to draw his dag-ger would be severely punished, but the warning had little effect. One, who had murdered his own brother at Philae, boasted that *he* would be the first to draw, and "swore by Alla and the Prophet that he would have one of our lives" and that his method was to stab people as they slept. "We however laughed at their threats, and told them they were more apt at talking of these matters than in executing them." Despite the dismissive words, the party must have felt vulnerable as they settled for the night. They always slept in the boat and Mangles says that each morning, they would see on the smooth surface of the sand ashore, "drifted by the night breeze, the tracks of the snakes, animals, etc., which had come down to the water's side during the night to drink."

At last, on 10 July, the two Cashefs arrived and set up shelters made of "a few sticks of date, the roof covered with grass", on the sandbank by the river. Mangles observed these arbiters of their fate with interest. Khalil was "a tall, handsome man, about 36 years of age, six feet high, very cor-pulent, and had a fine expressive countenance, with dark eyes: his dress was a large loose white linen shirt, with long sleeves hanging down nearly two feet, an old turban and slippers…Daoud Cashef appeared to be rather taller than his brother, though not so fat. He is a man about 45 years of age, and had a certain dignity and reserve in his demeanour that bespoke the chief:

he wore a loose blue shirt." It was settled that next day 60 men should start digging out the temple, paid two piastres a day each. The Cashefs made much of the fact that they had rejected the French requests to excavate the year before, and remained loyal to the English Consul.

On 11 July, nearly four weeks after leaving Philae, work began — briefly. There were only 50 men, who soon demanded *doura* (millet) as well as money, and refused to work more than five hours a day. By now the party was so fed up, they were "glad to give them any thing provided they would but work". They accompanied their labours with a merry song — an encouraging sound to their employers until the burden was translated to them: It is Christian money we are working for. Christian money is very good. We will get as much of it as we can. "This Nubian song," says Mangles drily, "though cheering to them, was not much so to us."

He described the task which confronted them: "...figure to yourself a flat excavated perpendicular surface, fronting the river, and hemmed in on one side by a mountain of sand leaning against it; the door in the centre of this plane surface buried in the sand, which rises on each side of it, increasing the labour and difficulty of digging down to a prodigious degree, for no sooner is the sand in the centre removed, than that on either side pours down." To excavate only a foot in the centre, the whole surface of sand which leaned against the temple must be removed — sand so fine "that every particle of it would go through an hour-glass".[13]

Belzoni contracted with the Cashefs that the temple should be opened, using 80 labourers, for 300 piastres. They imagined that the job would take no more than four days, "so little did we know of the real nature of our enterprize." The men worked with decreasing ardour, and in decreasing numbers, as the enormity of the task became clear. By the the third day "little more than nothing" was done. The Cashefs did not appear and old Mouchmar, one of their servants, who was acting as liaison, explained that they were fully occupied plundering a caravan passing by from Cairo to Dongola. Plundering over for the day, Khalil turned up, and with a supporting chorus of workers, demanded the half of the pay which had not already been handed over. Belzoni insisted that no more money was forthcoming until the work was completed; Khalil then tried to persuade Finati to give him his silk waistcoat, and Yanni to hand over his Mameluke sword, which in fact belonged to Salt, descending at last to asking for a certain pipe the crew had told him was in the boat. Meeting refusal on all fronts, he retired.

On one day, even the crew joined in, but soon, bored, Hassan, 'the blue devil', claimed that the boat was leaking and must return to Philae for repairs. There was no going back until the excavation was completed, was the stern reply. Then Ramadan began. As the Nubians could not eat between sunrise and sunset, they could not, they claimed, be expected to work. And so, "they left us with our temple, the sand, and the treasure, and contented themselves with keeping the 300 piastres", the balance of which had unwisely been paid over the previous day. The Cashefs suggested that the Franks had better go away and return in a month's time, when Ramadan was over. The Franks retorted that they would do the work themselves. Daoud did not care for this, fearing if they reached the door in his absence he would miss out on his gold, but was assured he would not be cheated.

The Europeans stripped to the waist and began to dig, with says Finati, only their hands for tools. The crew were so astonished and impressed that they joined in. A regime was resolved upon of working from dawn till nine, then from three till dark.

All agreed that this was a much more effective work force, and Finati allotted special credit: "...the two captains did each the work of ten Nubians in their own persons". Yanni concurs, "without the valuable assistance rendered by the above-mentioned gentlemen, we should not have succeeded in our undertaking." "Our hands certainly suffered a little by blisters," remarked Mangles cheerfully, "I had nine on one hand, and eight on the other." Over the next few days, varying numbers of locals joined in the digging.

The 'blue devil' fell out with Finati and chased him into the boat, with many imprecations. Finati believed the crew to be worse than the Cashefs and their people, "always in league with the worst of them...and became their ringleaders and advisers". But he adds, "I cannot help imputing also some little blame to the temper in which the work was conducted, since an over-punctiliousness upon little matters, which were not worth disputing about, and a determination to bind those strictly to the letter of their bargain, whom a very trifling present beyond it might have satisfied, led to almost all the difficulties and ill blood that occurred; as I took the liberty to represent more than once."[14]

Perhaps Belzoni, always so determined to resist being put upon, and the captains, accustomed to instant obedience from a crew, were unnecessarily unyielding — but they were operating in a remote place, without any personal authority, and may well have been right to suppose that any concession which could be construed as weakness might escalate their troubles into real danger.

One evening the leaders of a caravan passing by from Darfur came to visit the interesting strangers. The men wore their hair long, greased with oil and sometimes plaited. The caravan consisted of slaves and 4,000 camels laden with ivory, ostrich feathers, gum, tamarinds and rhino horns, bound for the markets of Cairo.

Despite Ramadan, the prospect of pay drew 64 labourers on 20 July;

the crew "stimulated them by example" which "coupled with our own personal attendance," produced a good day's work. On 21 July, with 40 Abu Simbel men at work, the bent right arm of the statue to the north of the door, much broken, appeared. That the arm was bent was very encouraging for it established that the figures were seated rather than standing, thus decreasing the depth they must dig to reach the door. But hope was soon dashed when they uncovered a roughly-chiselled projection from the wall, a possible indication that the structure was unfinished, and the temple, after all, but a castle in the air. However, they resolved to work on, to make certain beyond all possibility of doubt.

Crowds of men from both sides of the river flocked to the site the next day. The Europeans thankfully retired to the boat, leaving old Mouchmar to distribute 30 of the work tickets which were handed in for wages at the end of each day. It was soon discovered that he had only given out 20, reserving the rest to hand in on his own account. "While we were settling this with the old rogue", quarrelling broke out between the two sets of villagers about the sharing of the work, and "hostilities having commenced in a slight degree between the parties, the whole of them departed, shouting and hooting, in number about two hundred, the stronger party not permitting the Ebsambel people to work."

Towards evening, the Europeans returned to work on their own, soon joined by the crew and 20 volunteers. They had only three tools between them but before night fell they came to the chair of the statue. But there was still no sign of a door.

When 100 men appeared at dawn on 25 July, all but 20 were turned away, for it had been well observed by now that many hands did not make light work, but only considerable confusion. It was all or none, the men insisted, and after much noisy parleying, withdrew, taking all the tools with them, and threatening that Daoud and Khalil would be told of the crew if they dared to work. But "our sailors laughed at them, saying they cared nothing about the cashefs or anyone else." They were on their own again, with six tools they had made for themselves; but the crew of a passing ship joined in. Next day came a young Mameluke, travelling from Dongola to Cairo to visit his mother, widowed in the massacre of the Mamelukes in 1811. For five days until he left on a passing raft, he was very useful, for he understood the Barbarin tongue and could report what the locals were saying among themselves.

A spy sent by Daoud tried to prevent both crew and locals from working and threatened that old Mouchmar would have his head cut off for bringing bread to the party. Although the threats were as usual laughed off, Mouchmar told them that the villagers had been forbidden henceforth to help them or to sell them any food. Having sufficient provisions to last a few days, they decided to manage the excavation entirely on their own. Not included in the embargo, the sailors asked permission to go to the village for bread for themselves, but the 'blue devil' Hassan was caught stealing the party's *doura*, to which, with dried dates, they were now reduced. It was 112° Fahrenheit in the shade, and they were near the end of their resources.

But on 30 July they were secretly brought some milk. Better still, they dug down at last to an undeniable cornice. Beneath it was a smooth plane surface and a tablet inscribed with neat, highly-finished hieroglyphs; "the most favourable indication of a door we could possibly expect, and which much cheered our prospects." Towards evening, coming upon a "frize", surmounted by a *torus*, or moulding, they felt confident the door would be reached next day.

In the morning, they built a palisade to prevent the sand sliding back into the excavation, by driving in pilings of date trunks and pouring mud mixed with sand behind them. At sunset a corner of the door emerged. The sailors "expressed great signs of joy, uttering cries of 'backsheeish, backsheeish', and immediately asked us if it was not true, that we had promised them money whenever we should find the door." Not until we have entered the temple, was the uncompromising reply.

In high good humour, the crew set to work with a will to enlarge the opening, occasionally repeating their favourite words, "Backsheeish, tyep, tyep, [good, good]". By nightfall there was an aperture nearly large enough to admit a man's body, but Belzoni prudently decided not to attempt entry till next morning, in case of foul air within. Besides, they still had no idea how much sand was actually inside the temple; only too possibly a great deal of digging remained to be done.

As they went down to the boat for the night, Hassan lectured Irby and Mangles about the problems that lay ahead: the sand would fall on them as fast as they dug down...it was like trying to dig into the Nile...he would forfeit his beard if they succeeded. The rest of the crew joined in his assertions. Despite these gloomy prophecies, the sailors, still in great spirits, thought to profit by the occasion. They pressed the cook to hand over his new silk waistcoat, and Yanni to give them his new blue gown, but left the others alone, "thinking it best to wait till they got our backsheeish."

The crew were warned that work would start on the morrow before dawn, so that they should not think that the Europeans were out to steal a march on them, and secretly remove the 'gold'. The Europeans rose in the moonlight and called the crew, but did not press when there was no response. It was Friday, 1 August, the anniversary, Mangles noted, of Nelson's victory at the Battle of the Nile. Work began by flickering candle-light and the feeble rays of the waning moon.

Soon, there was a great noise from the shore below, the roaring voice

121

of the 'blue devil' plainly to be distinguished above all the rest, and the word 'Backsheeish' frequently repeated. Yanni went down to fetch another lamp; he was roundly abused: the pay was not enough, the work was too hard, they were leaving, they were too tired to stay any longer. Belzoni went down to collect a hammer; at sight of him, they all fell down on their knees and "began praying, bowing down, and kissing the ground according to their custom." Belzoni ignored the demonstration, but took all the weaponry back to the site. An envoy came to say that either the party embarked immediately, or they must land their effects and let the boat go, as the crew could wait no longer. Go when you please, was the indifferent response, but it would be their own loss, for "we would pay you nothing...for our part we were determined to remain till our work was completed."

The crew appeared in a body, dressed up in their turbans and gowns to give themselves consequence, and armed with sticks, pikes, swords, daggers and two rusty old pistols "more likely to kill the person who fired, than him who was fired at." They complained at length of how cruelly treated they had been, especially in the light of all their efforts to please, but did not neglect to utter threats as well, scraping the sand with their hatchets and swords. The *reis*, "in feigned paroxysms of anger, threw the sand up in his face, where the perspiration caused it to stick." The party listened calmly and replied "coolly and deliberately", advising them to behave more sensibly in their own interests.

Finati took no part in all this. "At that very moment, while fresh clamours and new disputes were going on with our crew, and the attention of all distracted, I, being one of the slenderest of the party, without a word said, crept through into the interior, and was thus the first that entered it, perhaps for a thousand years. Unlike all the other grottoes in Egypt and Nubia, its atmosphere, instead of presenting a refreshing coolness, was a hot and moist vapour, not unlike that of a Turkish bath, and so penetrating, that paper, carried within, soon became as much saturated with wet as if it had been dropped into the river."[15] As he made his way further into the temple, Finati found that the drifted sand extended only a short way from the door, and the chambers were clear. "With this favourable intelligence I came out again, still creeping flat upon my face...My first stay within had been very short, both for want of a light, and from the fear of fainting, or being stifled in that strange atmosphere."

When Finati emerged, the crew, seeing themselves completely foiled, allowed a mediator to disarm them, then stripped for action, laughing and repeating cheerily, "Tyep, tyep, berby, tyep [good, good, temple, good]."

Soon the hole was enlarged enough to allow the passage of even Belzoni — and "thus," says Mangles, "ended all our labours, doubts and anxiety."

Not quite. But for now, all was rejoicing and wonder, as they slid inside one by one and walked through the temple holding up their candles to illuminate "the finest and most extensive excavation in Nubia," says Belzoni jubilantly, "one that can stand competition with any in Egypt, except the tomb newly discovered in Beban el Malook [the Valley of the Kings]." He modestly forbears to mention at this point that it was he who was to discover that tomb, and also forbears to mention who was the first to enter Abu Simbel. Fortunately for historical accuracy, and for Finati, the captains confirm that "the janissary meantime had squeezed himself through the hole, and entered the temple during the debate..."[16]

For the next three days Irby and Mangles made minute measurements of the temple interior, and of the exterior as far as the thick covering of sand allowed. Only about three feet had been dug down from the lintel of the 20-foot high door. Two of the seated colossi on the facade were still buried up to their breasts, and the other pair, one broken and fallen down, remained almost completely hidden. They reckoned these figures must be more than 60 feet tall; the faces were seven feet long, the ears three foot six inches, the beard five foot six inches; they were twenty-five feet four inches across the shoulders.

While the captains measured, Belzoni and Beechey drew, suffering much in the steamy heat of the interior. "Mr Beechey spoiled his drawing-book, while only copying one of the groups; the perspiration having entirely soaked through it." They recorded their success on a wall of the inmost sanctuary.

The statues that were not too large or too damaged were removed to the shore to be taken to Salt, including two life-sized lions with hawks' heads, a monkey and a kneeling 'female' figure holding an altar with a ram's head on it in her lap.[17] Two villagers who came to examine the temple, gave it as their verdict that it "would make a good hiding place for their cattle, etc., whenever the Bedouins came to rob them".

While the Europeans were busy about the temple, the crew continued to grumble and mutter. Hassan tried to dissuade his fellows from loading the statues, but as their embarkation was a condition of payment, he had no success. When 40 piastres was handed over for distribution, the *reis* seized the whole as *his* share; "we, however, took it from him, and distributed it according to our original plan."

Early on 4 August they started down river, calling upon Daoud Cashef, who protested his ignorance of the difficulties his people had caused at Abu Simbel "even before we had mentioned the subject; this was certainly not very wise in Daoud, as nothing could tend more to prove his guilt..." Presents were exchanged, Daoud promised to keep the temple open for Mr Salt, and cordial farewells were made. Khalil arrived too late to be present at the adieux, and get his share of anything else that could be "squeezed out of us", but caught up with the boat next day at Deir, also professing to know nothing of the troubles at Abu Simbel. Told they had no presents left, he attentively examined everything in the cabin, but seeing nothing was to be had, took his leave.

On 8 August the crew brought "a scabby half-starved lamb as a present to us; we could not forbear from laughing, as it was really the most pitiful animal we had seen in the country; and in truth it must have put them to no small trouble to find such a beast. We refused the present most stoutly, but it was all in vain; they forced it into the boat."[18]

At three o'clock that afternoon, they came to Philae.

10

The Earl of Belmore and the Lordly Party

AS BRITISH Consul-General, Salt was at the beck and call of his countrymen or, at least, of those who considered themselves deserving of
his attention. There were clear class distinctions. The aristocracy and
landed gentry assumed they would be housed and entertained by the Consul
as His Majesty's representative; the slightly less well-connected expected to
call on and probably dine with the Consul; even the less distinguished would
'call' formally on their Consul and seek him out when they needed his help.
Many travellers in Egypt were of the class who deemed themselves worthy
of attention from the Consul and arrived with letters of introduction or sent
their requests for assistance ahead of them. The Reverend Joliffe, travelling
in Asia Minor and Egypt in 1819, advised travellers: "There are no inns —
and wherever you go there is a Convent or Consul to whom you should
resort...In Egypt the Consul-General will be informed of your arrival at
Alexandria. Send your letters of introduction to him...Cairo is a mile and a
half from the port; it will be necessary to call on [the Consul] before you
land your baggage...Of course he will provide you with lodgings, either at
his own house or elsewhere."[1]

Providing all this hospitality cannot have been cheap. Halls said that
Salt did not receive "the slightest remuneration for the expenses he
incurred" for looking after voyagers through Egypt on their way to and
from India, and he was inclined to believe that no such assistance was ever
offered.[2] These travellers were often officials of the East India Company; but
even more frequent were those who came to Egypt as 'tourists', and also
expected the Consul's hospitality.

Doubtless Salt enjoyed their company and, judging from their memoirs, they were often lively, intelligent and amusing, and a change from the
resident society of whom he complained, in an outburst to Halls' sisters, in
September 1817. "Really the society here is intolerable. If the women were
not *rather pretty*, there would be no enduring their company, as one is obliged to forget all one has learned in life — all mythology, all knowledge of history, all information, in short, that is acquired by reading, is utterly thrown
away upon them; but beauty it must be confessed makes up for a multitude
of sins."[3]

Not long after Salt was complaining of the local company, a party led
by the Earl of Belmore descended on him and absorbed many weeks of his
time. The Earl's physician, Dr Robert Richardson, a prolific writer, gave a

wonderfully detailed picture of how, if on a grander scale than usual, travellers journeyed in Egypt.

The leader of this lordly party was the gout-stricken Irish peer, the Earl of Belmore, with Juliana, his countess, who was also his cousin. He was 42, she about the same; their sons — Viscount Corry, and the Honourable Henry Lowry-Corry — were aged 16 and 14 respectively. With them were Captain Armar Corry RN, Belmore's half-brother, the illegitimate son of the Earl's father; Dr Richardson, the Earl's personal physician; Mr Holt, the Earl's chaplain and tutor to his sons. Miss Juliana Brooks, "the youngest but by no means the worst traveller of the party", had a somewhat unusual relationship with the family. She was born to Lady Brooks from a liaison with Lord Belmore while her husband was away at the Peninsular War in 1805. Juliana was 11 years old. The Countess had her lady's maid. There were several able-seamen and a couple of male servants. No grander British group travelled through Egypt until the Prince of Wales progressed up the Nile in 1868.

Early on 28 September the Belmores' boats from Alexandria tied up at Bulac, the port of Cairo, and the Earl forthwith despatched a messenger to "Mr Salt, His Majesty's Consul-General, to acquaint him of our arrival." Salt came in person to welcome them, bringing the only carriage in Egypt, that of the Pasha, to transport Lady Belmore to the Consulate, and a horse for the Earl. The others took donkeys from the donkey stands which were "nearly as common as stands of hackney coaches in London". Before long they arrived on "English ground...for the house of the representative of his Britannic Majesty is part of the British Empire." Richardson thought it a house worthy of the office of its posssessor: "an excellent house in itself, accompanied with the luxury of a small, but comfortable, garden, surrounded with a high wall, planted with trees, and intersected with walks."[4]

Mrs Elwood, wife of an East India Company officer, wrote a detailed description of the Consulate in 1826. The old Mameluke house was a rambling structure entered by an immense gateway into a courtyard surrounded by a sort of cloister, beyond which was the dining room with a curiously painted ceiling and a fountain at one end. This room looked onto a garden of oleanders, date and pomegranate trees, which opened onto the public promenade, where the Franks entertained themselves. A very narrow staircase led to the upper storeys which "seemed to defy all plan" although most of the rooms were "apparently constructed upon the principle of security and privacy. Many had curiously carved window frames, with painted glass and window seats. In the upper part of the Gran Sala, or reception room, was the Divan — an immense window-seat, filled up with cushions like a sofa." This comfort was somewhat compromised for the Elwoods by the fact that "the Consulate swarmed with every species of insect, crawling, jumping, flying, buzzing and humming about one, to a tormenting degree" giving anyone disposed to the study of etymology "a glorious opportunity".[5]

The Belmores were soon introduced to John Lewis Burckhardt and to Captains Irby and Mangles, recently returned from the opening of the temple at Abu Simbel. The Earl's view of Burckhardt was somewhat tainted by Lady Hester Stanhope's great distaste for him. She had written in a series of letters of advice from the Levant: "There is one man who might be useful to you, but whom I think vastly ill of...He is very plausible, but very false, very envious and [?] with the *mask* of sentiment and high feelings...I detest a man full of low intrigues and who wears half a dozen faces as he thinks to meet his purpose."[6] This was not the view of him held by Salt.

Richardson spent days wandering around Cairo. The city was about six miles in circumference, its wall entered by a dozen gates, some large and magnificent, others very inconsiderable. A canal leading off the Nile wound through the city, ending in the 'lake' of Esbecke. During the inundation from August onwards there were eight 'lakes' in and about Cairo. Although Richardson thought they had more the appearance of horse-ponds full of dirty water, they supplied water for all purposes, and in the evenings, "a place for sailing pleasure boats, where men can sit and make smoke under the artificial shade of an awning", while on their banks there were "fireworks pouring their light into the air, dancing dogs, dancing monkeys, dancing girls, and all the people making merry."

The population of Cairo was then about 300,000, divided into several different nations — all but one of which had at one time been masters of the country: Copts, regarded as the last true heirs of the ancient Egyptians; Greeks; other Christians or 'Franks'; Arabs; Armenians, Jews; Turks (the present rulers) and their Albanian militias. Each of these different 'tribes' had their own quarters enclosed by a wall and shut off one from the other from about eight o'clock each evening.

The most impressive sight in the city is the Citadel — from which Salt had painted his panorama in 1806 — crowning a rocky promontory jutting out from the precipitous cliffs of the Mokattam hills where the eastern desert breaks down to the Nile valley. The Pasha's house within the Citadel was in 1817 small, plain and without any exterior decoration though it had more glass windows than most Turkish houses. Richardson thought it more like an officer's residence in an ordinary barracks than the palace of a sovereign in the chief city of his dominions.[7]

* *

Belmore at last recovered from the gout which had plagued him since Delos. Early one morning Salt "and his usual attendants of Janizaries and grooms", took him and the men of his party to pay their respects to "the worthy successor of the Pharaohs" at his summer palace at Shubra. A traveller there in 1820, described it as "a pretty palace in the Constantinopolitan style", the rooms very high "and loaded with a profusion of gilding and mirrors". The ceilings were carved in wood and painted in lively colours; the floors covered with magnificent carpets. "If," she said, "the whole does not display much taste, the splendour and diversity of the ornaments...give an agreeable effect to the eye."[8]

The Pasha received them in a summer house by the Nile, his officers and men standing at a respectful distance. Mehemet Ali inquired about the purpose of their visit and then spoke of the prospect laid out before them: "the Nile, the grain-covered fields, the cloudless sky" and supposed that England offered no such prospect. He seemed convinced that England was under fog and snow for the greater part of the year and that they had come to Egypt because they had nothing so beautiful to admire at home. He offered them every possible facility for their journey up the Nile, but warned them that the Arabs were "a most thievous race" and must be carefully watched. However, Richardson reassured his readers that the Pasha had so established the internal tranquillity of the country that "the traveller may now visit every corner of Egypt unmolested."[9]

A few days later came the great occasion — the visit to the Pyramids in the company of Henry Salt. The Countess was disguised for this trip in 'Tirkish dress'. The Nile was still high and it was a day's journey by *cangia* across the river and along the Giza Canal where the wind fluctuated and the boatmen mounted their oars, singing as they rowed, each man in turn repeating a verse, the rest joining in the chorus. Ahead, beyond the luxuriant *dourha* and the palm groves, the party glimpsed their goal. However, as always, until one is actually upon the Pyramids "the eye always encountered something less than the mind expected to see."

When the party reached the base of the Pyramids, awed by their gigantic size, it was already mid-day and they quickly disposed of their belongings in the cave of the Sheik of the Pyramids, and took a hasty repast. With a couple of sure-footed Arabs "whose services we did not require", they entered the passage into the Great Pyramid and surveyed the discoveries of Captain Caviglia. Led by Salt, they went deeper and further than tourists go today and there is a note of relief from the doctor on regaining the open air. A short rest and they started to climb. Even Lady Belmore ascended the Pyramid "with the most perfect ease, and none of the party experienced the smallest difficulty or vertigo".

On the summit, Richardson was very censorious about the injury caused to the monuments by the knives and chisels of visitors who "anxious to perpetuate their arrival on this lofty station had left their names upon the stones". He obviously had no influence on this matter with the rest of his party — Lord and Lady Belmore both left their names here, Captain Corry marked every monument along the Nile and even Mr Holt, the chaplain, carved his name at Philae. Richardson, to give him his due, desisted — until Abu Sir.

They slept overnight in the Sheik's cave before visiting the Sphinx, Caviglia's excavations by now covered over. After further explorations they reboarded their *cangia* and set sail, reaching Cairo a little before sunset.

At the Consulate, they found several urgent notes from Burckhardt. He had consulted Dr Richardson about an attack of dysentry some days earlier — now his illness had seriously worsened. They could not go to him that night because the gates between the sections of the city were locked, and he lived far away in the Turkish quarter. Very early the next morning Richardson went to him and "rendered him every professional assistance in my power". It was too late. On 15 October Burckhardt asked Richardson to send for the Consul.[10]

Salt was deeply shocked and distressed to see the change in his friend. Only a week before Burckhardt, who was a large, even burly, man, had been walking in the Consulate garden, in perfect health, conversing with his usual liveliness and vigour, as he did every afternoon. Now he could scarcely articulate his words, often making use of one for another, was of a ghastly hue, and was clearly dying. "Yet he perfectly retained his senses, and was surprisingly firm and collected" as he asked Salt to take a pen and paper and write as he dictated his will.

He wished first to pay up his share of the costs of the Memnon head (this despite the fact that Salt thought he had already contributed enough); 2,000 piastres and his slaves and household belongings were to go to Scottish Osman; 400 piastres to his servant Shaharti; 1,000 piastres was to be sent to the poor of Zurich. His library of some 300 books and manuscripts he left to the University of Cambridge, apart from eight books on Europe which he gave to Salt. His papers were to be sent to William Hamilton for the African Association. "Give my love to my friends and let Mr Hamilton acquaint my mother with my death, and say that my last thoughts have been with her," he whispered, reaching out to shake Salt's hand in a final leave taking.[11]

Salt left the darkened room; Richardson and Osman remained until, a quarter of an hour before midnight, Burckhardt died "without a groan". He was just 33 years old. "The expression of his countenance," Salt wrote in the memoir of his friend, "when he noticed his intended journey…was an evident struggle between disappointed hopes, and manly resignation; but less of the weakness of human nature was perhaps never exhibited upon a death bed."

"The Turks," Burckhardt had said, "will take my body — perhaps you had better let them." So, his funeral was a Mohammedan one, conducted with proper regard to the respect in which he was held by the Islamic world. His body was buried in the City of the Dead and for years his friends, both Christian and Muslim, visited his tomb regularly. The question of whether Burckhardt was or was not a convert to Islam has never been settled with certainty; scholars were still making vehement statements on one side or the other years after his death. Perhaps he had simply come to accept that between two religions which shared so much history and myth there was no real need to choose.

To Salt his loss was a terrible blow, which "cast a shadow over the remaining years of his life". Burckhardt was "the only conversable friend I had in Cairo. Thus the hopes of the African Association are again blighted, and, I fear, it will be long before another plant will spring up so full of promise as the one that has been cut down." Every afternoon, between two and three, Burckhardt used to come to the Consulate, and the two still young men would stroll the shady walks.

Salt's words about Burckhardt say much about Salt himself and the attributes he valued. "As a traveller, he possessed the talents and acquirements which were rendered doubly useful by his qualities as a man. To the fortitude and ardour of mind which had stimulated him to devote his life to the advancement of Science, in the paths of geographical discovery, he joined a temper and prudence well calculated to insure his triumph over every difficulty. His liberality and high principles of honour, his admiration of those generous qualities in others, his detestation of injustice and fraud, his disinterestedness, and keen sense of gratitude, were no less remarkable than his warmth of heart, and active benevolence which he often exercised towards persons in distress, to the great prejudice of his limited means."[12]

There was little time for Salt to grieve. Lord Belmore had decided to extend his researches into Upper Egypt. Salt was to accompany the Belmores to Luxor and be absent from Cairo for some four months. He had been intending to travel to Upper Egypt for some time, but had been prevented by consular responsibilities.

Although some commentators have remarked that his consular duties were evidently so light that he could afford to be forever off to Upper Egypt, this, 19 months after his arrival in the country, was his first expedition to see for himself the wonders with which Burckhardt, Belzoni and the Captains had fired his imagination. Studying the antiquities and history of his station was considered to be an important part of a Consul's duties — a duty neglected, remarked the *Gentleman's Magazine,* by most, with the honourable exceptions of James Bruce, Nathaniel Davison and Henry Salt.

Autumn was the best time for travelling: as Salt put it, "the climate at present is that of a summer's day in England, and this will continue until

May." On 28 October in the late afternoon the company set out up river. There were five passenger boats: the Earl and Countess with Miss Brooks and two servants (the lady's maid and Lord Belmore's valet); Mr Holt with his two pupils, Lord Corry and the Hon. Henry and one servant (probably the one who carried Lord Belmore's guns); Dr Richardson was with Captain Corry, a sailor servant and the Nubian interpreter; the cook had a special boat with a Belmore servant as superintendent; Salt had his own boat but dined as a guest at the Earl's table.

The saying that everyone loves a lord was obviously also true of the Egyptians and the 'Turkish' governors, and the party was extremely well received wherever they went. The presence of HM Consul-General must have also encouraged this, but Richardson claimed all the credit for his lord and master.

At Siout they met Belzoni's old acquaintance, Mehemet Ali's son-in-law, the Governor, or Deftardar Bey, who received them in a low, cool room. They sat on mats and cushions as they took their pipes and drank coffee, and conversed about affairs of state. The Earl presented the Bey with a handsome brace of pistols, which gift was matched, on their return to the boat, by a present of sheep and salt butter and an invitation to a review of cavalry next morning. The display, led by the Governor, was a sham fight, in which the Bey, as might have been expected, was the conqueror. Then Captain Corry entertained their host by taking a meridian observation with his sextant to fix their latitude. Next the Bey announced target practice: horsemen galloping one after the other 300-400 yards towards the target — a small earthenware pitcher — and each firing as he turned, "manifesting no concern for his horse or his seat". The English were truly impressed and extremely gratified by the Bey's hospitality.[13]

One day the party rode on asses to the temple at Dendera. Salt had with him the *Description de l'Egypte* volume which covered Dendera, to compare the illustrations with the original. Richardson described them as "extremely elegant, and well-executed; but it is perfectly foppish, and not the least Egyptian in style and manner. It is besides extremely incorrect... in accuracy and feeling." Xenophobia appears to have guided these judgements and out-weighed appreciation of the tremendous work the French scholars achieved in a very short time and in trying circumstances. However, one can understand how the style of the French artists would have been unsympathetic to the more romantic English eye. (Hamilton had persuaded the French government "to furnish a copy of the magnificent *Description* for Salt's immediate use upon condition that it should be deposited with his marginal remarks in the British Museum. In fact, he passed it to his successor in his will.)

The party climbed the long shallow stairway to the roof past the wall carvings of which in the dim light Richardson wrote "everything seems to speak and move around you". On the roof, were a number of ruined huts, recently a considerable village. On the parapet they saw the names of Irby and Mangles carved, and Captain Corry added his own.

The party discussed why in England so little, except fragments, was to be seen of the wonders of Egypt. France on the other hand "had done so much to make the world acquainted with Egyptian antiquities." Should Egyptian antiquities be removed to England, or should there be a proper restoration of Dendera, before it was "trodden underfoot, and looked at in scattered fragments". Richardson admonished the English "where so many have the means" for not undertaking the great task of clearing the temples "taking accurate drawings or casts of the whole, so that it could be seen in England exactly as it is in Egypt."

Richardson's account makes the expedition sound amicable, but not far below the surface other feelings lurked. Salt later wrote sympathetically to Lord Belmore: "Your account of Dr R. did not in any way surprise me, the rudeness of his character was too evident, and as I felt no (need) of bearing with it, it lead me I fear once or twice to express myself more strongly than I ought to have done in your and Lady Belmore's presence, but it really was at times unbearable. Your patience must I am sure have been long exhausted before you parted, but it was far better, under all circumstances to bear with rudeness than have been deprived of his medical skill." He went on to express their joint concern about what the doctor might publish, though Salt thought that his short-sightedness and lack of profound observation would limit his judgement. Holt, on the other hand, Salt found reasonable company and Captain Corry "with his fine natural spirit and agreeable manners is absolutely formed for travelling".[14] Perhaps Dr Richardson did not notice how the others felt about him, for no sense of rancour comes across in his book.

* *

Onward up the river the flotilla sailed and on the evening of 16 November made fast to the bank by the fine spreading sycamore at Thebes. The next morning Salt's secretary, Henry Beechey, and Belzoni came to welcome them.

Belzoni and Beechey had collected Mrs Belzoni from Philae and returned to Luxor in September, when Irby and Mangles had sailed north to Cairo. At Luxor Beechey had been making drawings and Belzoni "recommenced [his] researches". There were two of Drovetti's men, both Piedmontese, working in Gournu, so Belzoni headed for the Valley of the Kings. In Salt's name he was given a *firman* to employ 20 men and set them to work. Herodotus had reported about 40 tombs in the valley; by Strabo's time only 18 were known, although the priests spoke of 47; Belzoni knew of only 11. He worked out where discovery seemed most likely — and his judgement was, as often, sure. Within days he was entering a long-lost tomb, converting a pole into a machine not unlike a battering ram to break in. There lay four previously undisturbed mummies. On 9 October he discovered the entrance to an unfinished tomb which had already been searched. Two unclothed mummies lay on the floor "quite naked, without cloth or case. They were females, and their hair pretty long, and well preserved, it easily separated from the head by pulling it a little."[15] A remark horrifying to any latter day archaeologist, but then perfectly acceptable to many, though not all, antiquarian explorers.

On 18 October there dawned for Belzoni "a fortunate day, one of the best perhaps of my life", a day which gave him "that extreme pleasure, which wealth cannot purchase, the pleasure of discovering what has long been sought in vain, and of presenting the world with a new and perfect monument of Egyptian antiquity." The fellahs had been working for some days to clear a newly-found entrance. Belzoni entered and immediately knew that he had come upon something very special.[16]

It was not easy to penetrate beyond the entrance corridors, but his engineering skills prevailed. Soon he and Beechey were in the wonderful many-roomed tomb. It was that of Pharaoh Seti I, but will always be known also as 'Belzoni's tomb'. As they advanced, the murals became ever more perfect. The tomb had long since been plundered and there was little there except for fragments and figurines, and one great, almost immovable object: a sarcophagus "not having its equal in the world and being such as we had no idea could exist...of the finest oriental alabaster...transparent when light is placed inside it...minutely sculptured within and without with several hundred figures...representing the whole of the funeral ceremonies."

Belzoni had made a truly important discovery. Word quickly spread. News soon reached the ears of the Aga of Keneh, some miles down river, that a great treasure had been found. He travelled for 36 hours with "a great many Turks, on horseback" who poured into the valley firing their guns. Belzoni, once recovered from his surprise, led the Aga into the tomb. He was totally uninterested in what he saw around him, "his views were directed to the treasure alone; and his numerous followers were like hounds, searching every hole and corner." They found nothing to interest them.

At last the Aga ordered his men out and turned to Belzoni. "Pray where have you put the treasure?"

"What treasure?"

"The one in this place."

Belzoni denied finding any treasure.

"I have been told," said the Aga, "that you have found in this place a large golden cock, filled with diamonds and pearls. I must see it. Where is it?"

Belzoni repeated his denial. The Aga sat down with his back against the sarcophagus to consider the position. At last he decided that Belzoni, with whom he was well acquainted, was telling him the truth, and rose to go.

"What do you think of this beautiful place?" Belzoni asked, pointing to the paintings on the walls as he walked to the entrance with the Aga.

The Aga glanced at them and laughed. "This would be a good place for a harem," he replied, "as the women would have something to look at."[17]

Four weeks after this momentous discovery the Belmores and Salt arrived at Luxor, news of their approach preceding them by the smaller, faster boats of the Egyptians.

Belzoni and Beechey led the Belmore party to the tomb on donkey-back. The road took them through a narrow defile into the mountains and was rough and disagreeable. The valley of the tombs was to Richardson "a most dismal-looking spot, a valley of rubbish, without a drop of water or a blade of grass...The heat is excessive from the confined dimensions of the valley, and the reflection of the sun from the rock and sand." As now, the valley was a place that "would hardly ever be visited by man or beast" if it were not for what it holds. The entrance to the tomb was not yet cleared and they had to prostrate themselves and crawl along through a narrow passage over rubbish. (Belzoni soon cleared this and on later visits they were able to use the flight of steps.) The sight that rewarded them was truly astonishing.[18]

Salt took great pleasure in announcing the discovery in a long letter to Mountnorris in January 1818: "a brilliant discovery...of a new King's tomb, exquisitely painted, and with the colours as fresh as on the day it was completed; it throws everything else, as far as colour goes, completely into the back-ground." He described the detail of the colouring and how the artists would have worked.[19] By this time Salt and Beechey were working together copying in the brilliant watercolours that still reflect the glory of the hues when they were first discovered. Salt was gaining a very close understanding of the skills of the artists. In Thomas Young's article on Egypt in the *Encyclopedia Britannica*, Salt's commentary is that of the artist: the colours used "are generally pure and brilliant, but intermixed with each other nearly in the proportion of the rainbow, and so subdued by the proper introduction of blacks, as not to appear gaudy, but to produce a harmony that in some designs is really delicious." Beechey's seldom heard voice joined in the praise: "One would think it was in Egypt that Titian, Giorgione and Tintoretto had acquired all that vigour and magic of effect."[20]

Salt's outlay, he told Mountnorris, had far exceeded what he intended, but, because of his father's bequest would "prove no very serious inconvenience". He then described the sarcophagus (using the words "I have found"). He was planning to transport it to Cairo and would not feel easy about it until he saw it safely there. He had already sent down river "the famous French stone" with eight figures, two on each side; a granite head, not so large as the young Memnon "but with a finer polish and entire", a marble sitting figure "of exquisite workmanship", 30 papyri, and "innumerable smaller items". Many of these items he felt able "to spare to" Mountnorris, and the rest "if the idea is approved," he thought of offering to the British Museum. This letter Salt sent unsealed through Hamilton to acquaint him also with the news and his plans. In a letter to Bankes also dated from the Kings' Tombs, he speaks again of 'my' discovery of a King's tomb — with no mention of Belzoni.[21] Undoubtedly he saw this discovery, made at his expense and with his *firman,* as work done in his name, as Carnarvon might have spoken of *his* discovery of Tutankhamun's tomb .

A few days after the Belmore's visit to the tomb, Bernardino Drovetti came to see what the English had discovered. Richardson found the 'ci-devant' French Consul (Drovetti was not yet re-instated in this post) an agreeable and intelligent man. He was the only Frenchman Richardson had ever seen completely run out of the small change of compliment and admiration. "Everything was so superb, magnifique, superlative and astounding that when he came to something that really called for epithets of applause and admiration, his magazine of stuff was expended, and he stood in speechless astonishment, to the great entertainment of beholders."[22]

* *

The Belmores' days above Aswan and in Nubia were especially successful. They hired boats above the Cataract and stocked up well at Aswan with the excellent bread available there, and sheep, poultry, two milch goats, eggs and melons. "The noble traveller had taken care to be well provided with a due assortment of the juice of the grape before the party left Cairo." The boats were smaller than those used lower down the Nile and, although each party breakfasted on their own boat, it was necessary to picnic ashore for other meals, sitting on the sand around a mat for a tablecloth, in the dim light of a candle. Before they set off there was a small drama. They intended to start early, but discovered the colours had been left at Aswan. "It was impossible to sail without them; they were our national banners, the badge and ensign of our country, which we were determined to display, wherever wind or wave would carry us." A British sailor was dispatched to collect them and they eventually set off mid-morning.

At Abu Simbel the temple entrance had already begun to fill up, though it had been cleared only a month before by Colonel Straton, and, while they were attempting to open it, an Arab rolled large stones down upon the boatmen working below from above the facade. He threatened that, should they continue with their labours, he would hurl more boulders on them. "There was no time for parleying for he might have been supported by hundreds." The Earl ordered an English sailor to fire a musket ball close to the man "so as just to let him hear the sound of it". It took several more shots to dislodge him, then he fled with their Greek interpreter in hot, but unsuccessful, pursuit. It appeared the man had agreed that the milch goats might graze on his barley field beside the river. In the morning the interpreter delayed giving him baksheesh. Thinking he would not get his reward, he became perfectly frantic and thus took his revenge. The Belmores were sympathetic to his cause. The boatmen soon opened the temple. They entered it briefly, but found it "a perfect oven". Belmore ordered large stones to be placed in the entrance so sand would not flow in before their return.

On 23 December they reached the Second Cataract. That evening they celebrated the 17th birthday of Lord Corry in style, accompanied by an Italian traveller they had met. In that barren and bare land, they had "plenty of French wines, and porter, and a bumper of the best Irish whiskey to drain to the health of that young and patriotic nobleman."

The next day they climbed the rock of Abu Sir. Travellers often observed and recorded the latitude and longitude of the places where they stopped. The French, as they swept through the country had done so, according to Salt, not always with complete accuracy: "All the latitudes engraved on the Propylon at Thebes are wrong; how they found out their error is known only to themselves." On Christmas Day, the Earl caused his own reading to be engraved on a rock by the Second Cataract, and they had their names, and those of the sailors, added to those already on the great rock.

It was time for the flotilla to turn north. Dr Richardson believed he might be "permitted to add, that the Earl of Belmore is the only English nobleman that ever was there, and certainly the first who carried his lady and family along with him."

They sailed into the new year of 1818 and "proceeded joyfully on their way to Thebes" where "the doors in the mountains of western Thebes loomed upon our sight, and like a smiling friend, invited our approach." They moored on 13 January by the great sycamore. Salt brought them sad news gleaned from a Greek newspaper. Princess Charlotte, only child of the Prince Regent and heir to the throne, had died in childbirth in November. The Belmores had watched her go happily to her wedding only 18 months before; it was "a calamitous bereavement that robbed the nation of so bright an ornament" and the gay spirits of the party were stilled.[23]

* *

While the Belmores were upriver, difficulties had arisen between Salt and Belzoni about their relationship. Belzoni's side of this disagreement is well established; Salt's less so.

Before Salt left Cairo he had been receiving couriers from Beechey and Belzoni for some weeks, each telling of some new discovery. He had left Cairo most anxious "to do all in [his] power to remunerate Mr Belzoni, and to promote his future prospects". Salt had offered Belzoni about £25 a month — twice what the Pasha paid his physician — and expenses on top of this. This payment was to date from Belzoni's departure from Alexandria after delivering the Memnon head. Beside this Salt would 'cede' to Belzoni any antiquities he could spare which might prove advantageous to him, and assured him that he would give him "other satisfactory proofs of my regard".[24] Belzoni expressed himself satisfied.

But four or five days later Salt made a casual remark to some Englishmen passing through Thebes about "the time in which Mr Belzoni has been in my employ" — and Belzoni exploded.

Up to then he seems to have given the impression that his dissatisfaction was financial, but now declared "in the most violent terms" that he had never been employed by Salt, but had been "working for the British Nation" ("being," commented Salt, "the first time he had ever started such a notion") and would be "satisfied to go without reward: that he was an independent man". Despite Salt's astonishment — probably as much at this display of public fury as Belzoni's brushing aside being paid a salary as having nothing to do with being employed — he answered quietly, and explained what had been arranged between himself and Belzoni. The whole party agreed, said Salt, that he had been liberal and should not be pressed into pledging more, as any further remuneration he might be inclined to make "must be left to contingent circumstances".[25]

Salt did not name the English travellers, but his account does not have to stand alone, for one was Colonel Straton (or Stratton) whom Salt had taken to the Pyramids and Belzoni had entertained with his discoveries a few weeks before and whom, one might imagine, he had given very much the impression of being his own man, so that Salt's words would be particularly galling. Belzoni recorded that Straton's party, on their return from Nubia, passed without stopping[26] — at the least some very disingenuous wording, as the remark is, in context, curiously irrelevant. Stay they may not have done, but stop they did, for, according to Halls, Colonel Straton (by the 1830s Major-General Sir Joseph Straton, CB, FRS) "speaks in terms of the strongest commendation of the temper and liberality evinced by Mr Salt under circumstances which might have excited considerable irritation in a less dispassionate and generous character."[27]

When the visitors had left, Belzoni continued to initiate "repeated and very unpleasant altercations, in which he unfolded pretensions to which I informed him I could never accede [how one wished Salt had been specific about these] while throughout he exhibited an unfounded jealousy of my assuming all the merit of these discoveries." In vain Salt assured him that nobody could value him more highly, nor be more disposed "to render him ample justice". In all his letters to England he would — and did — thus attest. He added that their relationship was analogous to that between a client and his architect: "having given the commission and supplied the means, whilst he...had all the merit of the actual discoveries."[28] In his statement Salt did not continue the analogy to its logical conclusion: the house, despite being the product of not only the architect's labour, but also of that immeasurable quality, his talent or genius, belongs to the man who paid for it, to be disposed of as he would. He did say this at least once, years later, to Robert Hay.

The discussion was suspended; Belzoni was sent down to Cairo with a cargo of antiquities, to take the opportunity to consult his 'friends', and then return with the necessary tackle to take out the wonderful alabaster sarcophagus from Seti's tomb. Salt gave him orders for his expenses and a promise of a thousand piastres a month for the future. Belzoni objected to this, but Salt insisted.

"You may give me what you please," Belzoni grumbled, "but this must be a distinct matter," and so, ungraciously, departed.[29]

Sarah had been living again atop the building in Luxor, and was delighted and relieved to be shaking the dust from the soles of her feet. The next time Belzoni went to Thebes Sarah went to Jerusalem instead, which is in itself a wonderful story.

But Belzoni did not return to Thebes when Salt expected him, and when at last the boat came back it carried not Belzoni but a young Tuscan doctor, Alessandro Ricci, whom Belzoni had engaged to help him make drawings in Seti's tomb. He carried a letter from Belzoni saying he would set off in a few days, "being detained by a little private business". Eventually hearing no more, Salt returned to Cairo himself.

The Belmores had missed this drama, though some of it must have reached their ears. Soon after their return from Nubia the lordly party was watched with cynicism by Count Forbin, who arrived in Luxor on 28 February: "Lord and Lady Belmour," he recorded, "had been visiting a part of Nubia, indulging themselves in all the pomp, parade, and grandeur, of luxurious speculation. Four large bateaux were in the train of the one which contained them: husbands, wives, young children, chaplains, surgeons, nurses, cooks, all, in various phrases, were anxiously talking of Elephantina."[30] Thither Forbin claimed he had himself planned to go. Whatever his intention, he was now overcome by an unfortunate illness, but rather than admit this, he blamed his retreat on the sight of the Belmores: "...with me now the illusion vanished...I even quitted Luxor much sooner than I intended, when, notwithstanding the dead and deep silence pervading its venerable ruins...I met with one exception, an English waiting-woman, in a rose-coloured spencer, a parasol in her hand, crossing me, at almost every turn. That very night I set out for Tentyra [Dendera]." One of those Forbin sneered at was Salt. "M. Salt, the English consul, with a numerous suite, had taken up his residence under tents in the valley of Biban el-Molouk...superintending researches...A number of presents and a yet more profuse distribution of money had overpowered the barren affections of the Arabs, and all his enterprises among them had succeeded in an amicable and wonderful manner." Drovetti, on the other hand, Forbin saw as nobly maintaining "a struggle with difficulty and persevering consistency."[31]

When Salt saw Forbin's book he wrote to Lord Belmore on 28 November 1820 that Forbin's words were a poor return "for the kind attentions he received during his short stay at Thebes, and the falsity of pretending to have run away from that place on account of your suite is too evident when we recollect that he stayed one day longer than he intended on purpose to spend it on board your boat." The bad taste left by Forbin's account did not only extend to the English. His countrymen too suffered. According to Salt "he had not one partizan in Egypt — his work being universally pronounced superficial, silly and woefully incorrect." He damaged the French interest by his comments on Mehemet Ali and Boghos and it "cost their Consul much pains to obliterate the remembrance of his visit."[32]

Another observer was complimentary and, because he was also French but was well travelled in Egypt, his testimony is of special interest. Frederic Cailliaud came from Nantes; his enthusiasm for mineralogy led him all over Europe and eventually to Egypt. He had an introduction to Drovetti in Cairo who, taking a liking to the young man, invited him to accompany him on a journey up the Nile together with Jacques Rifaud, the artist and collector and agent of Drovetti. Rifaud and Cailliaud were the men in the boat which Belzoni hired to carry the Memnon to Cairo. On their return, Drovetti introduced Cailliaud to the Pasha and he was commissioned to go into the Eastern desert in search of mines — most particularly emerald mines. Returning from one such expedition — loaded with ten pounds of pale green emeralds — in January he settled himself in a tomb at Gournu and set out to inspect the monuments and report the goings on of the various foreigners. At Karnak, the temple was covered with lines of demarcation separating the quarters of "the French, English, Irish, Italians etc". Some European ladies were traversing the ruins and making their way into the catacombs. Observing the undercurrent of rivalry between the various nationalities, he was inclined to think that the Arabs "foment these quarrels, which they could turn to some advantage." In the Valley of the Kings he met "the British Consul General...justly celebrated for his talents and knowledge, and by his travels in Abyssinia", with a numerous suite, some in tents, others lodged in tombs. He was shown Belzoni's tomb and introduced to the Belmores.

Cailliaud was impressed, firstly by their "very long suite" and then by their kind attentions. Lady Belmore "displayed courage far superior to her sex...every day exploring catacombs with great perseverance." She had so impressed Jacques Rifaud when she visited Karnak that he had offered to let her dig on territory that might have been considered 'French'. Fortune, he says, smiled on her and straightway she was rewarded with the discovery of a five foot long granite funerary boat, now in the British Museum. Dr Richardson was thronged about wherever he went by people imploring help with their infirmities. "In his endeavours to help he exemplified a degree of patience seldom witnessed."[33]

* *

While the Earl had been up river, the Greek who had been collecting for him had gathered many items of interest. These included an ancient door fully eight feet high in an excellent state of preservation. Belmore gave this to Salt who later sold it to the British Museum. After examining the haul, which included stone jars with animal-head lids, small statues and stones covered with deities, offerings, priests and hieroglyphics, Belmore rode to the Valley of the Kings where Salt and Beechey had been hard at work drawing the finest groups of figures in Belzoni's tomb. The watercolours of the temple's interior are now in the British Museum and, while the original faded, have kept alive the glow that first came to light in that tomb nearly two centuries ago.[34]

Inspired, Belmore returned to his own endeavours with enormous enthusiasm. "The man who toils for bread could not return more regularly to the performance of his stated task, than the noble traveller to direct and superintend the operation of his labours," commented Richardson. The collection he made attested to his success and zeal. Here indeed was a collector rampant, with the funds, position and energy to search out and remove whatever he wished with very little thought of a purpose. Many travellers at the time were as eager to collect their souvenirs of Egypt as the modern traveller is today — but the excitement of the activity as well as the size and number of the acquisitions was then far greater. Naturally the local people were only too keen to ransack the ruins to satisfy these demands. At this season the peasants had little work in the fields and were able to devote themselves "to opening and plundering the tombs of their ancient countrymen, of

140

every article that can tempt the European traveller to make his own". Belmore acquired an excellent papyrus from a mummy, which he unrolled himself with great care so that it remained perfect. How many papyri had been, and would be, opened by excited fumbling fingers to be destroyed or damaged in a few moments after two to three thousand years of security?

Although Richardson condemned the way in which the antiquities were being exploited, he must have whetted the appetite of future travellers with the words: "... the surface of Thebes is hardly searched, its mine of diamonds remain unexplored." However, he spoke harshly against the divisive exploration in the names of different nations. "It is a weak and wretched policy that makes one nation throw obstacles in the way of another in its search after knowledge; and the individuals who do it, have more good-will to self than to science." A statue buried, he pointed out, "can be useful to no man. But once uncovered...by whom it matters not...it is then the property of the world." This remains true, he said, whether it is transferred "to Paris, to London, to Rome, to St Petersburgh, to Vienna, or anywhere: still it is accessible, people can see it, study it, and derive from it pleasure and instruction. It is a lost child restored to the great family of science and art, which is of no country; whose home is the world, of which all its votaries are citizens united for improvement, and over whom religious and political differences should exercise no dividing influence or control."[35]

Today many will think the doctor well meaning but misguided, but, considered within the ethos of his times, it is a worthy, even noble, statement of how the world should be. The fact that it totally ignores the rights and interests of the local people and their country is hardly surprising. Egypt was effectively ruled by foreigners. Both rulers and people gave every indication of being uninterested in the antiquities except as a means of ready income. Mehemet Ali believed that the country was not yet ready to have its own museum.

Richardson's is the universal argument and justification of the collector, and his justification for the retention of the objects collected — so long as they are made available to the public view and not re-buried in some private hoard. What he did not understand was that this very scattering of objects would diminish the understanding of them and therefore their value to art and science. This was true even when the collector was far more scientific than Belmore is likely to have been. The provenances of parts of Salt's collection still remain unknown to the British Museum and scholars because the papers, if they existed, giving such details, and the objects became separated. Happily, the patient hours of drawing and recording by Salt and others on the spot and at the time of a new discovery, are invaluable to posterity.

The Belmores yearned to linger in Thebes, but they were warned that the plague usually entered Cairo in early April and that they should be away

141

from the city before then. So, at dawn on 10 February, they loosed from the bank and floated off down the river, leaving Salt and Beechey at Thebes, but carrying a message from Salt to Belzoni. On 12 March, after a diversion to meet Belzoni at the Pyramids, the Belmores' boats tied up at Bulac, and Richardson rejoiced that they had all returned in health and safety after four and a half months and 700 miles up river. Their luggage was dispatched to the consular house and their antiquities carefully packed and transferred to Alexandria to be forwarded to England.

Not all the collection arrived. Lord Belmore wrote to Salt from Malta in September 1818: "I have had the mortification to find a terrible wreck among my antiques…many of the best of my small figures broken to pieces — most of the papyrus ground to dust and everything laying jumbled together in the Lazaret [quarantine offices] as so much rubbish."[36]

The Belmores' travels were not yet over. Shortly they would set off to Jerusalem, but first they had to restore themselves to normality. Their beards and moustaches had "thriven so luxuriantly", their complexions had so browned, that they thought they might be mistaken for natives. Their clothes and shoes were in tatters from crawling into tombs and caves and walking almost constantly among sand and stony fragments. It was time too for those who had not yet assumed the dress of the country "to lay aside their European robes, and disguise themselves in the Turkish costume," for in Egypt a European could walk "unmolested in his close fitting garments… but the aversion to European attire [was] much greater in Syria, where it [was] even looked upon with a sort of disgust."[37]

On 25 March the party set off from the Consulate: the Earl rode the sheik of the caravan's own dappled steed, one of the sailors rode another horse with "the youngest traveller, Miss Brooks", before him, and Lady Belmore and the rest of the party were elegantly mounted on "Egyptian ponies, which were as loud in their bray as they were long in their ears".

"Such a procession in England," said Richardson, " would be gazed upon with astonishment, rather as if the Lord Mayor's Show were transferred to Cairo." And so they went, accompanied on the early stages of their journey by Mr Walmas of the house of Briggs, Shutz and Walmas, by Scottish Osman and, further than the others, by Belzoni.

In Jerusalem they were to meet with old friends and new: with Captains Irby and Mangles, with Thomas Legh and William Bankes, and "last of all, Mrs Belzoni, the wife of the celebrated traveller", who, disdaining other English company, accepted their invitation to travel with them to Nazareth. But that is another story, and one, alas, outside the scope of this book.

11

The Pyramidical Brain

THE BELZONIS and Yanni d'Athanasi, Salt's interpreter, arrived in Cairo on 21 December 1817. Belzoni had, he said, intended to return quickly to Thebes "to fetch away the sarcophagus and other valuable articles".[1] Salt certainly expected Belzoni to be back soon. But finding that he could not immediately despatch his 'little business', Belzoni sent Salt's boat back to Luxor, in the charge of the young Tuscan doctor Alessandro Ricci, "who was very clever at drawing, and who with a little practice became quite perfect in his imitations of hieroglyphics," instructing him to begin drawings of the newly-opened tomb. Sarah, despairing of ever persuading her husband to accompany her to the Holy Land — the ambition which first brought her to Egypt — set off there with James Curtin, both of them disguised as Mameluke youths.[2]

Belzoni was low in funds, but "the celebrated and veracious [sic] Count de Forbin" was in town and he managed to sell him the statues from Karnak originally destined for his home town. He would, he thought, be able to find some more to donate to Padua. Though he received what he thought only about a quarter of their value, it gave him enough to be going on with.

At the Consulate, where Belzoni lodged himself, the journals arrived from England, and Belzoni read them eagerly. To his great surprise — and chagrin — he found that all his "former discoveries and labours" had been published in the names of other people, while his own were not even mentioned. "It was not pleasant to see the fruits of and the credit of them ascribed to others, who had no more to do with them than the governor of Siberia, except as far as related to supplying me with money."[3]

He turned his attentions to the Pyramids. His record of his activities there does not always tally with Yanni's. Often regarded as suspect because he was devoted to Henry Salt and jealous of Belzoni, Yanni's account may well have been coloured by his personal view, just as Belzoni's words are, naturally, coloured by his.

Belzoni accompanied some Europeans to the Pyramids and took a good look at the second pyramid, that of Chephren. How could it be, he thought, that "in an intelligent age like the present, one of the greatest wonders of the world stood before us, without our knowing even whether it had any cavity in the interior, or if it were only one solid mass." He had heard rumours of a plan to raise funds to force a way into the pyramid with explosives, under the possible superintendence of Drovetti. It was seemingly impossible for one man to undertake, and the opportunity was more likely to be given to people of "higher influence". On the north side of the pyramid something caught his attention: just under the centre of the face was an accumulation of materials which had fallen from its coating. Belzoni came back the next day for another look.

He determined to take a chance, but to dig and to employ men to dig he needed a *firman*. Acting as interpreter, Yanni asked for a *firman* in the name of "two servants of the Consul-General of Great Britain, who were come by order of our master, to make a slight excavation around the pyramids." Yanni thought it dishonourable to "abuse the friendship of Mr Salt in such a manner", but was eventually swayed by Belzoni. It certainly seems unlikely that that such a *firman* would have been granted to Belzoni without using Salt's name.[4]

On 2 February 1817 Belzoni and Yanni set off to the Pyramids with a small tent and some provisions. Belzoni does not mention that Yanni was with him, but he clearly was — and being paid by Salt. In order to disguise his purpose, Belzoni put it about that he was going to the mountains of Mokatan on the east bank of the Nile. He had just £200 for the venture — his remaining money from Salt and Burckhardt and the money from Count Forbin. If he could not enter the pyramid before this was spent, he might simply be preparing the way "for others stronger in purse".[5]

Belzoni set 80 Arabs to work, with boys and girls employed at half the daily rate to carry away the rubble. For several days they laboured without success. He had excited his workers with visions of baksheesh both from himself and from the many visitors who would come to see the pyramid once it was opened. This vision began to fade as they sweated to remove the huge masses of stone and broke their hatchets on the mortar. However, as long as he paid them, they went on working, though with decreasing zeal.

At last, after 16 days of fruitless labour, on 18 February, one of the workmen saw a small chink between two stones. Belzoni thrust a long palm-stick into the chink. The Arabs were invigorated and the work started again briskly. They found an opening, but it was choked with rubble which they spent further days clearing. At last Belzoni, candle in hand, was able to look into what he realised was a forced passage. This entrance (now re-opened) was too dangerous: "the stones overhead were on the point of falling; some were suspended only by their corners...and with the least touch would have fallen, and crushed anyone who happened to be under them," or have collapsed behind them and buried them alive. Belzoni decided to retreat.

It was time to rethink the project. Belzoni spent hours examining the Pyramids again. Comparing the two, he noted that it was logical that the entrance to the second Pyramid would not be central, but about ten metres to one side. And there, 30 feet from where he stood at the centre, were marks that he thought might indicate the entrance. "This gave me no little delight, and hope returned to cherish my pyramidical brains."[6]

Belzoni set the Arabs to work again, but they had little faith in him and he heard them muttering "magnoon, magnoon" (madman) to each other as they laboured. The work was as hard as before and, in addition, they discovered larger blocks of stone in their way, besides the fallen coating stones. Another Italian turned up, whom Belzoni had met in Thebes: the Chevalier Frediani was the soldier and traveller who had been at Wadi Halfa with the Belmores.[7] He was just in time, Belzoni hoped, to be an impartial observer of the opening.

Yanni's account is rather different. According to him, after six days labour, Belzoni, wanting to go to Cairo, asked him to superintend the excavations. Up to that time, excavations had been proceeding on all sides of the pyramid, but, acting on the belief that, since the entrance to the first pyramid was on the north side, it might well be the same in this instance, Yanni concentrated all the diggers in that area. After three days, Belzoni returned, expressed his delight and praised him, then departed again for Cairo. Six days later, Yanni was able to send him the news that they had uncovered one of the black granite pillars of the doorway. Belzoni returned "full of delight".[8]

On 1 March they uncovered three large blocks of granite, two on each side, and one on top, standing in an inclined direction towards the centre of the pyramid — reminiscent of a gateway. On 2 March, at noon, "we came at last to the right entrance to the pyramid," Belzoni recorded. Through the entrance was a passage that descended for about 100 feet towards the centre, at an angle he later measured as 26°. The passage was littered with stones which took almost two days to clear.

At the end was a fixed block of stone, and, Belzoni thought, an end to all his dreams, but it was more like a portcullis than a solid wall. Raising it was very difficult, with little space in which to work so only short levers could be used. But, at last, inch by inch, it rose high enough for a man to pass. An Arab worker, Argian, says Yanni, was the first to enter. Argian was of gigantic height, but as thin as a stock-fish, and was able to creep and wriggle through the narrow opening. One can imagine the excited apprehension as they waited for his return. They were not disappointed.

"The place within," said Argian, "was very fine, with a great many apartments."[9] They raised the portcullis higher until there was better space for a man to enter. Here again the two men's stories diverge. Belzoni indicates that he was the next to enter. Yanni said Belzoni still could not enter "on account of his bulk" and asked him to go first. He stripped off and, after several efforts and suffering considerable scratches, descended into the pyramid and went as far as the chamber, which contained a sarcophagus. A couple of hours later, Belzoni was able to follow "to see with his own eyes that which he was not satisfied with hearing described by others."

Whatever the circumstances, after 30 days hard work, Belzoni entered the second of the great pyramids of Egypt and his countryman, Chevalier Frediani, was there to share the moment.

A shaft some 15 feet deep lay ahead. This they descended on ropes. Another passage ran downward and onward until they reached the door at the centre of the large chamber. Belzoni's words send a tingle down the spine: "I walked slowly two or three paces, and then stood still to contemplate the place where I was. My torch, formed of a few wax candles, gave but a faint light..." Where he had expected a sarcophagus at the west end of the chamber, he was at first disappointed, but then he found it, buried in the floor — and empty — and he knew others had been there first. They peered around the chamber in the flickering light. On the west wall was inscribed an announcement in Arabic: The Master Mohammed, lapicide, has opened them ; and the Master Osman attending this opening ; and the King Alij Mohammed from the beginning to the closing up.[10] Belzoni and Frediani, and almost certainly the unmentioned Yanni and the workmen, wandered around the interior — the first men to have been there for centuries.

Frediani returned to Cairo and quickly spread word about the great discovery, and visitors started arriving. A young Italian from the counting house of Briggs and Walmas rummaged through the rubbish in the sarcophagus and found pieces of bone, which turned out to be those of a bull.

Just ten days later the Belmores arrived from Upper Egypt, and Belzoni was delighted that again the Earl and his family should be the first British people to see his discovery, as they had been at Seti's tomb.

It was now, Belzoni belatedly decided, time to return to Thebes.

* *

In early March, Salt, disappointed that Belzoni had not returned, decided to leave Thebes. At much the same time a certain Captain FitzClarence, on his way home through Egypt, reached the Nile at Kenne and was told that the Consul was only a day ahead of him. He followed in hot pursuit, hoping each day to catch up and sending despatches ahead.[11]

On the evening of 7 April, FitzClarence reached Bulac, put on his red uniform coat, his sword and his pistols and set off to what he had been told was the British Consulate. On arrival the doorman told him, as he understood, that this was the Russian (Rossi) Consulate. By this time it was late and FitzClarence, determined not to be turned away, forced his way into the

1. Henry Salt, aged about 20, by John Hoppner, c. 1800

2. Henry Salt, by John James Halls, c. 1815

3. Henry Salt in 1815 by an unknown female artist in Geneva

4. View at Trinchinum, India, by Henry Salt

5. The manner of crossing a river between Point de Galle and Colombo, Ceylon, by Henry Salt

6. William Coffin in the war dress of Abyssinia, by John James Halls, c. 1830

7. Nathaniel Pearce in Abyssinian dress, by Henry Salt, 1806

8. View of the stele at Axum, by Henry Salt

9. The residence of the Ras at Antalo, Abyssinia, by Henry Salt

10. Mehemet Ali, Viceroy of Egypt, from John Madox's *Excursions*, 1826

11. Sir Joseph Banks, Chairman of the Trustees of the British Museum, by
T. Phillips, 1810

12. John Lewis Burckhardt disguised as Sheik Ibrahim, by Henry Salt

13. Giovanni Battista Belzoni by Gauci, from Belzoni's *Narrative*, published in 1820

14. William John Bankes MP, by Sir George Hayter, c. 1832

15. The Sphinx uncovered by
Captain Caviglia and recorded by
Henry Salt, 1818

16. Dr Madden attending a lady of
the harem, by Henry Salt, 1826

17. Reproduction of a scene in Seti's tomb in the Valley of the Kings, by Henry Salt, 1818

18. The sarcophagus of Seti I in the Sir John Soane Museum, from J. Britton's *The Union of architecture, sculpture and painting exemplified by…the house and galleries of John Soane*, published in 1827

house and up the stairs. He burst in on three startled people in Turkish dress. He feared he had intruded upon the harem of some jealous Turk, but soon discovered this was the house of the Austrian consul, the aged Mr Rossetti.

FitzClarence had not shaved for four months and sported a long beard; the Rossetti family must have had a nasty shock. However, as soon as they realised he was an English officer, they treated him most kindly, offered him a bed for the night and, when he refused, sent him on his way on his donkey to the British Consulate guided by a man with a paper lantern, through streets, at this late hour, almost empty of people, but full of "hundreds of yelping dogs".

The British Consulate was in "the most strange, out-of-the-way place imaginable", but when at last he reached it, FitzClarence learned with pleasure that Salt was at home. He jumped off his donkey, and, passing through a narrow passage, entered a small courtyard. There he might have fancied himself in the catacombs had he not recollected "that he was in the sancto sanctorum of an inveterate and most successful antiquarian". The lantern lit up extraordinary figures along the walls. FitzClarence, eager to meet his host, brushed past two large wooden figures "like porters, from the tombs of the kings at Thebes" at the door, and mounted the stairs.

There was the Consul-General himself, seated at a table, having just finished his meal. Away from home for five months, he returned to find a mound of letters, and had not yet opened any of FitzClarence's despatches. Yet he made his unexpected guest immediately welcome and offered him hospitality for the duration of his stay. He could, in fact, hardly have done otherwise. FitzClarence was the eldest son of the ten children of the Duke of Clarence, later King William IV, and his mistress, Mrs Jordan. He was aide-de-camp to the Governor-General of India, Lord Hastings, and was in Egypt on a mission from Hastings, carrying a message to England about the successful Mahratta campaigns. Another messenger had been sent by way of the Cape to see which route was quicker. In short, FitzClarence was on government business. However, once in Cairo, he could not be in any great haste for there was plague in Alexandria and it was unlikely that any ship would call there for some time.

While FitzClarence was at supper, Belzoni, huge in his Turkish costume, appeared. He was, FitzClarence thought, " the handsomest man I ever saw... above six foot six inches high, and his commanding figure set off by a long beard. He spoke English perfectly", and was bursting with news of his entry into the second pyramid. Salt for his part spoke "in raptures of his late discoveries at Thebes and said he intended to return the moment he could to Upper Egypt." FitzClarence at last retired, full of anticipation about the next few days, which would, he knew, "always form an epoch of my life".[12]

At breakfast there was Belzoni, and FitzClarence clearly understood that "he was not only resident with, but in the pay of Mr Salt." Again they talked of their finds and of the tomb at Luxor where Salt had been working. After breakfast Salt brought out a box full of curious and interesting objects he had collected at Thebes: "beautiful specimens of papyrus which he had himself taken out of the mummy wrappers"; a small leg and thigh made of wood "most correctly carved, and equal to, if not surpassing, any thing [FitzClarence] had previously seen"; a piece of linen covered with hieroglyphics "which appeared exactly as it had been printed"; and a "most curious and valuable scarabeus, its flat side entirely covered with beautifully executed hierglyphics". Salt spoke with enthusiasm of other finds, not yet arrived: a great quantity of dried fruits from Thebes; a whole dress formed of a kind of bugle (or glass bead). He and Belzoni were both "in raptures" about the alabaster sarcophagus. They must have enthused not only about its beauty, but also about its potential value, for FitzClarence was aware of this too.

Then the three men went into the courtyard through which FitzClarence had hurried the night before. Here were the four statues of black granite "as large as life with women's bodies and heads of lions, seated with the emblematic key of the Nile (the ankh) in one of their hands", Belzoni had discovered "in company with about thirty others", deep under sand at Karnak, "deposited there without regularity, as if to be concealed."[13]

In the afternoon, Salt took his visitor to see the Pasha. FitzClarence was impressed by the respect in which Salt was obviously held by Mehemet Ali. The feeling for "the British name and character", which must have been based to some extent on the reputation of the Consul-General and his predecessor, was so strong throughout Egypt, FitzClarence reported, that "individuals of a rival nation, when on the Nile, being challenged from the shore by the police, have been known to call out that they are Inglaize." Together the men reclined on sofas, smoked and sipped coffee. They discoursed on the threat of the 'Wahabi pirates' who had over-run 'the Indian sea' and about how the Pasha's son, Ibrahim, had defeated the Wahabi army in the south and was even then only 40 miles from their capital.

On 9 April FitzClarence finished what would become Chapter XXXI of his *Travels* with the words "Tomorrow we are to visit the pyramids." On their way, early in the morning, Salt pointed out to him Selim, one of the French soldiers of Bonaparte who had deserted and become a Mameluke. There were only two dozen of these men remaining and most of these, after the slaughter of the Mamelukes in 1811, lived beyond the Cataract. There had been at one time, Salt told him, three English Mamelukes, "worthless drunkards, who, for the honour of their country, are fortunately dead."[14]

It was not until they reached the banks of the Nile, now at low water, that they caught their first sight of the pyramids, with the sun shining on them. Mounting the waiting donkeys, the three men proceeded between green fields of corn. FitzClarence noted the separation between the desert and the cultivated land as "a sharp line on a bank, one side of which is green and the other sand." From fertile fields, one takes a few steps into the sand and inhospitality at the desert's very edge. This sand, FitzClarence complained, as they left the donkeys and trudged the 900 yards or so to the Sphinx "is most painful and fatiguing to pedestrians".

They moved on over the rocky and uneven ground to the second pyramid, "the great object of Mr Salt's visit".[15] FitzClarence, as they moved around the site, was fully aware of his privilege: "to hear on the spot, the remarks of one gentleman who had deeply studied the subject, and of the other who had immortalized himself by discovering the entrance to the chambers contained in the enormous mass before us."[16] The three men entered the pyramid through the long, granite-lined, passage, and then "taking off every thing but our shirts, and the lower parts of our dress" and each receiving a wax candle, they went on and downward: Belzoni first, Salt second and FitzClarence bringing up the rear. At last they reached the great chamber on a level with the base of the pyramid. "On the wall, immediately opposite where we entered, Belzoni had inscribed, in the Italian language, in large letters, which extend from one end to the other, his name and the date of his discovery." FitzClarence also noted that Belzoni had carved his name on the block of granite across the entrance outside. "Certainly no one had a better claim to be indulged in this innocent vanity," he commented tolerantly.

Belzoni had warned FitzClarence that he was likely to suffer extreme fatigue as a result of the day's endeavours, but he was still determined to follow the tradition of climbing the Great Pyramid. Leaving Salt and Belzoni, he started up accompanied by a few Arabs. He was soon exhausted both with the strain and the sandy desert wind. Looking down, he was almost overcome with nausea, but persevered to the top, knowing the regret he would feel if he did not. There he found the names of the Belmores and the ubiquitous Captain Corry inscribed, along with that of the Countess's lapdog, Rosa.[17]

Belzoni took him through the Great Pyramid: "a most distressing and fatiguing perambulation". FitzClarence says of himself that he was a stouter man than Belzoni and his "spirit of perserverance and research was fast giving way to heat and fatigue". At last he gratefully settled in the shadow of the Sphinx and partook of some cold meats and Madeira. When they mounted their asses for the return journey, he bravely declared that his mind was as much delighted as his body was fatigued by the experience.

The time for parting was fast approaching. FitzClarence encouraged Belzoni to write an account of his opening of the second pyramid for him to take to London. Belzoni wrote in Italian, which Salt translated and added a covering letter highly praising Belzoni's work. Curiously, Belzoni wrote of this arrangement: "Mr Salt, the Consul, took the opportunity of FitzClarence to send an official account of my operations in Egypt and Nubia to the ministers in England...I suppose because he had no opportunity of sending any correct account before that time."[18]

During his last days in Cairo, FitzClarence visited the sights. He found no difficulty apart from "occasional hooting of children at my cocked hat, as those of Christian parents would probably do at the turban of a Turk in the streets of London". One evening Salt took him to call on Signor Rossi, where he had deposited some interesting items brought from the neighbourhood of Thebes, including a head of 'Orus', "10 feet from the top of the mitre to the chin, having a band at the bottom part of it not unlike a turban ...made of red granite...and in a very fine state of preservation...an arm 18 feet long of the same statue with the fist clenched."[19]

****

FitzClarence tactfully gave no hint of difficulties in the relationship between Salt and Belzoni, although Belzoni's evidence shows that he was to some extent aware of them. The fact was that Salt found Belzoni no less disgruntled than he had been in Thebes. Apart from the awkward question of whether being paid a salary and expenses by Salt (and having taken up residence, presumably free, in the consular house) was or was not the same thing as being employed by him, Belzoni again complained bitterly that Salt was claiming honour and glory rightfully his, and stated he had believed everything he collected was for the British Museum. In this, of course, he was correct. The only question was how would it become the property of the British Museum.

How much of Belzoni's obsessive determination to have the greatest part, if not all, of any honour and fame to be bestowed by the 'British Nation' had been fuelled by the lavish praise of the Belmores, FitzClarence and others (including Salt himself), the dumbfounding in Seti's tomb of the arch-rival Drovetti, and even perhaps some wifely proddings, one can only conjecture. Certainly he had every reason to have grown in confidence in his own powers and authority as an antiquarian. Indeed, it is fair to say, that at this time he was *the* authority on discovering the secret places of the ancient Egyptians. The tower of righteous fury facing Salt at Thebes was not the same Belzoni as the man, lately dismissed by the Pasha, without resources or forseeable future prospects, who had been sent to fetch the Memnon head, however conveniently he forgot this when he wrote his *Narrative*.

That Belzoni deserved and should receive the highest praise and honour, it was not in Salt's nature to deny. To Salt, James Bruce's most unforgivable conduct, in his account of his adventures in Abyssinia, was in suppressing the presence of his companion, Balugani, at his supposed discovery of the source of the Nile, to the extent of falsely pretending the unfortunate young Italian was already dead, thus denying him any share in the credit. It is inconceivable that Salt could behave in a similar way: he spoke of Belzoni with the most enthusiastic praise in letters to his friends, and the articles in the *Quarterly Review* to which, said Halls, Belzoni "owed much of the popularity and celebrity he experienced on his first arrival in England", were based on Salt's correspondence with William Gifford, the *Review*'s editor, and to such other influential people as William Hamilton.

Salt patiently "continued in the same quiet line of remonstrance and forbearance, doing justice to his merits, and succeeded at last, (as he thought), in some measure, in calming his perturbed spirit." He proved to Belzoni that he had never had any reason to believe that all he collected belonged to the British Museum, as it was Salt himself and not the Museum, who had "borne the whole expense". Eventually they came to an amicable and final settlement, and this time the agreement was carefully written and signed by the two parties:

Cairo April 20th 1818

Whereas it appears that some erroneous idea has been entertained by Signor Giovanni Baptista Belzoni with respect to the objects collected under the auspices and at the expense of Henry Salt Esquire in Upper Egypt [this form of wording, said Salt, he consented to, as 'Mr. Belzoni seemed to think it of infinite importance'] as being intended for the British Museum, and whereas it has since been satisfactorily explained to Signor Belzoni that such ideas were altogether founded on a mistake, it has been agreed and determined between the above parties in a friendly manner, to terminate, and they do hereby terminate all differences between them by the present agreement.

In consequence of the zeal displayed in his researches, and the many valuable discoveries made by Signor Belzoni in Upper Egypt under the auspices of Henry Salt Esquire and at his expence, it is agreed by the said Henry Salt Esquire on his part to pay to Signor Belzoni (all actual expences having been settled) the sum of Five Hundred Pounds British money within the span of one year from the present date.

And further that the said Henry Salt Esquire shall make over to the said Signor Belzoni (in addition to the two already disposed of) one of those Statues with a Lion's-head now standing in the consular Court Yard.

And further that he shall concede to the said Signor Belzoni the cover of a Sarcophagus found by him in one of the end-tombs of the Kings at Thebes with such other objects as he may be able to spare.[20]

Further that the said Henry Salt Esquire stipulates that whenever the Sarcophagus lying in the King's Tomb discovered by Signor Belzoni shall be disposed of — the said Signor Belzoni shall be considered as entitled to one half of the surplus of whatever price may be given for the said Sarcophagus exceeding the sum of Two Thousand Pounds sterling — it being understood between the said parties that the said Henry Salt Esquire shall offer the said Sarcophagus to the British Museum at a fair valuation within the space of Three Years from the present date.

And further the said Henry Salt Esquire promises to give his assistance to the said Signor Belzoni in making a collection on his own account during the present season at Thebes.

On the part of Signor Belzoni — he, the said Signor Belzoni hereby agrees to the above said arrangements and further on his part engages to go to Thebes and to do all in his power to bring down for the said Henry Salt Esquire, at the expence of the latter — the two Sarcophagi now remaining under Mr Beechey's charge at Thebes and to give such other assistance to Henry Salt Esquire's Agent there as may appear to him (Signor Belzoni) advisable. And further it is agreed by the respective parties above mentioned Henry Salt Esquire and Signor Belzoni that this friendly agreement shall be considered to all intents and purposes binding on both parties and also as a final settlement between the said parties.

In confirmation whereof the said parties above mentioned have mutually interchanged copies of this agreement written respectively in their own hands — to both of which copies they have in all due form jointly affixed their signature and seal — this twentieth day of April in the year of our Lord One thousand, eight hundred and eighteen in the consulate-house at Cairo.[21]

"Thus," wrote Salt, "all our differences, as I thought, being happily adjusted, Mr. Belzoni departed, to fulfil his part of the contract, to Thebes; after shaking me heartily by the hand at parting, with the expression, 'I hope we shall continue the best friends.'" Belzoni, too, at the time, was satisfied with his arrangement with Salt. He wrote in his own hand — and inimitable spelling — to Lord Belmore, who was by then in Jerusalem, on 18 April. This letter, long hidden in the Belmore family papers, makes it only too clear that he was happy:

I have the honor to aquint your Lordship that on the arrival of Mr Salt in Caira My Affer with him took the Good Tourn I most hapely could wish we mad arrangements satisfactory to both parties and all ended in most frendle termes...the works of discovery in Upper Egypt have been declared due intirly to my own Indistry and Exersion and that Mr Salt has paid the Expenses for the works as I employed my little capacity for the sayd discovery.

Captain FitzClarence has been mediator of our silly, little differences.

Now going entirely at my own expense to make model of temble at Biban el Malook and intend to have it built in London on the same scale as the original.

A declaration by Mr Salt of all my discovery in the Upper Egypt and openeing of the Pyramid taken by FitzClarence and will publish it in my name.[22]

Even Salt's fiercest detractors would have to admit that Belzoni had the best of this contract, at any rate in any business sense. Of course, no contract could assure him of the public's applause — the *Quarterly Review* and his own efforts were to do that for him. Beechey, who spent more time with Belzoni than any other man in Egypt, told Halls that he had found him "of so suspicious and dissatisfied a disposition, that it was in some respects difficult to keep on any terms with him." Certainly these terms were not enough, and as later, unfortunately for Salt, would be clearly shown, Belzoni's spirit was not enduringly freed of its perturbation.

On 7 August 1818, Salt wrote to Valentia, now the Earl of Mountnorris, to whom a few earlier letters had evidently miscarried, answering some queries about Belzoni, and again praising his strength, his ingenuity, his indefatigability and zealousness; "and joining to all this, a very intelligent mind". After enumerating all that Belzoni had achieved ("for me", writes Salt repeatedly, not "under my auspices"), he continued rather sadly: "As to his monopolizing the credit of these discoveries, I have no objection to it, for I have only the merit of having risked the speculation and paid the expenses; and besides, the experience of life has taught me to estimate at its just value the opinion of the multitude. I shall in time produce proof of my benefiting, at least, by these discoveries, by the drawings I have already made; but I am dubious as to farther publication. I want nothing from Ministers, nor from mankind. My mind is settled as to the course of my future life, which I do not expect to be a long one, and the world may pursue its own course as it pleases for me. My only hope is a small independence, some ten years hence, on which I may retire; and if I do not succeed in securing this, I can stay where I am."[23]

12

Collections and an Expedition

COLLECTING and studying the antiquities of Egypt had become an absorbing passion for Salt, but were to bring him perhaps as much pain as pleasure, and almost to cause a breach in one of his oldest and most valued friendships.

Asked by Mountnorris to collect antiquities for him, Salt had employed a Mr Riley to make purchases for him in Upper Egypt. Soon he told Mountnorris he would shortly send him "a pretty satisfactory description of antiquities already collected for your museum. Whenever you can pay two hundred pounds on this account...you will oblige me, as I have already expended fully that sum in purchases for you."[1] He would sketch everything before he sent it off, a sensible precaution when artefacts might be lost or damaged in transit.

Mountnorris expressed resentment of Salt's own collecting. "You say you are sorry I did not give you notice that I meant to collect," wrote Salt in October 1817, "but the fact was I had no intention of the kind. Circumstances which occurred after I arrived led me to think it might be done and I was tempted to make a bold push — before Drovetti's eyes were opened...My ideas of collecting have been brought on," he explained, " by finding it the only solace of existence in this place for as to the society it is most wretched. I also think that it may be possible to collect a few things of such value that if ever I should be obliged to quit Egypt from ill health or an inclination to retire it might furnish together with my father's bequest the means of living in some nook or corner in Europe — as you must know that I have received official notice from the Office that no Pensions are ever allowed to Consuls...if I should be lucky in this way you will own that it is more reasonable that I should reap the advantage than even my best friend..."

Had he willed Mountnorris his collection? "As to your having them by my death — I consider this during my stay in Egypt as no improbable circumstance, life in this country is very precarious and my constitution is none of the best." He added, "I will try to send you a mummy but it is difficult and to tell the truth I dislike having any thing to do with them myself."[2]

Mountnorris continued fractious. His complaints of May 1818 gave Salt "much vexation and concern," but on re-reading, he realised a letter not reaching England had led to the Earl's mistaken notions, "though a little patience and reliance on me might have prevented such a letter". The missing letter had contained a list of all he had collected for Mountnorris, with careful notes of the place where each article was found — a concern with provenance in advance of his time. He had not forwarded the best articles until he had tried the route, fearing, with good reason, as Lord Belmore discovered, that packets were not handled with care at Malta.

He had collected for Mountnorris up to June 1816 with no thought for himself, but then "began to speculate on a larger scale for myself", hoping to offset the expenses incurred in removing the Head. Of the articles he had commissioned Belzoni to acquire for him, "I allotted you what I conceived a very handsome proportion namely all the small articles and two lion headed statues of Isis (nearly perfect) and which are much finer than any now in Europe, which I estimated...at £400."

He had kept for himself two of the same statues and the seated statue of 'Jupiter Ammon', hoping these were of sufficient value to cover his expenses of that year — "this I considered myself fully entitled to do as indeed you fully admit in one of your last letters." If this arrangement did not please the Earl, he would give him £300 for "your two lion headed ladies and leave all the rest of the collection (which you will allow when it has all reached you to be of considerable value) as a present in your hands, having been always most desirous of shewing the friendship and esteem I shall always feel for your past kindness...though I must again repeat that I have been hurt by the contents of your letter as I never made any promise (to my recollection) to collect exclusively for you but merely offering to do so as a means of obliging you...I have not forgotten you, but have collected many articles — especially two perfect papyrus — which I shall offer to your acceptance and this I shall continue to do so long as I collect and you write me no more letters like the last." He hoped to send most or all the articles direct to England in about two months in a ship of Briggs and Co., "and trust you will then renounce your opinion 'that you believe you have received the trash and that what was worth keeping has found its way into my own collection' — otherwise 'we must measure swords and part'".[3]

Salt had been urged by Sir Joseph Banks to take advantage of his situation to collect antiquities for the British Museum, a request, according to Halls, later "enforced by letter". It would be interesting, in the light of subsequent events, to know exactly what Banks said. Salt's first effort to enrich his country's national collection had been, with Burckhardt, to present it with the Head of Memnon — and somewhat equivocal thanks he was returned for that. Though the head reached England in early March 1818, five months later Salt had not even received notification of its arrival. Admiral Penrose in Malta, who *had* received an acknowledgement from the Foreign Office, so informed Salt in June, but Banks' letter did not reach him until November. It is true that Sir Joseph may have written as early as May.

A factor which again and again complicated events and made them both more hurtful and more harmful to Salt was that between a letter leaving England, his reply, and the reaction to it reaching him again, from nine to 18 months could elapse, while letters that never arrived at all led inevitably to misunderstandings.

When he began to collect for himself, Salt had little money to lay out. The £4,000 with which he had left England had been largely disbursed on his European travels and in fitting up the Consulate. With a salary paid months in arrears, had he not been able to borrow from Briggs and Co. he would "have had a hard run having been put to many unlooked for expences and Egypt being no longer the Cheap country it used to be."[4] The cost of Mountnorris's antiquities had come entirely from his own pocket, as had half the cost of getting the Memnon to Alexandria and Belzoni's 'present' for doing so, all the cost of opening Abu Simbel and the Theban tombs, and the recompense given Belzoni (not, of course, to be referred to as a salary); he was also sending Pearce in Abyssinia goods and money to the value of £50 or £60 a year. But on 27 May 1817, his father died and by his will, probated 3 December, Salt shared equally with his sisters, Jane de Vismes and Bessy Morgan, the sum produced when the estate was settled. £1,000 of his £5,000 inheritance was "locked up" for some unexplained reason.

Concerned about the money already expended, Salt had a compelling reason by June 1818 to approach the British Museum to obtain the recompense of which he was under the impression he had been assured. "I am sorry," he wrote Hamilton, "to hear that the Trustees (for I am aware of Sir Joseph Banks' influence among them) do not wish for more Egyptian antiquities."

Not a very propitious moment to offer his collection, but attitudes might harden further and it seemed wise to test the water at once. Rather than address the Trustees of the British Museum directly, he wrote privately to Hamilton, asking for his "friendly advice" on how to act: "I have gone to great expense in collecting, chiefly with a view to throw some light on the sculpture of the Egyptians, and have fortunately discovered, by digging, about twenty specimens, not very bulky, that will prove their claim to great excellence in the art, and which satisfactorily demonstrate that the Greeks borrowed the rudiments, if not more, from this extraordinary people..." He also had various wooden sculptures, "which they carried to a perfection unknown in any other country", and "besides these is the sarcophagus of alabaster, *unrivalled* in its delicate workmanship".

Now if the Government would take these (the latter for the British Museum, and the *statues* for the Royal Academy) at a fair valuation, I shall be glad to

put them at their disposition at Alexandria, it being a great object to avoid farther cost in the transport; and it would be easy for the Government to secure
their safe passage, at scarcely any expense, by ordering one of the transports
coming for corn here, to take them on board.

As to the *value*, I would most willingly leave *that* to yourself, or any
other persons the Government might appoint to be settled after the arrival of
the articles in England. The Conte de Forbin, when here, pressed me much to
let him have a portion for the King of France, and I know that they would be
disposed to pay a handsome price; but I should be sorry to see such articles out
of England.

If the Government would not take the collection, would Hamilton help him
to get it to England, "as I have already embarrassed myself much with the
expenses incurred." He begged forgiveness for troubling Hamilton, "but, as
it affords the only prospect of a return some day or other to Europe, the
matter is of course of deep interest to me." Of his £5,000 inheritance, half
was "*already* disposed of in forming my Collection; if, therefore, I could
repay myself and add something to the sum, it might afford a reasonable
prospect, after six or seven years, of enabling me to retire from office; otherwise, I must be forever condemned to remain here, which you will allow
is no very desirable lot, since saving out of my salary is totally out of the
question, so long as a due regard is paid to keeping up the respectability of
the Consulate."[5]

He must expect to wait eight months or more for an answer. About this
time William John Bankes arrived in Cairo, and plans were hatched for a
joint expedition.

* *

"I have seen two obelisks in the island of Giesiret-ell-heif [Philae]. The one
is of white marble and standing, but without any hieroglyphics: the other,
which is of granite, lies upon the ground; and has a row of hieroglyphic figures on each face."[6] The year was 1738, the observer Frederick Norden, a
Danish naval captain, in Egypt on a fact-finding mission for King Christian
VI. In 1799 Napoleon's savants recorded the obelisks in their plans and elevations of the Temple of Isis for *La Description de l'Egypte*. In 1801 William
Richard Hamilton noted them; Burckhardt saw them in 1813 and suggested the British Museum should procure them — but the Museum Trustees did
not "think it expedient". Belzoni, in 1816, formally claimed the prostrate,
unbroken obelisk in the name of the British Consul before the Aga of
Aswan, and gave him four dollars to guard it until he should return.

But it was William John Bankes who finally took action. On his first
visit to Egypt in 1815, he told his father that he was obliged to travel with

a "brigade" of workmen and apparatus, "in case I choose to remove a Pyramid or the Statue of Memnon."[7] Though he failed to remove even the obelisk, he excavated its pedestal and found Greek inscriptions on the lower stone.

Bankes left for the Holy Land in December 1815; Finati, already in his service, accompanied him, but returned to Egypt when Bankes sailed for Cyprus in June 1816 and eventually became Salt's janissary. In November 1817, Bankes, back in Syria, asked Salt to send Finati to him. As Sarah Belzoni, with James Curtin, was about to go to the Holy Land, Belzoni asked that Finati might escort them. Towards the end of March 1818, Bankes, Sarah, the Belmores, Captains Irby and Mangles and Thomas Legh were all in Jerusalem and Bankes, the Captains and Legh made an expedition to Petra, the first Europeans since Burckhardt to enter the hidden city. Legh, Irby and Mangles departed for Constantinople, but Bankes remained in Jerusalem to commit sacrilege. Disguised as an Albanian, he obliged Finati to accompany him into the Muslim holy enclave, and not only entered the Temple of Solomon, but there obtained an official certificate that he had done so. Finati was terrified; had they been found out, Bankes, a rich English milord, might have got away with it, but he, a Muslim who had knowingly introduced an infidel into the Temple, would probably have been executed. They left for Egypt in some haste.

After some exploring in Lower Egypt, Bankes was received very kindly by Salt in Cairo, kindness he was in need of, for he fell prey to opthalmia. During his enforced inactivity he laid plans for an expedition to Upper Egypt. He wrote to his father, "a large boat is already engaged for me, and our consul...will accompany me in another at least so far as Thebes and probably to the furthest point of my voyage...I can do all at my leisure and shall probably make many new discoveries, of which you shall hear whenever there occurs an opportunity (which the consul's being with me will render pretty frequent)."[8]

Salt had been obliged to refuse Lord Belmore's invitation to join him in Naples for the winter, since it was impossible to obtain permission from the Foreign Office in time, but, with the Pasha soon off to Alexandria, and the reliable Samuel Briggs to deputise as Consul, a jaunt in congenial company was an attractive and useful idea.

Bankes "is a most delightful companion," he wrote to Mountnorris, "from his extraordinary powers of memory, and the opportunities he has had for observation."[9] And to his sister Bessy, "Of all the men I have ever met with, I consider [him] as being gifted with the most extraordinary talents; born to family and fortune, he has dedicated his whole time to learning and the arts, possessing a fund of anecdote and good humour, which renders his society the most agreeable and entertaining that can be conceived."[10]

Born in 1786, William John Bankes was the son of Henry Bankes M.P., the cultivated and scholarly possessor of estates in Dorsetshire, including Kingston Hall (now Kingston Lacy). Brilliant, charming, whimsical and witty, William was a social success at Cambridge University, where he formed a lasting friendship with Lord Byron, who described him as "the father of all mischiefs". He set out on his travels in 1812. In Spain and Portugal, at the military headquarters of the Duke of Wellington, a family friend, he began to acquire an art collection — not always, despite his abundant funds, legitimately. The Duke is said to have remarked firmly to his officers, "Gentlemen, I will have no more looting; and remember, Bankes, this applies to you also."[11] Sailing through life on a magic carpet of brilliance and charm, Bankes could be arrogant and at times careless of the sensibilities of others. Faults that he himself admitted were indolence and a disinclination ever to settle down to the dull business of arranging and ordering his notes and sketches into publishable form. It recalls Salt as a young man — but Salt disciplined himself to publish his Abyssinian travels, and there is evidence he produced other work in Egypt, now lost, while Bankes never produced the erudite work of which his friends were always expectant. Bankes had another characteristic, graphically illustrated by his intrusion into the Temple of Solomon: he "loved danger as some men love one woman: in spite of reason, warning and experience".[12]

About the middle of October 1818, the expedition departed up the Nile. The progress was very slow, recounts Finati, "for every quarry and every tomb in the ridge of the Mokattam was examined and explored". In the tombs at Beni Hassan they discovered murals which Bankes considered "the most curious in Egypt as to their details". Reaching Thebes about 1 November, they stayed more than two weeks. Belzoni, Beechey, Ricci and Yanni had just returned from 40 days in the desert, exhausted after nights passed on the backs of their camels. Belzoni believed they had found the ruins of the lost city of Berenice. The trip, taken at Salt's expense, yielded the Consul nothing but a fragment of a tablet, but he bore the outlay philosophically.

Belzoni had a new complaint. By their contract in April, Salt agreed to help him to collect on his own account; as Belzoni claimed this was impossible because all the potentially fruitful sites already belonged to Salt, he amiably proposed that Belzoni should be free to dig in any he "thought hopeful", being paid his expenses and a third share of whatever was found. According to Salt's accounts, he spent about 1,500 piastres, "without finding, as he reported to me, a single article".[13] No wonder Belzoni expressed himself "fully satisfied" with this arrangement.

On 14 November the two crossed the Nile to Luxor, where they ran into Drovetti, who accompanied them to Karnak as witness to the various sites which were to be allotted Belzoni. He told them of a man, dressed like Belzoni, who lurked in the temple ruins, intending, he claimed, to do him an injury. Salt, laughing, said that Belzoni could not be so easily imitated, but Belzoni, ever alert for intrigues (often rightly, when dealing with Drovetti and his agents), suspected the tale would make a fine excuse to fire upon himself, and told Drovetti he hoped he would tell his people to be sure, if they shot, it was on the sham Belzoni, "as it would not be quite so pleasant or satisfactory to me if the mistake had been found out after." Having successfully teased his rival, Drovetti replied that the person had now been sent away from Thebes.

Bankes engaged Belzoni to go up to Philae to remove the obelisk which, though claimed in the name of the British Consul, Salt had ceded to him. Drovetti, regaling Salt and Belzoni with sherbet and lemonade at his house among the ruins at Karnak, exclaimed angrily that he had paid the "rogues" at Aswan to bring the obelisk down for *him*, but they had failed to do so. Belzoni replied firmly that they had no right to, as he had claimed it in 1816 for Salt. Drovetti answered that he had been much deceived but, graciously, as the obelisk was intended for Bankes, he would not say a word about it, and "voluntarily ceded it to him".[14] His actions were to belie his words. He enquired politely when they would set off.

The day they left Thebes, 16 November, Salt wrote to Sir Joseph Banks on Belzoni's behalf, in reply to Sir Joseph's suggestion that the Italian might be employed in collecting officially for the British Museum. Belzoni calculated that the expenses would amount "on the most economical system" to £1,500 a year. As he presumably based this on his experience, it throws an interesting light on how much Belzoni's operations were costing Salt. He left it to the Trustees to decide "on whatever recompenses they may think propur [sic]".[15]

A positive fleet sailed from Thebes. Bankes had a *cangia* of 14 oars, Salt a larger but less manageable *maash*, while a smaller boat had been engaged for the Baron Sack, Chamberlain to the King of Prussia, and a renowned naturalist, who, recommended to Salt by the Foreign Office, had begged to accompany the expedition.

A fourth boat carried the servants, the kitchen and the provisions, including sheep, goats, hens, geese, ducks, pigeons, turkeys, and donkeys, which occasionally "joined the chorus with the rest of the tribes, and accompanied the fleet with a perpetual concert". The commissariat was Salt's responsibility, as he wrote to Lord Belmore: "We have our separate boats...but the provisions being on board my barque I shall now take the lead, instead of being a mere visitor as last year when your kindness saved me both the expense and trouble of keeping a table on board."[16]

Belzoni looked upon the catering arrangements with the scornful eye of a traveller inured to short commons and a camel's back for a bed: "Yet it was arduous travelling, living in that manner, destitute of every commodity of life; for even at table we had not ice to cool ourselves after the hot repast, which was concluded with fruits, and only two sorts of wine. In short, our lives were a burthen to us from the fatigue and dangerous mode of travelling. We were not like travellers who live on the best of every thing they can get, and write at home the hard life they undergo. O, no! O, no! we would scorn to travel in such an effeminate manner."[17]

The other members of the party were the Scotsman, Osman, as dragoman, and a young Frenchman, Linant de Bellefonds, who had arrived in Egypt with the Comte de Forbin in 1817 and when Forbin left, stayed on, working for a while for the Pasha. He offered his services to the expedition and Salt engaged him as an artist. At Thebes, Belzoni, Beechey and Yanni joined and Bankes took on Dr Ricci, as both physician and artist.

"The party [consisted] only of very *pleasant* and *agreeable* people," wrote Salt to Julia Hanson, Halls' youngest sister, "Mr Bankes is one of the most delightful companions I ever met with, high-bred, well informed, and possessing an inexhaustible fund of humour; the Baron Sack full of little anecdotes, such as Halls delights in, of armadilloes, flamingoes, field mice, and monstrous snakes which he had collected in the course of a long residence in Surinam; withal very credulous, and permitting himself to have a goose's egg foisted upon him for a crocodile's, yet infinitely amusing and *good-humoured*;" and himself, "a traveller, still fond of gibes and merriment, and now and then, when conversation slacked, introducing an *Abyssinian* story to while away the hour; while the *secondary* planets were content to shine in their respective spheres, and looked up with all *due* deference to the more *brilliant luminaries*."[18]

Every site was examined and drawn. Salt gave Julia a charming sketch of "the infinite variety of matter to be found at all the principal ruins...Now it was the plan of a garden, painted without perspective, but showing all the walks, trees, flowers, vineyards, and even little ponds, that delighted us. Then a procession, coming from the interior of Africa, with leopards, lions, cameleopards, and blue monkeys sitting on their backs...led by negroes, bearing on their shoulders elephants' teeth and sandal wood...enchanted us...at other times we were seen running after the representation of a chase...a set of dancers, playing on the tambourine, flute, and harp: a couple of learned clerks, with their pens behind their ears..."

On 21 November, at Edfu they found Drovetti's agents excavating, and learned that one of them, Lebolo, had received a dispatch from his employer a few days since and left hastily for Philae. Just before Silsili, they sighted Lebolo sailing down again, and hailed him; but he did not stop. Belzoni, full of suspicion, left the others at Kom Ombos and, with Osman, hurried up river to Aswan, where his fears proved well-founded. Despite being told by the Aga of Aswan that the obelisk had been under guard for the British Consul for three years, Lebolo had convinced the people of Philae that it belonged to Drovetti's ancestors, and so to him. Leaving his claim with one of the Philae sheiks Lebolo departed hastily, "as he thought his face could not be impudent enough to meet us". Belzoni was told that the French had several times tried to remove the obelisk, the latest attempt only two months earlier, when the cataract had been thought too low to allow its passage. It was even lower now. When Salt arrived, it was firmly established in his official presence that Belzoni's was the first claim on the monument. They encamped on Philae, and Bankes' liberal presents persuaded the local sheiks to provide labourers, and a boat *reis* to ferry the obelisk. With its pedestal, which had been half-buried under rubbish, it was moved from in front of the propylon to the waterside. At this moment, the Aga of Aswan brought a letter, with Drovetti's own seal, ordering the Aga, translated Osman, to prevent anyone removing the obelisk. Salt asked the Aga to send Drovetti his compliments and tell him that "we were going to remove the obelisk". Seldom can the Anglo-French rivalry have come so near a direct confrontation.

Bankes also employed men to clear the ground within and around the ruins, and pull down the crude brick structures which had obscured them. Some new chambers were discovered in the temple, but they were devoid of either ornament or objects.

While Belzoni was inspecting the hazards of the cataract, the workmen building a pier to slide the obelisk from shore to boat took the opportunity to skimp on the foundations. With the whole weight of the stone upon it, pier, obelisk and some of the men "took a slow movement, and majestically descended into the river, wishing us better success." Belzoni's first horrified thought was for the loss of such a monument, the second, "the exultation of our opponents", and the third, "the blame of all the antiquarian republic in the world". Wretchedly, he contemplated the current eddying about the corner of the obelisk that showed above the water. Though Bankes said mildly that "such things would happen sometimes", Belzoni saw "he was not in a careful humour himself"; Finati says he was "evidently disgusted". But Belzoni assured him that a few days would retrieve the situation.

According to Yanni, another unpleasant scene between Salt and Belzoni took place at Philae. Belzoni "had the audacity to demand of Mr Salt, as the price of his services" the sarcophagus of Seti. He needed it, he said, as part of the tomb he planned to erect in England. "He thus had the modesty to fix upon the choicest and most valuable article of all that Mr Salt had been able to procure, after an outlay of some thousands of piasters. Mr Belzoni knew very well that he had already been liberally rewarded by Mr Salt for his services." This "extraordinary demand" led Salt to dismiss Belzoni "without receiving any further gratifications than his regular appointments as far as Alexandria."[19] As neither Salt nor Belzoni mentions such a monumental row, it is hard to know what credence to give the account.

The party left Philae; Finati was to follow when the obelisk had been rescued, which pleased him, as he could prolong his honeymoon with a young Nubian he had married. By ingenious levering and propping up with stones, much of it done underwater by the skilled local swimmers, the obelisk was brought triumphantly to shore. Since the boat would not take both pieces at once, Belzoni ferried the pedestal to the mainland, where it remained forlorn for nearly three years. One of Drovetti's agents made a last attempt to stop the operation, but the Aga said firmly he had orders from his superior, the Defterdar Bey, not to meddle with either party; attempts to bribe the sheiks and the labourers were rejected "with disgust".

Halfway through the inundation, the cataract was 300 yards long, falling at a 20 to 25 degree angle amid randomly projecting rocks. Down this, the 22-foot obelisk must pass, an operation demanding all the skill and experience of the whole tribe of Nubians stationed ready to pull or slacken the guide-ropes as necessity arose. Finati paints a vivid picure of "the great boat wheeling and swinging round, and half filling with water, while naked figures were crowding upon all the rocks, or wading or swimming between them, some shouting, and some pulling at the guide ropes..." "It was one of the greatest sights I have seen," says Belzoni. At its fastest, the boat was travelling at about 12 miles an hour, slowing as it neared the end of the cataract and gliding at last "smoothly and majestically onwards with the stream." The obelisk had passed the most perilous yards of its journey to a Dorsetshire garden.

Leaving the boat to sail to Thebes, Belzoni made his own way more quickly overland. On 23 December he found Sarah ensconced in their former home among the tombs at Biban el Malook, and passed Christmas "in the solitude of those recesses, undisturbed by the folly of mankind". Each had much to tell. The most daring and dangerous of Sarah's adventures in the Holy Land had been her clandestine entry into a mosque in the Muslim precinct in Jerusalem, not "the Holy of Holies on the platform" (the Dome of the Rock), but the one in the south-east corner.

A few days earlier there had been a very heavy downpour of rain. Before Belzoni went south, he had filled up the well that barred the way into the chambers of Seti's tomb so that he could bring the great alabaster sarcophagus across it. Unfortunately, the well formed not only a deterrent to thieves, but a means of diverting just such deluges, and though Belzoni had started, in early November, to dig a channel outside the tomb to turn away any downpour, on the arrival of Salt and Bankes, he stopped the work.

Water and mud had run into the tomb and steam rising from the damp cracked walls had detached plaster. Sarah had the mud cleared away, but inestimable damage had been done by this surprising oversight of the 'hydraulics engineer'.

The peace of Christmas was soon disturbed. "I must now enter into new contests with evil beings…foul deeds of malice" writes Belzoni dramatically, and not without reason. "Our opponents, with their commander, Mr Drovetti" were settled among the ruins at Karnak. The obelisk in its boat at Luxor was "rather too close under their noses, as they expressed themselves", and they laid a plan to pick some difference with Belzoni which could justify a quarrel. On 26 December, near Karnak, Belzoni was set upon by Drovetti's two Piedmontese agents, Lebolo and Rosignani, leading some 30 Arabs. Lebolo seized Belzoni's bridle with one hand, his waistcoat with the other, demanding what business he had to take an obelisk that did not belong to him, robbing the agent of his third share of the profit from its sale in Europe. Rosignani shouted abuse and levelled a gun. Then up rushed Drovetti with more Arabs and more loud accusations. Behind Belzoni a pistol went off and he dismounted hastily, prepared to sell his life dear — but "the kind Mr Drovetti" assured him he was safe. Next day, a French traveller, Edouard de Montulé, sketching at Luxor, saw Lebolo speak to his interpreter, who asked permission to cross the Nile. Pressed, the man admitted it was to join Lebolo and Montulé, guessing his intentions, forbade him to go. The 'colossus of the left bank' had a luckier escape than he knew.

Montulé was very critical of the Salt-Drovetti carve-up of the sites. His indignation was less than disinterested, stressing the fact that, however many presents a person might make to the locals, let him "only proceed to attack a pyramid, a temple, the isle of Phile, [sic] &c. &c," and he would find it already "the exclusive property of M Drovetti, M Salt, &c. &c." Every day increased the Anglo-French rivalry, and "Thebes ultimately became the theatre of the grand engagement which was to prove decisive, and where M Belzoni really underwent those dangers of which he speaks." Montulé considered that it was not Salt, Drovetti or Belzoni who were to blame, but their agents, who were frequently rewarded with a share in the value of their finds, and "consequently nourish mutual animosities".[20]

Belzoni had had enough. "I could not live any longer in a country where I had become the object of revenge." He wrote a full account to Salt, but did not ask for redress, "as I could not expect to have any in that country". He finished his sketches and models of Seti's tomb, removed and loaded the sarcophagus onto the boat; as well, "all that I had accumulated on my own account" joined the obelisk.

On 27 January 1819, feeling more on leaving Thebes "than any other place in my life", he embarked with Sarah on a boat laden with treasures.

At Rosetta the cargo was off-loaded on to a *djerm* for the voyage to Alexandria, with the addition of his four or five 'lion-headed ladies' stored in Rosetta; possibly also the sarcophagus lid he had found hidden under rubble in the Valley of the Kings. A friend of Belzoni told Yanni he had already sent 40 papyri to Europe for him; if, as Yanni claims, found while in Salt's employ, somewhat dubiously accumulated. There were also "specimens of antiquity which Madame Belzoni collected on her own account."[21]

At Alexandria, Belzoni found a letter from Salt, advising him not to leave Egypt till he had an answer from England (about collecting for the British Museum) and also had had "redress of the outrageous behaviour of those gentry" at Thebes. Salt had asked Peter Lee to present depositions to M Roussel, the French Consul. Belzoni, while "glad to see that my cause had been taken up", was pessimistic about the outcome. Drovetti was in Alexandria, staunchly defending his agents and naming Salt as his accuser. It was agreed the matter must be postponed until Salt's return. Unwilling to sit about, Belzoni deposited Sarah in Rosetta and departed into the western desert, in search of the temple of Jupiter Ammon.

It had taken just over three months for the obelisk to voyage from Philae to Alexandria — it was to be long before it set forth on its travels again.

* *

Finati bore the tidings of the obelisk's safe passage of the Cataract to Bankes, whom he found at Kalabsha. The researches were still so painstaking that they stayed at each site from three to ten days, measuring, mapping and sketching. Salt wrote to Julia Hanson, "All but the baron, who was chiefly engaged in killing frogs, snakes, beetles, and such like game, were enthusiastically fond of the arts, and really vied with each other who should produce the best sketches; being generally occupied *hard at it*...from nine o'clock in the morning till dark."

On 13 January, just above Korosko, they encountered another party of Europeans. Of these men, Wyse, Godfrey, Baillie and Barry, the one well-known today is Charles Barry, a young architect, upon whom Egypt was to have a great influence. He had already toured France, Italy and Greece when in Athens he met David Baillie, who was so impressed by the beauty of his drawings that he employed him as his artist. In Syria, they joined forces with Godfrey and Wyse, had been up the Nile as far as the Second Cataract, and were now on their return down river. At Abu Simbel they had cleared the sand which already had sealed the door. When they fell in with "the Consul's flotilla", they breakfasted on the low sandy bank and spent the day together. "Mr Salt showed me the whole of the sketches that he had made since leaving Philae, in pencil and very numerous, the production of himself, Mr Beechey and Mr Linant," recorded Barry. He also looked over Bankes' and Ricci's drawings, "which on account of their great number he keeps in a basket".

Barry described the *cangias* of Salt and Bankes. "A cabin in the stern was large enough to contain comfortably two travelling bedsteads lighted by lattice windows on each side before which is a white linen hanging as protection from the wind. Behind the cabin was a smaller room for shoes and lumber and behind that a place for the steersman." There were two small lateen sails, and the 12-man crews could lay to the oars if the wind was contrary.

Salt and his companions continued slowly up to Abu Simbel, where they spent over a month. The presence of the Consul, and possibly a more emollient and liberal treatment of the locals, ensured there were no labour troubles. As the entrance to the temple had been so recently cleared, a more ambitious project was undertaken, the uncovering of the southernmost of the four colossal figures down to the feet, which took almost three weeks. A few Greek letters were found scratched on the legs. Bankes was convinced that the legs nearer the door would carry more so the sand from that figure was rolled away, to cover again much of the first. They uncovered a Greek inscription written in the time of Psammeticus, valuable proof, Salt recognised, that the temple had been built "before that remote period". The second giant was in its turn reburied, as the northernmost head was revealed for the first time, so that a general drawing of the complete quartet could be made.

The interior of the temple was lighted with small wax candles, fixed upon clusters of palm branches, which were attached to long upright poles, and spread like the arms of a chandelier more than halfway to the ceiling. They enabled Bankes and the other draughtsmen to copy all the paintings in detail, as they stood "almost naked, upon their ladders".[22] The atmosphere was like a Turkish bath and must have been almost unendurable.

Unlike many other travellers, Salt and Bankes felt no need to record their presence at every temple they visited; but Abu Simbel was different, and here there are three inscriptions. The first, on the left flank of the southernmost colossus, reads:

Wm BANKES
OPENED (THIS) [very faint]
(COLOSSUS) [defaced]

And on the adjoining wall is painted:

(SALT) [defaced] H. B. M.
CONSUL
GENERAL IN
EGYPT

The other inscription is to the north of the figures:

THIS TEMPLE WAS
OPENED AUGUST 1 1817
BY ORDER OF
(HENRY SALT) [defaced]
H.B.M. CONSUL GENERAL
IN EGYPT
THE SOUTHERN COLOSS-
US LAID OPEN TO ITS BASE
BY Wm BANKES Esq (IN 1818) [defaced, presumably because wrong]

The whole is within an outline, outside which appears AND 1819, the actual date.

The Deftardar Bey from Siout, on his way to examine how far the Second Cataract was navigable, in preparation for the Pasha's proposed expedition against Dongola, paid a visit. In uncomprehending astonishment that so many people should occupy themselves in such discomfort, he could only repeatedly ask the perennial question: "What treasure have they found?"

A traveller who arrived on the evening of 14 February had been pursuing Salt's party up the Nile. John Hyde landed at Alexandria on 29 November, accompanied by William Rae Wilson.[23] From Cairo, Wilson departed for Syria, but Hyde hired a *cangia* and set sail from Bulac on 2 January 1819.[24]

Near Niguade, Hyde met Belzoni's boat; Sarah exchanged a few oranges for a quarter of an antelope Hyde had shot. At Luxor he was hailed by the sculptor Jacques Rifaud, who was at work modelling the "most interesting of the temples" and drawing the rest, and forming a collection of flora and fauna. In Seti's tomb Hyde picked up some broken fragments of the lid of the great sarcophagus, but was driven out by a "sick headick" brought on by the atmosphere. Halfway between Esne and Edfu, Godfrey, Wyse, Baillie and Barry spent an hour with him and gave him a map of Nubia made by Thomas Legh.

Hyde came up with the flotilla at Abu Simbel, presented his letter of introduction, and was given a "most friendly reception" by Salt. Four days later they sailed for Wadi Halfa, pausing frequently to examine the Greek

167

and Coptic churches on the banks for inscriptions, "with the most minute attention". On 22 February, the party climbed to the Rock of Abu Sir and Hyde added his name to the others already there. As it was Bankes' ambition to continue south as far as Dongola or even Meroë, at Wadi Halfa what Finati calls "a tedious negociation" began, to obtain the protection of Hussein Cashef. As at Aswan, though Bankes might be able to make lavish presents, it was Salt who indisputably possessed the authority to negotiate. He caused Turkey carpets to be laid out on the shore, with a canopy held over them, and the principals sat down, ringed by 50 or 60 of the Cashef's guards. The Cashef agreed only with great reluctance to provide camels and an escort, saying "The Duty of a Prince is to keep his Friends out of Danger — I will afford you my protection *so far as I can ensure your safety.*"[25]

If Salt had intended to continue up river, he was prevented by falling dangerously ill. None of his companions ever expected to see him alive again. Linant and Osman turned back with Salt; Baron Sack may have left them even earlier.

Had Salt been with them, the expedition might have succeeded; mere travellers could not command the respect due to a Consul if only because of his privileged access to the Pasha. Bankes' expedition failed. When they were 150 miles above Wadi Halfa, their 'protectors' abandoned them, taking the camels; Hyde fell so ill that sometimes they despaired of keeping him alive; finally, at Amara, the Cashef flatly refused to let them go further, saying that should they "persist in going forward to the upper country we should find 'our graves were already dug for us'."[26]

On 19 March, three weeks after they had started out, and travelling mainly on foot, they were back at Wadi Halfa. There in a day or two, they were joined by Captain Foskett, Mr Fuller and Nathaniel Pearce.

* *

In the spring of 1818, Pearce had informed Salt of the turbulent state of affairs in Abyssinia and his own precarious situation and asked permission to join him in Egypt. Salt replied warmly, "Nothing will give me greater pleasure." He would provide him with an easy job, "such as looking after my garden, or collecting antiques…and if anything happens to me I have left you *by will* fifty pounds a year for your life and that of your wife." Pearce, he suggested, had a potential source of income in his journals, which were "very clear and very amusing…I feel no doubt…of being able to make of them a very excellent book which may do you great credit in the world, and be the means of putting some money in your pocket." Salt also promised that if Coffin wished it, he would help him to get to England.[27]

For some time after Salt left Pearce and Coffin in Abyssinia in 1810, they prospered under the Ras's protection. But the Ras, of whom Pearce wrote to Salt in 1815 as "just as Young as ever", grew old and feeble. He died on 28 May 1816. Coffin wrote, his Dorsetshire burr sounding in his shakily phonetic spelling, "the ole of the nyte whos kept very style and sakrit in washing the body and performing there ushill serimyoney with...the preastes...[the] body whass taking out in the Garding Closte to the rum that he Dyde in whar thar whos A tent piched belonning to his friend Mr Salt which whos formerly giving to him and never taking to any whars as a toking of his only friend Mr Salt as hea never forgot always of talking of him till the Day of hiss Deth." Coffin "could not forbeare spelling a tear or two for my old friend and master." The Ras had ruled for 28 years.[28]

Almost before he was buried, rioting broke out, as the contest for succession began. Pearce and Coffin were nearly killed by some soldiers of Subagadis, the man whom Salt had judged so intelligent and capable that he would probably succeed the old Ras, as, eventually, he did. After Subagadis himself rescued them, they fled in different directions, losing touch for more than a year. When they met, Pearce persuaded Coffin to leave Abyssinia with him, though it would be no easy thing for them to get away with their lives. Back with his family, Coffin's heart misgave him, and he sent Pearce a message that it was "nothing but madness". Pearce determined to go alone and when Salt's letter and passport arrived, fled under cover of darkness, with his wife Tringo and her little servant, and made a slow way to Suez, where he learnt to his "severe mortification" that Salt was not at Cairo.

Two gentlemen were staying in the Consulate, the Reverend William Jowett, travelling to sell Bibles to the Egyptians, and a tourist called John Fuller. They were sitting after dinner on 24 January, when they heard a voice in the court, loudly demanding to see Mr Salt. The Italian servant ran in, "begging us to interpret the meaning of the stranger, whose vehemence seemed to have thrown him into great alarm; and we ourselves were a little surprised, when we saw him followed in by a man of very wild appearance, whose figure in the dusk looked almost gigantic. His head was covered with close curling hair, his chin with a short tufted beard, and his nose flattened to his face gave a most ferocious character to his aspect. His legs and arms were bare; the remainder of his person was covered with a flowing white drapery, over which was thrown the skin of some wild animal. A short sword hung by his side, a small round shield over one shoulder, and he brandished a spear in his hand, while he attempted with impatient gestures to explain his meaning to the astonished Italian."[29] Salt must have spoken often and warmly of him, for Jowett said at once, "Is not your name Pearce?" and told the servant to assign him a room.

When Fuller and Jowett later paid him a visit they found the floor strewed with Abyssinian arms and curiosities, including a civet cat in a cage.

Tringo, "though of a deep copper complexion and though worn down by the fatigues of a long and perilous journey, retained some traces of beauty, which joined to an air of deep melancholy gave her altogether a very interesting appearance." She sat cross-legged on a mat; crouching, half hidden behind her, was her servant, a "little woolly-haired half-naked girl, called Cullum, who seemed full of fun and gaiety, and delighted with the novelty of the scene."

Pearce soon became "quite uneasy, not knowing how to proceed to my master; I was so much afflicted that I could not sleep." Jowett, going to Upper Egypt with Fuller, offered to employ Pearce and, though Tringo wept bitterly at being abandoned, she was persuaded to stay in the care of Salt's women servants.

Pearce and Fuller put on Turkish dress. Fuller did not "recommend its adoption, except in those places where the prejudices of the people render it necessary"; and, putting his finger on the unadmitted motive of many a European, "although the superior dignity and grace which it gives to the figure may flatter the personal vanity of the wearer, its cumbrousness will constantly check his activity, and multiply the temptations to indolence which in a hot country are always sufficiently abundant. There is one circumstance, however," he added, less straight-faced, "which may recommend it to some travellers; — the change of appearance effected by the resumption of Frank costume is so complete, that it will enable them, on their return to Europe, safely to avoid noticing those persons with whom in the East they may have been connected by the ties of familiarity or obligation, but whom it may not be agreeable to recognise in more polite countries." Pearce and Jowett in one *cangia*, Fuller in a second, set sail on February 6.

Three days later, going ashore, they saw walking towards them a man "of colossal size, dressed in handsome Turkish clothes, and with a fine flowing beard." Belzoni invited them aboard his boat and showed them the antiquities with which it was laden. Pearce, as nobody introduced him, withdrew, regretting being unable to speak to Sarah. "I greatly wished to pay my respects to her, she being the first Englishwoman I had seen for a great many years." But Belzoni, inquiring about this "person of a strange appearance", called him back and showed him the utmost kindness. "If ever pity and compassion were shewn to a traveller, I received them…from these benevolent persons. Mrs Belzoni was at a loss what to put before me to eat, and indeed I was so much at a loss for English, that I could neither inform her, nor express my gratitude as my heart wished." When he left, Sarah followed him, "and stood with me on the ancient stone they had brought [Bankes' obelisk!], and promised, though she had no particular business at Mr Salt's house, to go thither purposely to see Tringo and console her, and have something killed for her by a Christian before her face": one of Tringo's chief

170

fears was of having to eat of meat killed by a Mohammedan. Pearce was quite overcome, "wishing that my voyage could have been with beings so humane and affectionate to a fellow-traveller". The Belzonis often said: "We know what it is to travel; every one is for himself in this part of the world, but we think it our duty to help others when it is in our power."[30]

At Aswan, Jowett turned back — having met with little success selling Bibles in Egypt, he expected none in Nubia — and Fuller's dragoman refused to go further south. When Pearce offered to take his place, Fuller gladly accepted his services, "having had many opportunities during our voyage of learning their value".

Hiring camels, they rode into Nubia, and the following day, 10 March, saw some tents pitched near the temple of Kalabsha, on the other side of the Nile. They fired pistols, and a boat came to ferry them over. From one of the tents Salt emerged, wan and weak, to receive them. There must have been an affecting reunion between Pearce and Salt, but Fuller says nothing of it. Pearce's journal comes to an abrupt end on 28 February at Luxor, but he recorded the occasion in stone, on the pylon of the temple: "It is here I met H Salt Esqr after being left by him on his service to Abyssinia the last time May 1810 (10) March 1819."

13

"If Friends Thus Traduce Me"

HOWEVER much he may have longed to stay with Salt, Pearce was committed for the moment to Fuller, and they continued upriver, transferring to a boat at Deir. Captain Foskett, overtaking them, gave them a tow. At Abu Simbel the entrance to the temple was already almost choked with sand and, suffering the usual exhaustion from the enervating heat of the interior, they were unable to stay within for more than three-quarters of an hour.

On 21 March they anchored at Wadi Halfa by a small flotilla "belonging to to Mr Bankes, Mr Beechey and Mr Hyde". The failure of their expedition persuaded Fuller to abandon his plan to go further south and the entire fleet left Wadi Halfa three days later. The Bankes party settled in again at Abu Simbel, but Fuller and Pearce sailed north, to land on Philae on the evening of 30 March. Pearce, less enthralled by antiquities than Fuller, occupied his time and his knife in carving the inscriptions that were, more than 170 years later, to arouse such curiosity in two of his countrywomen that they set forth on the long and fascinating journey that culminated in this book:

> N Pearce
> Five months from Addwar in Abyssinia,
> after being in that Country
> 14 years in the service of the Earl of Mountnorris and H SALT Esq
> March XXXI MDCCCXIX

They reached Cairo on April 29. After a few days in separate quarantine, for the plague had begun, they joined Baron Sack, Jowett and Salt, who had more or less recovered from his illness. The party was "occasionally enlivened by Belzoni...when in good spirits a most agreeable companion".[1] On 12 May he came to settle his accounts with Salt, who, finding a balance owing of £169, made it up to £200. He also went over his collection with him and gave him everything "I could spare, which he gratefully accepted, and — as Mr Fuller...can declare — seemed quite a satisfied man, and expressed a hope in parting that we should continue friends." But "the Alexandrian air brought on his fever again, for there he once more began to talk of my taking all the merit to myself of his discoveries, &c., and on my going down to Alexandria broke out, why or wherefore I know not, into an open rupture."[2]

Belzoni's discontent was fuelled by the frustrations of his lawsuit against Drovetti. Still enraged by the affair of the obelisk, despite having ceded it to Bankes, he persisted, Belzoni told Bankes, "in his claims of the obelisk, which he has no more right than the Governor of Siberia." The French judge had demanded 1,200 dollars for taking depositions at Thebes about the attack; when the French consul ruled that, as the accused were not French subjects, but Piedmontese, Belzoni could only obtain redress in Turin, his sense that he was unjustly treated may have reawakened his 'fever' against Salt — but he neglects to mention either that he quarrelled with the Consul or that, even after that, Salt continued to do "all I could to serve him, and, as the last act of friendship, paid for him all the expenses of his lawsuit."[3]

* *

After an attempt to travel to the Holy Land, aborted by their being robbed on the second night out, Fuller and Jowett retired again into quarantine. Incarceration in the Consulate had its compensations: it was "a very comfortable prison. We had a house with spacious and cool apartments, a shady garden arranged in the English style, a library well stored with books, an endless variety of drawings, and sketches, a large collection of Egyptian antiquities; and though last, not least in our esteem, an excellent billiard table."

Bankes and his companions journeyed slowly to Luxor, from where he wrote on 1 June, that the best news a letter from Salt had brought was of "an amendment in your health, I should hope that the uniform habits of life and quiet of a quarantine might contribute materially towards completely reestablishing it...you will be more than ever sensible of the value of your garden though it be no longer the promenade of any fair two legged creatures besides the Crane and the Peacock. By the by, I am bringing a companion...a very fine young ostrich (which I got in Nubia) though I am afraid that he will hardly be trusted among your shrubs...I think you will think your court a better place for him. This is the only inhabitant of our *cangia* that you are unacquainted with, so I speak of him first."[4]

Soon after quarantine was lifted on St John's Day, 24 June, Bankes and Beechey reached Cairo, with the unfortunate ostrich. His keepers, "observing his great propensity to hard substances, mistook unfortunately for his natural and ordinary diet things which were only the objects of his luxury". His daily diet was a little corn and nails, with an occasional knife or razor, or a few buttons, pulled from the coats of his attendants. "This metallic system did not however succeed; the poor bird drooped gradually, his strength just lasted him to walk with a stately step into the court of the consulate, and he died in about an hour afterwards." His post mortem found most of the iron to be dissolved, the immediate cause of death being a three- to four-inch nail which had perforated his stomach and mortified.[5]

The days grew intensely hot. Even by excluding all light and air in the daytime, the temperature in the house could not be kept lower than 84°, while outside the thermometer "flew up directly to 105° or 110°...We accommodated our hours to the climate and the general manners of the inhabitants: Rose at four o'clock, and rode out for an hour or two before sunrise, dined in the middle of the day, and then slept or reposed for two or three hours. After this we walked out or paid visits, supped soon after sunset, and went to bed about midnight."[6] This, except that it does not include the hours devoted to duties and a voluminous correspondence, is probably a fair account of how the Consul also spent his time.

Part of his correspondence resulted from, at last towards the end of May, receiving a response to his letter to Hamilton of 11 months earlier, asking his advice about his collection — but it was hardly a welcome one. He had spoken warmly in the letter of the "great excellence" of Egyptian art, from which the Greeks had "borrowed the rudiments, if not more". Should he have been more cautious in his appraisal of the artistic merit of Egyptian sculpture? His opinion was ahead of his time, and even to infer that his collection might be comparable to the Greek and Roman artefacts in the Museum probably did him no good with the Classically-educated Trustees.

If it was a tactical mistake, he made a much worse one. He quite properly appended an inventory, "a rough list from which you may form some slight idea of the value of the Collection; all the minor articles, which are very numerous, not being included, though many of them are singularly curious as illustrating the arts of the country. Opposite the chief articles I have put a rough calculation of their *supposed* value; but in this I am liable to be *much mistaken*, as I do not at all know how such antiquities might sell: indeed *such* as these have never been seen in Europe." How could such cautiously named prices be construed as positive demands, particularly as in his accompanying letter he said so clearly, "As to the *value,* I would most willingly leave *that* to yourself, or any other persons the Government might appoint to be settled after the arrival of the articles in England."[7]

How Salt arrived at his prices is unknown, but certainly not entirely by himself. Halls thought some of the 'foreign Savants' in Egypt advised him. Forbin had given him good reason to be sanguine, and there was a fellow collector who valued his own acquisitions very highly indeed — M Drovetti. He and Salt, despite their necessary political rivalry, at times exchanged artefacts. Who more likely to suggest or encourage generous values for another's collection, when these could only serve to enhance his own (as both he and Salt considered) even finer one? It is pleasant to fancy the two gentlemen agreeably appraising the antiquities together over a glass or two of good French wine.

Unfortunately, though Salt's letter was meant only for Hamilton, seeking his disinterested opinion and advice, as a wise and experienced friend, Hamilton most unwisely, and one must say thoughtlessly, passed it to Sir Joseph. There should have been no harm in that. But Hamilton also sent the list, and Banks chose to assume that the prices named, by Salt's careful admission possibly mistaken, superseded his offer to accept an independent valuation. The result was disastrous.

Halls was enraged on his friend's behalf. Banks, who had been "the chief adviser of Mr Salt as to forming a Collection, now became the loudest in his condemnation; and from the great weight he possessed with many influential persons, excited for a time no small degree of prejudice against his former protégé." Banks treated the list as a public document, and "not being very conversant in matters of art, and having no notion either of the great merit of Egyptian sculpture or of its *value*, he appears, without waiting for explanation, to have formed a very rash judgement upon the whole affair, and to have *acted* with equal precipitancy. But he was then growing old, and his temper, which was at no time distinguished by suavity, had become soured by infirmity. He has been well characterised as a 'Man of a *word* and a *blow*'; and, in the instance in question, the blow seems to have taken precedence."[8] Halls adds cuttingly that though Banks was a man of good general abilities, and "somewhat distinguished" in science and natural history, "his knowledge in the Fine Arts was extremely limited; and yet on these subjects, as well as on those he really did understand, his authority seems to have been regarded as paramount."

Banks wrote Salt a decidedly cool letter: "Though in truth we are here much satisfied with the Memnon, and consider it as a *chef-d'oeuvre* of Egyptian sculpture; yet we have not placed that statue among the works of *Fine Art*. It stands in the Egyptian Rooms. Whether any statue that has been found in Egypt can be brought into competition with the grand works of the Townley Gallery remains to be proved; unless however they really are so, the prices you have set upon your acquisitions are very unlikely to be realised in Europe." The collections of Greek and Roman art were housed in the Townley annexe to the Museum. The Egyptian Rooms, also in the Townley Gallery, in Banks' opinion, did not contain 'grand works'.

"I cannot help being sorry," he continued, having cut the Memnon down to size, "that you have abandoned your original intention of placing yourself *in the hands of the public*. I dare not, however, offer you any advice on the matter, as though I differ entirely from you in estimating the gain you are likely to make by the sale of what you have procured, *in Europe,* you may have prospects which are utterly unknown to me." His harshness was somewhat softened by his final paragraph: "I have written very freely on what I consider as a very great miscalculation of yours; but I beg you to be assured, that no miscalculation can alter the good opinion I have always entertained of you, or change the sincere regard with which I sign myself Your faithful servant and well-wisher, Joseph Banks."[9]

Hamilton wrote: "The enclosed from Sir Joseph Banks will explain to you, more fully than I need enter upon the subject, the views entertained at the Museum respecting your proposals for their taking the lead in the farther progress of your antiquarian speculations. I can only unite with Sir Joseph in recommending you not to dip too deep in search of hidden treasures of Egyptian sculpture, for in these economical times, John Bull may be easily induced to withold his purse-strings, even at the risk of losing the unique monuments which you have discovered."[10]

Neither letter, though discouraging, could really alert Salt to the storm he had unloosed on his head. The 'unfortunate list' was passed around, and "poor Salt was accused unheard of being a dealer, a Jew, *a second Lord Elgin.*" It was even suggested by some that he should forfeit his Consulship. Very hard, comments Halls, since he had taken a considerable risk with money entirely his own, no part being of his Consular salary, and when "the only sin with which he was charged amounted to nothing more than his having stated *privately* some very *vague* calculation as to what he had good reason to suppose might be the value of his Collection."[11]

The reference to Salt as a 'second Lord Elgin' was relevant, not only because of the parallels to be drawn, but also because the aftermath of the Elgin controversy provided a very powerful reason for the Museum Trustees to be unwilling to lay out money on the collections of gentlemen in the foreign service.[12]

The public outcry was not likely to be soon forgotten, either by the public or the Trustees of the British Museum.

* *

Two weeks before he knew the trouble he was in Salt had written to Hamilton that he had for now ceased collecting, as he could not afford it, but would send what he had to the Museum, "and shall be content to receive whatever may be deemed a modest recompense. I have no doubt, that in our fit of enthusiasm we have greatly exaggerated the value of these remains, but still they are such as will do honour to any Collection." He hoped to replace the money he had spent, which "with interest, will amount to something more than three thousand pounds." Bingham Richards, a long-time friend, now Salt's man of business in England, estimated that the cost, in principal and interest foregone, was nearer £4,000.

As transport and insurance would be very expensive, Salt asked Hamilton to obtain him an order from the Admiralty to the Admiral at Malta to assist, "for though I know him very well, yet it would be pleasanter, both to him and to myself, to have it done by an order from home" — the Consul did not like to presume on his status. For the first time, he named a price: "If the Museum would give me £4,000 and take the risk on themselves, I would gladly send them all I have. In remains of sculpture in *wood*, in mummies of animals and birds, in vases, as well as papyri, independent of the statues and fragments of statues, I will venture to say it is the best Collection ever made, except that of Monsieur Drovetti's, and he would not part with his for £10,000."[13]

It was not until he received what must have been a very plain-spoken missive from Mountnorris that Salt truly grasped the trouble he was in, and even then at first made light of it. "...I should be much inclined to smile at the construction which has been put upon my unfortunate letter and list, and which it seems has gone nigh to stamp me with the character of a Jew. As you, however, seem to think the matter of real importance, I will endeavour to throw a little light on the affair."[14] He asked the Earl to show his explanation to Sir Joseph Banks and Yorke; his uneasiness must have increased, for on the same day he wrote to them also.

He told Banks that he felt "most exceedingly hurt and distressed at my meaning, expressed in a letter to Mr Hamilton, having been so completely misunderstood. It was undoubtedly my own fault...in enclosing, at the same time I asked his advice about offering my Collection to Government *at their own valuation*, a foolish list of my private estimation of the value of the different articles, which list, however, I by no means wished to set up as a standard for the Government to go by."

To prevent, he continued, any future misunderstanding, "I now take the liberty of offering, through you, my *whole* Collection to the British Museum...without any condition whatever, and shall feel a great pride hereafter in rendering it complete." Should the Trustees decide to reimburse him, in whole or in part, his heavy expenses, he would "receive it as an obligation, or otherwise shall rest perfectly satisfied in the idea that my services in this respect may not be ultimately overlooked by the Government." He begged Banks to make his proposal known to the Trustees, and "with your usual kindness to explain away any disadvantageous impression as to my intentions with regard to this Collection which may have gone abroad."

He mentioned the terms of his agreement about the alabaster sarcophagus with Belzoni, who had "estimated its value at something preposterous" — that it should be offered to the British Museum within three years of April 1818 at a fair valuation, and that Belzoni should receive half of any amount in excess of £2,000 which it might fetch. It was therefore necessary to have a separate valuation of it made "by any persons the Trustees may appoint, for the sake of getting rid of this claim. As far as I myself am concerned, I wish the sarcophagus to be considered as being, with the rest of the Collection, at your disposition."[15]

To Yorke, he again regretted the "foolish list", never intended as a guide to any valuers. He now felt his ideas had been over-enthusiastic, but it must "be observed in my excuse, that in Egypt the mania was at that time so strong that I had been offered by Monsieur Drovetti (through Mr Bankes) ten thousand dollars for the sarcophagus — any price I pleased for a small and entire statue, for the King of France, by the Count de Forbin — prices not likely to be given in England — all which I rejected, as determining not to place myself in the light of a dealer."[16]

Salt avowed generously to Mountnorris that he did not blame Hamilton — to whom "I am most grateful…for his many acts of kindness, and feel satisfied that I have not a better friend in the world" — but himself, for sending "the Christie-like sort of list, as you term it, without sufficient explanation."[17] Hamilton was less complaisant about his part in the sorry affair than the victim, writing to Mountnorris, "[I] most willingly take upon myself any share of the blame arising from the incautious manner of communicating his former notices respecting his Collection of antiques. I ought certainly to have suppressed the catalogue, as it was priced, but as it was referred to in the body of the letter, I let it pass without discrimination."[18] Indeed.

That such a close friend as Mountnorris could so misconstrue him was pain enough to Salt, but there were other hurtful remarks in his letter — recurring resentment that his protegé should collect for any but himself, now coupled with a suspicion, having seen the 'infamous list', that *his* statues were being offered to his country. On 1 June, Salt wearily took up his pen again: "I cannot let [this packet] go, though fatigued to death with writing without giving you a few lines in answer to the more private parts of your letter. There is one paragraph totally unworthy of you and which has given me real pain — I can forgive such unjust suspicions but they are not easily forgot. I must have been a rascal indeed if I could offer for disposal to one what belonged to another."

He explained carefully that the two best of his 'lion-headed ladies' were destined for Mountnorris, the next two for the Museum. A fifth he had given to Belzoni, who sold it to Baron Sack for £105, a sixth went to Drovetti in return for "some little things he gave me" and two more had been given the Pasha's interpreter, who sent them to the Emperor of Austria, "where they made a great noise…Besides I am neither dealer nor Jew as you will ultimately find. If friends thus traduce me what must I expect from enemies. But I have done; I hope and believe from the general *kind* tenor of your letter that you did not intend offence."

One often gets the impression that the Earl behaved to Salt like a fond but domineering elder brother, upon whom the younger, goaded too far, will occasionally turn. Salt had been urged by Mountnorris to produce a publication, but,

> you must allow me to be my own master on that point...and if any thing had been wanting to deter me from it, it would have been your last letter. I have done a good deal and hope to do more, but if I ever publish it will be in my own way and at my leisure. I want not profit — I want not the ordinary fame that attends modern publication but I wish to leave something behind me that may deservedly perpetuate my name. This is not to be done in a hurry — neither my time nor my occupations are my own — and the letter writing I have intra my official duties pretty fully occupies my time. I shall when opportunity arises occasionally send my drawings to England but certainly not to be published till I retire. You are in the thick Vortex of life and attribute more value than it deserves to the momentary applause of the day. To make a work on Egypt better than Mr Hamilton's will not be an easy task whoever undertakes it and as to all the ephemeral productions of Light — Legh — Dr Richardson — and all the rest of the travelling authors who — as the Indian expresses it — 'take walk — make book' — I envy them not their fame.
>
> Neither life nor its concommitant enjoyments have any strong hold upon me — I have suffered too deeply and seen too much of the vanity and uncertainty of it ever to make myself a slave to its whims. You advise me not to ride the high horse — but I shall continue to go on mounted as I always have been and whether it be with an income of £500 a year or one — my feelings and actions will not change. As long as I can keep at peace in my own breast I am satisfied.

After various digressions, Salt returned to the sore again.

> I have given [Belzoni] a note to you that you may see what a strange being it is. Why should I object to his copying and publishing — it was he that made the discovery though with my money — and surely he deserves to be remunerated. I repeat to you again I am not a Jew — nor have I ever been the slave of Mammon...I will sacrifice any thing if you will but let me live in quiet — and if I cannot obtain what I seek in any other way, I will close my commerce with mankind, by giving up, at once, all but my official correspondence...[19]

When Salt's letters reached England, Hamilton, Yorke and Mountnorris all wrote to Sir Joseph urging him to ensure that the Museum obtained the collection. Feeling that Salt had fully exculpated himself from the accusation "which we both thought he deserved" Mountnorris trusted that "this explanation will restore Salt to your esteem, which I know he values above every thing." He added that he had shown some small statues and bas reliefs Salt had sent him to the sculptor Francis Chantrey, "who without hesitation pronounced that the Greeks were evidently the pupils of the Egyptians, and that he could trace it from the works I showed him to the Athenian works of Phidias. I cannot put down the Egyptians as Barbarians, or consider their Statues as Curiosities only for the Antiquary."[20]

Yorke wrote with his customary warm enthusiasm, "...although '*a rigid oeconomy* is so much the *order of the day*', I cannot help hoping that the House of Commons may be induced to supply the Museum with adequate funds...to enable the Trustees to secure for the British nation the most important and curious of the antiquities which have been obtained by Mr Salt...It would be an indelible disgrace if such articles as these were either permitted to find their way to any foreign museum, or were to become a *ruinous charge* and a *subject of regret* and mortification to those who have had the Spirit, the Intelligence, and the Perseverance to obtain them. Surely this can never be; and, even should the House of Commons prove so tasteless and supine, I trust the Prince Regent will never suffer so great a Blemish to fall on the National Honour. In any case, I trust that high-spirited individuals enough may be found to rescue their country from such a disgrace: should it be necessary to form any subscription for this purpose, and to defray Mr Salt's Expenses and fair loss on his Capital, I for one will very readily (though not rich) and cheerfully deposit my proportion."[21]

Only Banks was grudging in withdrawing his disapproval. "Mr Salt wishes to discharge from your mind, as well as from mine and others of his friends, the opinions we entertained on perusing his schedule of valuation of his Egyptian Collection," he wrote to Yorke. "He has certainly removed it, which is a good measure on his part; but he does not appear to me to establish on any good ground his reasons for having originally sent it."[22]

Nor had he put the list out of his mind when he wrote to Mountnorris, enclosing the letters from Yorke and Hamilton ("both of whom are ardent well-wishers to Salt"). "One of Salt's statues has arrived: it is the one he values at £800; consequently, in his opinion, the best he has." This was the 'Jupiter Ammon'.[23]

Knowing he could hear nothing of the reaction to his explanations for many months, Salt had to carry on his everyday life, but, however much occupied with friends or duties, there must have been a constant apprehension at the back of his mind, which can have done both his easily depressed spirits and his health no good.

He took Fuller one evening in Ramadan to visit the Pasha at Shubra. Fuller thought he "had not the dignity either of appearance or manner which generally belongs to a Turk of high rank. He talked with great freedom, seemed fond of treating every topic en bagatelle, and sometimes pushed back his turban from off his forehead, and gave himself up to an unconstrained fit of laughter." Fuller had a rare view of the Pasha at ease in his country retreat with a man he liked and trusted. Salt's attitude to Mehemet Ali, however, even if he felt a personal liking, was, judging both from his official and his private comments, a constant wariness of his ambitions and a frequent disapproval of his actions.

As was his custom in the hottest season, the Pasha went down to Alexandria. About the middle of August Salt and Beechey followed him and the rest of the party gradually dispersed. Fuller and Baron Sack departed together for the Holy Land, Hyde left for Sinai. Bankes lingered in Cairo, unwilling to tear himself away from the conversation of Pearce, whom Salt had appointed major domo of the Cairo Consulate, where he proceeded to carry out his duties with his usual combination of competence, zeal, plain speaking and a ferocious rectitude daunting to any hopes of the consular servants to cheat him. Salt noted, with affectionate amusement, that he had "completely adopted the character of a feudal follower — whatever I command he is ready to execute; but nothing can induce him to express a wish of his own, his only answer to any proposition made by the travellers here, being 'If Mr Salt wishes it, well and good; if not, I can't think of it', or some such downright phrase."[24]

In his care for his master's interests, Pearce did not spare himself. Salt wrote on 1 September, rallying his steward: "I am sorry that you did not apply to Mr Walmas for money, as I mentioned to you in my last, and that in consequence you have been put to some inconvenience, but hope this letter will arrive in time to set all to rights…I suppose, by your having reduced yourself to three, and *even two piastres a day*, that you have some intention of following up the system of the Frenchman with his horse, who had just brought it to live upon one oat a day, when it died. If you have particular pleasure in this, it is all very well; but I shall feel perfectly satisfied if you do not exceed two hundred piastres a month, which is the sum I meant to allot you for your household expenses. I suppose Turinga, on your late plan, does not by this time weigh more than ten pounds, and Cullum not more than five. As for yourself, I imagine, what with starving and medicine, that you are reduced to a reasonable size; but at least you ought, though it may agree with you, to have some compassion on the women."[25]

When Bankes finally departed from Egypt, he left Salt with a legacy to keep him in mind for years to come. The obelisk lay at Alexandria but its pedestal still languished on a sandbank near Philae, and an even weightier problem had been added. On his way back from Nubia, at Maharraka, Bankes had spotted a twelve-foot square, three-stepped granite platform he thought would form a splendid base for his obelisk. He took it to be an obelisk pedestal, but modern opinion is that it was one of the detached solar altars often found near temples. Whatever it was, it was unquestionably exceedingly heavy and awkward to move.

14

Romance and Diplomacy

IN MAY 1819, Salt wrote nostalgically to Mary Halls of the "fireside coteries" of friends and family they used to enjoy in England. "Such delights as these, which after all form the chief charm of existence, are utterly unknown in this blessed land, where neither morning nor evening is ever ushered in with the glad countenance of a friend, but all is outward courtesy, too generally and too justly mingled with contempt for one's company." At present, however, the plague was keeping away "a great number of our 'enemies', for that designation will much better suit the generality of our acquaintance than that of friends."[1]

The cry of loneliness and frustration might have risen from any overseas posting, and the solution is often the one that Salt had hinted at to Mountnorris, in another fit of depression the previous year: "The greatest want however which I feel is that of a wife — my affections are strong and I want objects around me whom I could love — had I children I should be happy — but to stagnate at a distance from all literature, arts, knowledge, delicacy or taste...is...a punishment almost sufficient to drive one mad. But think what we will of it, the wheel must go round."[2]

Once Mary of Birmingham, whom he had wooed in 1815, had finally decided never to join him in Egypt, Salt had little opportunity of meeting a companion of "delicacy and taste" with whom to share his life. But it is not to be expected that a man of Salt's warm feelings for women would live an entirely celibate existence. By the nature of such relationships, it is unlikely that any record would survive. Yet we have found one piece of second or even third-hand gossip, a few sentences in letters from Salt himself, an article based on private (and untraced) Consular papers, Salt's will, and a missionary record.

In 1824, James Burton's friend, Greenough, quoting Charles Sheffield, one of Burton's entourage in Egypt, noted, "Salt had a slave girl whom he got with child and then made her over to a Mussulman, abandoning his progeny."[3] Knowing Salt's attitude to slavery, it is most improbable he would keep a slave in his household; but there might have been no way of confuting or explaining this gossip, but for a letter from Salt.

On 1 September 1819, writing from Alexandria to Pearce, he requested, "Pray ask Osmeyn [sic] how Makhboube is going on and send me the particulars".[4] In 1934 Bryn Davis saw private Consular papers when researching an article on Salt. He commented on "the question of Salt's son by an Abyssinian woman called Mahbubeh who had run away from the Consulate ten years before (in about 1818) and had since been living with Osman, a kind of factotum who kept the servants' accounts for Salt."[5] It is difficult to be sure if 'Mahbubeh' is the mother or the child.

On 13 August 1825, Salt added a codicil to his will, leaving "two thousand five hundred dollars out of the proceeds of my house in Alexandria" to "the benefit of my reputed son in the hands of Osmeyn as a provision for him."[6] So the Mussulman to whom Salt "abandoned his progeny" was William Thomson, or Osman. Osman had married Burckhardt's Abyssinian slave and had, by 1820, a son called Ibrahim;[7] in his home, Salt's child would have young companions, and the oversight of a foster-father who, despite his enforced conversion to Islam, Salt probably felt could be trusted to instil Christian principles in his son.

When, after Salt's death, the Consulate was concerned with the child's affairs, the house cannot yet have been sold. Osman was requesting compensation for keeping the boy; this was finally assessed at two piastres a day. From May 1829, the child "was taken care of by some missionaries at Alexandria". The rest might have been silence — but, in 1851 a young man of 32, a silk reeler of Shinfain, calling himself Henry Salt and claiming Salt as his father, was married in the British Consulate in Beirut to Julia Karabetts, daughter of an Armenian bishop.[8]

* *

In August 1819 a letter arrived for Pearce from his brother Joseph, saying he would be very glad to see him in England — something Pearce, it seems, had doubted. Forwarding it from Alexandria, Beechey asked Pearce to send down to him by courier his cocked hat and feathers — "they are in one of the top drawers of my bedroom", where the servant had forgotten them. In Alexandria, he said, they missed the garden, "for there is no such thing here." He sent greetings to Tringo and, "Pray let me be kindly remembered to Osman and tell me who [?he] beats [?him] now at billiards." Beechey's execrable writing obscures the message here.[9]

Attacked by the dreaded opthalmia, Salt had to depend on Beechey to write his letters for a while. The first use he made of his recovered eyesight was to fall in love. Halls hints that he met the young lady in "interesting circumstances…which appear to have seized on the imagination and romantic turn of Mr Salt's mind, and to have greatly influenced his apparently hasty decision."[10] Mr Pensa was a respectable merchant from Leghorn with business affairs in Alexandria, who had brought with him his wife and two daughters, for the elder of whom, it seems, a marriage had been arranged — but one she found unacceptable. How Salt met and courted her we do not know, but the contemporary gossip was repeated by Martin de Tyrac, Comte de Marcellus, in his memoirs.

Marcellus, a young French diplomat, had been in the eastern Mediterranean for some years.[11] He reached Alexandria in the heat of July 1820, to be greeted by the *caquets de la ville* still eagerly repeating last year's scandal about the British Consul-General, by now probably well-embroidered by constant telling.

This was the story. A certain Austrian merchant of Alexandria had added a postscript to a letter to his correspondent in Leghorn suggesting that if he knew of any young woman having nothing to do in Europe, who was of a suitable age and in other ways matched his tastes, he would be glad to receive her. Soon there arrived an Italian girl who more than met his most ambitious demands — a 17-year-old Venus who so impressed him that he wanted to wed her as soon as she had overcome the fatigues of the journey. Her views were apparently not consulted, but, before the marriage could take place, the British Consul-General, "passing under the window of the charming Italian, was so struck by her beauty that he declared himself the rival of the Austrian, and himself made her a proposal of marriage which was promptly accepted."

The merchant, understandably, "threw out fire and flames, but in the Orient what is an angry man's anger against the authority of a Consul-General?" The complainant went to the Austrian Consulate and the question was treated as one of commercial principle:

1. Codes and treaties of commerce allowed Paul to take over the merchandise sent to Nicholas and landed on consignment — until it is in the shop.

2. However, Paul must not dispossess Nicholas of the value of his investment.

It was a serious matter. There was a long exchange of notes between the Austrian and English chancelleries, and finally a third chancellery was chosen to arbitrate. The decision was that the article in question should be taken by the English Consul-General, but that he be obliged to reimburse all the expenses of shipment from Leghorn, disembarkation fees at Alexandria and other fees occasioned by importation of the article. Judgement was strictly executed. "And that," wrote Marcellus, "was what happened in 1819 in the town of Cleopatra."[12]

However it was, Salt's instant attraction may have been that to him the girl bore a marked resemblance to Mary of Birmingham. There were few European ladies of suitable status and character in Egypt and those who were came and went like "birds of passage", as Halls commented, so that a man "must be sudden in his proceedings and determination, or the prize will surely elude his grasp".[13] And to the parents of the pretty young woman (whose first name no one ever mentions), the British Consul-General must have seemed a far better catch than the one they had planned. Salt told Mountnorris that he had met a young lady of Leghorn who so strongly took his fancy that he was "induced to enter into holy bands of matrimony (to which I was perhaps much inclined by the desire of rescuing her from a most distressing situation into which her friends had involved her)."[14] It was irresistibly romantic.

The courtship was brief. On 19 September, Salt wrote to Pearce in Cairo that he was "on the point of being *married*" to a young and very amiable lady. He urged Pearce to do all he could to put the house and especially the garden in order for her arrival, "but," he added, "I hope to arrange every thing comfortably without too much change."[15]

The marriage was celebrated with a public dinner in Peter Lee's garden, probably on 10 October 1819, with Beechey and Bankes, on the eve of their departure, in attendance. On 11 October, Bankes wrote a final note to Pearce, saying that he had given Mrs Salt diamond earrings as a wedding present and that he expected Pearce was "very impatient to see Mr Salt's Bride, she is very young and very pretty."[16]

A few days later Beechey and Bankes set sail from Egypt: the one, though not perhaps the best of secretaries, a man of an agreeable disposition with some excellent qualities, who had shared many experiences with Salt in the last three years; the other, a man in whose entertaining and cultured company Salt had revelled. The departure of the Belzonis (considerably more encumbered with baggage than on their arrival four years earlier) the previous month, though apparently in friendship, was, in time, to produce further trouble.

Despite the speed of his courtship, Salt was never to regret his choice of bride. Peter Lee's wife, Emma, told Halls that there never existed a happier marriage or a more devotedly attached couple. But from the first, a shadow hung over them. Though Salt was only 39, and "a fine-looking man capable of partaking in all the enjoyments of life", on the very day of his wedding he was struck down with a bout of the illness which continued to dog him for the rest of his life, and on this occasion brought him "to the verge of the grave". To help him recover, an immediate change of air was recommended, and Salt and his bride set out by sea for Cairo. Their boat was driven back at Aboukir and they had to wait for the Governor of Alexandria's carriage to be sent to carry them to Rosetta, nor could they go on until a surgeon came from Cairo to accompany them. Salt was in such pain that he could only travel for part of each day and his agonies were followed by fainting fits. In Cairo, he lay in this dreadful state for two months, his life given over to the attentions of the doctors. His young wife must have been terrified, constantly fearing that this near stranger who was her husband would die before she ever came to know him. It was not until January 1820 that he gradually began to recover his strength and spirits. His wife was always beside him, and he told friends that her unceasing care did more to restore his health than any of the doctor's medicines.[17]

A wedding present awaited Mrs Salt in Cairo, from the Sultana, chief wife of the Pasha: five cashmere shawls, "a splendid present, if the high price, even in this country, as well as the exquisite beauty of the shawls, is considered."[18]

The weather that January was exceptionally fine, Pearce had heeded Salt's instructions about the garden, which was in "high beauty", and the close of the carnival season was particularly gay. Salt's own pleasure in weather, garden and gaiety were doubled by seeing his wife's happiness. A great cloud must have lifted from her. Her piano stood in the *sala* and one can imagine their evenings together with the music he had missed for so long.

In February, hearing that a collection of his antiquities awaiting a ship at Rosetta was in jeopardy, Salt dispatched Pearce to deal with the problem. On 2 March he wrote, "I am happy to find that you have succeeded in saving my antiquities from the imminent danger they ran of going to the bottom of the Nile," and suggested that Pearce await the expected ship in Alexandria, to accompany the collection to England. The impediment to Pearce's return even to visit his own country was that, on the Admiralty registers, he was still marked as a deserter, and therefore in danger of being seized back into the Navy. Salt now assured him that "proper measures have been taken to set *all right*". Some very eminent people had concerned themselves in the matter. Charles Yorke, a former First Lord of the Admiralty, wrote to Sir Joseph Banks, "I trust there will be no difficulty in getting the Broad R [for Renegade] taken from his name at the Navy Board. I shall be glad to intervene if necessary."[19]

In fact, Pearce was soon back in Cairo, for in March Salt fell ill again and had need of him. This time an attack of dysentery complicated his chronic pains and reduced him to "a mere skeleton". The Pasha was so concerned that he offered the Salts his house on the bank of the Nile in Old Cairo, and here Salt was again restored to health. But for weeks a lethargy hung over him which deterred him from any exertion and even from his normal correspondence with friends and family. During his illness, without Beechey's help, and despite Pearce's manful efforts to deal with them, applications for the Consul's attention mounted up, worrying him more and more, but it was not until June, at last on the way to recovery, that he returned to the Consular house.

During this time, tragedy had struck Pearce. Tringo had been ill for weeks, with bouts of vomiting, but her most incurable ailment was homesickness. Fuller says, "of all the slaves brought to Cairo, the Abyssinians alone seem to be melancholy and to regret their native country; they have a great sensibility of disposition, and almost all of them sooner or later fall victims to the *maladie du pays*", and in a footnote, "This was the case with Pearce's wife, Tringo."[20] Salt sympathised — "Poor Tringo's wish to be taken to Abyssinia is very characteristic of that attachment which the Abyssinians bear to their country: but you must be aware that it is a thing impossible." Pearce's life would almost certainly have been forfeit had he set foot in his old haunts. Salt was most concerned that all should be done for Tringo's comfort, instructing Pearce that he should put even such important guests as the family of Bokty, the Swedish Consul, in rooms other than the Consul's own, "on account of not disturbing poor Turinga". It seems the Pearces were either occupying the 'master suite' or accommodated close by. But a safe and comfortable dwelling and warm regard from the strangers she lived among were not enough. She died in early May 1820.

There was now nothing to keep Pearce from returning to England forever (though he seems to have entertained an idea of being employed to explore the interior of Africa in due course).[21] Salt wrote several letters recommending him to the protection of his influential friends: to Lord Belmore; to Yorke — "His sufferings have been great; but he has never ceased to maintain the high character of an Englishman; and I am glad to say that he carries home a journal that will do him credit in the eyes of all who know how to estimate a vivid narrative of facts"; to Sir Joseph Banks — "He is the bearer of a box of plants, partly collected by Mr Bankes and myself in Nubia, as also a few minerals collected by the late Mr Burckhardt." To Halls he sent a portrait of his wife, executed by his new secretary, Mr Santini — "not a very favourable likeness...neither so young nor so handsome as the original." Intended eventually for Bessy Morgan, the picture has not, it seems, survived. Salt could not resist a chance to enthuse about his darling — "My lady has a good deal of spirit and character, but tempered by a very excellent disposition...[I am] much happier in the state of matrimony than single...I hope that you also have gained by your change of condition"; Halls, then aged 43, had married, on 2 December 1819, Maria Anne Sellon, daughter of an eminent lawyer.

To Mountnorris, Salt wrote, "I am *very happy*, I can assure you...my wife is a very amiable girl, and we live very happily together".[22] All this enthusiasm rather suggests that Salt was consciously countering any criticism of the hastiness of his marriage to a very young lady. In fact, the only adverse comments on record are from William Hamilton. Hearing of the event from Mountnorris, he replied gloomily: "...an event for which — taking place in that country — I augur no good — for his health — finances — or Domestic Comfort."[23] But, as Halls (whose own wife was nearly 20 years younger than himself) remarks, "after all, a man ought to be left in these matters to his own discretion."[24] And the enthusiasm was not forced — Salt was truly enchanted by the lively Italian girl; he ended a letter to Halls with an exclamation which sounds, for once, like the sparkling young man of pre-Consular days: "What a *fine world it is*!"

But all Pearce's letters of introduction had to be added to, with tragic news. In late May, with £100 in his pocket from Salt, he and his valuable baggage had boarded a ship which was then detained for lack of sufficient cargo, and Peter Lee advised him to await a ship of Briggs and Co., and meanwhile live at less expense than aboard in "a commodious garden-house belonging to the Consul". Here he fell ill with a severe bilious fever. By the time, on 10 August, that Lee took a visiting East India Company doctor, Mr Henderson, to see him, he had been ill 15 days and was reduced to such a state of exhaustion that there seemed little hope of recovery. He was determined to bid farewell to Salt, after which, he said repeatedly, he should die content. Stubborn to the end, he managed to fulfil his wish. Salt arrived from Cairo later that day, and was able "to pay him those last attentions for which the important services he had rendered in Abyssinia, and a long and faithful attachment, had given him so just a title." He died in the early hours of 12 August, and was buried in the evening within the precincts of the Greek convent, "carried to the grave by six English sailors, which from his love to the Navy, in which he had served, he had always anxiously desired." Two English Consuls and many other "respectable persons" formed his cortege.[25]

The Navy deserter, the Abyssinian warrior, the Consular steward, was truly mourned by many friends. John Fuller wrote of him, "He was altogether an extraordinary character. Great warmth of temper, and an unbounded spirit of enterprise were the sources of all his errors. His good qualities were courage, activity, intelligence, and zeal in the service of his employers...I am happy to pay this tribute to the memory of a humble but most valued friend."[26]

Salt, who felt severely the loss of a friend with whom he had been through so much, concluded his obituary with words which would have pleased Pearce deeply: "He has left a brother and sisters who loved him...they will long cherish his memory; and it will forever be held in respect by all those who knew his sterling worth, and who admire an honest English heart joined to a true English spirit."[27]

In his will Pearce left his journals and papers to Salt, "for whom these facts were originally collected and that he may publish them in whatever form he thinks proper." Salt intended to edit and publish Pearce's adventures, but was never able to finish the task; at his own death, he left Pearce's and his own Abyssinian papers to Mountnorris, and eventually it was John Halls who prepared and published Pearce's story, in 1831.[28]

Pearce's other main bequest was that all his clothes and money not required to pay his funeral expenses ("if the civilised civilized world deem this not sufficient, let my funeral consist of Arabs, but at least be buried where Europeans in general are who die in this country") should go to "my dear girl Cullum", with his blessing and a recommendation to Reverend Jowett, "in whose family she may be employed and perhaps be a means of getting her back to her native country."[29]

* *

In early August, Marcellus, having enjoyed the gossip of Alexandria, had gone to Cairo to sight-see, and on his last day was invited to the English Consulate. As was the custom at this time of year, to avoid the great heat, he was invited at *point du jour*. Salt received him in his little museum and showed him his collection of papyri, statuettes, mummies and hieroglyphic inscriptions. He described the work he was doing at Thebes, which seemed to Marcellus to be largely concerned with contradicting the observations of Napoleon's savants in the *Description de l'Egypte*. "He exulted at the difference he found in some lines of a statue, and showed rather more of the malign jealousy of a rival, than the zeal of a real *ami des arts*." He had, of course, been specifically commissioned by the British Museum to compare the work of the savants with the originals, but can he really have been so impolite as to "exult" at French errors to a Frenchman who was his guest?

They were still examining the treasures when the sound of a song by Rossini played on the piano floated down to them. A pretty and accomplished voice took up the words. Salt seemed apologetic about the diversion. "It confuses me," he said, "such a European distraction in the middle of ancient things and so little related to Asia or Africa." But soon he took the Comte to the salon and introduced him to a young woman with a charming face framed by long blonde hair which fell to her bared shoulders, large blue eyes, a delicate complexion and a sweet expression. A sturdy little figure in a toilette more Italian than English completed the ensemble that was Madame Salt. Salt left them alone for a few minutes while he attended to another matter. "I must admit," said Marcellus, "to thinking that such a Helen would be worth the effort undergone in the pleasure of winning her."

She spoke with an unaffected vivacity in an accent reminiscent of the Florentine, and answered his rather impertinent questions with engaging frankness and enjoyment. "I am happy here — all the oriental ways and customs are so new that they amuse me and sometimes make me laugh to myself. I miss, it is true, the sweet language of my country — and I still don't know two words of English, but at eighteen one can accustom oneself to anything."

189

Salt returned and she served refreshments with a typical Italian grace, and then sang several songs for them. When the Comte left, Salt accompanied him out, and said to him quietly, "I was alone in Cairo...I wished to people my solitude, and liven my old age. You don't blame me like the others, do you?"

The Comte made haste to say that Salt's position seemed to excite envy rather than blame. And he waited 20 years before telling the world about his glimpse of Salt's personal life.[30]

* *

In autumn 1820, Salt decided he would like to show off his wife to his family and friends at home. He had been in post four years and he had personal affairs to attend to, including several things he wanted to publish — and he also needed to recover his health. Accordingly, in September he asked the Foreign Office for a short leave of absence. Mails were as slow as usual and it was not until December that Lord Castlereagh, the Foreign Minister, gave his permission, mentioning with enthusiasm Salt's "zealous endeavours to be useful in *all ways* to his country".[31] Castlereagh's recognition of his work — both consular and antiquarian — must have been gratifying, but the permission to leave arrived at a bad time, when considerable apprehension of a rupture with Russia made Salt feel his presence in Egypt was essential. He appears to have accepted the disappointment with his usual equanimity, though he still hoped at least to get to Leghorn to visit his wife's family.

Consular diplomatic duties were building up. He was asked by the East India Company to approach the Pasha about some unresolved trouble of three years earlier. A dozen ships had been sent to block the Imaum of Senaa's ports which, Salt told Mountnorris, "has occasioned a great sensation in the Red Sea...I hope, however, with prudence to be able to steer clear of a quarrel." Robert Wilson, a former surgeon in East India Company ships, witnessed part of the negotiations with the Pasha. Wilson, dressed in his "best Mamlouk attire and mounted on a horse belonging to the Consul, accompanied him in full uniform with all the Janizaries of the British Consulate."[32] After some conversation about Wilson's plans, the Pasha turned to Salt and the serious business in the dispatches from the Government of India "respecting the outrage committed against the English at Mocha". Having listened "with great temper", the Pasha discussed the situation with much acuteness. As he had 25,000 men in the vicinity, the Porte would expect him to give their allies support. The Porte was already looking jealously at English acquisitions in the Persian Gulf. He spoke slightingly of the Governor of Mocha — a renegade Italian–Muslim who had once been a menial in his employ. He would send dispatches to solve the problem. At a later audience with Wilson, the Pasha spoke of the prosperity brought to Egypt and the advantages that could accrue to the Abyssinians and Dongolese if their countries were united with Egypt.[33]

In June 1820, Salt had informed Joseph Planta at the Foreign Office that Mehemet Ali had sent his second son, Ismael, on a great expedition to extend his power fully into Nubia and beyond the Second Cataract. Salt feared the gossip about Egypt's intentions to the south, which he had picked up the previous year, was proving true. By early November the Egyptian army of 10,000 men, with 12 pieces of cannon, had advanced as far as Dongola and were preparing to march on Senaar. Salt wrote, "Some idea has been entertained here that Abyssinia is the ultimate object."[34] Two clerics from Cambridge, who travelled far into Nubia above the Second Cataract, spent much time on the fringes of the army. George Waddington and Barnard Hanbury recorded, "The ambition of Mehemet Ali is to possess all the banks of and the islands of the Nile, and be master of all who drink its waters, from Abyssinia to the Mediterranean." He also had designs on Abyssinia, but abandoned them "on a formal assurance that an attack on a Christian state would probably involve him with the English Government."[35] That formal assurance was Salt's, though he was concerned that he was exceeding his powers in giving it.

On 20 November 1820, Salt had an important discussion about the expedition with the Pasha. Their audiences usually followed a pattern. The Pasha, seated on his divan, would beckon his 'friend' to sit beside him; the interpreter would stand nearby, courtiers and others would stand around, probably listening, possibly talking to each other. That was how this audience began.

"I hope," observed Salt, "that your son has no thought of penetrating as far as Abyssinia...the obstacles he would meet with are scarcely to be overcome by so small a force."

"Then I will send a larger one," the Pasha countered.

"Twenty thousand would not be sufficient."

"Then I will send thirty," said the Pasha and, half in jest, half in earnest, "I am determined to see at last what can be done. If I can conquer it, I shall make a great name." He questioned Salt about the country, and the number of horses there.

"In Begunder," Salt replied, "the governor can raise forty thousand."

The Pasha smiled. "They will do well for my cavalry."

So far the conversation had been almost bantering. Now Salt felt it favourable to take on a serious air, and told the Pasha frankly that he would be truly sorry to hear of his intention. "I am sure it would be displeasing to the British government," he warned. "Abyssinia is considered, after my last mission, as in some degree under our protection."

"You must be jesting!" exclaimed the Pasha. "Of what consequence can Abyssinia be to England?" The tone of the meeting now altered. The Pasha gestured his attendants to leave the room and his son, Ibrahim, who had been seated at a distance, came close to his father where he might hear more distinctly.

Salt felt he should press his position strongly. "Abyssinia," he pointed out, "is the only country in Africa which has retained the Christian religion. It has resisted for ages with effect all the attacks of the followers of Mahommed. You cannot expect now that the nations of Europe, but more especially Great Britain, will look on quietly and see it, without provocation, attacked. On the contrary," he added, "I was myself employed at great expense to visit that country, with a view to establishing amicable relations with its rulers. Many persons in England have become interested in Abyssinia's favour. The Bible Society has, for example, published a part of our Scriptures in their language for the sake of improving their condition. I am sure, on the first notice of your intention to invade Abyssinia, it would produce a very unpleasant impression against Your Highness in England." He let this sink in, then pressed the Pasha on "the impolicy of the attempt. You will, Your Highness, find a whole population, when inspired by religious enthusiasm, difficult to conquer."

By now the Pasha realised that Salt was very much in earnest. His tone changed, and in his most impressive manner, he reassured him: "Though the country were full of gold and jewels, and the conquest certain, I would at once relinquish all thought of it, rather than be compromised for a moment with the British government."

Now Salt smiled. "I am most happy to have so solemn an assurance from you."

The Pasha repeated his statement with emphasis and Salt promised to relay this message immediately to Lord Castlereagh. "I am certain," he added, "that his lordship will find your words most satisfactory."

Mehemet Ali explained more particularly what he asserted to be his real views on the expedition. "I have troops who have been troublesome to me — in this way they are employed on other matters...and the expedition will gain information respecting the course of the Nile...it has baffled the researches of a great many men, since the time of Alexander. I also hope," he added, "to render the cataracts navigable. I have sent up able engineers for this purpose. I hope to open a free trade in this way with the interior."

"Such objects," approved Salt, "will excite much interest in Europe. If you succeed in these ventures, Your Highness, you will render your name glorious."

In his report to Castlereagh, Salt suggested there might be yet another motive, "namely that of providing a secure place of retreat, in case he would be attacked by the Sublime Porte" — which at the time seemed not improbable. He had made what he hoped was Britain's position very clear to the Pasha, but he did not necessarily believe that would deter him. Although he could not conceive that any attack on Abyssinia could ultimately succeed, he estimated that if the Pasha's troops were assisted by the Muslim forces of Senaar, "it must produce trouble and bloodshed throughout the country." He had done what he could and sought Castlereagh's instructions so that he might pass on the British government's sentiments, further to deter the Pasha, "should he still entertain any such a wild notion." The letter only reached London in July 1821, some eight months later.[36]

Despite the Pasha's assurances, given almost hand on heart, Salt did not entirely trust him. His informants had told him that some Egyptians had been taught to imitate the Coptic manner of signing the cross and other ceremonies and that these men accompanied the army. He also heard that Ismael Pasha, for his own information, had had a part of Salt's *Travels in Abyssinia* translated into Turkish. But, for the present, Salt felt that his remonstrances had arrested the Pasha's intentions and he admitted that he had never known the Pasha to give his word if he did not mean to keep it. Whether it was his action which halted the invasion, whether the Pasha had never intended it, even if his sons had, we cannot be sure — but Salt certainly had reason to believe that he had helped to save from attack the country in which he took such a lasting interest.

The constancy of Salt's attachment to Abyssinia is remarkable. Pearce's death had removed one link, but he was still in touch with William Coffin and he had an Abyssinian priest living in the Consular house: "a good quiet soul, who contented himself with reading his Bible aloud for ten hours in the day." He could not write, so Salt had asked Subagadis, now Ras of Tigre, to send him two priests "from among the best informed, who I think will be acceptable to the Bible and Missionary Societies."[37]

Another matter giving Salt concern was the unsettled state of the eastern Mediterranean following uprisings against Ottoman rule in Greece. "Hundreds of poor Greeks" arrived daily at Alexandria, "passing into cruel slavery." At first those who arrived on British ships were bought and freed by members of the European comunity, some even with financial help from Mehemet Ali himself, but there were too many. Salt told his Lichfield friend Sir Francis Darwin that he believed Europe and Russia had missed their chance and the Greeks were paying for this weakness.

Not all the work that engaged the Consul-General was so significant nor so interesting as negotiations with the Pasha. He described to his 'niece' (as he playfully called Mary Halls) the more mundane tasks of his office. He congratulated her brother Tom on his promotion to the police magistracy, a situation he felt, had he not been Consul, would have "exactly suited" him.

However, his present job also required him to sit in judgement: "scarcely a day passes over my head that I have not to decide upon some dispute, settle some commercial controversy, or pronounce judgement on some delinquent, occasionally for serious offences." He explained that whereas in "civilised countries" foreigners were subject to the laws of the state they live in, "in these barbarous regions the Consuls are a sort of Kings. Every Consulate *here* is a little Government, and all those residing in the country are considered to be under its exclusive protection." Occasionally, if a very serious crime had been committed, the Pasha would cut off a European's head, "but otherwise he leaves everything that concerns our subjects...to our wiser jurisdiction." So Salt would try cases of murder, assault and robbery, and decide between contenders in cases involving hundreds of thousands of piastres.

In Cairo he had about 300 "subjects", who included Maltese, Ionians "&c,&c", and about as many again at Alexandria, mainly under Peter Lee's rule, but able to appeal to his superior 'worship' ("as Dr Richardson, in his *Travels,* calls me"). It was, he thought, a strange system, "and one that was certainly never in the contemplation of the Government at home", which meant that no regulations or proper rules of guidance were laid down. "We do our best, sometimes proceeding as far as imprisonment, fining and whipping; but you may be sure we never, however hardened the criminal, or terrible the offence, proceed to the extremity of hanging."[38]

* *

One 'crime' which Salt failed to prevent or even detect until too late was the theft of what was believed to be one of the greatest treasures of ancient Egypt.

When the Pasha's advisers suggested that he speculate in antiquities on his own account or form a collection in museums locally, he replied that he considered the state of Egypt "not sufficiently ripe for such establishments". In fact, he used permissions to search for and carry off antiquities as a way to "allure" Europeans to Egypt. So wrote Sebastien Louis Saulnier, a collector based at Nancy. For some years a correspondent of the ubiquitous Yussuf Boghos, from whom he had received "several packages from Thebes", in 1820 he embarked on a more ambitious venture — the acquisition of the bas-relief planisphere in the upper temple at Dendera, the finest and least damaged of the three zodiacs then known.[39]

Denon, travelling indefatigably with General Desaix's army in 1799, was the first to draw the Zodiac; Napoleon's savants proclaimed its importance — though Salt was correct in his suspicion it was of later date than they believed, linking it stylistically to Ptolemaic mummy cases. Saulnier considered the Zodiac would in some measure compensate for the absence from the French collections of such "distinguished relics of antiquity" as the Rosetta Stone, the Head of Memnon or the Obelisk of Philae.

When Saulnier's agent, a young stonemason, Jean Baptiste Lelorrain, arrived in November 1820, he claimed that Salt and Drovetti had assumed "a kind of exclusive right to what remains of the superb heritage of the Pharaohs and the Ptolemies...where they have struck their shovels or pick-axes, becomes their legitimate property"; a treaty had been concluded by which the Nile was the boundary of their respective "domains". If true, then Dendera was in Salt's domain. Most Europeans used their *firmans* to collect openly, if somewhat surreptitious when actually cutting bits off temples; Lelorrain's operation had to be entirely covert.

The Zodiac was 12 feet across, about three feet thick and Lelorrain estimated it weighed about 20 tonnes. With stone saws and a little gun-powder, its thickness was halved, it was cut into two parts, lowered down the side of the temple, dragged six miles to the Nile and loaded on a boat. Saying the river was too low, the *reis* refused to set sail, but a bribe soon cured this impediment, really caused, Lelorrain suspected, by rivals plotting to delay him. Later they were hailed by another boat, and, on the orders of the Kaya Bey, told to move the Zodiac no further. Lelorrain, who claimed to recognise one of Salt's agents, replied he had the Pasha's permission and any interference would be an offence to the French flag at his masthead. According to the *Quarterly Review*, this was "no more than his pocket handkerchief", but the ruse worked and he sailed on, protected by "this humble and probably not very cleanly, representation of the French flag".[40]

He later claimed that Salt himself had been "concerting measures" to carry off the Zodiac, arranging that Bankes send him the necessary imple-ments. The *Quarterly Review* thundered that this was entirely unfounded — "it never once entered the head of Mr Salt to commit so barbarous an act as that of destroying the most perfect monument that remained on the banks of the Nile; and so far from making any attempt to prevent M Lelorrain from taking the sacrilegious prize out of the country, he did not even know that such an infamous theft had been committed till it was at Alexandria." Salt's wry comment was that he saw from the French papers that he was credited with attempting to foul Lelorrain, but the truth was that he had known noth-ing about it until too late. Had he discovered the theft in time, he told Bankes, he would "through the Pasha's interference have prevented it alto-gether". Bankes too was extremely indignant at the accusation that he had connived with Salt to take the Zodiac. In a letter to the *Quarterly Review* he stated, "I have always deprecated, in the strongest manner, any spoliations of existing and entire monuments, such as that temple is." He strongly denied sending any equipment to Salt *"for this or any similar purpose."*[41]

On 18 July 1821 Lelorrain embarked the Zodiac for Marseilles, rescuing it, claimed Saulnier, "from the destruction and danger to which it was exposed" not only from the "natives" but also from "certain Europeans… that appear zealous for the preservation of antiquities." Eventually on exhibition in the Louvre, it cost Louis XVIII some £6,500 — a far larger sum than Salt was to be paid for his legally acquired treasures.

* *

Salt had heard nothing about his collection from Banks, Museum or Government since May 1819, and was increasingly alarmed for the sarcophagus of Seti. Fearing there might be difficulties in passing the sarcophagus through English customs, Salt asked his agent, Bingham Richards, to approach Joseph Planta at the Foreign Office for assistance. Two people recommended by Planta had recently been given "every attention" in Salt's power in Cairo, and Salt now wrote to ask Planta's protection for "our celebrated sarcophagus of alabaster". He indicated that his concern was not only for "this very precious relic of antiquity", but also whether he had been wise patriotically to refuse two offers of 10,000 dollars he had received for it — one from the Prussian Baron, Minutoli, the other from Drovetti.

The Pasha about this time expressed an interest in buying two frigates from Britain. He did not want new ships, just "as good as new, handsome and in perfect order…so as to please at first sight". On such a deal, Salt suggested to Hamilton, depended keeping up a good understanding with the Pasha. Drovetti had recently been re-appointed French Consul-General and Salt was well aware that he would make the best use of the situation should Mehemet Ali be disappointed.[42]

* *

The family Salt so longed for was not easily achieved. He told Mountnorris in early November 1820 that his wife was in a *promising* way — she had previously miscarried at two months, but was now safely past the third. In June 1821, as Lelorrain was sailing down the Nile, Salt was more concerned with babies than antiques. He proudly announced that his wife had been safely delivered of a fine girl, "a charming child, beautiful as an angel and very engaging". They named her Georgina Henrietta Annesley, as a compliment to her godfather, Mountnorris.[43]

196

15

Negotiations

AT A MEETING at the British Museum on 19 February 1820, Charles Long, Henry Bankes and Lord Aberdeen were asked to communicate with the Admiralty about transporting Salt's collection. Possibly Sir Joseph Banks's death on 19 June put the matter out of mind, for it was not until after a Trustees' meeting on 13 January 1821 that the letter was written. A month later the Secretary to the Admiralty replied that when an opportunity offered, a proper vessel for the purpose would be dispatched. Fortunately for Salt, left hanging without a word "in any shape" from Sir Joseph, the Museum or the Government since his letters of May 1819, he did have an unofficial notification, "which I think Mr W. Bankes was good enough to make me", that a ship was to be sent. But before that, alarmed for the sarcophagus, which was "in daily risk of being broken" at Alexandria, he asked the Pasha to have it carried, with some other articles, on the frigate *Diana*, which Mehemet Ali was sending to England for repairs.

In September 1821, when the *Diana* docked at Deptford, a very large exigent Italian presented himself before Salt's agent, Bingham Richards.

When he left Egypt in mid-September 1819, Giovanni Belzoni went to Italy to visit his family, but on 31 March 1820, *The Times* announced that "the celebrated traveller Mr Belzoni has arrived in this metropolis..." By that time William Hamilton had met Belzoni more than once, and commented to Mountnorris, "He is as mild in his manners and as unpretending in his accounts of himself, as he is Gigantic in Stature, and gifted with extraordinary perseverance and activity. I was pleased to see that he took. Every opportunity of speaking of Salt as of one with whom he was on the most friendly terms — and perfectly satisfied, and he does ample justice to the richness of Salt's collection of Egyptian antiquities."[1]

Determined to establish his reputation, Belzoni decided to write up his exploits. He was soon to be found in the "little back parlour" in Albemarle Street, London, where the publisher John Murray's "four o'clock visitors" gathered. Not only distinguished writers, such as Byron and Sir Walter Scott, but also "the less than literary, whose chief merit was that they had travelled in unfamiliar places" were encouraged by Murray.[2] Belzoni proved a particularly good 'catch'.

He refused any help with writing his memoirs, other than the correction of his spelling. "As I made my discoveries alone, I have been anxious to write my book by myself...the public will perhaps gain in the fidelity of my narrative, what is lost in elegance." He was right — any loss in style is more than compensated by the character that comes bursting through. Well reviewed, the book ran into several editions, and was translated into French and Italian.

Despite his remarks to Hamilton (whom he knew to be Salt's friend), and proclaiming that he could say far more if he would, Belzoni accused Salt of having attempted, by claiming to be his employer, to take credit for achievements that were his alone. Nor did he scruple to slander Salt even more thoroughly in conversation. The journalist Cyrus Redding wrote in *Celebrities I Have Known*, "It was reported that Salt, having aided with money a public work, wished to engross the credit of it." This 'public work' was the gift of the Head of Memnon to the British Museum. Belzoni, Redding wrote, wished it to go to the Museum, and Burckhardt thought it an excellent idea, "for he was above all meanness". He spoke to Salt, "who had been a sort of clerk or secretary to an Irish peer, Lord Valentia, who, it is probable, procured Salt, a Lichfield man, the consulship of Egypt...Salt at once agreed, on the application of Burckhardt, to aid in getting the Memnon to England by a pecuniary advance — no doubt comprehending well how he should get remunerated." But when the head reached the Museum, was Belzoni mentioned? No, he was "passed over by Mr Valentia Secretary Salt, who wished, in more cases than one, to obtain notoriety through the labour and ingenuity of others. In the synopsis of the Museum, too, the name of Belzoni was carefully excluded." No doubt at the malign suggestion of Salt! "That priceless gem, the sarcophagus of oriental alabaster, was the property of Belzoni alone."[3]

Redding's book, not published until 1868, may be equally inaccurate about his other celebrated acquaintance; in Salt's case, it renewed in the latter half of the nineteenth century an idea still prevalent today: that he had behaved disgracefully to an honest and enterprising man.

In fact, Salt had frequently written to his friends acknowledging and praising the zeal and intelligence that had led to Belzoni's great achievements, had acted generously towards him, well beyond the call of obligation, and had thought they had parted on amicable terms. When, even before Belzoni's book was published, rumours reached Salt of what he might expect, he wrote, in the course of a letter to John Murray, "I do not mention anything about Belzoni because although he has behaved foolishly and ungratefully towards me, I shall always admire what he has done. I shall never commence the attack but if he is impudent enough to begin with me, which I understand he intends, I shall feel myself justified in exposing his weakness and folly for which I have ample documents *in his own writing in my hands*."[4]

Once he saw the book, what Halls styles "the insidious attacks" directed against him, both there and, as he had heard, "through other channels", determined him that he must put his own case forward. Unlike Belzoni, Salt refused to publish his 'Plain Statement of Facts' at large, to injure his traducer in the eyes of the world, but sent it to Hamilton for a very limited circulation only — "I wish to avoid publication or putting myself in opposition to a mountebank" — an epithet probably referring both to Belzoni's early career and his present conduct.[5]

Salt was insistent about this; to Colonel Leake he wrote that Hamilton had made "a slight mistake" in thinking he wanted the statement published — although he had given him permission to publish "*should he think it necessary,* I expressed myself anxious to avoid that step, being only desirous that it should be shown to my valued patron Mr Yorke, and others of *my friends* in England, and also, I think, to the Trustees of the British Museum, that they might be able to form a fair judgement of my conduct towards Belzoni, whose ingratitude, I will confess, has given me much pain. But a man of his disposition and character, though he may deceive the world for a time, as he did me, will sooner or later unmask himself and appear in his true colours." He asked Leake to forward the paper to Bingham Richards, with written instructions only to show it to "any of my friends he may think right".[6]

How many friends were shown it is a matter of conjecture. One must hope the Trustees were, for Belzoni was being feted in London society, and it was surely not only Redding who was regaled with tales of the despicable conduct of the British Consul in Egypt. Halls saw the statement for the first time when it was given to him when he was writing Salt's biography. Less forgiving than Salt, he felt that Belzoni's behaviour was such that "common justice requires that the memory of Mr Salt should no longer suffer from the suppression of a document which gives a wholly different colour to the transaction and places his good feelings in a most favourable point of view." On the score of imprudence, however, "(in first giving his confidence to a foreign adventurer, and secondly in the great sacrifices he made to appease his capricious selfishness and overweening vanity) Mr Salt, it must be conceded, cannot be so readily acquitted".

Halls was told by Henry Beechey, who spent more time in Egypt with Belzoni than anyone, and witnessed some of his altercations with Salt, that "Belzoni was of so suspicious and dissatisfied a disposition, that it was in some respects difficult to keep on any terms with him." When gathering material for the biography, Halls consulted Beechey, who replied, "I am glad to hear that you have undertaken to write the Life of our excellent friend Salt — a better man never breathed...Belzoni (poor fellow! he had many good points about him,) was often in the habit of using very violent language, and frequently declared that he was not employed by Mr Salt, though it would have puzzled him very much to prove the assertion...There never was a man better treated, in every respect, by another than Belzoni was by our poor friend, though he never would allow it, and I verily believe that he persuaded himself it was otherwise. In fact he was, on some points, more than half mad, and this was decidedly one of them. Captains Mangles and Irby could furnish you, I believe, with a good many anecdotes in confirmation of this. They knew Belzoni thoroughly, and would amuse you very much with his oddities."[7]

On 1 May 1821, Belzoni opened his exhibition of two reconstructed rooms from Seti's Tomb, together with a scale model of the whole, based on the drawings and models that Dr Alessandro Ricci, with some help from himself and Beechey, had made at Thebes in 1818. It was mounted, appropriately, in the Egyptian Hall in Piccadilly, and the *Gentleman's Magazine*'s review described how "the visitor...is deeply impressed with the awful solemnity that surrounds him."[8] It was a great success as people from all walks of life jostled for a view.

Closed for a few weeks in the summer, the exhibition re-opened in the autumn. What better encouragement to a second visit, by adding an amazing new lustre to the show than the actual, the genuine, the priceless, alabaster sarcophagus? Belzoni hastened to request Captain Walker of the Pasha's frigate *Diana* to detain the sarcophagus while he addressed a memorial to the Trustees of the Museum asking permission to take possession of it and place it in his Tomb.

Richards must on several occasions during the negotiations for Salt's collection have wished his friend had not made him his agent, and this was surely one. Salt had instructed him to deliver the sarcophagus to the Museum, with a receipt for its deposit. Belzoni, who had the right to a half share of any sum it fetched above £2,000 and claimed to have a buyer willing to pay £3,000, suspected that if the sarcophagus were once in the clutches of the Trustees, without a previous valuation, he might never get his share. Richards also felt that delivery without a valuation might compromise the interests of both Belzoni and Salt.

Unable to consult Salt himself, Richards turned to his friends and to his own father. Though the reasons given were various, the verdict was unanimous: Salt's instructions must be complied with. Indeed, Theophilus Richards, sceptical about Belzoni's claims, advised that even if Belzoni came with £3,000 in bank notes, "I do not think you would be justified in deviating from your instructions, and you might be liable for damages by the Trustees of the British Museum."[9]

A few days later, Richards received a characteristic note from Belzoni: "Sir, Having seen Mr Hamilton since I saw you, I was not a litle surprised to find, that you made a complaint against me in consequence of the delay of the alabaster sarcophagus, from the *Diana* frigate. Though it is immaterial to me to whom you complain, I beg you for the future to be more cautious in making use of my name on such unfounded insinuations and intrigues."[10]

The sarcophagus was delivered to the Museum on Friday, 29 September 1821, to form a large indigestible lump in the negotiations that followed.

* *

In May 1821 the Naval transport *Dispatch* was at Alexandria, taking on a load of antiquities. Bankes' collection, including his obelisk and its pedestal (fetched down by Yanni) were embarked, and, over six days, 92 cases of Salt's collection. It was the plague season and in the reigning confusion two cases of mummified animals were left behind.

Salt sent with the cargo a complete list of the contents of 128 cases of antiquities (of which four were already in the Museum and seven had been transported in the *Diana*), identifying the provenance of most of the objects, though not as precisely as modern archaeologists would wish, and the finder/purchaser of the most important ones. Thirty cases, containing mainly objects found or bought by Belzoni, included most of the largest statues and the vases. Of the other cases, nearly half held objects found or bought by Salt, including some large statues, while the rest of the articles were either gifts to Salt or from unidentified sources, the latter mainly small objects. Acquisition of the contents of three cases was credited to Yanni D'Athanasi.[11]

In 1821, Yanni had only recently become Salt's agent in collecting, but his role in obtaining the majority of the antiquities in Salt's second and third collections tends to be underrrated. The mantle of Belzoni fell on Yanni's shoulders, but the mantle of Belzoni the *celebrated* discoverer of Egyptian antiquities has effectively cloaked Yanni's less spectacular but still significant achievements. Barely 21 when he took on his role, and lacking the impressive presence of his predecessor ("an active little fellow," observed John Madox), he opened no major tomb or pyramid — though, just because of his meagre build, he was the first European to enter both Seti's tomb and the pyramid of Chephren. But he discovered more than one commoner's tomb, with the contacts fairly intact, and procured Salt "upwards of a hundred" papyri, many fine mummies and countless artefacts.

In the shifting of great weights, if Belzoni is justly famous, Yanni should be also. Belzoni moved the obelisk of Philae, Yanni its more awkward pedestal; Linant de Bellefonds moved the largest stone of the platform of steps at Maharraka, Yanni the other three. He moved two sphinxes, each weighing 250,000 pounds, from Salt's excavation behind the colossi near the temple of Memnon. "Mr Belzoni...boasts of having removed a monolith weighing twenty or five-and-twenty thousand pounds...He would have been overwhelmed with astonishment on learning that in less than a month these two sphinxes were removed...Mr Belzoni required forty days to remove the head of the younger Memnon..."[12] Unlike Belzoni, Yanni had experienced workmen and proper equipment; the achievement is still impressive.

Yanni's financial arrangements with Salt are not known, but it seems probable that they were, as in the final contract with Belzoni, expenses and a share of the finds. Certainly Yanni was dealing on his own account in Thebes. How large his share was must be conjectural, but, referring to the posthumous sale of Salt's third collection at Sotheby's, he says, "I had with his executors an equal interest."[13] Could this mean anything but a financial interest?

The *Dispatch* reached England in November, but the delivery of the collection to the Museum evoked not even an acknowledgement of its arrival from the Trustees. Though nearly three and a half years had elapsed since Salt's initial approach through Hamilton, they could not realistically start negotiating while only a few articles had been seen. Once everything had arrived, there could be no reason for further delay.

Were it not for the sarcophagus. In April 1822, Salt received a complaint from Belzoni that their agreement that the Consul would offer the sarcophagus to the Museum at a fair valuation within three years had now outrun by nine months. He claimed that he had an offer of £3,000 "standing" with money ready from some Continental speculators, that he had so informed the Trustees, and that he would pay £2,500 to Salt's bankers on delivery of the sarcophagus to the purchasers. The Trustees had replied that his memorial would be laid before a general meeting once Salt had made his official offer to them. "Under these circumstances you must be aware. that if the chances of selling the said sarcophagus are lost, owing to your delay, according to agreement, and with the documents I possess, I shall claim the said loss to be reimbursed to me by you...I sincerely hope that you will take this matter into consideration, and make the said offer according to agreement...so that all may end in an amicable manner, as it is my wish that differences of this kind should not be brought before the public."

Salt replied at once that he had made the offer to Sir Joseph in May 1819, 13 months after the agreement, but would now write again "to prevent any further delay, which is, you must be aware, more prejudicial to my interest than yours."[14] He addressed the Trustees the same day, probably glad of an excuse both to let them know he was aware the whole collection was now in England and to repeat his unconditional offer. Since the original offer in 1818, he had acquired new responsibilities — "...I feel it necessary for my interest to state that, this Collection has been made by me at great expense (upwards of three thousand pounds) at the imminent risk of the funds employed, out of private property left me by my father, to which alone (in case of any disaster occurring to me, and my health has been for some years and continues to be very precarious) my family has to look for support. I have therefore, to throw myself entirely on your liberality, and shall be perfectly satisfied with whatever you may determine in my favour."[15]

Almost as he wrote this, Henry Bankes was laying before his fellow Trustees a letter from Salt to his son William, dated 6 January 1822, to say that now all his collection was in England, Salt hoped the Trustees would come to a decision about their purchase. William Bankes was often used by the Trustees as a liaison between themselves and Salt, a rather peculiar way for an official body to conduct business. They resolved, on 11 May 1822, that Bankes should "state, in his answer to Mr Salt", that the Trustees wished him to appoint someone on his own behalf to make a valuation of the Collection. "The Trustees decline the alabaster sarcophagus, on account of the very high value put upon it by Mr Belzoni."[16] Bankes told Richards that "the utmost value set upon the sarcophagus in a meeting of the Trustees…was *considerably under one thousand pounds*. Mr Salt, therefore, by their official note being set at full liberty to seek another purchaser, appears to me to owe it to himself and his family to accept the best offer that has been made; and I have no scruple in recommending you to do so in his name, especially as by this expedient so unpleasant a sort of partnership is done away with."[17]

* *

While Bankes exerted himself on Salt's behalf in England, Salt was much involved with Bankes' affairs in Egypt. The obelisk and its pedestal were in England, but the great platform of steps Bankes wanted as a base to his monument still lay at Maharraka and because Ismael Pasha was waging war in Nubia, boats were difficult and very expensive to obtain. Linant brought down one stone towards the end of 1822, but an unexpectedly rapid fall of the Nile prevented him moving the others.

By February 1823 the 11-ton stone was at Salt's country house near Bulac, waiting to go to Alexandria. Salt warned Bankes that it was so heavy and awkward that "no common merchantman will undertake to carry it" to England. He suggested hopefully that Bankes might abandon the other three stones, as this one "would make a sufficiently fine front-stone and the rest might be built with other stones."[18] But Bankes was not prepared to forgo any of his stones — "it would cost more to make the stones in Scottish granite…if you upon the spot and with all the influence of your public situation can not bring about what to me appears so simple, *I am sure that I* can not suggest any [illegible word] but must sit down content with a disappointment."[19]

203

Linant was also causing problems. Commissioned by Bankes in 1820 to investigate and copy the inscriptions on the supposed temple of Jupiter Ammon at the Oasis of Siwa, and then go to Meroë in Nubia, the goal Bankes himself had been baulked of reaching, Linant instead went to Sinai, where he made, Salt said, some beautiful drawings. Bankes was not pleased. Linant finally set off for Nubia on 15 June 1821.

Salt had great difficulty getting a *firman* for the expedition, as Ismael Pasha had induced his father not to grant any, especially to the English. It took three meetings with Mehemet Ali before Salt at last "drove him to grant it by declaring that if he did not, it would put an end to all friendly communications between us — and that I was sure it would be taken very ill by our Ministers at home."[20]

On the Sinai trip, Linant had fallen ill "near to death", and was still so weak that Salt felt he could not send him off without medical advice. Alessandro Ricci was to supply the advice; the arrangement displeased both young men. Linant thought Ricci's presence quite unnecessary, and recorded in his journal that from the start of the journey, Ricci sulked and refused to speak. At Damer in Nubia on 7 November, he had been sulking for days, Linant could not think why. Finati, acting as their dragoman, said, "Il faisait un museau dure [a stiff muzzle]." That day Ricci refused to go any further with Linant, who told him he was mad, left him two of the camels and secured all Ricci's drawings in his own luggage. Four days later they met at Shendi, but Ricci still persisted in proceeding alone.[21]

The bad behaviour of the pair pained Salt. He was sorry "the Doctor with Linant has behaved so ill...I hope you will be assured that I have done everything for the best — these young men have since you left Egypt given me much trouble and cost me no inconsiderable sum but I am really fond of both of them and especially Linant and should have been truly sorry, not to have obtained for you the completion of this voyage, which you have so much at heart."[22]

Far from coming to grief, Ricci caught up with Ibrahim Pasha at Senaar, and treated him successfully for dysentery. Ibrahim made him his temporary first physician and wrote to Salt "in the handsomest terms...assuring me that it would be no detriment to the mission but on the contrary that he would send up for Linant and take him also in his company."[23] Ibrahim fell ill again, so desperately that Ricci declared only an instant return to Cairo could save him. Leaving Linant, they travelled at such a pace that the voyage took only 36 days, "a thing almost incredible", Salt commented. Ricci, travelling in Ibrahim's *cangia* in constant attendance, managed to save him.

"Everybody from above speaks most highly of the great exertions of Linant and of his drawings and charts of the Nile, and by his letters it appears that to complete his works at the true Meroë he ran great risk of his life," wrote Salt, softening Bankes for the bad news. "You must expect a considerable demand upon your purse...Yet though the expence may exceed what you have calculated upon, I feel assured you will have reason to be highly satisfied with the undertaking...I am certain it will prove not only the best work, but the only one worth having, upon Meroe and the countries above Hanbury and Waddington's expedition — and even where they have been, his pencil will make up for the want of novelty in description. I can only say that I envy you as sole author and patron of the expedition — for it is one that might have done honour to the Government."[24] Linant was back in Cairo on 24 July 1822 with, among other things, the first drawings of the brick pyramids of Meroë.

Linant continued to give Salt trouble. Bankes wanted him in England with his drawings and journals, but Linant procrastinated. On 7 February 1823, Salt wrote that arrangements for his departure were complete, and he had persuaded him, with difficulty, to go directly to England. He commented indulgently, *"Young men*, though amiable as is our friend Linant, have always their vagaries, and without they are in some degree indulged nothing satisfactory can be obtained."[25] Next day he had to write that Linant was refusing to leave without additional money, which Salt thought unreasonable. He made a limited offer, but three days later felt he must accede to avoid further delay. Linant still lingered in Cairo and missed his passage.

Bankes was disgusted. "I was to pay his expenses travelling, but not to keep him for his own wish and pleasure all his life! This is quite unreasonable!...Surely this was strangely managed, when you might have presumed that every day's delay subjected him to this risk, and meant an increase of expense," he reprimanded. Linant's expedition to Sinai, "which I have always been utterly unable to comprehend...was, so far as my views were concerned, so much time lost"; if he had been made to go to Meroë when Bankes had intended, "the impression on his mind of friendship and gratitude towards me would have been stronger and more active...I write perhaps a little out of humour, but you will hardly be surprised at it when I remind you that I am left either to infer that my letters do not reach you or that you do not take the trouble of reading them or paying the least attention to them." He had the grace to add later in the letter, "I am expostulating, my dear friend, and not scolding, which I have no title to do."[26]

Salt was requested to be firm with the wilful young man, "but I beg at the same time you will do everything in the most gracious and conciliating manner." The letter is among the Bankes papers, and may be the rough draft for a less acerbic communication; as it stands, it suggests Bankes had something to learn about gracious and conciliatory behaviour.

Linant finally appeared at Soughton Hall, Bankes' house in Wales, in

November 1824, "still wearing his Eastern habit and with his Abyssinian lady," recorded Finati, who was already there, summoned by Bankes as a witness in James Silk Buckingham's lawsuit against him for libel (a fascinating affair, unfortunately outside the scope of this book). Finati eventually returned to Egypt with Lord Prudhoe in 1826; Linant, in the employ for a while of the African Association, in 1825.

In his letter about Linant, Bankes also turned a scolding eye on Salt's affairs. "...I more easily excuse in a friend his little attention to the contents and purport of my letters where they are upon my own business when I discover the same total disregard of them where his own interests are materially concerned; for I must remind you that...after advising you to cut short your connection with Belzoni by letting him have the sarcophagus for what he offered or pretended to offer for it, I went on to recommend to you in the plainest terms that you would name values upon your part for the remainder (making Mr Bingham Richards a party with them) and naming me if you thought proper, along with any other collector or person of vertu (and I hinted at Mr T. Hope and Mr P. Knight for the purpose)... Of this you took no sort of notice, but in your answer to Mr Bingham Richards seemed to leave it to the Trustees altogether, which I have told you from the beginning was the worst way possible, being both awkward and invidious for them, and by no means likely to tend to your advantage." He sent kind remembrances to Mrs Salt, "who I suppose can now understand them in English."[27]

In fact, in May 1822, before Bankes' original recommendations had reached him, Salt had told Richards that if the Museum should ask for a valuation on his behalf, "you may apply to Mr Fuseli, Mr Chantrey, Mr Flaxman, or Mr Westmacott, of whose judgement I have a very high opinion, or any other persons you may think right; or advise with Lord Mountnorris or Mr Halls. In fact, I leave you full powers to act for me throughout this affair when it may be necessary, being highly satisfied with the prudence, judgement, and attachment to my interests, which you have hitherto shown." He enclosed a formal power of attorney, and added, "It may be right to tell you in confidence, that I hope to get four thousand pounds from Government, or otherwise I shall feel myself aggrieved. Should it be five thousand, I shall be highly satisfied."[28]

Bankes and Salt suggested very different types of valuer. Thomas Hope was a wealthy authority on, and collector of, antique sculpture, art and vases, while Richard Payne Knight's reputation was as a connoisseur, "the arbiter of fashionable vertu", whom Bankes seemed unaware had given evidence against the purchase of the Elgin Marbles, had put an extremely low value on them, and had once told Elgin he had wasted his time bringing them to England; furthermore, being the Townley Trustee at the Museum, Knight could surely not be considered impartial. Salt's suggested arbiters were not connoisseurs, but working artists; all but Fuseli were sculptors, and as Chantrey thought highly of Egyptian sculpture, it is a great pity he was never asked to act — nor, indeed, was anyone asked to value on Salt's behalf. The greatest pity of all, perhaps, is that Salt was prevented by the precarious state of affairs in the Eastern Mediterranean from taking up the permission Yorke had obtained for him to pass a year in Europe, during which he could have visited London to look after his interests. Richards had to deal with the Museum alone.

Despite the Trustees' vigorous rejection of the sarcophagus, Salt's friends still hoped they might be induced to change their minds. On 8 January 1823 Richards approached them again, writing that though it was not necessary for them to enter into the question of Salt's contract with Belzoni, if they would state what proportion of the whole sum "they conceive may be paid for the sarcophagus, it would certainly set the matter between Salt and Belzoni at rest." If they did not wish to do so, "it is quite immaterial, for if Belzoni can prove that the sarcophagus would have sold for more than two thousand pounds, he may claim half the excess of Mr Salt. I hope therefore that the Trustees may be disposed to recommend it to Parliament to grant the sum of five thousand pounds for the purchase of all Mr Salt's Collection, not merely on the score of the separate value of each item amounting to that sum collectively; but also as a repayment of money actually advanced with the best intentions and judgement, and as a testimonial of the desire of the Trustees that the British nation should possess the best Egyptian Collection extant."[29]

His letter was referred to the next general meeting, on 8 February, when a sub-committee was appointed "to consider the purchase, leaving out the sarcophagus."[30]

Richards assumed that the Trustees, as they had themselves valued the sarcophagus at less than £1,000, could, if they still refused it, in all honesty deduct only that sum from the £5,000 he had suggested and offer four. He was wrong.

Immediately after attending the sub-committee on 13 February, he wrote a memorandum. The President stated that the Committee "wished to make arrangements for the purchase of Mr Salt's Collection, leaving out the sarcophagus, which appeared, by an offer in the room, to be valued at £3,000." Would Richards consent to take £2,000, for the remaining part of the Collection? Before replying, Richards inquired about the offer for the sarcophagus, and "found that one of the gentlemen had *a letter from Mr Belzoni* to a Mr Brown, of Trinity College, Cambridge, *containing the offer* and an assurance that *the money should be paid* (deducting £500) to the bankers the moment the sarcophagus was delivered up by the Trustees. Belzoni's power of attorney was also on the table."[31]

Rapidly assessing the situation — that the Trustees, not over-eager to purchase, might withdraw altogether — that Salt had, by making his offer unconditional, enabled the Trustees to act as they pleased — that Salt needed to recoup his funds — that if a further £2,000 could be obtained for the sarcophagus, he would receive the £4,000 he hoped for — Richards felt he must accept the offer. Henry Bankes assured him that the sum would be paid during that session of Parliament.

"Now I hereby declare," Richards noted, "that I went prepared to accept any offer made by the sub-committee, in the full confidence that if it should not be thought adequate to Mr Salt's deserts, it would be increased by the assistance and recommendation of his friends at a *General* Meeting." His assent had established an agreement to purchase at a specific sum, and he felt convinced, that if the sarcophagus were ultimately to be kept by the Museum, £3,000 must be paid for it, as the sub-committee had deducted that sum from the £5,000 he had named.

Richards explained his actions carefully to Salt. "So much has been said of *economy,* and so little in *approbation* of Egyptian antiquities, that I was almost afraid you would be left *in the lurch* entirely." There had been no question, "not even a hint", as to a separate valuation, and indeed, with no standard to judge by, one could not have been satisfactory to either party. Had the valuation been high, the Trustees would have rejected part or even all of the collection, had it been less than £2,000, Salt would have had not only to accept it, but to pay the appraisers a percentage. "I do not think, considering all things, the Trustees have evinced any disposition to be liberal towards you, and I do not expect that either yourself, or your friends, will be satisfied; but there is time for the latter to bestir themselves in your behalf, while you, through my representation, remain inactive, certain of having acted in a most honourable and disinterested manner throughout the business." He had writen to Yorke, Mountnorris and William Bankes "to urge them to take all possible steps in obtaining all you go for."[32]

There were two hopes for a better final outcome: the sarcophagus was released for sale elsewhere, and Salt's friends were extemely indignant about his treatment.

"It could not possibly have happened," Bankes reproached Salt, "had you made me or any other collector a party, as I would not have acceded on any account to the proposal, upon your part, and would indeed have outbid them myself at such a price. But as you left the matter; for *me* to act was impossible, it would have been a completely unauthorised interference. All that I could do I have done. I have protested both privately... and publicly to every person who has spoken upon it, against so inadequate an award and against the principle on which the estimate was made." As Henry Bankes' son, "it is quite impossible for me to be the first mover of any supplemental grant upon these grounds in the House of Commons but I attended several times this last session for the express purpose of supporting Mr Hudson Gurney in a proposition which he was ready to bring forward on your behalf (and did once mention) but found no proper opportunity. Either in that way or in some other I will take care that it shall be considered in the next session, unless the Trustees shall of themselves come forward and in truth I make little doubt of being successful in bringing the compensation up to what in common reason and justice it ought to be. But should we fail, it is yourself that you may thank for having missed your opportunity."[33] One must really hope that this Job's comforter of a letter never reached Salt in quite such a candid form.

Salt wrote optimistically to Hamilton, now Ambassador to Naples, in October 1824, that Bankes had told him he felt "certain of getting me from Parliament, next session, another thousand pounds, as he has already tried his ground, and finds both Ministers and such Trustees as are in the House, inclined to accede to the proposition."[34] But no concerted effort was ever made on Salt's behalf, so that for the Collection which had cost him, as Richards estimated, in principal and interest, £4,000, he received half that amount.

As for the sarcophagus, rejected because of "the very high value" put upon it by Belzoni, Salt asked Richards to offer it to Belzoni, "on his paying me the sum of *two* thousand pounds on my account, *as I do not wish to intrench upon any profit* he may be able to make above that sum. You will give him a reasonable time, if necessary, to find a buyer for this sum." He suggested that, should Belzoni have no success, Richards should write to General de Minutoli, and if he refused, then to the French Government through the Comte de Forbin (who had made an offer for the sarcophagus in Thebes) — but all this only if Richards could not "find a buyer at £2,000 in England. At all events, sell it soon if possible, at the same time taking care that you do not get me into any scrape with Belzoni. Even should you not be able to get more than *one thousand five hundred pounds,* it will be better to sell it than to remain longer without the money. I cannot help feeling that the Trustees of the Museum have much compromised my interests by not coming immediately, on Belzoni's making the proposition to them, to a determination, as in that case he would have been obliged to abide by his offer, which he will now, I doubt not, find means to evade."[35]

The sarcophagus remained in the Museum. Belzoni, in Paris arranging a showing of his Tomb, was justifiably cross about the Trustees' dilatory behaviour. Halls unkindly reproduced the letter he dispatched to Richards in all the glory of its original spelling:

As I acquinted them and you long seince that I have offers from other quarters where it may be disposed of advantagiously for both party, Mr Salt and myself, for ready money and much aboue what the Trustees will offer at any time or circumstances, notwisstanding the said Surcophagus been depriciated in the house of Comon by the worthy Mr Bankes the friend of Mr Salt — I expectad that the worthy president Mr Bankes would have esued the above order without Eistatson... I cinciarly wish that this matar may comes to an end in a friendly maner, but I fear it will not be so oweing to the eroneous prociding taken by the honorable Messrs Bankes against me, I hope also it will not be necessary to Inforce the Low to obtain what is justly due to me, for such Mass of facts would apear before the publick, that would rise the Indignation of every onest Inglishman, and I am realy astonished how an honorable body of Men like the Trustees of the British Museum can late themselfs be persuaded away by the wrong sugestions of two or three Indiuiduals, whose motiues for so doing are euident, I hope Mr Bankes will reflect that the low in Ingland is adminstrated for a Stranger on the sam scole with an Inglishman, though he may be related to poiple of influence, as he, Mr. B — , boast to be.[36]

Having rejected the sarcophagus in May 1822, it was not until 15 March 1823 that the Trustees informed Richards he could remove it. As Belzoni had departed to Africa, Richards wrote to Sir John Copley, the Solicitor-General, who held the power of attorney given by Belzoni to the Reverend Brown of Cambridge, requesting he would tell him he was ready to treat with Belzoni's purchasers. Browne replied that it was unlikely that he could get in touch with Belzoni for a considerable time and he did not know the name of the purchaser. Belzoni was on his way, like Burckhardt, to search for the source of the Niger, and was, on 3 December 1823, like Burckhardt, to die of dysentery without reaching his goal.

Was the purchaser a fiction (as Bankes, Richards and Salt all suspected), or had there been an offer, perhaps made once and never renewed? Or did Belzoni's unfortunate temperament prevent him trusting even his own appointed agent? Even Sarah cannot have known, for she was fully capable of addressing Richards or the Trustees on her own account. If there *was* a purchaser, and at £3,000, this was the worst lack of consideration for her interests that her husband ever showed.

In 1824 it looked for a moment as if some of the Trustees, stung by the idea of the sarcophagus falling into the hands of foreigners, and, with some others, ashamed of "the undignified parsimony which, in matters of this nature, too frequently regulates the proceedings of our great National Institution", would persuade the Museum to enter into fresh negotiations. On 14 February 1824 Richards, summoned to a general meeting, was told that £2,000 "might be now named for the sarcophagus". He replied that he must stand out for the Trustees' original estimate of £3,000, at least until he could consult Salt. He inquired whether he "might acquaint Mr Salt there was a desire to purchase." The evasive answer justified his decision not meekly to accept a hypothetical offer; "The chairman did not very well see how I could do that. No proposal being farther made to me, I retired." In the anteroom, he found William Bankes awaiting the outcome, and disappointed to hear what had passed. He advised Richards to offer the sarcophagus elsewhere for £4,000, "according to my orders from Salt". "It appears certain," comments Halls bitterly, "that they [the Trustees] at no time evinced any great desire to possess the Collection, nor to act with the slightest degree of liberality; their proceedings uniformly bearing a much stronger affinity to the trading spirit of a retail dealer than to the broad and enlightened views that ought to influence the managers of a splendid national institution."[37]

When Richards informed him of the latest developments, Salt's reply was uncharacteristically irate and unkind. He was ill and utterly dispirited by the whole affair, so it was excusable, though unfortunate, that poor Richards, who had faithfully done his best in almost impossible circumstances, should suffer the blast.

> I cannot understand upon what grounds you are acting. When there was a moment for taking a high tone, when the Trustees offered the miserable sum of two thousand pounds for the whole of my Collection, excepting the sarcophagus…you made no opposition; accepted the money, and compromised me completely on that head: and now, that you have nothing in hand but the sarcophagus, the sale of which you will find more difficult than you suspect, and on which I never laid any extravagant value — now, that conciliation was so necessary for my interests, you take up a high tone and demand for the sarcophagus three thousand pounds, adopting as your basis, not my instructions, but the offer of Belzoni. [He added in a footnote: Nothing vexes me so much as the circumstance that you should have, by this line of acting, given the Trustees reason to suppose that I have been in collusion all the time with that prince of ungrateful adventurers — God knows, on the contrary, that I always believed his offer to be a fictitious one, and that I have but one wish, never to have my name coupled with his. Why then ground your demands on his offer?] Look back to my letter; is there any thing of this kind in my instructions?

He requested Richards to send a lawyer's letter to Belzoni's agent, demanding that the £3,000 be paid down, or the agreement considered to be null, and "unworthy your farther notice…I could almost fancy you had been bitten by Belzoni or his agent! Offer it for four thousand pounds! where will you get half the sum?"[38]

"Where will you get half the sum?" The answer, unbeknownst to Salt, had already been given. The eccentric architect Sir John Soane, "a spirited individual and liberal encourager of art", very concerned lest this treasure should be lost to England, not only offered £2,000 but consented to allow two years for Belzoni to produce a better price. For a final time, on 10 April 1824, the sarcophagus was offered to the Trustees, and again declined.

211

Richards had been right to distrust the tentative offer of £2,000.

Shortly after this, news of Belzoni's death reached England, and no further delay was necessary. The sarcophagus was delivered to Soane on 12 May, and the disposal of Salt's collection, first set in train six years earlier, was complete.

There is no doubt that the Soane Museum's gain was the British Museum's loss; there is also no doubt that Soane got a great deal more fun out of his acquisition than an institution ever could have. During March 1825, he held three soirées and, when all the lights were dimmed, a lamp placed within the translucent sarcophagus illuminated its delicate beauty. Sarah Belzoni was present one evening, and received "every attention from the guests". Was Salt's name ever heard among the murmurs of admiration for Belzoni's wonderful discovery?

Salt had finally recouped his outlay. Compared to Lord Elgin, who was down about £39,000 in his dealings with the British Museum, he had suffered financially no worse than if he had put his patrimony in a sock under his mattress. But nothing could heal the feeling of betrayal inflicted by the treatment meted out to him — "the wound is within".[39]

16

Scholars, Travellers and Tourists

FROM 1809, the *Description de l'Egypte* of Napoleon's *savants* had begun to appear in its vast, heavy volumes. There was a flood of other writing about Egypt in travellers' tales and journals. The Rosetta Stone and other inscriptions were beginning to yield their mysteries to the efforts of the hieroglyphists. Interest in Egypt quickened, and as the discoveries of Salt, Belzoni, Caviglia and Drovetti became known, and were regularly discussed in the journals, it was to many young men, interested in both antiquity and adventure, like news of a gold rush. The Greeks' bid for independence made the classical world less welcoming; Egypt under Mehemet Ali was safer. An increasing number of travellers saw Egypt as an attractive route to and from India. It was taken by Major Moyle Sherer in 1823, when he noted that "the ground...has been trodden and described by a hundred travellers, and is, for all useful purposes of description, as well known, perhaps, as any road or province in our native country."[1]

Significant among the travellers was a group of young artists and scholars who came to stretch their wings: to discover, to collect a little — but, most importantly, to record. Some stayed or kept returning for a decade or more. Among them were men well known in the annals of the exploration of Egypt like Edward Lane and John Gardner Wilkinson; but there were also several who made their mark elsewhere: Joseph John Scoles, architect of a number of Catholic churches including the flamboyant Jesuit Church of the Immaculate Conception in London's Farm Street; Algernon Percy, Lord Prudhoe, later the fourth Earl of Northumberland and a Trustee of the British Museum, to which he gave the Nubian lions who welcome the visitor to the Egyptian Galleries; Frederick Catherwood, the recorder of the Mayan empire, and tiny Joseph Bonomi who became keeper of the Soane Museum. A third group are less well known because they published little — though they recorded much: Robert Hay, a Scottish laird who employed many of the others to draw and record with him along the Nile (Bonomi, Catherwood and Lane among them); and James Burton, reprobate, mineralogist brother of the architect Decimus Burton, with his somewhat disreputable companions Charles Humphreys and Charles Sheffield. Most of them often travelled and lived together, usually sharing the excitement of their finds.

These young men arrived in Egypt from 1821 onwards. They were in their early 20s and, although undoubtedly studious, also undoubtedly high spirited and ready to enjoy the freedom of this exotic new society. Robert

Hay might purse his lips in disapproval at some of their conduct; James Burton was only too happy to take on the role of master of the harem. They were at times a worry to their Consul and certainly often a nuisance — although Salt also admired them and, on the whole, appears to have wished them well, though, as a family man with an important official position, held himself somewhat aloof.

George Gliddon, son of an Alexandrian merchant, was accepted sometimes into the young men's circle, and his family was well known to Salt, whom he admired. Looking back in 1840, he wrote: "every temple, every tomb, contained something unknown before; and which these gentlemen were the first to date, and to describe with accurate details. A more intensely interesting field never opened to an explorer — every step being a discovery."[2]

* *

Standing, shadowy, behind some of these young men as an influence and guide was one Sir William Gell.[3]

Gell was knighted in 1814 after a successful mission to the Ionian islands for the British government. He became chamberlain to sad Caroline of Brunswick, Princess of Wales, when she left England to remove herself from her husband, the Prince Regent. He arranged her tour to the Near East but did not accompany her. Gell possibly fell on hard times as a result of his loyalty to her. By the 1820s he was settled in a beautifully situated and elegantly arranged villa in Naples, where he drew to himself a group of scholarly, gossipy younger men, whom he entertained, encouraged, flattered and amused. He enjoyed a circle of English and Italian acquaintance of whom Salt's friend, William Hamilton, when he moved from the Foreign Office to become Ambassador in Naples, was one. Gell interested himself in many cultural matters including those of ancient Egypt. From Naples he made a study of the study of hieroglyphs, passing news and letters between Egypt and the rest of Europe, describing himself to Dr Thomas Young as "purveyor-general of the hieroglyphs."[4] He was always keen to pass on to others the knowledge he had gleaned from his correspondents, of whom Salt was a regular.

Gell never went to Egypt. He always had an excuse when opportunity offered: the weather, his health, his finances, the political state of the world. Perhaps his procrastinating is best summed up in a letter to Wilkinson in August 1824: "I cannot go unless I have every convenience and that does not seem at present the probable case."[5]

For some reason Gell did not care for Henry Salt and took every opportunity to alienate his young protegés from the Consul and to encourage them to scoff both at his public persona and his archaeological and scholarly pursuits. His animosity shows most clearly in the poem he wrote in the notebook of James Burton before he left for Egypt:

If you travel in Egypt 'tis reckoned a fault
To be seen on the Nile without letters for Salt,
But be sure when you shew your credentials to say
What dropp'd from your intimate friend Castlereagh
Whom you met at the Travellers' Club t'other day.
Who seem'd quite consoled when he thought that at Cairo
That good fellow Salt rul'd instead of old Pharaoh
Who he felt quite assur'd would take you by the hand
When he knew how allied to the Marquis you stand
That Sidmouth and Harrowby both were your cousins
And you reckon'd your friends in the Household by dozens.
Add that Hamilton once forc'd upon you a letter
But to burn it dear Liverpool hinted was better
Than that persons connected like you with the Court
Should be troubl'd by things of such little import.
Not a word of Mountnorris — that interest is past
Sense of favours conferr'd is not likely to last.
And hint not oh hint not one word about painting
Unless you would set the great Consul to fainting
But lock up your papers and hide all your drawing
If you would be safe from his pilf'ring & clawing
And whatever you do hold your head up in Alt
Or you're likely to profit but little by Salt.[6]

As the many insinuations in this poem have sometimes been absorbed uncritically, they need examination. It is clear that Salt was held in high esteem by Castlereagh who, when appointing him, told him he considered him the man most capable for the job. As Consul-General, Salt was indeed obliged to entertain the visiting gentry and to pay particular attention to those of high birth; however, he also went out of his way to be kind and helpful to such unimportant young men as Linant, Ricci, Wilkinson, Lane and John Madox. The poem implied that Salt had cast off a patron he had no further use for, but the evidence is clear that the awkwardness between himself and Mountnorris was only passing, and caused by Mountnorris rather than him. As to the suggestion that he was ashamed of his artistic background, evidence shows how far from the truth this is. The nastiest accusation — and one James Burton apparently believed without any personal experience — was that Salt would pilfer others' work and present it as his own. It is possible that this was a very early reaction to his relationship with Belzoni, but Salt appears if anything unusually scrupulous in acknowledging his sources and helping others to share his researches.

Whatever the other young men thought of this clever poem, it certainly influenced Burton. In March 1822, on his way to Egypt, before he had even met Salt, he wrote to his father that he could not agree that the House of Briggs & Co. could give letters of introduction to Salt equal to those of Lord Londonderry (Castlereagh). "The verses which I have inserted in a letter to Greenough [his close friend with whom he corresponded regularly over the years], will give you his character."[7]

****

The first scholar to arrive was John Gardner Wilkinson.[8] Wilkinson and an old university friend, James Wiggett, making 'the Tour' before entering the church, decided to travel together. At the end of summer 1821 they were in Naples where Gell took them under his wing and put the idea into Wilkinson's head of going to Egypt as more than just a traveller. "Why do you not take up some branch of antiquarian research...?" Gell asked, and offered to tutor him. Wilkinson agreed and "devoted himself to the study of the monuments and topography of that country." James Burton was also in Naples, preparing himself to work as a mineralogist for the Pasha, and they studied Arabic together.

By December Wilkinson and Wiggett were in Cairo, with a letter of introduction from Gell to Salt, who took Wilkinson to meet the Pasha, accompanied him to the Pyramids, and showed him the work done, under his sponsorship, by Captain Caviglia. Osman soon took him to buy Turkish clothes, for "nothing is to be arranged without Osman, who keeps the rogues in order." This question of how to dress in Egypt was to be a cause of awkwardness between Salt and Wilkinson in the future.

Before long Wilkinson and Wiggett were off up the Nile to Thebes, which became Wilkinson's main base in the years ahead. They went on into Nubia and, back at Thebes, met Linant and Ricci returning after nine months beyond the Cataract. Wiggett soon fell desperately ill with dysentery, and they sped to Alexandria to seek Ricci's help. He and Linant were reporting to Salt on their expedition. Eventually Wiggett recovered enough to be sent home; Wilkinson might have left too and taken up his commission in the army, but he did not. He was firmly set on his new career and was not to leave Egypt until 1831.

****

Salt was working hard on his collection of copied and original inscriptions, on papyri and other objects. In September 1822, when he wrote to Halls' sister describing his work as Consul, he added "the little time I have to spare besides, is spent poring over Greek manuscripts, and in the study of Egyptian antiquities, in which, as you know the sort of burrowing facility I possess, like that of a mole underground, you will not be surprised at my having made considerable progress."[9] Over the next year he gradually pieced together an interpretation of the hieroglyphs from his records from many places in Egypt. By March 1824 he had completed work on an essay outlining his conclusions.

From time to time, as Wilkinson became more knowledgeable, Salt discussed problems of the decipherment of the hieroglyphs with him. Wilkinson fulsomely acknowledged this help in his own work on hieroglyphs published in 1828: "the kindness of Mr Salt, our Consul-General, who has ever been ready to give one assistance in my pursuits, whose fame as an antiquarian is well known, and with justice highly appreciated in the literary world."[10] Salt shared his ideas and progress with Gell too and sent him material. He studied Young's and Champollion's work as it arrived in Egypt. He had one great advantage over them: the monuments were to hand and his own copies were at the time the best available. Modern scholars acknowledge that Salt's great contribution to the study of hieroglyphs was that he made the first accurate copies. The *savants* allowed their artistic training to influence their reproductions, though Salt himself admired their accuracy.

Salt admitted quite candidly to Halls that he had been "wrong in ridiculing" the ideas of Champollion's phonetic system underlying the hieroglyphics, which he had at first met with "a very decided prejudice". But, believing that Champollion and Young would not waste their time on vague conjecture, he seriously examined the theory. Before long this led him to "a complete conviction of [his] error" and his own work, following their hypothesis, gave "a new lustre to this interesting discovery". It was the realisation he came to that scholars, far apart, not in contact, were coming to the same conclusions that made him decide to publish. He found, he told Halls, the phonetic alphabet "was not only applicable to the Roman and Greek Conquerors of the country, but also the Ethiopian Sovereigns who had ruled over Egypt." He found out several names, including ancient kings and queens, private individuals, and gods, from the many names of different deities he had collected in Upper Egypt.[11] But — with his manuscript all but ready — needing only recopying and correcting — fate intervened.

* *

Another, rather more unusual, scholar arrived in Egypt in 1821 and Salt gladly offered him hospitality. Joseph Wolff, a German Jew, turned first Catholic and then, after a ramble through the choices of Protestantism, chose the Church of England as a working compromise. He came to the East to convert other Jews to his beliefs. He arrived in Alexandria in early September 1821 and met Mr and Mrs Salt with the Lees. Wolff was a scholar of some standing. He had been to university in Germany, attended a seminary in Rome and studied at Cambridge. His study of languages of the East had been paid for by the Scotsman David Baillie, who employed Charles Barry in Egypt in 1819. In Rome Wolff had met Niebuhr, Bunsen and Akerblad. In Salt he recognised "a man of deep learning, very skilful in reading inscriptions and most eminent in drawing — cold in manner but kind in heart." Mrs Salt he found strikingly beautiful.[12] At the Cairo Consulate he met the traveller John Carne and together they went to Sinai. In late November he returned to Cairo and was welcomed by the Salts in their own home, where Mrs Salt's mother, Madame Pensa, was also in residence. When Wolff left in mid-December Salt promised "to take all pains to establish a Bible Society in Cairo." Wolff travelled on to the Levant, but returned to Alexandria in October 1822 and was again warmly greeted by the whole Salt family.

The autumn months Mehemet Ali often spent at his palace by the sea and those consuls who lived most of the year in Cairo followed him, no doubt also glad to escape from the heat of the capital. Salt's daughter continued to enchant him and he wrote proudly to Mary Halls that, at 16 months she had been vaccinated against smallpox, had had the measles and had no fewer than 16 teeth "which is a great matter for a child to have got over at so early an age."[13] At the end of 1822 Mrs Salt was again pregnant, with a baby due in May 1823, while Georgina was, in her father's opinion, "one of the handsomest and most engaging children I have ever seen." Salt liked children and they liked him. Wilkinson reports him buying children's toys in the market because of their charm and design, and perhaps also to give to his daughter.[14]

The next baby was born prematurely in March and lived only 16 days, to be buried on 26 March. Her name was Julia. Salt wrote a poem in her memory which he sent to Mountnorris with the words of deprecation with which he tended to introduce his public efforts, "You always smiled at my poetry, but I think you will be pleased with the following lines, written a few days after the death of my little girl":

Grand Cairo
Dear suffering child, to thee it was not given
To breathe the balmy fragrance of the spring,
Nor view, at morn, reviving nature's bloom;
Open'd thy eyes in agony, not to know
Thy weeping parents; nor a mother's care.
Nor all the fond anxiety of friends,

218

Could save thy wish'd for life. Sweet angel now,
(So to thy father's inward sense thou seem'st)
Lift up thy little hands before God's throne
And ask for us that bliss thou there enjoy'st.[15]

* *

James Burton did not follow Wilkinson to Egypt until late March 1822 and soon went off into the desert to explore under the command of Mehemet Ali's senior French officer, Colonel Seve. He had been kindly received by Salt, but, with Gell's poem in his notebook, was very distrustful. He wrote to his friend George Greenough in February 1823 asking him to write up and make public notes that he had passed through Salt, as he was worried because: "He is a gentleman... who is accustomed (*on dit*) to attribute much more than he might to himself and may also forget to add my name in the account."[16] Burton's dislike of Salt continued even when he came to know him better, and Salt may well have been aware of it. According to a friend of Burton's, Salt only once asked him to dinner and that because "James happened to call just as the table was serving." Burton was very critical of Salt's lack of hospitality compared to that of Peter Lee in Alexandria: "a very honourable man [who] does great credit to the nation, but I cannot praise so much Mr Salt...who is quite the reverse. He never gives a party to the English...while Mr Lee is constantly giving dinner parties and balls."[17] Burton's information does not tally too comfortably with others', and his lifestyle made him an unlikely guest in a family home.

Late in 1823 a group of scholar-tourists, all trained architects, arrived at Alexandria, who were inadvertently to be of great concern to Salt at a very difficult period. They were Henry Westcar (who kept a diary of the journey), Henry Parke, Joseph Scoles and Frederick Catherwood. In Cairo they presented themselves at the Consulate. Salt was, as usual, welcoming and indeed suggested that they join him up river at Manafalout where the Pasha had arranged a military spectacle.

Salt reached the great encampment on 9 December, and the young men arrived three days later. Tents were laid out in a wide half moon with the green tent of the Pasha in the centre. Salt's tent nearby was "green without and red within", with two rooms and very commodious. Not far away, nicely balanced on the other side of the Pasha, was the tent of Colonel Drovetti. Close at hand were the inevitable camp followers in a makeshift market "where all things were sold" by Frank traders who, attracted by the great gathering of 4,000 soldiers, had ascended from Cairo.[18]

The soldiers wore dirty maroon coloured jackets and large trousers gathered into gaiters; their 'centurions' wore scarlet ornamented with gold

219

"and looked very well". The officers, Westcar noted, were mainly French. Their commander, Joseph Seve (known as Sulima Pasha), had recently 'turned Turk', a conversion Salt disparaged, indicating that if an Englishman did this "he would not own him as a countryman in case of need" — an interesting remark in light of his patronage and trust of Osman and his close friendship with Burckhardt. He reported to the Foreign Office (tantalisingly saying he was using an extract from his journal which does not appear to have survived, although correspondence with the editor of the *Quarterly Review* may give its content). "This morning [11 December] the troops were drawn out on a plain where they were reviewed by the Pasha. At the end they kept up a running fire for ten minutes that astonished us." In their exercise of arms he judged then "nearly as perfect as European troops" and in their marching "somewhat inferior to the British but nearly equal to the French troops I have seen." "It gave," he reported to the *Quarterly Review*, "the best idea of a battle I have ever witnessed, always excepting the Duke of Wellington's famous review on the plains of Mont Martre."[19] The troops — Mehemet Ali's four new regiments, formed under the direction of Colonel Seve from black slaves, a few Berbers and a great number of conscripted fellahs — were gathered before sailing to take part in the suppression of the Greeks. Some believed that the purpose of this military exhibition was to let the Sultan in Constantinople know of the stature of the Pasha of Egypt. Tartar messengers from the Porte were there to witness the occasion and carry news of it to their master.

Salt returned to Cairo, having promised his wife — who was again pregnant with, they hoped, a son — that he would be with her by the new year. The young men turned south up the Nile.

Even at the 'durbar', Salt followed his antiquarian interests. In August, the traveller John Madox had come to Egypt, been offered transport in Salt's *cangia* to Cairo, accompanied Yanni d'Athanasi to Upper Egypt and was now with Yanni at Gournu. Salt wrote to him about two stone boats Yanni had discovered, asking him to look also at the boats found by Giuseppe Passalacqua (who had come to Egypt to buy horses), "as he may be a little jealous about showing them to me in Cairo". Salt wanted to see Passalacqua's boats so he could restore his own in the correct manner.[20] He gave Madox details of what to observe. "I envy you," he wrote wistfully from his red-lined tent. "the enjoyment you must have among the noble ruins of Thebes"; but duty, both consular and connubial, called him back to Cairo. As a postscript he sent news to Thebes that he had secured the freedom from slavery of the father of his domestic, Moosa, who would soon be returning home to Gournu: "If my voyage here had had no other result, I should feel happy in having made it, as the poor man has children yet young, and no one else to provide for them."[21]

* *

At Luxor at the turn of the year the four young architects met Yanni and John Madox, who was kind enough to "lionize two of them over the ruins". Continuing up river, into Nubia, at Kalabshe Westcar recorded what might have been a serious accident. Scoles, "who has a very large bum", in measuring part of the temple, was obliged to mount a wall, "but on account of the weight of his posterior", lost his balance and fell on a Nubian dwelling, "which, unable to stand this close bombardment", collapsed. Fortunately the fall led to nothing worse than levity. Soon they were faced by a more serious problem. News came in March 1824 of rioting in Egypt with the fellahin rising and killing Franks and Turks from Kena southwards. They were caught between Nubia and the riots. News grows as it travels and they heard that the governors of Esne and Homs had been killed, that "Mahomet II, brother to the Prophet" was leading the revolt and, later, that Yanni had also been killed.[22]

Madox, after crossing the desert to the Red Sea, returned to Gournu on 14 March, with a young Quaker, John Fowler Hull. They found Yanni alive but very anxious. A dozen Arabs had been sent by the sheik who claimed to be Mahomet II to seek guns, having heard that Yanni had 200 at his disposal. Yanni handed over one, and feared they would return. In the evening the sheik sent a message that "… the English were their friends, and that he was a friend of the English, and would protect them, swearing by the sword and the Koran, that if any one robbed the English, even of the cord of a camel or an ass, he would restore them a camel or an ass for it." His role, he went on, was on the order of God and the Grand Signor (in Constantinople) "to dethrone Mehemet Ali". The local Arabs then settled down around the house with their long spears, to defend it. Yanni and his household were left unmolested, though 17 local people were killed and thrown into the Nile during the night.[23]

The troubles continued, with threats against foreigners, which were always denied by the sheik. By now Madox felt himself in a trap. On one side were the Arabs who might plunder or murder them; on the other, Salt had written on 28 February warning of the increasing threat of the plague, which had broken out a month early in Cairo: "I have to recommend you, in case of your returning, to come up directly to my house, without touching or having communication with any one, and in this case we shall be happy to receive you; though, perhaps it may be necessary, to satisfy the ladies to put you in quarantine in your chamber for a day or so. Be careful in this case to have your box well packed, so as not to have anything outside that can be susceptible." This was a very generous offer — and most family men would not have made it. If, on the other hand, Madox decided to stay up river, Salt asked him to send for what he needed and to pass this message on to "the other Englishmen aloft". He added that he was contemplating going to Europe with his family in May: "Perhaps you may like to join us."[24]

Once the Pasha's troops were in place, battle raged up and down the river. Rumours were rife, the most fantastic being that 4,000 English had arrived at Cairo and taken the Pasha prisoner, at the request of the Grand Signor. In truth, as Madox learned a few days later from three horse-dealers, the Pasha had retired to his palace at Shubra in quarantine from the plague.

On 21 March another disaster shook Cairo. Fire broke out in a large building (described by the *Gentleman's Magazine* as Mehemet Ali's palace) near the arsenal and, despite efforts to quell it, towards sunset a magazine of gunpowder exploded with a shattering noise and a shock which was felt all over the city. The fire caused further explosions and word spread that underground vaults full of gunpowder were threatened. The danger of the plague was forgotten as people fled from the city to the western Nile or to gardens near the town. Salt received the consuls of Naples, Sweden and Spain and their families as well as some of the Pasha's staff into the Consulate. Gradually the danger receded and life returned to normal once Salt and others were convinced that the fire could not penetrate to the gunpowder deposits. The Pasha stayed the whole time at his palace on the Nile, sending a reward of one hundred thousand piastres for those who risked their lives to extinguish the fire. Madox was told when he returned to Cairo in July that up to 5,000 people "were deprived of life by this most lamentable accident".[25] The number would have been far greater if the Pasha's troops, returned from Manafalout and preparing for an expedition against the Greeks had not been prevented by the plague from occupying their quarters very near the arsenal.

Not many days later, on Good Friday, the worst tragedy of Salt's life struck. On 10 April Mrs Salt was delivered of another daughter. On the first day both mother and child were perfectly well, and the Salts and Madame Pensa could celebrate the new addition to their family. Then on the third day Mrs Salt was seized by puerperal fever. The plague was still raging, with 250 people dying daily and everyone shut up in their houses. Dr Cimba, a medical man from her home town of Leghorn who had attended her delivery, was called away to his own wife who had fallen ill and, once gone, they could not permit him to return to their house for fear he would bring the dreadful disease with him.

Salt persuaded Dr Martini (a young Tuscan physician who had accompanied Comte de Forbin up the Nile) to come. Martini, fearing that they might be infected with the plague too, was quick and careless. He diagnosed a slight gastric fever and fled. The medicines he prescribed hastened her illness.

They recalled the doctor who, finding her much worse, begged her to take comfort. "You will soon recover," he assured her.

"No, I know I shall die; but, sinner that I am, I trust that God will in his mercy take me to himself!" she replied. She had already recommended Georgina and her mother to her husband's protection. It was Good Friday, 15 April 1824. She was dead before evening. She was just 20 years old.

"It is impossible," her distraught husband wrote to his sister Mrs Morgan some three months later, "that anyone could die with more piety and resignation in the will of God than my angel." Whatever the circumstances of their meeting, theirs was undoubtedly a real marriage of lovers. "She was one of the most perfect beings I ever knew, her whole happiness being placed in her husband, mother and child." Young as she was, she had foreseen her early death. She often said to him: "When I am gone who will take all this care of you?" He always replied that she would, he trusted, live long after him. But she would answer, "No, I know that I shall die young."[26]

17

The Years of Change

IN EARLY April Henry Westcar and his party had decided to run the gauntlet of the insurgents and on 12 April Yanni reported to John Madox that they had passed Luxor without stopping. Madox was very annoyed, having hoped to escape with them down river.

"Ecco!" Yanni exclaimed, "la maniera di vostri compagni Inglesi!"

The next day a letter arrived for Yanni telling how the four had fared. Their situation in Aswan becoming very perilous, "and everything going on badly in Nubia", they had escaped after hearing at Aswan that he, Yanni, and all his family were killed. Now, knowing he was alive, they asked him to join them. Madox sent word for them to wait, warning them of the plague which lay ahead.

But the threat increased. Achmet Pasha, leader of the army, was coming to Gournu. Unexpectedly Yanni became hero of the hour. He dressed himself in European style "with pistols etc", mounted his horse, which was finely caparisoned in scarlet cloth, and, attended by his cook, "also well mounted, having a sabre and plenty of pistols around him", set off to confront the young Pasha. Achmet received them politely and advised them all to leave, and on 16 April Madox and Hull sailed away in the approaching dusk from a scene of "perfect confusion: cases of mummies, statues and antiques of all sorts lay scattered in every direction."[1]

By 22 April Westcar's group were with Wilkinson, who had been up river with his female slave, when Madox arrived amongst them at Keneh. News of continued unrest came in from all directions. Soldiers returning from five years in Arabia had been ambushed and killed or wounded, and their English officer wounded. The Pasha's Tartar cavalry, unable to take the mutinying army at Aswan captive, cannoned down 500 of them. On 4 May the English party at last left Keneh, slipping away by moonlight, accompanied by a gunboat. On 14 May Yanni caught up with them and gleaned "the melancholy intelligence of the death of Mrs Salt" in a local town.

Westcar's party eventually reached Cairo on 20 June, but it was not until 4 July that Madox and Hull landed there early in the morning "and Osman came to us", Mr Salt being in Alexandria. Salt, when he heard they were all safely returned, recorded his relief in the midst of his sorrows.

* *

Salt had been unwell at the time of his wife's lying in and afterwards was struck down by the old malady that laid him low at times of stress and grief. With her son-in-law so ill, Madame Pensa probably took the lead. Within two weeks of the tragic Good Friday they had moved, with a surgeon attending Salt, and with Georgina and the new baby, to Alexandria. Salt's life was in shreds. With no house of his own, the family were taken in by Peter and Emma Lee. In many ways this was a satisfactory solution. Despite earlier awkwardness between them about the division of the roles and responsibilities of the two consulships, the two men were fond of each other. The Lees had a houseful of children to sweep the motherless, three-year-old Georgina into their lives. The baby, moved from one wet nurse to another, survived only briefly. After this latest tragedy, Salt decided to send Georgina to Leghorn, away from "the unhealthy clime of this detestable country". With her grandmother and the banker Pietro Santoni, the husband of his wife's younger sister, his daughter would be well cared for, the proof being "the education of my beloved wife, who never left her mother," and the fact that the family "doat on the dear child."[2] Sympathy at the time came from an unexpected quarter. Salt wrote to Colonel Drovetti on 11 June 1824 thanking him for the Biscuit (a dry viand for seasick passengers) that the French Consul had procured for "le depart de Mad. Pensa et de ma chere Georgine." It was a favour he would never forget.[3]

This dreaded parting with Georgina over, Salt slowly recovered his health, comforted by the Lees with whom he continued to lodge. He gained some relief by completing a long and somewhat pedantic poem about Egypt, which he published in Alexandria on 10 July. It was the first book in English to be published in Egypt. He intended it for friends and to encourage the printer, Alexander Draghi, rather than to bring himself any fame. As the compositor was entirely ignorant of the language, the difficulties of correcting the proofs may easily be imagined. Mountnorris might have smiled at his friend's effort, but it was no worse than much that was published in the journals in Britain. His introductory disclaimer could hardly be more humble: "This poem was printed with a view to divert the Author's attention whilst suffering under severe affliction, as well as to give encouragement to a very worthy man, the Printer." (Sadly the printer did not include the intended notes, for they might have revealed much.) "Should the contents of this little work bring back any agreeable recollections to the minds of travellers, of the various scenes they have noticed in passing through Egypt, the object of its Author will be, in great measure, attained; beyond this, the only satisfaction he can promise himself consists in the gratification of those friends to whom it was dedicated."[4] He sent 15 copies for named friends in England. In distributing the poem he exposed himself to the criticism of those who read it, although he thought that by not selling it he would not be "overhauled by the critics". A few lines give a flavour:

How pleasant, too, along thy stream to sail,
And catch the fragrance of the morning gale;
Watch the bright orb of day in glory rise,
Taking his cource aloft through cloudless skies.
....
Here, too, Karnak, thy glorious temple rears
Its pile, the wonder of past circling years,
Tread lightly, traveller, tread, nor dare disturb
The awful silence of this solemn scene :
If thou have passions, learn them here to curb,
And banish from thy mind all earthly spleen.

* *

Salt had to bear his grief and loneliness at a time when the situation in the eastern Mediterranean was far more insecure than it had been for most of his years as Consul-General. The events leading to this go back some years.

In April 1821 the mainland Greeks of the Morea had rebelled against their Turkish overlords, ruthlessly massacring many of the 20,000 Muslims living there. Massacre was followed — in traditional Balkan fashion — by retaliatory massacre and in Constantinople the Greek patriarch and four bishops were hanged. The rebellion spread to the islands. For a time Mehemet Ali stood aloof, unwilling to come to the aid of the Porte, and occupied with his own affairs in the south. However, in 1824, the Sultan offered to cede Candia (Crete) to him if he would reduce it to submission. Mehemet Ali could not resist. It was no easy task and it was two years before the last Cretan chiefs were hanged. His son, and general, Ibrahim Pasha, marked this achievement by sending a bagful of Cretan ears to be nailed to the Great Gate of the Seraglio.[5] The reward — or next temptation — came early in 1824. The Sultan bestowed the *pashaliq* of the Morea itself upon Mehemet Ali in return for active support on the Greek mainland. The demonstration of military power that Salt beheld in Manafalout in December 1823 was not unconnected with this recognition of Egypt's power, and the troops massing in Cairo when the explosion and fire in the Citadel had caused such havoc in March 1824 were already intended for the Morea.

On 10 July a great Egyptian expedition set out from Alexandria: 16,000 soldiers, 100 transports and 63 armed vessels under the command of Ibrahim Pasha, with the task of recapturing the Morea from the insurgent Greeks. Ibrahim Pasha's task was made more difficult by the Sultan, who in his convoluted manner, had appointed as admiral, or Capitan Pasha, to the expedition, Mehemet Ali's declared enemy, the very Khusrau Pasha whom he had unceremoniously driven out of Cairo in 1803. With his commanders at loggerheads, the Sultan might expect to retain control. It was not until January 1825 that Ibrahim Pasha at last landed on the Greek mainland and it took him a further six months to quell the fierce resistance. This despite those qualities of leadership which Salt had described to Joseph Planta of the Foreign Office in 1818: "undaunted firmness, or rather cruelty, to those who oppose him, a command of money and being celebrated for scrupulous adherence to his word." These qualifications Salt thought "peculiarly requisite to gain influence over the Arabs,"[6] but likely to be less popular with Europeans, and the Ottoman Turkish rulers.

By the end of July Salt had put the finishing touches to the manuscript of his essay on the "phonetick" hieroglyphs of Young and Champollion to send off to Bingham Richards to see through to publication.

Salt's studies over the years had been both extensive and detailed, and based on proofs of the interpretation as far apart as Abydos, Edfu, Dakke, the granite sanctuary of Karnak, and at Philae. One of his contributions was that he showed that the names suggested were "in perfect agreement...with the dates of the edifices on which these names have been deciphered."[7]

His researches were published with his copious footnotes and even more copious ones from William Bankes (who on this occasion acted with some expedition) under the title *Essay on Dr Young's and M. Champollion's Phonetic System of Hieroglyphs*. Salt financed the publication himself, intending it mainly for circulation to friends and interested acquaintances, but Sir William Gell wrote critically of it to Thomas Young, dismissing it on the grounds that, as he had sent all Champollion's discoveries to Wilkinson, "Salt profitted by these also and though he might say he never saw Champollion's book [*Précis du système hieroglyphyque des anciens Égyptiens*], he had seen from me all it contained and whenever he went alone was mistaken." In 1826 he wrote again to Young: "...as to Salt's claims to originality, they were only fit for Humbugia, for myself I have sent to Egypt all the inventions of yourself and Champollion as fast as they came out."[8] Gell overlooked the fact that sending documents to one person is no proof either that they arrived or that they were shared straightway with others. Salt was obviously nervous that such claims might be made against him, and added a postscript to William Hamilton on 9 October, asking him for a copy of the letter he had written on 8 March, as "it *proves* the fact of my having discovered the application of the phonetic alphabet, to the names of the gods and ancient kings, prior to Champollion's last work having reached Egypt, about which some people may be unkind enough to express a doubt."[9]

A chronology of the movements of travellers in Egypt confirms this point. The last contact Salt could have had with Wilkinson was on 28

February 1824 when they were both in Cairo, and Salt showed his essay to him. Wilkinson later claimed that he had not actually read the material as, he told Gell in December 1826, when Salt had sent him "his Opera, I skimmed it over as anyone would with the ophthalmia. He afterwards asked my opinion of it. One could not say otherwise than excellent. But the fact is I had not looked into it properly."[10] Salt could not know this, assuming it to be true, and by June, when Wilkinson returned to Cairo from Upper Egypt, Salt had been for several weeks in Alexandria where on 3 August he received the document from Mr Anastasi, four days before his own material was sent off to England.

Whatever Gell's motives or his or Wilkinson's attitudes to Salt's essay, others were impressed. In December 1826 the *Edinburgh Review,* in a scholarly 50-page article, considered various works on the decipherment of the hieroglyphs, bracketing together the work of Salt and Champollion, who "have not only conclusively settled" certain matters relating to names and titles, "but we think have established that this sort of hieroglyphic writing was much more extensively employed..."[11]

Champollion himself was full of Salt's praise. He was then treating with Pietro Santoni in Leghorn for Salt's second collection on behalf of the King of France and told Santoni that he was writing an article "rendre justice entiere" to Salt in an important scientific journal. In January 1826 his article appeared in the *Bulletin universal des Sciences et d'Industrie.* The most useful contribution to the debate on interpretation of the hieroglyphs, he remarked, "is not always that which adopts the divergent view". While others in Europe were struggling in the vague region of theories, not based on the facts, "an English savant, M. Salt, was advancing an impartial and reflective view, and, with my work in hand, goes to prove the theories on the entire monuments of Egypt themselves." Champollion congratulated himself on this proof and recommended it to those who still believed that one could arrive at a solution by several other routes than those he had proposed. Salt had, he noted, frankly admitted that he had at first disagreed with the phonetic theory, but "being able to consult the original monuments and a number of collections of the 'designs', he had soon acquired a complete conviction of his error, and confirmed the principals and sign values Champollion had established." Using this theory, Salt recognised new names on the inscriptions on temples in Upper Egypt, and had even been able to correct Champollion on some points, "having the original monuments under his eyes". Champollion praised Salt's analysis of new forms, and his important contribution of three further letters in the hieroglyphic alphabet. He found it a remarkable coincidence that two people far apart at different points of the globe with slow communication between them, should arrive by deduction at the same conclusion. These circumstances seemed to him to give strong proof of "the solidity" of his phonetic interpretation of the hieroglyphs. In conclusion, he acknowledged publicly his gratitude to Salt and recommended his work as being very precious in the elementary study of Egyptian archaeology and to those who were contributing to the establishment of the true principles of its study.[12]

There is no evidence that Salt ever saw this article, and Wilkinson apparently did not know about it. In July 1827 he wrote to Gell, "How Champollion must laugh at Salt's work. I am sorry that Salt himself is inclined to think there is anything in it."[13] The matter is now obscure academic gossip, of little interest to modern Egyptologists, and Salt himself was only marginally important in the deciphering of hieroglyphs, but his contribution might have been more enthusiastically recognised if the 'purveyor' of hieroglyphs had chosen to encourage it to be so. As today, a distant amateur's commentary upon a subject with which academics are struggling carries little weight. However, in 1827, the *Essay* had appeared in Paris and its translator, L. Devere, commented that if there were people who still did not believe the phonetic theory, Salt's essay would dissipate their doubts.[14]

* *

Sailing down from Cairo in August, Henry Westcar recorded the strange circumstance of seeing a boat carrying Mrs Salt's coffin also travelling northward. Is it possible that her body had been embalmed in order to be taken to her last resting place in the Latin Convent in Alexandria where their marriage would have been consecrated?[15]

Salt, this final duty to his wife completed, was due to resume his duties in Cairo. In mid-September disaster struck again. Peter Lee fell ill and in only ten days was dead. Salt "with all his wounds torn open afresh" had to comfort the very people who had comforted him so recently and to whom he acknowledged he owed "in a great measure, my recovery from the deplorable state into which I had fallen."[16] Mrs Lee and her five children were left almost destitute, unless the Levant Company provided for them, which Salt thought unlikely. There seemed to be no alternative but to return to England where the Lees had not lived for many years.

Sadly Salt saw them depart and returned, alone, to the empty house and a double burden of work as Lee's duties as well as his own now became his responsibility. He was left "without any one whom I could look to for consolation, in case of need, or whom I could call a friend in the country." Lee's job was both less interesting and more burdensome than his own. He described the duties to Bingham Richards that November as "being more like those of a Bow-street magistrate than any other Christian office: gales of wind daily and gales among the seamen and captains — I have no less than seven seamen in prison at the moment." "The disagreeable and worry-ing nature" of the work left Salt little time, commented Halls, "for the indul-gence of his favourite pursuits, and still less to devote to correspondence with friends."

For most of the year the Pasha spent only brief periods in Alexandria and Salt, unable to return to Cairo, watched anxiously as Drovetti held increasing influence over the Pasha: "wherever Mehemet Ali goes — to Cairo or Alexandria — Drovetti is free to go." Salt, with no house of his own, was lodging with Robert Thurburn, and frequently urged the Foreign Office to make a new appointment so he could return to his proper post. It was now even less likely that he would be able to go on leave to Leghorn. He eagerly awaited the frequent reports of Georgina from the Santonis and Madame Pensa, and was delighted by their good accounts of her. They made him much happier "than if she were remaining here, as she is out of the way of plague, fever, ophthalmia, and all our blessed disorders." Her portrait, now missing, hung over the door of the main *sala* in his later Alexandrian house where he could see her as he passed in and out.[17]

For company, apart from passing travellers, there were few like-minded people. All the British captains expected to be invited to dine when they were in port (presumably creating some of the jollity that Lee's hos-pitable home was known for), and there were the consuls, described by his friend Robert Madden as "so wrapped up in their own importance, that they affect to be worshipped as little demi-gods by their subjects and are ridiculed as foolish persons, doting on their gold lace and dressed only in a brief authority, which renders them conspicuous, but not respectable." Some of them were in debt in one way or another to Mehemet Ali, who handed out bribes in the form of "a cargo of beans...credit for produce...permission to dig for antiquities at Thebes..." to persuade them to turn a blind eye to his own actions.

Of Drovetti, Madden commented, Mehemet Ali "allots the pay and privileges of a privy counsellor...so Drovetti has more influence over him than any other European." It was, after all, Drovetti whose "prudence and dexterity seated Mehemet Ali on the throne", and Madden considered him "the most perfect courtier in his manners and appearance...the elegance of his address is only surpassed by the depth of his dissimulation, and the skil-fulness of his subterfuge." Madden found "something terrible in his counte-nance; and as he stalks along the plain of Alexandria every evening, muffled up in his white *bernoux,* the Franks are seen to retire with a sort of deferen-tial horror, and whisper as he passes, 'Make way for Catiline.'" Madden, and possibly Salt, thought that Drovetti was luring Mehemet Ali along a disas-trous route. Salt, Madden noted, had less influence "because he condescends not to intrigue with the menials of the court, but he is more respected."

Besides the consuls for company — or lack of it — there were the merchants of the nine English houses of commerce in Alexandria: those of Briggs and Thurburn, Bell, Harris, Muir, Casey, Joyce, Shutz, Gliddon and Hayes. Of this commercial community Madden lamented "the mercantile jealousies which debar all social intecourse between them." However, as individuals, he could not speak too highly of their respectability.

Of other foreigners in Alexandria, Madden had little good to say, except for the missionaries, whose work he deplored although he admired them as men, speaking of the resident minister in Alexandria, Reverend McPherson's "unaffected piety and worth."[18]

* *

In November 1824 a minor Scottish nobleman arrived in Egypt. Robert Hay's work is possibly as important to the recording and study of ancient Egypt as that of either Edward Lane or Wilkinson, but Hay only published *Illustrations of Cairo* (a collection of drawings by himself and other artists). He retains little recognition, though during his years in Egypt he produced many volumes of manuscripts and drawings (49 in the British Museum collections alone) and collected more than 200 cases of antiquities and casts, many of which were purchased by the British Museum after acrimonious negotiations. In later years he employed artists and architects in a 'studio' in one of the tombs of the Valley of the Kings to draw plans, sections and elevations of the monuments, and even on his first expedition he took his own assistant.[19]

Hay had met Joseph Bonomi in Rome. Bonomi was three years older, the son of the architect Joseph Bonomi Senior who left Italy to work with the Adams brothers. Bonomi, a tiny man, "tending almost to dwarfism", studied drawing at the Royal Academy, and, after many years in Egypt and with many unsatisfactory false starts, due largely to financial problems, would eventually be thought of as the best recorder of hieroglyphs of his time.[20]

Together the two young men with a couple of friends spent a long, pleasant summer in Italy and Malta. There they met Frederic Catherwood and Henry Parke, who gave them useful information about Egypt. They arrived in Alexandria on 7 November, and called on Henry Salt the next morning. He received them coolly though politely, but asked them to return to dine, giving Hay more time to observe him: "I was greatly surprised by Mr Salt's manner and he does not seem to be quite the man he has been represented — but don't judge too quickly. There was only another gentleman beside ourselves and both seemed conversable." It is hard to tell from this what Hay had been told, but almost certainly he liked Salt better than he expected — one may surmise that his prejudice may have come from Sir William Gell, whom he met in Naples, though Catherwood and Parke may also have provided an unsympathetic account.

Conversation turned to Belzoni, whom Salt (his earlier forbearance now quite worn away) accused of ingratitude, saying "that his money had supplied Belzoni in all his operations and that the excavating of the Temple of Ypsambul cost him, Mr Salt, two hundred pounds — presents given by Belzoni were also from his pocket, and in fact 'Belzoni was no more than an architect employed to build a house and employed as many men as he chose'." The account given by Captains Irby and Mangles in their book "is strictly correct", Salt said. He hinted that he would publish himself if he could expect fair play from the press. At three his guests took their leave and Salt took "his usual nap".

At the Consulate in Cairo Hay and Bonomi met a man who appears only at the very fringes of Salt's life, although he was quite an important part of it for some years: the Chancellor (or treasurer) to the Consulate. Charles Sloane did not impress Hay and indeed he seems an improbable figure in Salt's entourage. "Mr S. sat almost clumsily in one corner of his sofa," wrote Hay, "dragging instead of drawing a burnous that was not the whitest I have seen, about him, up to the very chin in a very awkward manner, as if he was quite naked below and wished to conceal it... some peep of a hand or rather a paw stretched out for paper...Dirty stockings...made me almost think it was a pig wrapped up in a Bournous instead of an Englishman."[21]

The 'pig' introduced them to Osman, with "his manners perfectly of a Turk", who took them to James Burton's house, where one of Burton's ladies was peering out. "For he lives like a Turk in that respect — though in this he was not alone." Hay found him a pleasant well-educated man who "takes great pains to dress well in the costume of the country, and wears a most magnificent shawl Turban. His face is rather thin, his nose acquiline and on the whole he makes a very good Turk, wears no beard, only moustaches."

With the help of Osman, Hay went into the bazaar to prepare to dress "in the style of the country". This was easily achieved for ready made clothes "are of a kind that will fit any body". He bought a handsome suit of scarlet cloth and returned later to buy material for a cloak. To a young man noted for his unusual dress in Europe — where he flaunted a white top hat in the Mediterranean countryside — it must have been great fun, like a child let free on a gorgeous dressing-up box.

Not long before a problem had arisen over the Consul's responsibilities for certain British subjects and protected persons, particularly the Maltese and Ionians, and Salt had consulted the Foreign Office about his role. Canning's response of March 1824 was that these people should be treated like "His Majesty's natural born subjects", but that "a wide distinction exists between British Subjects residing in Egypt in an independent character for the prosecution of commercial or other pursuits" and those who were in the service of the Pasha. "The latter naturally diminish their claim on the immediate protection of their own Government, and if they choose to abide under the control of His Highness, they must do so at their own risk and peril."[22]

It was not until late October that the Consulate acted on this letter. When "Mr Salt caused a notice to be pasted upon the walls stating that he would not protect any British subjects who appeared in the Turkish costume, or much to that effect." Burton and Wilkinson, "the only two in Cairo under these circumstances" copied down the actual words of the notice and their scrawled copy (in Italian and English) still remains among Burton's papers in the British Library.[23]

Burton and Wilkinson speedily demanded to know why the Consul was removing their rights as Englishmen to his protection. While one cannot sympathise with their tone, one may sympathise with their comments, particularly as they would have known that many British travellers, including those directly enjoying the hospitality of Salt, took to Oriental dress up country. Salt probably did not approve of Europeans wearing Oriental dress, unless for a proper purpose as when travelling, but on the other hand there are reports of young Englishmen visiting the Consulate in Turkish dress. It is only too possible that misunderstanding or misinterpretation were significant in this incident.[24]

Hay — whom Salt does not appear to have advised on dress — was not satisfied with the answer his new friends received and wrote in his diary that "whatever my dress may be, I shall insist as long as I bear the passports of my country and as long as I call myself a British subject, on being protected as such, by those paid by the country for the good and welfare of all those belonging to it, whatever may be their pursuits." Indeed, whatever Salt's — or Sloane's — reasons for posting this notice, almost all travellers in Egypt adopted the 'Turkish' dress when out of Cairo.

Despite the tone of Burton and Wilkinson's letter, Salt was surprisingly conciliatory. He wrote to Burton "trying to lay all the blame on his agent Mr Sloane as not understanding him — that it was only those employed under the Pasha" (of whom, of course, Burton had been one) "that were expected to appear in their own costume, or stand the consequences of whatever might happen while wearing the Turkish dress; it had nothing to do with travellers..." "Curious indeed if it had," commented Hay tartly. "Englishmen dictated to by their Consul as to the dress they are permitted to wear would be something quite new and not a little laughable!" He then described in some detail the full Turkish dress which he now felt free to don — having cannily waited until the matter was resolved.

Hay dined at the Consulate when Salt was back in Cairo, as did Burton and Humphreys (contradicting Burton's claim that he never dined there), to meet Lord St Asaph and his companion Captain Grace who were going up the Nile. ("For why I do not know," commented Hay. "He seems however a gentlemanly man and devoted to his pipe.") Sloane was asked to show Salt's drawings to Hay, who was not impressed. "Notwithstanding the kindness I cannot say that I was not greatly disappointed with the meagreness of the display besides the careless manner in which most were done; and all that I could learn from them is that much is to be found along the banks of the Nile, worth giving greater pains and time to than he seems to have bestowed." The young men stayed late in conversation with their host.[25]

Hay soon met Wilkinson, to whom he carried a letter of introduction from Gell. He found him dressed as a Turk and looking much like one, and avoiding Franks as much as possible. On Christmas Day, Hay, having squabbled about his bill at the Consulate, was seen off up the Nile by Osman, with Bonomi and Hay's manservant John, and a cooked turkey but no wine for the celebrations.

In late February they caught up with Lord St Asaph at Thebes. After a day together at Karnak and a comradely dinner aboard, St Asaph proposed that they should excavate in company, employing a hundred men between them. However, instead they spent the days idling together until it was time to separate. One evening they entertained themselves on Hay's boat quoting to each other excerpts from "that *beautiful* poem from the pen of Mr Salt on the Nile and its wonders." One can imagine their irreverent laughter ringing out merrily across the water:

> Hail to thee, lonely valley of the dead!
> Compass'd with rugged mountains, where the tread
> Of man is rarely heard, save his who roams
> From foreign lands to visit thy lone tombs —
> Tombs of long perish'd kings, who thus remote
> Their sepulchres have set in barren spot,
> Where not a blade of verdure ever grew:
> To me that hast a charm for aye that's new,
> For I have cast, for days, for weeks, for months, my lot
> Among thy rocks secluded — oft at night
> Hath the still valley met my awe-struck sight,
> Lighted by silver moon that seemed to cast
> A lingering look upon thy 'antres vast',
> While many a blast blew, not unmix'd with dread,
> That bore, methought, a chiding from the dead.

However humble Salt's introduction to his poem, and however sad the circumstances of its creation, it must be admitted that it was a work which

234

would inevitably create hilarity in clever young men who had been enjoying a companionable dinner.

Salt's experience with the British Museum had been bitter and might have been disillusioning, but few wounds are deep enough to cure a collector once the addiction has taken hold. He employed Yanni d'Athanasi as his collecting agent at Luxor, and Hay and Bonomi frequently visited him to view his finds which, despite being Salt's agent, he was sometimes prepared to sell on his own account for ready cash — perhaps making some think it was Salt who was the 'dealer'. On Hay's first visit the principle exhibit was a mummy, "the cases of which were well painted and the face and beard beautifully executed." On another occasion, when Yanni had been excavating at Karnak, there were many bronzes and a silver statue which he allowed Bonomi to draw. Once Hay went to Yanni's as a buyer. Yanni had just received some fresh supplies from Karnak, and Hay purchased a large bronze statue of Osiris, which he thought had had some restoration by Yanni himself "as he is too fond of using the file to give [them] an appearance."

18

A Friend, The Louvre and Growing Danger

FORTUNATELY for Salt, in June 1825 Dr Richard Robert Madden arrived in Alexandria. Born in Dublin in 1798, he read medicine in Paris and London and had already travelled extensively. He spent several months in Naples with the Irish aristocrats, the rich and cultured Blessingtons. Having travelled through Greece and the Levant, in Candia (Crete) he met Ibrahim Pasha, to whom he took a strong dislike.

There are few descriptions of Ibrahim, and Madden's does not always match others. He saw a man, only in his mid-40s, who was "so corpulent as to be unable to go any distance afoot, and possesses neither dignity of feature nor of figure...His eyes are small and twinkling, of that peculiar grey which Lord Byron supposes characteristic of cruelty; and the *tout ensemble* of his countenance is exceedingly vulgar." Madden was disappointed that a man, much praised as a soldier, should not be more impressive, but acknowledged him a person of "great personal courage, and of extraordinary ferocity."[1]

Madden, like so many other travellers, intended to write about his travels, but regretted that he was not one "who affected to be a learned traveller...it is difficult to carry Herodotus, Hamilton, Strabo and Sir William Gell, Pococke and Pausanius in one small head, albeit enveloped in a turban."[2] His interests were less with the ancient world than with the world around him. It was the plague season and, he had developed theories about the treatment of this terrible disease. He proposed to Salt and Thurburn that he should attend plague patients to test his ideas.[3] Both men made unenthusiastic representations on his behalf, but soon the plague itself imprisoned them in their homes, and they dissuaded him.

Salt wrote to Jane Morgan (Bessy's niece by marriage) more contentedly that June. Although he still longed for home, they would find him strangely altered: "quite the old gentleman of forty-five, with a serious face, grey hairs, and an increasing corporation, my health for some months back having been better than it has been for years...besides this, you will find me afraid of the cold, very regular and old-batchelorlike in my habits, and fond of having everything comfortable around me."[4]

At some time after Madden's arrival, probably before September, Salt, who had been lodging with the Thurburns, took over an 'excellent' house outside the crowded city. Madden moved in as medical attendant to his household, and together the two men created a pleasant garden, as Salt had done in Cairo, and there was laughter again in Salt's life. Madden made two unsuccessful attempts to climb Pompey's Pillar, but a Miss Talbot, "an Irish lady of some verve", managed to ascend it and breakfasted on the summit. From there she wrote a letter to Mr Salt, dated "from the top of Pompey's Pillar" and he sent an answer purporting to be from "the bottom of Jacob's Well", but which Madden says "he confesses was written in his parlour".[5] In Madden's *Travels* is a light-hearted portrait by Salt of the doctor, in Turkish dress, attending a Muslim lady, of whom only a small hand appears from behind the harem curtain for the doctor's diagnosis. They discussed the possibility of moving the obelisk known as Cleopatra's Needle to England, the Pasha having graciously proffered it to the British nation some years earlier. The British government had inquired if it was worth the expense; Salt felt it was not, although he was assured by the Pasha, through Boghos, that "The Obelisk may be removed at any time which His Britannic Majesty may judge most convenient."[6]

Madden was not only good company but a man after Salt's own heart. He supported liberal ideas: the abolition of slavery, the regeneration of the people who had been enslaved, respect for the cultures of other peoples and races, and a concern for people as individuals. In his *Travels* Madden spoke out in the strongest terms about other men's racism: "It is the fashion here, as well as in our colonies, to consider the negroes as the last link in the chain of humanity, between the monkey tribe and man; but I do not believe the negro is inferior to the white man in intellect; and I do not suffer the eloquence of the slave driver to convince me that the negro is so stultified as to be unfit for freedom."[7] Madden — possibly reflecting Salt's real thoughts — was very critical of Mehemet Ali's schemes. Drovetti, he thought, by his subtle counsel, was leading the Pasha down a false route. "He mistook the genius of the people; overrated their necessities and estimated falsely the interests of a country which is purely agricultural." He was highly critical of the many building projects, "resembling palaces", and the vast investment in machinery imported to make products to compete with the rest of the world, but costing more than the export value they could produce. In addition, "the Frank parasites" had lured the Pasha into believing that he had the finest troops in the world. As a result "armies were raised and fleets built, which the revenues of Egypt were unable to maintain", with the consequence that neither fleet nor army were paid. The war in the Morea was draining the coffers of the state yet further.[8]

Salt was immersed in the mundane business of the Alexandrian Consulate, but political matters concerned him, and he frequently urged Lee's replacement. It could not have been a worse time to get a decision. In 1824 it had been decided that future holders of Levant Company consulships should be appointed by His Majesty's Government, but it was not until

May 1826 that the Company formally surrendered its charter, and consular appointments began to be made.

In August 1825 a crisis suddenly recalled Salt to his political role, and his report to the Foreign Office gives a vivid picture of a strange and tense few days. In the evening of 10 August an enterprising Greek captain attempted to slip up on the Egyptian ships in the harbour. A pilot's suspicions were aroused and he called out to them, "Dogs without faith, I know you — anchor directly or if you approach those ships of war they will soon sink you to the bottom!" It was too late. A Turkish man of war was set afire and sank. The Greeks escaped. "It was," Salt wrote, admiringly, "certainly a hardy enterprize but ill executed...It might have produced most disastrous consequences...and it could have been difficult to restrain the populace from turning their vengeance on the Franks."[9]

Thomas Galloway, scion of a London engineering family in the employ of the Pasha, sat with his employer overlooking the harbour at the Ras-al-tin Palace and witnessed the incursion. Immediately Mehemet Ali, in a violent rage, galloped off on his mule to the battery on the point, hoping to fire on the invader. Failing, he ordered several ships out of harbour to give chase. To add to the insult, news came on 12 August that the Greeks had set fire to a cargo boat within sight of one of the Pasha's ships. The Pasha exploded, lifting off his turban and promising the wrath of Allah, he rushed down to the waterside and commandeered a ship. Boghos had scarcely time to send on board a cushion or two and an interpreter, some money and provisions before he sailed, and, for a week, the Pasha sought both the Greek ships and his own with no success.[10]

The very next day a fleet of 16 frigates, many large corvettes and brigs — altogether some 40 sail — appeared off Alexandria. It was the Pasha's old enemy Khusrau Pasha, the Capitan Pasha of the Ottoman fleet, arriving, battered, from the siege of Missalonghi. Word was that he had blocked the entry to Damietta and Rosetta and was come for Mehemet Ali. The Pasha had disappeared, his most able troops were far away across the Mediterranean and his greatest enemy was at the gate. His ministers were aghast. Hurriedly they called a council meeting and consulted both Drovetti and Salt. It was agreed that the ships might enter harbour, but that under no circumstance should the Capitan Pasha land. Salt and Drovetti feared for the safety of the Franks. Everyone made it their business to keep the Capitan Pasha in good humour "by sending him a profusion of everything the Country afforded". No one, not unnaturally, could believe that Mehemet Ali had gone off on his madcap adventure, but believed he had withdrawn to Cairo, hearing of the Capitan's approach. At last, on 20 August, before dawn, Mehemet Ali slipped back into his palace, and Khusrau Pasha was invited to present his compliments at the palace. Salt was present to watch this clash of Muslim Titans.

"A struggle ensued who should pay the greatest attention to the other." Salt watched enchanted as each tried to take off the other's burnous first. This was "at last compromised by their pulling them off together." Each tried to induce the other to take the seat of prominence in the corner, until at last "our Pasha placed the other there with gentle violence...Each attempted to take the fly-flapper in hand to drive away these teasing insects from each other's face which was put an end to by our Pasha, for he is the taller of the two, holding it out at arm's length."

Mehemet Ali agreed to provision and repair the whole fleet and provide ammunition of every sort. He even arranged to pay the crews up to the day of their arrival. He gave his old enemy 80,000 dollars for his private use. In all this, observed Salt, "he showed himself using every means in his power to evince his magnanimity and desire to promote the interests of the Ottoman Porte. Thus his greatest enemy was seen as a supplicant at his feet" — a fact, Salt suggested, that the Capitan Pasha "can neither forget nor forgive." Nor, thought Salt, did it seem likely that the Capitan Pasha would "cordially cooperate in any measures that may redound to our Pasha's glory." This "undisguised rivalship" of the different Pashas throughout the Ottoman Empire, he commented, "has indeed contributed materially and must contribute to its ruin."

On 19 October, the two Pashas parted "in appearance as brothers and friends", but Salt doubted that very cordial feelings existed between them. The Capitan Pasha left for the Morea accompanied by a further 1,500 horsemen, 8,000 infantry and the Pasha's new ships to support Ibrahim in the siege of Missalonghi, and Alexandria returned to "perfect tranquillity".[11]

Early in 1826, with these reinforcements, Ibrahim stormed the port, and before long captured Athens. Mehemet Ali became full of exciting visions of power. "The sword," he told a French officer, "has delivered power into my hands, and I should be indeed ungrateful if I did not continue to employ it for the service and salvation of the Turkish empire."

"But," said the officer, "will the English give you time to accomplish these great designs?"

A most pertinent question. Without at least an understanding with Britain, Mehemet Ali's dreams would be hard to achieve. The Pasha above all was a realist. What was needed to make cooperation attractive to both parties? On his side, such a falling out between him and the Porte that Egypt's independent status might be recognised; on their side, enough offered to be more attractive than the Porte's offerings.

Salt had yet another concern that autumn: that of Lord Cochrane entering the Greek service. Thomas Cochrane, tenth Earl of Dundonald, was a brilliant but unruly naval officer, constantly in trouble with officialdom but supported by his many admirers. In 1817 he had accepted command of the Chilean navy and helped secure the independence of Chile and Peru from Spain. He moved to the Brazilian navy and helped secure Brazil's independence. In 1826 he had reputedly been recruited by the Greeks. Mehemet Ali suspected that the British were behind him. His information about Cochrane was correct: he served — as a freelance — as admiral to the Greek navy in 1827-8.

Salt wrote to the Foreign Office that if Cochrane were permitted vessels and steam-boats (which were just going into commission at sea), "he would soon be able to cut off Ibrahim Pasha from his resources, and at once annihilate every hope on the side of the Turks of a prosperous issue of the contest."[12] Salt feared that Cochrane would blockade Alexandria and cut off trade with Europe, "with very evident results". In this situation Britain could well be blamed — and His Majesty's subjects suffer. Both Pashas had said to him repeatedly that "had it not been for the English, the war would have been terminated and they would be in possession of the Morea". The Turks, he felt, were unlikely to understand "the nice distinction of a Nation being at peace and its subjects being permitted to carry on a war".

Cochrane, for all his record in South America, found it almost impossible to get the Greeks to collaborate effectively, and thus had far less effect than expected. Further, his own lack of cooperation with General Church, who acted with Greek forces on land, would further limit his effectiveness.

* *

On 19 September 1825, while the Capitan Pasha was still in Alexandria, another young Englishman arrived in Egypt. Edward Lane was seriously intentioned, and, as an Arabist rather than an antiquarian, he would make a lasting contribution to the understanding of the modern life of the country.

Within hours of arriving he came to Salt's house near the Bab-es-Sidr, in the old Arab city half a mile from the modern town: "a delightful retreat", and the garden "appeared like an oasis in the desert, though in another situation it would have possessed few charms." Salt received him like an old friend, perhaps recognising in this young man something of Burckhardt in his determination to learn from the people of the country. Captain Caviglia was staying with Salt and told Lane about his understanding of magic which had led him, he believed, into the pyramids. Linant de Bellefonds was staying too with his Abyssinian wife, whom Lane had met in Malta on their way back from England.[13]

* *

That autumn a presence entered the political arena in the eastern Mediterranean. Under the new Tsar, Nicholas I, Russia was turning her attentions again to the Turkish empire. The British, loath to allow the Russians to get embroiled, called for joint Anglo-Russian mediation, into which the French joined, in an attempt to arrange an armistice between the Greek rebels and the Porte. The Sultan maintained that the Greek rebellion was an internal matter in which the European powers had no legitimate interest. He would not listen; Mehemet Ali, however, was intrigued.

In early April 1826 Salt wrote distractedly to the Foreign Office urging them yet again to appoint a replacement for Lee. He was stuck in Alexandria looking after the petty affairs of merchants and sailors while Drovetti was free to see to affairs of state. "He goes wherever Mehemet Ali goes — to Cairo or to Alexandria — and is trying to persuade Mehemet Ali to replace all Turkish officers with Arabs." This, Salt believed, would mean that the Pasha would have no back up if the local people revolted. "His behaviour to the natives makes them look forward to a French invasion" — England's worst fear. The economic situation was dire after "two bad Niles". The country was reduced to a great state of distress, "as the cultivators are made to fulfil their engagements to the Government". Pharaoh, Salt added grimly, "by the advice of Joseph, contented himself with a fifth, but the Pasha is scarcely content with two thirds." Furthermore Mehemet Ali's attention was distracted because he had taken over the active administration of affairs at Cairo and was actually sitting in judgement from eight to ten hours every day. So concerned had Mehemet Ali become about the plight of the country that he had sent out 'distinguished persons' to look into the state of affairs. Salt thought it unlikely they would report truthfully.

Boghos had been made superintendant of Commerce at Alexandria and was *de facto* governor there. Salt found him much easier "to treat with than a Turk", but this did not stop abuses in inferior departments. Salt went on to describe the placement of troops around the country, and then turned again to his regret that he was so completely tied down at Alexandria that he was prevented from being near the person of the Pasha, affording "a still freer rope to the intrigues and machinations of the French Party — now become so powerful in Cairo." Drovetti was attributing all Mehemet Ali's failures in prosecuting the Greek cause entirely to the English — "so that we are looked upon with a very jealous and, I may say, evil eye throughout the Country." He did not sense any immediate danger, but was sure that the British should be wary. French naval ships were often seen at Alexandria, "but we seldom see a British Man of War here so that the Pasha conceives that the British Government does not take any interest in the concerns of the country."[14]

The letter reached the Foreign Office in July. Their reply must have irritated Salt further. They were surprised, considering the interesting nature of what he wrote, that he had not "considered it necessary to address to this Department more frequent communications of what has lately passed in Egypt." But his letter had, at last, had the desired effect. They had appointed as Peter Lee's successor, Mr John Barker, lately Consul in Aleppo and an old friend of Burckhardt, Bankes and other travellers. "Once Barker is established, you will, of course, return to Cairo," the letter said reassuringly.[15]

But before Salt received this letter he wrote again, after visiting Cairo, about the financial affairs of the Consulate. Even in his absence the Consulate had to provide hospitality for many visitors and money was running out. He had not been able to pay the Cancelliere and his assistants, nor the two dragomans and two janissaries. He had had to pay £200 to the agent in Cairo (probably Mr Maltass) who was carrying out the government's business. Typically, in the midst of his own financial concerns, Salt asked too for help for a dragoman of "thirty years faithful service" and now retired, to whom a pension of £60 a year "would place above want."[16]

* *

Madden, Linant and Lane were not the only travellers who relieved Salt's loneliness. Less than two weeks after he had written his desperate letter to the Foreign Office, two very welcome guests stayed briefly with him. Anne Katharine Elwood and her husband, Charles, a major in the East India Company army, were making their leisurely way to India by the overland route.[17]

Mrs Elwood gave a charming picture of Salt's domestic arrangements. The house was built very much in the Italian style, with a long *sala* down the middle and a flat, terraced roof. The upper part of the *sala* was furnished with deep sofas and thick cushions, and here the Elwoods sat in the mornings and Salt received his many visitors. On their arrival he offered them coffee in little china cups on filigree gold saucers "which would have delighted any old dowager in England", handed on a silver salver. From the window they looked over a garden of date palms to Pompey's Pillar, to which the Cancelliere in Alexandria, a young Venetian, escorted them in the cool of the evening. The next day, it being Sunday, there were many callers; on weekdays the visitors were of all nations: a stately, dignified Turk, a Greek adventurer, an English sea captain or an Arab fellah with a complaint.[18]

One evening a parcel arrived from Yanni at Luxor and they gathered around to see it unpacked. There was a silver figure of a Persian king, very rare and sadly over-cleaned by Yanni, necklaces from mummies, several scarabei and other trinkets, some of which Salt pressed upon his guest.

She found Salt "a rather fine looking man, with a considerable degree of lassitude", and they were not long gone when he succumbed again to a bout of his chronic illness. But when conversation turned to literature, politics and the arts, he cheered up and displayed his "great powers of entertainment". He showed them his paintings and his poetry; "it seemed a refreshment to him to turn from the price of Cotton, or from the trifling disputes of English Captains or Arab Fellahs to the works of Madame de Stael or Walter Scott."

On 19 April the Elwoods sailed for Cairo to stay at the Consulate for two weeks, entertained by the Vice Consul, Mr Maltass. Here, too, there was a constant flow of visitors of all nations all day long. Anne Katharine sat at Mrs Salt's grand piano which was still "in very tolerable tune" and entertained the company with quadrilles and Irish melodies she never expected to play in Grand Cairo.[19]

****

On 18 June 1825, Salt had written to Bingham Richards that a collection was now in Leghorn: "antiquities to the value of four thousand pounds: the finest collection of papyri existing, the best assortment of Egyptian bronzes, several paintings in encaustic, and rich in articles of gold and porcelain, — in fine, what would make the collection of the Museum the choicest in the world, as an Egyptian collection."

The question of a pension still troubled him, but he had a possible solution. This collection he would "willingly *present* at once to the Museum, could I obtain a pension of £600 like Hoppner on which to retire.[20] This, of course, is a very confidential communication, and only to be made known to such friends as Mr Bankes and Mr Yorke. Could the matter be brought about, I should be a happy man for the short term I have to live. I have already fortune enough for my child; and with a certain income, I should be able to live somewhere in Italy, or London perhaps, and employ myself in finishing my sketches, and in arranging my Notes on Egypt, &c. These are probably day-dreams, but your being acquainted with my wishes may be of use."[21]

His dreams seem modest enough; yet James Webster, a visitor to Cairo in 1828, commented that he "was remarkable for his love of money, which he indulged so far as to become a trader in antiquities."[22] On the contrary, the evidence rather reveals a man, who though concerned about how he was to manage financially, was unusually humble in his aspirations.

Although Salt was ready to strike a bargain directly with the Government — collection for pension — he was firm about one thing: "It would be a great pleasure to me that it should go to England; but no more dealings with the British Museum — the Soanes are the people for me."[23]

243

A month later Salt hastily wrote again, for the whole situation had changed. Ironically, the French Consul, Drovetti, had suffered the rejection of his collection by the French government, but having refused offers from England and Germany, in January 1824 sold it to the King of Sardinia for 400,000 lire (about £13,000). The collection was placed in the Royal Museum in Turin, where it was seen with admiration by Jean Francois Champollion, the decipherer of the hieroglyphs.

Champollion heard that in Leghorn there was another collection awaiting a buyer. It was in the charge of the banker Pietro Santoni (husband of the younger sister of Mrs Salt), who was rather reluctant to display it — but Champollion's name opened all doors. He was stunned by the richness of the collection, which was, except for the lack of statuary, better, he thought, than Drovetti's. The French government could obtain this magnificence for 250,000 francs (about £10,000).

"I have just received notice from Monsieur P. Santoni," Salt wrote to Richards, "that Monsieur Champollion has been at Leghorn to see my collection, sent by the French Government with a view to purchase it; that he was much delighted, and that it is likely to be bought at a very advantageous price for my interest. I think it right to apprise you immediately of this, that I may not be compromised in any offer you might make on my part, through my friends, to Government...as it certainly will not be possible for me, after what I have suffered in England, to sacrifice my interests farther with a hope of any advantages that *might* accrue in that country."

However, the tempting course of claiming that negotiations with the French had gone too far to be stopped was not one Salt would pursue. "Of course it being understood *clearly,* that if any arrangement should have been by chance made before this reach you, I shall most *strictly* abide by it, and you will in that case, and in that case only, write to Santoni to suspend all treaties for the collection."[24]

For once fate did not act against Salt's prospects. On 12 April 1826, Pietro Santoni happily informed Richards that "the papers concerning the sale to his Majesty the King of France of the collection of our dear friend Mr Salt, were signed at Paris on the 18th of February. He left this affair entirely to my management, and without giving me any distinct orders as to price, was nevertheless continually soliciting me to complete the sale, writing to me repeatedly that, as long as his acquisitions were placed in such a situation as their scientific merit demanded, he should be content with even less than 150 thousand francs...I have now been enabled to obtain for him 250 thousand francs, payable...in four years, by equal yearly instalments, to commence the first of July next.

"You may imagine my satisfaction in having been able to procure such an advantage, upon a point of interest, for a friend so dear to my heart."

Had Salt "required more than 150 thousand francs, my demand would… have exceeded 250 thousand francs; and I have no doubt we should have succeeded, because the collection is most desirable indeed in its kind. I have moreover the pleasure of stating to you that this affair has been treated by me, and brought to its end, with all possible delicacy, and although the name of Salt did not appear in it, all the world knew he was in fact the proprietor of the museum."

On 15 March 1826, Champollion arrived in Leghorn to catalogue the 4,014 objects in the collection and supervise its transfer to the Louvre. Some of the officials in Paris had questioned the value put on this acquisition, but, in October, as the objects emerged from their cases, the most sceptical marvelled at the diversity and richness revealed. There were exquisite gold statuettes, bronzes ornamented with gold and silver filaments, mummies, papyri, musical instruments, tools, and a powerfully sculpted portrait head of painted limestone, still known as the 'Salt head'.

Champollion saw France's acquisition of Salt's collection as a revenge against the English. Santoni might have agreed, though for different reasons. He bitterly resented Salt's treatment: "As to the Directors of your Museum, they have, in truth, conducted themselves very ill, in every respect, with regard to our friend. Salt might well have been to his own country what Champollion is to France. His acquirements and talents are, however, known and esteemed by foreigners. They might well have afforded to be somewhat liberal for the benefit of one who is worthy of the highest esteem, both on the part of his Government and of the whole nation, as is abundantly proved by his admirable conduct in the highly conspicuous station which he occupies."[25]

* *

Not long after the Elwoods' departure, Salt was again so unwell that Madden encouraged him to take a journey on the Nile to Cairo. Salt wished to superintend the raising of his splendid consular *cangia* which had sunk the previous season precipitating two unnamed English travellers into the Nile. Luckily, Madden recorded, they were expert swimmers, and only suffered the loss of their baggage, books and papers. Madden praised the public works he observed — such as the Mahmudiyah Canal — but criticised the use of forced labour in completing them. The further south they went the more they were annoyed by flies, fleas, ants, cockroaches and mosquitoes. Salt had a mosquito curtain, but Madden "was doomed to diet the murderers of sleep". Despite these marauders, Madden found that Salt's knowledge and good humour made their journey the most delightful he could conceive.[26]

Salt had a quantity of splendid presents from the executors of an Indian Nabob to present to Mehemet Ali in return for his sanction for the building and endowment of a mosque in Mecca. Madden's description of the occasion was not flattering. The Pasha was surrounded by "fierce looking Albanians, with their feet bare, variously accoutred; a crowd of slaves; a host of Christian parasites, meanly cringing." These last were Greek and Italian merchants currying favour with the court. Into this scene Mr Salt entered with his hat on, complaining of the cold, and wore it throughout the audience. The Pasha treated him with much kindness, inquiring into his health and suggesting that, rather than discuss business, they talk about Salt's English gardens and his new house in Alexandria. Salt and Madden settled themselves on the divan beside the Pasha and the Nabob's presents were brought in: heaps of Indian shawls, embroidered muslins, gold-worked silks were thrown at the Pasha's feet. The articles of greater value were treated with more care: the snuffboxes set with diamonds, clocks and watches of curious workmanship and a fowling piece which discharged 17 shots in succession. It was this last that caught the Pasha's fancy. His "penetrating eye sparkling with pleasure as he cocked it to his shoulder".

The conversation turned to India and the recent siege of Bhuratpore.

"Is it true," asked Mehemet Ali, "that the English have taken the city and massacred the garrison?"

"There is no doubt that they took the city," Salt replied carefully. "The garrison refused quarter and thus many lost their lives."

The Pasha burst out laughing. "Oh," he said, "you are clever people in England; you go to war in India; you massacre garrisons; you do as you like with your prisoners, and no one talks against you; no one points at your red swords; but my people kill a few *giarours* [Christians] in Missalonghi, and all *Franguestan* [Frankland or the West] cries out 'Murder'; every Christian calls my son Ibrahim a bloodhound."

Salt politely responded that he had never heard anyone make this accusation. He turned to Madden to confirm this view. "I could not," said Madden, "hear anything which my Consul heard not; but the Pasha believed neither of us." He had a French newspaper at his side which someone must have been translating to him, for when Salt asked for a private audience and the others withdrew, Mehemet Ali began talking about the Pope.

"And so people kiss his toe? How extraordinary to kiss a mufti's toe. If I went to Rome, would they compel me to kiss his toe?"

Salt assured him that he might go to Rome whenever he pleased without kissing any part of his Holiness, and that the English had a Mufti of their own, or at least a head of their church, but his toes were never kissed.

Mehemet Ali continued to ask questions about religion in England. Had the English not punished, with the sword, those who rebelled on religious grounds? Yet the Sultan never interfered in another country's religious wars. "We never asked you why did you trample on these dogs? And now tell me what right have you to send money and arms to our people [the Greeks] to rebel against their masters? And why do you ask the Sultan to set them free?"

Salt confessed to Madden later that he found it difficult to respond to these awkward questions. However, he expounded on the disinterestedness of British policy, and the toleration expressed in British laws at some length. The Pasha listened "with great gravity and good humour, as if he believed every syllable of it; for Turks are extremely polite in argument, and had rather appear to be convinced than have the trouble to repeat their dissent."

While Salt's audience continued in private, Madden was surrounded in the antechamber by all the officers of the court eager to consult the Consul's *hakkim* on matters of health. He only escaped at last by promising "to physic the whole court, gratis, the next morning," and thus had time to look around at "the most magnificent palace in the Mahometan empire" with marbles and statuary from Italy, looking-glasses from France, and carpets from England. Thomas Galloway, of the London engineers, had supplied gas lighting in which Madden could see the frescoes painted by Constantinople Greeks. A workman told him that the palace harem was calculated to receive 800 women.[27]

Madden spent time with Galloway, going in the evenings to Arab *conversazioni* with James Burton and Osman, in each other's houses. They talked far into the night of the science and literature of Egypt. Each man brought his own pipe and tobacco, while the host provided coffee and sherbet. One matter of discussion was the possibility of building a canal from Cairo to the Red Sea, linking it to the Mediterranean with consequent trading benefits. Galloway had been deputed to look at this possibility. The Pasha, the year before, was delighted by the project. However, the British government was considered hostile to it; "the Consul did not sanction it", and eventually Mehemet Ali withdrew his consent.[28]

When Madden visited the Pyramids, having spent several months with Captain Caviglia while they both lodged with Salt, he had interesting opinions about the purpose of their builders. He thought it likely they contained the secret of the religion of ancient Egypt, which Salt, in his interpretation of the hieroglyphs, had not found in the papyri. It was, Madden said, the opinion of Salt ("and two other individuals of great Egyptian erudition") that the great secret was "the knowledge of the creation," and that the Egyptians had, whether by revelation or tradition, a more ancient and detailed account of the first history of man than any other people before the Jews. Madden climbed to the summit and acknowledged that "thousands of people in England would have given more than I was worth to have been in my place."[29]

By July the waters had risen to the proper height in the Nilometer and the *kadridge* was opened "with all the customary pomp which, from time immemorial, has ushered in this festival." The Pasha, however, had received bad news from his son in the Morea and absented himself, though his court joined in the celebrations. Soon after this event Salt was well enough for Madden to set off toward Nubia. He bore with him a *firman* from the Pasha announcing him as "the prince of *hakkims,* the most learned among the learned, and the friend and *hakkim bashi* [most senior medical man] of the English Consul; the friend of His Royal Highness." He had several small missions to perform for Salt. At Antinoe, he stopped to record an inscription from one of the tombs in the mountains. Reaching what he thought was the tomb Salt had indicated, he sent the reis 80 foot down into its well, which he believed no European had ever visited. Returning from the darkness, the *reis* brought a paper with pencilled notes on the back, made by Dr Bromhead, a friend of Madden's who had been in Egypt two years before and had since died of fever near Aleppo.

At Luxor, where he met Hay, Madden had another matter to attend to for Salt: to search out a Copt who had returned to his village to become a priest. If he had not yet entered holy orders, Salt wished him to return to his old office as *valet de chambre* because of his great honesty. Madden met him with his bishop — a fat old man, who sold Madden a scarab, but would not release the young man, though his mother and sister begged him to take him to Salt. After an attack of excruciatingly painful ophthalmia, Madden returned to the Cairo Consulate in "a sorry plight" but soon travelled on north and in five days had "the pleasure of meeting Mr Salt and his other Alexandrian friends". In early 1827, he departed for Palestine and Syria, not to return until October, and was not there to support Salt during the political turmoil of the next months.

19

Mr Consul-General Salt

THE REBELLION in the Greek Archipelago escalated and by 1826 was sucking in the great powers of Christendom. In April Salt told Mountnorris that "the Greeks' downfall seemed inevitable...a catastrophe which must sooner or later ensue if they are not assisted by some European power." He continued to find his own situation frustrating, with no replacement for Peter Lee and the Pasha much in Cairo, "surrounded by French Agents and Partizans".[1]

Stratford Canning, cousin to George Canning the Foreign Secretary, arrived in Constantinople as British Ambassador to the Porte on 27 February 1826 to find a grave situation. "The Greeks were pretty well run to earth, and the burthen of war was thrown almost entirely upon Egypt, whose Pasha, the famous Mohammed Ali, commanded in Candia, and by means of his son Ibrahim and a powerful squadron threatened the principal holds of the insurrection. The Turks were about to triumph at little cost to themselves. Why should they compromise?"[2] The only alternative to a Turkish conquest might be if the Pasha of Egypt be used 'to shake' the Sultan. This became the purpose of British policy in the region: to divide the Pasha from the Sultan and encourage him into a position of neutrality so the Greeks might be able to gain their independence.

On 10 June Canning wrote to Salt suggesting that a share of the tribute that it was proposed the Greeks should pay to the Porte, and a pashaliq in Syria for Ibrahim, might be more profitable to Mehemet Ali than to exterminate the Greeks at great cost to himself.[3]

Salt's reply at the end of August shows the respect in which he held the Pasha: "such flagrant violation of Muslim sentiment as supporting the Greek cause could not possibly be looked for."[4] His respect must have faltered when he discovered that the Pasha's sentiments and ambitions were more self-seeking than Islamic. Without at least an understanding with Great Britain, any dreams Mehemet Ali had of independence would be hard to achieve. He was above all a realist. What did he need to bring him English cooperation? Such a falling out between him and the Porte that Egypt's independent status might be recognised; and, in return, so much offered that it was more attractive than the Porte's offerings.[5]

The rebellion of the janissaries in Constantinople on 15 June altered the balance of strength between the Sultan and the Pasha. The rebellion, brought about by the restrictions placed on this special army by the Sultan, failed and

249

the rebels were "mown down by the Sultan's artillery and burnt to death in their barracks or cut down as they dispersed...The Sea of Marmara was mottled with dead bodies". By 22 June all was quiet again — "as quiet as the bow string and sabre can make it." With his janissaries destroyed, Sultan Mahmoud had to create a new regular army, under his control, to replace them. For the moment his military power was greatly weakened.[6]

Meanwhile Ibrahim's methods of putting down the rebellious Greeks were seen as grossly cruel. Indeed they were bloody — and became bloodier with retelling. The men were slaughtered and their womenfolk carried off — often to fill the slave markets of Cairo. Salt was as opposed to slavery as any man, but he too was a realist. On 12 August he wrote to the Foreign Office: "It must be remembered that this is not a particular feature of the present contest. It is the same course that has been practised by the Turks in every war they have carried on." Nor, he suggested, could the Pasha effect a change. "It is only by strict conformity with certain of these deeply rooted prejudices of his subjects that he has been able to accomplish so much."[7]

In mid-September Mehemet Ali arrived in Alexandria. He and Salt had several private conversations, following which Salt wrote to Foreign Secretary Canning in some alarm. He found the matter of "a nature so delicate, so confidential and, as I conceive, so important" that he felt entirely at a loss how to act. There were no men-at-war due to sail to Constantinople with whom he could entrust a report to Stratford Canning and he felt he must make an official report to some authority. Suddenly he was burdened with diplomatic responsibilities beyond his experience, and feared he could not be sufficiently explicit in his responses, and yet was in danger of being deemed to be "meddling with matters of too high import for my charge". Mehemet Ali's enthusiasm for Stratford Canning's suggestion Salt believed to be sincere.[8]

At the first meeting with the Pasha on 16 September, Salt suggested that, if the British Ambassador were to support the Pasha's views at the Porte, Mehemet Ali might be prepared to favour British views.

The Pasha replied that it was his anxious desire to serve the British Government and to act, if possible in union with it, but it was not in his power to assist — matters were too unsettled, the feelings of the ruling party at Constantinople were violent in the extreme against any concession.

"But," he went on, "I am interested to hear more from the British Government — about what they might have to offer to tempt me..." He appreciated the limitations on Salt's powers. "Perhaps a person might be sent from London charged with full powers to come to an understanding. Such a person might pass easily as a traveller," he mused. But it would not be easy even then. "You must be aware how many opposing interests I have to consult, how many prejudices to surmount, how delicate is the affair! If the matter comes to the attention of the Porte, I would give it a blank denial. I could," he admitted, as a strong mark of confidence, "have finished the Greek contest before this, had I given more naval backing to my son, Ibrahim Pasha, but instead I gave him orders to loiter about in the interior and I have delayed — as you must have seen — the expedition from Egypt."

Then he turned to another matter, also with great frankness: the appointment of Lord Cochrane to head the Greek navy. "As to Lord Cochrane, if he is *alone*, be assured it is a matter that does not give me any uneasiness...Tell therefore the Ambassador — if you should write to him of what I have said — that it is not for this I am inclined to change my line of conduct. It does not, be assured, in the least influence me."[9]

Salt realised that it was more than possible that the Pasha would co-operate with Canning's proposal. They met again on 24 September and Mehemet Ali sought Salt's views on the possible Russian intervention. "Come lay aside the Consul and tell me as a friend what you think of Russia."

Salt thought Russia would fulfil her existing agreeements; Mehemet Ali, rightly as it turned out, thought her more 'accommodating'. To turn the conversation, Salt asked if Mehemet Ali had heard of the Porte's plans to cir-cumscribe the power of the Pashas.

"They have enough on their hands without that. But," Mehemet Ali gave a very significant smile, "Mehemet Ali is no Pasha — has no title — is plain Mehemet Ali. I have never put on my seal any other inscription than — Mehemet Ali. I have little left, as you may see, of the Pasha except my *chiaouses* with silver sticks and my divan — Mehemet Ali is little but will be free." Later he dwelt again on this, adding, "England and Egypt as friends might be of use to each other — there is nothing I desire more."

They spoke of affairs in the Morea. Salt remarked, "I should be glad if you could bring your son and his troops back to Egypt. Then I would have no fear of Your Highness being other than good friends with England."

"Yes," Mehemet Ali replied, "but that is not so easy a matter — but if there are those who desire it, they will know how to accomplish it..."

"Once Consul Barker arrives," Salt said, "it would give me great plea-sure to make a visit to England that I might be able verbally to let our Minister know the exact state of things."

"No, no! You and I will stay here," the Pasha replied. "If anyone were to come, your presence would be necessary. Your Government has confi-dence in you [such, Salt noted aside, 'is his flattering opinion of me'], and I have great confidence in you. No, no, you must stay here."

This conversation, Mehemet Ali assured Salt was "not between the Pasha and the Consul, but as between two friends". ("This is a favourite mode of speaking with him and at such times his manner has a charm that it is difficult to conceive without witnessing…" Salt added.) In Salt's opinion, "The Pasha is 'resting on his oars', waiting to see what advantage he might draw from the present state of affairs." The French, on the other hand, had, he suspected, put Mehemet Ali on his guard by their over-enthusiastic activities. By Britain keeping always aloof — and representing the French Consul-General as entertaining views of conquest on Egypt, Salt believed he had served "greatly to enhance in his eyes the value, if it could be obtained, of our friendship".

At dawn on 29 September Mr Boghos called Salt to Mehemet Ali's garden. The Pasha had heard that Lord Cochrane was at Malta, acting under the name of Campbell Blair.

"Will your government arrest Lord Cochrane?"

"I don't think they can." Salt explained that Cochrane travelled as a private individual and, in any case, would not step ashore.

"If Lord Cochrane is unsupported by your government, I can cope with him," said Mehemet Ali. "I will have no secrets from you. The fact is that I now hold my foot in two stirrups [a Turkish expression meaning 'I have two lines of conduct before me'] — in balance until the spring."

"Your retiring from the contest," said Salt, "would be very satsfactory to England, but I am not sure what we have to offer in return, Your Highness. What services would you expect?"

"I will have no reserve with you. Money is not my object — I do not want it — I despise it…" But, the Pasha suggested, England might help with his navy. "I want ships and she might furnish me with them — to be paid for, of course — nothing, I know, can be done without payment in England — but she might give me credit for a year or two — This might be of use to me. If England does not, France and Austria will — but I'd rather have the obligation to Great Britain." After a pause, he added, "I should also require that the world leave me free scope to aggrandize myself, if I should find occasion, on the side of Arabia [by which, Salt indicated, he meant the Yemen]. And I'd wish to have this last in writing — Above all I'd wish for secrecy — that whatever might be agreed upon should be unknown to the other powers as well as the Porte… Now you know my mind, be discreet in your communications."

"I'll only communicate what you wish," offered Salt. "The rest I will introduce as my own speculations."

"No," Mehemet Ali said, "I have no objection that you let your Ministers know that I cannot save them at Constantinople, but that in the other way I might be able to meet their views. If any influential person were to be sent — as a mere traveller under pretence of visiting the antiquities you are so fond of, I could easily arrange our conversations at Cairo without exciting a suspicion of the object of his visit." He then explained his immediate strategy, which was mainly concerned with repelling any Greek attack on Alexandria.

Salt reported that the fleet's unnecessary delay was already causing surprise. Mehemet Ali made excuses, but they might be considered frivolous. But Salt reckoned he wanted more. "He has at heart the gaining from our government some general assurance of sanction of his independence, should any circumstance drive him into rupture with the Porte," but, Salt emphasised, "he carefully abstained from touching on this point."[10]

Two less important, but time consuming, matters also demanded Salt's attention that autumn: a gift to the King of England; and the new Consul at Alexandria.

* *

Although a showman had imported a white camel to England in 1810, given it artificial spots, and exhibited it in Piccadilly as a 'cameleopard', no live giraffe had been seen in Europe at that time. Drovetti had indicated that one would be a very welcome gift to the King of France. In mid-1826 a giraffe had been killed by Egyptian troops in Senaar and her two offspring sent by camel caravan and boat to Alexandria. Mehemet Ali offered them to Salt and Drovetti for their respective monarchs. One was larger than the other so the two consuls drew lots. The smaller animal fell to Britain, but Salt was assured by a high official that "the smaller one is by far the handsomest of the two." It was then about a year old, "perfectly domesticated", and stood about ten feet in height.

Before long the giraffes were on their way. The French animal wintered in Marseilles before proceeding on foot to Paris, with a chic poncho and bonnet for wet weather and enthusiastic crowds to cheer it on its way. The English giraffe, with two Arab keepers, an interpreter and two Egyptian milch cows (and their calves), "in the character of wet nurses", wintered in Malta. It was May 1827 before the English party boarded the merchant vessel *Penelope;* 11 August before the giraffe landed in London near Waterloo Bridge. It was lodged in a roomy warehouse, and that night a noisy crowd gathered outside. Disturbed by their noise, the animal looked anxiously around; but "he no sooner bent his elegant head down to his keeper and ascertained that he had a friend close by his side, than he became quite composed and easy."[11] The next day he was transported to Windsor where the King hastened to inspect his extraordinary acquisition.

* *

Although Salt had known of John Barker's impending appointment for some months, it was not until 25 October 1826 that he arrived in Alexandria to take over the burdens of the consular work from Salt after two long years. Barker was 54, an age when most consuls were looking for their pensions rather than a new posting. Both Burckhardt and Bankes had enjoyed his company at the Consulate in Aleppo, and Salt must have been looking forward to his coming for this alone. The reality was a severe disappointment.

Barker started complaining almost as soon as he landed. He wrote a long list of complaints to the Foreign Office: the accommodation was unsatisfactory, the costs in Alexandria high. Mr Salt had told him he would have to pay rent and give presents to certain Turkish officers, not to mention making donations for charitable purposes. The Consul, he reported, was always expected to take the lead: "a fête with a Ball on the King's birthday and one or two balls in the carnival given to all the Europeans in Alexandria, which a consul can hardly avoid." Peter Lee had enjoyed (and paid for) this social round; Salt hardly mentioned it. In addition there were dinners for captains of the King's ships and "entertainment in my house to travellers of distinction who I could not permit to put up at an Alexandrian Locanda." All this would leave him little of his £1,000 'nett' for the maintenance of his family. If the pay was inadequate, so was the job and the place. He would find himself shut up for six months every year for the plague, and at other times having to face "the most unpleasant business of magisterial interference to settle the disputes or punish the misdemeanours of drunken sailors, cut throats and prostitutes."

But his greatest complaint was that Salt did not intend to retire quickly. He had applied for the consulship because he understood that Salt was planning to retire — and he could take over. Now he found Salt intended to take a short leave but not retire for a further three years. "But," Barker remarked, "you know how easily the resolution of quitting lucrative situations are postponed from Spring to Autumn, and from Autumn to Spring." He added a postscript: he had just seen a despatch from Joseph Planta to Salt and "perceived that he had misunderstood what Salt told him and that this Consulate would now be on the same footing as Smyrna" because of the report Salt had made to the government the year before. Barker would therefore benefit where Salt had not. He still sent the letter full of its complaints and insinuations.[12]

On 3 December, Barker wrote to "his devoted friend William John Bankes" (via the Foreign Office and Bingham Richards) "on a point on which I and Mr Salt shall probably not be agreed". Mr Salt was in Cairo and he had not been able "to learn his ideas on the subject". It was a matter of whose pocket should receive the National Fees — his or Salt's. Having urged Bankes to help him to obtain the Alexandrian job, he now would prefer to be transferred to Smyrna, his birthplace. He wrote also of "some ancient marbles" belonging to Bankes which were to be moved to Malta, but "Mr Salt had forgotten to mention the subject", so he did not know which 'marbles'. Fortunately, Mr Caviglia had sorted that out for him, but he still did not know whether they were to be sent by merchant or naval ship. It might be thought that a note to Salt would have been a better way to find out than by grumbling to Bankes in England several months away. Barker's motives in asking Bankes to help him get the post become only too clear in a letter at the end of 1827: he had heard that Salt had acquired a large fortune by collecting Egyptian antiquities and accepted the situation in the hope that Salt "would soon retire upon a Pension and he [Barker] would be preferred to his situation of Consul-General", a position from which he, too, might make his fortune.[13]

****

Meanwhile Salt was dealing with more complex matters of diplomacy than he had faced in his whole career. But the British government, beset by internal changes, moved slowly. and for months no reply came from London. Mehemet Ali began to seek other ways to gratify his ambitions and to play the European powers off against each other. On 24 November 1826 a French brig landed Generals Boyer and Livron, with a 'phalanx' of senior officers and subalterns in Alexandria. They were a very important 'trade and aid' mission, and their arrival was greeted by 500 rounds of fire. Mehemet Ali knew exactly what he wanted from them: help with training and equipping his navy to vanquish the Greeks — or any other enemy. In December Boghos provided the French mission with a shopping list of Egypt's needs.[14]

From Constantinople, Stratford Canning watched with alarm, believing the Sultan was endeavouring "to re-animate the zeal and loyalty of his Vice-Roy — with a fair prospect of success." At the end of a report to the Foreign Office in February he added a hurried postscript: "The Sultan has offered to place the whole conduct of the war in the Archipelago under the Vice-Roy of Egypt."[15] Now the plan to separate Mehemet Ali from the Sultan, at least into a state of neutrality, became more urgent. Mehemet Ali was delighted with his promotion, particularly as it was at the expense of the Capitan Pasha. "In a few words," he told the acting French Consul, with an air of extraordinary pleasure, "the Sultan has given me *carte blanche* to return the Greeks to their obeisance."

The next visitation to Egypt came from the Porte itself. On 7 March 1827 Suleiman Pasha and another Ottoman emissary arrived. Suleiman was warmly welcomed in Cairo, where a grand cortège escorted him to the Citadel on 16 March, and Mehemet Ali came out to the head of the stairs to receive him. Five days later there was a great review of 14,000 men, and on 22 March Mehemet Ali was invested with the *pashaliq* of Candia.

In April he was in Alexandria inspecting his growing fleet. The port was alive with activity. Ships came and went between Alexandria and the Morea continuously. Some returned for repairs and revictualling; others brought news. Merchant ships had to linger beyond the harbour before coming into the Old Port to unload. An extra mole was built for a further dozen frigates. Fifty-five men-of-war were assembled already. More ships, newly built or repaired, arrived from the shipyards of France and Italy. On 13 April Mehemet Ali wrote proudly to Ibrahim, "These vessels are both good and beautiful; never has a Mussulman nation seen their equal."[16] But still they did not sail.

Drovetti had not been well and, after 24 years in Egypt, had asked for leave in France. It seems strange at this moment, when his experience and his influence were of such value both to France and to Egypt, that his request should have been granted. He left Cairo on 20 May 1827, to be replaced by Consul Regnault from Sidon, a pompous man, out of his depth in the diplomacy of this posting.

Drovetti's departure made Salt restive. In May, in Cairo with Madden, he wrote to Bingham Richards, that unable to take leave because "my presence here being required during the continuance of the Greek War," he begged Richards and others to enable him to retire — "the rest of my life cannot be a long one."[17]

Not many days later there arrived in Cairo a traveller whom it truly cheered Salt to receive. William Coffin carried a letter from Subagadis, now the Ras of Tigre, dated 24 April 1827 and addressed to His Majesty George the Fourth.

> There was about 16 years ago a servant of yours, Henry Salt Esq, came to Ras Walataulose and brought him many things for his churches. I have also four churches and should like to have the same knowledge of Your Majesty as your Father had formerly of Ras Walataulose. [To this end he was sending one of his servants with Coffin to confer.] Our countries are afar off but our Religions are the same. If Your Majesty could send me one hundred of your Light Horsemen for one or two years, as we have plenty of horses but no good and brave Riders like your Countryman who returns to your servant Henry Salt Esq with this Letter. If you could send me a Doctor, Painter, and Carpenter, or any other Tradesmen, some paints, saws, Carpenters Tools, and some lead to finish the Churches I have built.

There followed some suggestions about how these items might be shipped — perhaps reflecting the knowledge of a supercargo in such matters. The letter ended: "I have sent my Shield, Spear and Knife: likewise Skin and five dresses as a token of Friendship and Christian like feeling."

Salt and Coffin were delighted to be re-united after nearly 17 years, but Coffin was shocked by Salt's altered appearance, and in the months ahead often urged him to leave Egypt. Salt responded that "while he felt he had strength enough left to be of service to the interests of his country", he should stay. Coffin's son John, then about 11 years old, accompanied him. He was, according to Robert Hay "very dark but his features are sharp and intelligent."[18] Salt, who enjoyed the company of children, diverted himself by skirmishing with the boy in the Abyssinian fashion, or fencing with sticks. John was devoted to him.

Hay noted Coffin's arrival: "He is a tall, good-looking man...with a prepossessing expression of countenance. His dress is a plain white sheet with a red border at the bottom, apparently of the same manufacture as that worn by the Nubians — it is thrown on in the same manner. His shawl (used as a turban) is very flat and picturesque. On his feet he wore sandals. His beard he had suffered to grow, but in Abyssinia they wear it cut with scissors but do not shave it..." At first Coffin had difficulty expressing himself in English after so many years, but soon he changed his clothes, saying he was "ashamed of his sheet" and returned to his West Country English. Like Pearce, Coffin entranced everyone with his tales. He confirmed Bruce's story of meat being cut from living animals when soldiers were on a march, which he had witnessed. He later exhibited how it was done for Madden and Lord Prudhoe.

* *

Despite outward appearances, Mehemet Ali was still not hurrying. He made leisurely preparations for a summer campaign and, with his ships lying ready at Alexandria, again pressed Salt for an answer to his proposals. On 11 June he suggested that, if the British and French really intended to intervene, they should send their fleets to Alexandria and thus appear "to compel His Highness to desist from war"; he would then oblige, "wanting only a fair pretext for taking such a step."[19] Salt passed on this message, but received no response during the hot summer weeks. On 15 June there was a flurry of excitement. At dawn a flotilla of 23 ships arrived off the coast. They were assumed to be merchantmen from the Levant. It was not until evening that suspicion arose, and it was realised that here was no less a person than Lord Cochrane, new Admiral of the Greek navy, testing the waters. The Greeks set fire to a small brig and then departed before the Egyptian ships could follow.

On the morning of 18 June Salt went to see the Pasha. He found him exultant. He had had the advantage of Lord Cochrane.

"It is folly," he said, "for Cochrane to join with the Greeks where the confusion must resemble the Tower of Babel. I have ordered my captain to follow the Greeks to Rhodes."

"Perhaps he will not need to go so far," Salt responded.

So it turned out. Cochrane slipped away from his pursuers and on 1 July the Pasha's ships returned empty handed. But Salt found it hard to explain away this invasion by a British naval officer and aristocrat.

As they entered July, no word came from London. But matters were moving on. Britain and France had drawn up a treaty in which they agreed to work together in the matter of the Greek war. Stratford Canning waited anxiously for word of the treaty being signed but it was weeks before he received official confirmation. However in mid-July, in London, instructions had been given to a certain Major Cradock to go to Egypt with all speed to negotiate with the Pasha. The Foreign Secretary, Lord Dudley, himself wrote the instructions, explaining that the Cabinet's views would have a greater appearance of "earnestness and consequence by being conveyed by an individual charged to bear them directly from His Majesty's Government than if they came exclusively through the usual channel of the British Consul-General in Cairo."[20] Such an envoy had, of course, been Mehemet Ali's own wish and suggestion.

* *

Cradock was to make haste overland to Corfu and then proceed on a man-of-war to Alexandria. There his efforts were to be directed to secure the neutrality of the Pasha in the struggle "betwixt the Turks and the Greeks. This he should do by employing such language — excluding however absolute menace — as, in his judgement, would be the most efficacious." He was advised that the Pasha was "wary, astute, neither a fanatical Mussulman nor a devoted servant of the Porte, and was guided almost entirely by the dictates of his personal interest or ambition". Cradock was to indicate that the allies (Britain, France and Russia) were supported by "the good wishes of Christendom in this endeavour to bring about the pacification of the Levant," and that the Pasha "would recommend himself to the strongest party" if he assisted. The forces of Europe were now ready to move and, although "the Allies do not mean war while they talk of mediation", yet very quickly a naval force could "appear in those seas irresistible to any thing the Ottoman Empire and its provinces could oppose to it". Cradock should assure the Pasha that "it had been principally out of consideration for himself and the difficulty of his position — the Porte having given to the authority of the Pasha of Egypt the character not so much of province as of an Empire — that they had so long delayed returning any answer to His Highness's overtures through the British Consul." In reality, it had been necessary to have the treaty between the allies signed and the fleets brought into place. This action, Dudley suggested, would "afford the Pasha an excuse with the Porte, the validity of which cannot be gainsayed."

The Honourable John Hobart Cradock was an excellent choice for this mission. Son of the second Baron Howden, who had been one of the chief officers on the British expedition to Egypt in 1801, he had followed his father into the army. He was only 28 but had plenty of useful diplomatic experience: as aide-de-camp to Wellington in Paris, and later ADC to Marshal Beresford in Lisbon, before becoming ADC to Salt's acquaintance Sir Thomas Maitland, Governor of Malta, in 1820. In 1823 he had visited Egypt, gone up the Nile (and carved his name inside the propylon of the temple of Philae in April). He had probably accompanied Salt to an audience with Mehemet Ali for George Canning noted that he was acquainted with the Pasha. In 1824 he had exchanged to the diplomatic service, as attaché at Berlin for a year, and in the Paris Embassy from June 1825. It was from this post that he was ordered to Egypt. He was a preposessing young man — nicknamed by the ladies of Paris 'le beau Cradock'.[21]

* *

Mehemet Ali was week by week less able to excuse his inactivity to the Sultan. He diverted attention and amused himself by taking short sailing excursions in the new ships he received from Europe. On 23 July noticeably well-equipped and well-drilled men came from Cairo and started to embark. By 4 August several ships of war and transports stood out to sea. At midday the cannon fire of a naval exercise was heard from the shore. An hour before sunset the public street criers called the troops on board.

At last, on 5 August, the entire Egyptian fleet sailed and was soon out of sight. During August Sir Edward Codrington's fleet had reached his station off the Morea, in preparation for the three allied squadrons to block supplies from Egypt or Turkey into Greece. The allies still clearly saw their intention being "to avoid, if possible, anything that may bring war..."

On the evening of 8 August HMS *Pelican,* commanded by none other than Captain Charles Irby, sailed into Alexandria with Major Cradock on board. The Pasha had set out for Cairo that morning. They had missed each other by little more than six hours.

Cradock lost no time in consulting Salt, whose pleasure in meeting Irby again was overwhelmed by the gravity of the occasion. They consulted Boghos early the next morning. He asked that Cradock set out his instructions on paper, to be conveyed immediately to Cairo. Cradock and Salt should not follow until the next day "to prevent discussion and suspicion among the Beys"; Cradock's visit must appear one of "simple curiosity".

Salt was not optimistic. En route to Cairo he wrote to Stratford Canning "We have to ask from him [the Pasha] a neutrality which may compromise him altogether with the Porte, and have nothing specifick [sic] to offer in return."[22]

At four o'clock on the afternoon of Thursday, 16 August the Consul-General and the King's envoy were ushered into the Pasha's presence. All but Boghos were ordered to withdraw. Cradock explained the position of His Majesty's Government, particularly where "the Pasha's own interest, present and future was directly concerned." Later, Salt said he believed it would be impossible for the Porte to refuse Mehemet Ali the Pashalik of Syria and its tribute should he remain faithful in the present crisis. Cradock thought differently. He believed the Pasha was looking to his ultimate independence. Probably both ambitions influenced Mehemet Ali.

The Pasha listened carefully. "I have considered your note with attention. I acknowledge the weight of your many observations. But you are quite wrong where you talk of the exhausted state of my country." This was, he assured them, solely occasioned by two years of 'bad Nile'. Indeed the Greek war had been of "the greatest service" to him. He spoke of the great confidence he always placed in the British government — "beyond all others".

"I always desire to conform to the wishes of the English government. Has not my conduct with regard to Abyssinia not been proof of this? But now, I am placed in a very difficult situation. I am perfectly at a loss what measure to adopt that will satisfy England — and not be dangerous to myself. Perhaps," as he spoke shifting his hands with a sort of convulsive movement, "perhaps there will be no hostile termination — no collision. Surely the Porte will accede to the propositions of the Allied Courts? Yes — that is so…the Porte will agree. There is no hazard of hostilities. As a subject of the Porte, I am sure," he added uneasily.

Cradock observed that the Pasha perpetually referred to himself as a Subject or Dependant of the Porte, "with a sort of studied affectation". Cradock thought he showed considerable anxiety and reported to Stratford Canning that "though cunning be so prominent a feature of this Chieftain, he has not yet learnt to control the expression of his eye and convulsive movement of his hands." One may imagine them — the powerful but emotional Albanian with the two Englishmen, allowing no feature to indicate reaction or strain, facing him down.

Cradock did not reassure the Pasha. "There is a very generally held opinion," he said, "that the Porte will *not* accede."

"But," Mehemet Ali retorted with peculiar emphasis, "I have reason to know that it will." Cradock pressed him to devise some measure to ensure the neutrality of his fleet. He gave no direct reply, but suggested he needed time to give the matter more deliberation.[23]

Cradock and Salt were ushered out with ceremony — but no actual assurances. The next day Cradock called on Boghos, hoping for a recall from the Pasha. None seemed likely. Was Mehemet Ali waiting for a response from the Porte? Cradock pressed the urgency of the matter. Boghos was obviously not in a position to hurry his master. Salt then suggested that the Pasha might be prepared to see him privately. Cradock, having observed the respect and confidence with which the Pasha invariably treated the Consul-General, agreed that this might have a good effect. On Sunday 19 August Salt went alone to the Pasha.

Again the courtiers withdrew; only Boghos remained. Formalities performed, Salt laid out his agenda. "As the British government has paid you the compliment of sending the Honourable Major Cradock from England on purpose to conciliate Your Highness, I trust Your Highness will be prepared to give such an answer as might prove satisfactory to our Minister."

"I do not see what answer I can give," Mehemet Ali replied. "Is Major Cradock authorised to give any specific reply to these propositions he has hinted at to me ? Has he any advantages to offer me for the sacrifices I should be called upon to make in favouring your views?"

"You will appreciate, Your Highness, that the propositions are not of a nature for our Minister to have given any direct instructions relative to them. But, sir," Salt spoke carefully, "may I venture to advise you, if your answer must depend on that point, do not lose the opportunity that now presents itself of speaking out clearly. It might never again occur that you can explain in precise terms your wishes to the British government. Of course," Salt added, "you may be assured that every delicacy will be used respecting such a communication. It would — we assure you — be kept a *profound* secret."[24]

"Ah, Mr Salt, but there will — according to my calculations — not be time for such communication. No answer is possible before the crisis has already taken place. It will take at least 20 days." In this estimate Mehemet Ali was extremely optimistic, although it probably was just possible for the Ottoman Tartar messengers to reach London and return in this time.

Salt agreed. "It is indeed likely to be the case. But in the meantime Your Highness might find means to delay the operations of your fleet — and take such precautionary measures as might prevent any unpleasant collision until the moment when you become acquainted with the final resolutions of our Cabinet."

The Pasha was not happy. "This would be difficult. I have waited and waited and delayed — under one excuse or another." As indeed he had. "The Porte has become greatly dissatisfied with my proceedings. Even if I were disposed to give such orders to my own fleet, the Grand Signor — commanded by bigots, I well know — will not be easily brought to second my purpose. Even my son — even Ibrahim — might be supposed 80 per cent to attend to my directions — but for the remaining 20 per cent even he will have a will of his own. Your government — the British government — must have seen my situation — they (had I been worthy of their notice) must have known how to draw me honourably out of the business."

Salt would have sympathised. He too had waited anxious months and well understood the Pasha's quandary. He repeated his earlier argument. "No stronger proof of my government's amicable intentions could have been given than that of sending Major Cradock hither. Everything, Your Highness, must have a beginning. The opening now presented appears to me — speaking as an individual — the most favourable that could have occurred. I think you know, Your Highness, that I have your interests and those of Egypt at heart. I would not give the advice I do if such was not my real sentiments." Salt resumed a more official stance. "If ever an opportunity of ingratiating yourself with the European powers were permitted to slip by, you could never expect to find a similar one. It is, sir, the part of a wise man to make the most of such rare occasions."

Mehemet Ali assumed a more easy — and more confidential — tone. "I am convinced of your wish to serve me. I have always found your advice good and am truly glad to find — as Boghos has informed me — that you stand so well with your government." He added, "I will tell you the truth. I have already — to satisfy their *amour propre* — had some discourse with my Chief Officers — but I have not disclosed to *them* my real intentions. My determination is this. Let Major Cradock proceed directly to your Admiral. Let him recommend to the Admirals of the combined fleets to send immediately an officer with a letter from them addressed to Ibrahim Pasha to tell him that matters are now brought to a crisis — and he must not think any longer of attacking Hydra, as they are determined if he does so to prevent him by force — in fact, to beat him off. Do not let the officer charged with this letter wait for an answer. Let him merely deliver it into the hands of Ibrahim Pasha."

At last Salt knew that the negotiations were succeeding, but he was still cautious. "This is well, but I still have fears."

"What fears?"

"This letter will have little effect if not backed by secret instructions from Your Highness yourself."

"Leave all that," Mehemet Ali said, with a very expressive look, "to me. I am going to act a dangerous part. If I were to remain by the Grand Signor on this occasion, I might, it is true, lose my fleet, but I should be certain to gain Syria and Damascus. Whom else has he to lean upon? He would be obliged to give me my own terms. You will see — I will shortly have some great personages sent from Constantinople to make me propositions. It is a great thing I am doing to satisfy your government. You know the difficulties I have to contend with — but I rely upon the friendship of England. Let England stand by me and I shall be repaid. I have long wished ardently for her support — and to form a lasting league of commerce and amity with her. She must, I should hope, now feel that she is bound to aid me."

"As far as my private opinion goes," Salt responded, "when the occasion comes — should Your Highness carry this business successfully through — England would not desert you. Let me say that already I see you as — in everything but form — independent."

"Yes," the Pasha replied. "Yes, as the Turkish saying goes, every man is a King in his own House, but Egypt is but a small kingdom. Syria and Damascus and Arabia are in fact at my disposition. I will speak out. I will — for once — boast like a Bedouin or a man from the mountains. If I should not have what I seek — I could raise up a religious war that should rage for 50 years." He seemed about to set off into one of his romantic tirades, but reined himself in. "But this is not a thing to speak of — this is a private discourse between ourselves. If your government supports me — as I hope — if it will acknowledge me when occasion comes — as an independent prince, I shall be satisfied." His face lit up and his eyes flashed as if the fate of Empires were already in his hands. "You will some day — not far remote, I trust — reside here in another capacity than that of Consul."

Salt thanked him for the promotion he was disposed to bestow. "I can assure you, sir, that whatever might be the issue, I should be perfectly ready to attach my fate to yours." With thoughts of retirement, Georgina and Italy, he surely cannot have said this wholeheartedly.

"When does Major Cradock depart?"

"When he knows your decision, Your Highness."

"I shall be happy to see him. As to my answer it cannot be otherwise than a declaration of my being obliged to look to the Porte as the guide of my conduct. The rest must be secret."

At Cradock's final meeting with the Pasha next day, 20 August, as a mark of unusual favour, he was invited to dine. Mehemet Ali spoke of the delicacy and difficulty of his position. "The British government promised support if I angered the Sultan. Undoubtedly if I now withdraw my fleet, I would be stamped as a Rebel. Yet, my friend, you come with no guarantee or protection if compliance embroils me with the Porte. I have thought the subject over in all its bearings." He paused. "I hope earnestly and request," he marked the words emphatically,"that what I am going to advise, as coming from me, may be kept a profound secret — both by your Minister at home and your Ambassador at the Porte." Cradock sat silent and Mehemet Ali continued, setting out the same method of approaching Ibrahim Pasha as he had outlined to Salt. "The letter," he said, "should be couched in the strongest terms. It should represent to him the danger of exposing himself to a collision with the Christian powers, and dissuade him from any hostile step — particularly from attacking Hydra — which was to be the first object of his fleet." He paused to consider. "I wish the letter to be dated off Hydra — it will carry more force with it." There followed more details about the delivery of the letter. "It must," he emphasised,"appear entirely the act of the Admirals." He repeated the instruction, "No answer to this letter must be requested. Leave all the rest to me."

Cradock urged the Pasha to tell him what means he intended to use. Mehemet Ali avoided answering until Cradock felt it impolitic to press further.

"We Turks," said Mehemet Ali, "have a way of doing things among ourselves — depend upon it, the event will be as you desire."

Salt, with years of experience of the ways of the Pasha, would have believed him, but Cradock continued to express dissatisfaction with this as a reply to his government, although he agreed that such secrecy, even towards himself, was necessary. "Your reply is not as precise as I had reason to hope." Salt can hardly have given him such reason, except his own belief in the Pasha's word in these circumances. "It puts me in an uncomfortable situation," Cradock insisted.

The Pasha was firm. "I am sure that Ibrahim Pasha, on receipt of the Admiral's letter, will take no step without communicating both with Constantinople and Cairo. At all events, a delay will thus be gained. That will be the equivalent of neutrality."

Cradock concluded that Ibrahim Pasha already had secret instructions on all possible contingencies — just as the British commanders had — and that the Pasha had known, even before Cradock's arrival, of the projected articles of the Treaty.[25]

Before leaving Cairo on the evening of 21 August, Cradock had a brief meeting with Mehemet Ali. The question of independence was not raised. Then, taking Irby's advice, he set off with all haste for Smyrna, to find Admiral Codrington's flag ship, the *Asia*. They were joined by two travellers who had been staying at the Consulate: Lord Prudhoe (heir to the Duke of Northumberland) and his friend Major Orlando Felix were happy to take the opportunity of travelling to Smyrna.

Prudhoe and Felix were not the only guests at the Consulate during those hot, fraught days. Mr and Mrs (later Sir Moses and Lady) Montefiore were on a long projected journey to Jerusalem in the cause of Judaism and, while they awaited a ship for Jaffa, had made their way to Cairo. Montefiore sought an audience with the Pasha, and Salt arranged for Vice-Consul Maltass to accompany him. On his return he found Salt "much alarmed at the non-arrival of a despatch from an English sloop-of-war. He understood the Porte had refused the mediation and the English Admiral had orders to act. Mr Salt would see the Pasha in the morning and then set off for Alexandria."[26]

* *

After the crisis of those days in Cairo, matters took a slower course. Codrington had left Smyrna, where Cradock found Admiral Byng ensconced in the French Consul's house. Byng agreed to join Cradock in search of the fleet. The French admiral, de Rigny, also accompanied the *Pelican* and off Navarino on 21 September, as Cradock completed his report, he added "the Squadron of Sir Edward Codrington has just hove into sight."

The letter to Ibrahim Pasha was prepared, expressing the allies' wish to "prevent the useless effusions of blood" and that the Pasha would "feel the expediency of refraining from any steps which might entail so disastrous a circumstance as a hostile meeting between the Ottoman and Allied fleets." The letter was sent into Navarino and an invitation came back for Codrington to meet Ibrahim at his tent on 25 September. The interview took place in the presence of "the whole of the Turkish-Egyptian Chiefs". The outcome was an agreement that the Turko-Egyptian fleet should remain in port until Constantinople and Alexandria sent orders. This the allies regarded as being, in effect, the armistice which had been sought.

* *

Between these events, on 3 September, Commander Peter Richards wrote to Salt in Cairo that his ship the *Pelorus* was anchored at Alexandria. From 31 August the port was blockaded, as part of Codrington's orders should there be no satisfactory response from the Porte by that date. Richards fortunately had a good understanding of events. He explained that should the Egyptian fleet withdraw and then be attacked by the Greeks, perhaps led by Lord Cochrane, Admiral Codrington would regard the Egyptian ships as under his protection. It was, said Richards, for Salt to decide the next action.

On 6 September Salt replied that, having on the previous day been bled twice, he was too unwell to go to see the Pasha. However, he had sent Mr Walmass with Richard's letter to the Pasha to alert him, and asked him either to come down himself to the Deftardar Bey's garden where they could meet discreetly or to send his carriage to carry Salt to the Citadel. Mehemet Ali chose to work through a messenger. Early next morning he sent Walmass to Salt to say that he would send a general reply, but, if Salt's health would permit it, could he remove immediately to Alexandria where they could act through Mr Boghos, and by letter, as this would be more secret than meet-

ings, which "might give occasion for rumours of various kinds in the town."
Salt left Cairo on 7 September and reached Alexandria three days later, "but
in a state of such severe indisposition" that he was unable to meet Richards
and Boghos until the following day.

On 11 September Boghos explained that Mehemet Ali was uneasy
about suggestions the French had made about a possible way forward and
expressed the view that "on the contrary, the Pasha has never explained himself to the French in the frank and open manner he has to the English, particularly Mr Salt and Major Cradock." Indeed, "the excessive impudence"
of the French admiralty and agents had, in Drovetti's absence, stirred up
trouble for Mehemet Ali in Constantinople for having detained the fleet.
The Pasha, Boghos said, was sure the English would understand the difficulty of his position and "how impossible it was for him to recall any part
of his force, or act in any way as if he had an interest separate from the
Porte." But, if there was a way he could cooperate he would do so — indeed
"it was clearly in his interest that the Greeks should be free...His Highness
is," Boghos sadly declared, "between two evils — it was better for him to
suffer the loss of his fleet than draw on himself the whole weight of the
Ottoman Power, the hatred of all Mussulmen, and thus sacrifice all he had
been so long endeavouring to establish."

Salt and Richards must have wondered where all this was leading:
Boghos soon made it clear. "I believe His Highness is prepared to hear of the
destruction of some of his ships. Nay," he spread his hands, "he may perhaps think a little damage might be of service in the eyes of the Porte. Even,"
Boghos surprisingly added, "if he sustained a total loss it would not cause
any change in his sentiments towards the English. The Consuls and merchants may be assured," he emphasised, "that themselves and their property would be respected. Even if orders of a rigorous nature come from the
Sultan, His Highness will find means to protect them and ensure them a safe
residence should they choose to remain."

For Salt, concerned for the British subjects in his care should matters
fall out ill for the Pasha, this was welcome news. Richards wrote to assure
Lord Dudley, "the most perfect tranquillity exists at Alexandria and the
British residents, nothwithstanding the present aspect of affairs, are under
less anxiety about their safety than for some time past."[27]

20

The End

DR MADDEN returned to Alexandria from Syria in early October. The Montefiores had come down from Cairo, determined to set off for Palestine, undeterred by the troubled times. He arranged to await their return to travel to England.

He found Salt in a wretched state, suffering from severe symptoms of his recurring illness. Despite all his other concerns, he had managed to ship out his third collection to his brother-in-law, Pietro Santoni, in Leghorn, On 7 October he wrote to Santoni: "You will do the best you can in the sale of it. It has cost a large sum, and should not be disposed of for less than one hundred thousand francs. It would suit England particularly, as there is all that they want, and it has not that which they have." Thurburn also had written to Pietro Santoni to warn him that Salt was seriously ill with "internal hemorrhoids", and that, unless his health greatly improved, he would have to go at once to Europe.[1] Madden and Thurburn agreed that a change from "the damp and unwholesome atmosphere of Alexandria" was the only chance for Salt's recovery, and prevailed upon him to go on an excursion on the Nile. Barker took it upon himself to inform the Foreign Office that, as Salt was too ill to conduct the work, he was taking over responsibility. It is not clear why he took this decision, nor whether Salt instructed him to do so.

Before they set out Salt sealed up and destroyed several of his manuscripts and papers. Madden remonstrated, but he insisted. As they sat together before the fire, Salt observed that "he was fully sensible of his approaching death." Madden begged him again not to destroy the papers.

"If I were a young man," Salt replied, "they might procure me notoriety [in the sense of being widely known], but that sort of notoriety can do the dying no good." He paused, "Were I desirous of being better talked of after death than I have been living, there are other papers I might be more desirous of giving to the public. These letters," he took up a packet, "are part of my correspondence with Belzoni. They could exhibit the secret of that jealousy that induced him, while carrying on his researches, to load me with imputations which, in health, I had neither the inclination nor the leisure to refute — and now, in sickness, have still less." He handed them to Madden. "Burn them with the rest — my remembrance of the quarrel shall be buried with their ashes."

Madden held the packet for a few moments, reluctant to commit these letters to the flames. Salt snatched them from him and threw them into the grate. "Doctor, you would not have done for Brutus' freedman; you have forced an author to be his own executioner."[2]

The next day Madden and Salt, Coffin and his son John, Yanni d'Athanasi and Salt's servants set off from Alexandria. At the village of Dessuke it became apparent that they should go no further. They set up home in the house of the Aga of Dessuke and, for several days, Salt seemed to be holding his own or even mending. Then there was a change for the worse and he recognised that death was fast approaching. He was calm, spending hours discussing religion and other matters with his companions. Madden frequently read to them all from the New Testament which Mrs Rudland had presented to Coffin in 1812. Later John Halls wrote down Coffin's own account of these days by the Nile, and read it slowly over to him to avoid the possibility of any mistake.[3]

Madden urged medicines on Salt, but he was convinced that, though medicines might delay his death, they could not cure him. "It is in vain to alter my opinion. Your kindness now is more valuable to me than the skill of 20 doctors." Then he asked everyone to leave the room except Madden. To him, he dictated his last wishes as codicils to his will, weeping profusely between the words. He had already, on 13 August 1825, bequeathed funds for the care of his "reputed son in the hands of Osmyn". Gerard Shutz, a colleague of Briggs and Thurburn from Alexandria, joined them and was witness to Madden's signature. Salt spoke repeatedly of Georgina, far away in Leghorn: "Will no one talk of her!" But no one could, for none of his companions, with the possible exception of Yanni, had ever seen her.[4]

Madden knew the end was now very close and called a missionary clergyman to Salt's bedside. They prayed together and then Salt sank into a state of delirium and delusion. But the end was still slow to come. Every now and then he would rally and the men's hope would be rekindled.

One night Yanni and an Arab servant were sitting up with him, but had both fallen asleep. Somehow Salt tottered from his bed to Madden's couch in the next room. He sat himself down on the sleeping doctor, locking his fingers into his beard, shouting, "Doctor! Doctor! This is no time for sleeping!"

"Why have you risen ?" the shocked Madden asked.

"To show you the power that is left — the superhuman power that has enabled me to conquer death — I am saved — I am well."

Coffin, roused from his mattress on the floor, tried to separate Salt's fingers from Madden's beard and urge him back to his own bed. But Salt cried out, "Get the boat ready, and let us immediately be off, or throw me into the water."

It took a great deal of persuasion and struggling to separate him from

Madden, who lost part of his beard in the scuffle. Nothing they could do would prevail upon Salt to return to his own room. They talked gently to him, listening to his mumbled words as he told them of the nightmare he was living through. He seemed to believe he was pursuing his own funeral, till he had at last overtaken the corpse, which he imagined to be in the room he had just left. They brought him, at last, the key to the room and he kissed it repeatedly, gradually growing calmer, until he allowed them to lay him down on Coffin's mattress on the floor. As he lay there he caught sight of Coffin's snuffbox lying on a bench. He seized it and took a large pinch of snuff, forcing it with great eagerness into his nostrils. Then he sank down almost lifeless on the mattress, and lay there for a long time before returning to his normal self.[5]

The horrific scene in the Egyptian darkness reduced the men to a state of shock and dread. When at last they got Salt back to his own bed, he lay tranquilly for a day or two and seemed to be recovering, although Madden had given him up for dead. Years later in *The Infirmities of Genius,* a discourse on literary men and medical matters, Madden recalled how Salt exhibited "the lightness before death" in which people may show a sudden mental vigour before they pass. Salt spoke in various languages to his attendants "some of which, as the Amharic, he had not used for many years". Coffin and his son John might have been less surprised by this, and Salt had often had Abyssinians around him during his time in Egypt. Also "he composed some verses that referred to his previous sufferings" and repeated them with great energy to Madden.[6]

One day Salt appeared so much better that the men allowed themselves a break from their vigil and went walking in the neighbourhood. When he returned Coffin was shocked by what he found. While they were away Salt had suffered a frightful discharge of blood of the most alarming nature. Coffin rushed to find Madden.

"It is all over," said Madden quietly.

Yet Salt lingered one more day. That night he again managed to drag himself from his bed and was found struggling with one of his attendants on the floor. "He's dead," he muttered, as he pressed his fingers into the man's eyelids. Madden pulled him up and heard his last words: "Oh! Doctor, this is Frankenstein!"

He died a few hours later in the dawn of 30 October 1827, in his 48th year. The distraught John Coffin mourned the passing of his friend in the manner of his homeland, lifting his white garment above his head and crying out loudly.[7]

****

The desolated men found a carpenter to make a coffin in which they placed Salt's body once it had been washed and properly laid out. The coffin went aboard Shutz's swift sail-and-oared boat down to Alexandria with Salt's household servants. Madden, Coffin and John followed in Salt's own boat.

For a day his body lay in the hall of the consulate house, where so many visitors had met and talked with him, constantly watched over by his servants. The flags of all the European nations were hoisted as a mark of respect. Because the precise reason for his death was not certain, it was agreed that Madden and some other medical gentlemen should open the body to find the cause. It was as Madden had long suspected: the spleen alone was diseased, otherwise all was well.[8]

On Thursday, 1 November Salt was buried in a corner of his own garden beside an ancient slab with a Greek funerary inscription which Madden and he together had positioned on a little hillock. He had wished to be buried in the Latin Convent next to his wife, but, "he being a Protestant", the Catholic church refused permission. Mr Montefiore had returned from Palestine and described the funeral in his diary: "All the foreign Consuls were present in full uniform, also Capt. Richards of the *Pelorus*, with his officers, and many others. The procession was headed by two handsome horses of the Pasha, without riders, then followed 12 of his janizaris, 12 English marines, with arms reversed, and the British naval officers. The coffin was carried by six British sailors, and the pall was supported by six consuls, Mr Barker acting as chief mourner, and being followed by other consuls, merchants, captains, etc. After the funeral service the marines fired three rounds. The *Pelorus* fired minute guns during the procession." The distance was nearly half a mile, and the dust and heat so unbearable that Montefiore was apprehensive of getting the fever.[9]

Later this corner of Salt's garden was walled in and became a small Protestant cemetery. A handsome cenotaph, surmounted with a funerary urn, was erected, carved with words written by Salt's friend and cousin, the Reverend Thomas Butt, whose father so long ago had introduced him to Lord Valentia:

Here sleep the mortal remains of
Henry Salt Esq
A native of the city of Lichfield,
His Britannic Majesty's Consul-General in Egypt.
Twice he penetrated into Abyssinia,
with the hope of restoring the long-broken intercourse
between the nations of England
and that barbarised Christian land.
His ready genius explored and elucidated
the Hieroglyphics and other Antiquities

270

of this Country.
His faithful and rapid pencil,
And the nervous originality of his untutored verses,
conveyed to the world vivid ideas
of the scenes which delighted himself.
In the midst of his important duties and useful pursuits,
he was in the 48th year of his age,
and after a short illness, summoned, as we trust,
to his better and eternal home, on the
twenty-ninth day of October
in the year of our Lord 1827.
His only child, Georgina Henrietta,
has been permitted to appropriate this Garden
to the interment of European Christians.

These words followed in Arabic :

Profane not this ground, where the bodies of
believers in Jesus rest in sure and certain hope
of blessed Resurrection.[10]

21

Aftermath

TEN DAYS BEFORE Salt's life slipped away at Dessuke, on the other side of the Mediterranean, the naval forces of the allies and the Turkish fleet had met in Navarino Bay and the action that day gave Navarino its place in naval history, as the last great naval engagement under sail. Even by August, when Salt and Cradock conferred with Mehemet Ali, too much time had passed, and it was already almost too late to stop the plan of action decided between the Western powers. On 1 September Stratford Canning wrote to Lord Dudley that, there being "no response from the Porte, so instructions to the Respective Squadrons are announced..."[1]

On 8 September Admiral Sir Edward Codrington sent a message to the fleet that the armistice had been recognised by the Greeks but not the Turks, but still great care should be taken "that the measures adopted against the Ottoman Navy do not degenerate into hostilities..."[2] More than a month later he was still holding back, believing that every inducement should be given to the Egyptians to withdraw their ships and guaranteeing them safe return to Alexandria if they carried away troops. Instead he heard that the Egyptian army was brutally attacking ports elsewhere. Three days later Codrington sent Cradock into Navarino with a letter signed by the three allied admirals accusing Ibrahim Pasha of violating the armistice. Ibrahim was not available. The allied fleet gathered outside Navarino Bay. Within the bay the French military advisers still working for the Egyptian navy ordered the ships into place in a great crescent. Then they departed, their work done.

There was a simple choice for the Egyptian fleet: to sail out into the waiting fire of the allies or to remain in place. Codrington was well aware of this. By mid-day on 20 October his ship, the *Asia*, headed straight into the bay, followed by the French and the Russians. Two hours later they were anchored within range of possible Turkish fire. The allies continued to give every sign that no act of hostility was intended. Indeed Codrington ordered the marine band to muster on the poop deck of the *Asia*.

The tension was immense — too immense. A Turkish ship fired on HMS *Dartmouth* and all hell broke loose. What followed was not a battle but an engagement of individual ships.[3] By six, when the early dark of the Mediterranean fell, 174 allied sailors were dead, and 475 were wounded (including Cradock). Sixty enemy vessels were destroyed and Codrington estimated 6,000 Egyptians and Turks had died. Out of delay and chaos had come destruction and victory.

Commander Richards, who had taken over the negotiations with the Pasha in Egypt, reported on 31 October that just as he rose to go from a session, Mehemet Ali said, "Yes, yes, it must be so. There will be a naval engagement but it will be trifling. Your Admiral will sink three or four of the first of our ships; the others will turn back and the affair will end."[4]

* *

The day after Salt's funeral a Turkish corvette brought news that 13 of the Pasha's finest ships and 32 of the Sultan's had been sunk in Navarino Bay with a loss of 6,000 to 8,000 lives. "All the Franks in Alexandria," Sir Moses Montefiore recorded, "are in the greatest alarm, dreading the revenge of soldiers and Turks."[5] But the Pasha kept his word to Salt and no harm befell them.

Mehemet Ali was amazingly magnanimous despite the understandable fears of the Europeans. Madden, reflecting on the dangers, wrote: "No one unacquainted with Egypt can form an adequate idea of the loss of Mr Salt at such a moment. The Battle of Navarino had just taken place, and though the Pasha appeared little affected by the destruction of his fleet, his real feelings were unknown, but many distrusted his intentions. Mr Salt had considerable influence over him, and possessed his confidence, and during his illness Mehemet Ali absolutely refused to communicate with Mr Barker, who he found obnoxious".[6]

On 12 February 1828 Cradock, now promoted to Colonel, returned to Alexandria to join Richards' negotiations. He was received most graciously by Mehemet Ali who he found grown old and extremely nervous, yet still not compromising. Cradock's message was that, unless the Pasha evacuated the Morea he exposed his son to total destruction. On 30 March Cradock's final report from Alexandria has a tone of great exasperation: "I conceive it entirely useless to attempt any further negotiations with Mehemet Ali, as his determination is evidently to persevere in his present system, and to admit no argument but the appearance of unanswerable force."[7] Would Salt, perhaps, have achieved a more favourable reply where His Majesty's envoy failed?

* *

The tale of Salt's collections was not yet over. A third collection was in Leghorn to be disposed of by Pietro Santoni. He sent the collection to England sometime late in 1834, accompanied by Yanni d'Athanasi to explain it, and it was sold by Sotheby's in a great nine-day event in March,

1835. "It appears," commented the *Gentleman's Magazine*, "that the desire to possess objects of such remote antiquity and high interest is considerably on the increase in this country." The prices obtained for the third collection, "made by our late spirited countryman," were "very liberal". In total, the 1,083 items, which included mummies, statuettes, papyri, tablets, right down to "A bow, with 3 Arrows", fetched £7,168 18s 6d. At more than £4,500, the British Museum was the major purchaser.[8]

* *

On 28 May, 1829 Reverend William Krusé of the Church Missionary Society wrote from Cairo to a colleague in London. Among other matters was the following paragraph:

> On the 18th of May the boy Henry Salt, natural, but illegitimate son of the late British Consul, was delivered over to our care until an opportunity presents of sending him to Europe — We long ago desired Osmann [sic] Effendi, under whose charge he hitherto has been to send this boy to our School, but he [Osman] was not inclined to do it. — When Mr Tod was here in Cairo, we spoke to him about this boy, telling him we thought it our duty as missionaries to look for the boy that he does not become a Muslim. Mr Tod spoke to Mr Thurburn, who immediately wrote to Mr Maltass, the Consul's Agent, that Osmann shall deliver the boy over to him, and that he, Mr Maltass, shall give him under our charge till he can be removed to Europe. — The boy is now in our house, eats at our table, and we care for him as for our own child, for its almost certain, that Maltass as well as Osmann will leave Cairo soon, and the poor boy has then nobody in Cairo to take care of him. — How long he is to stay with us I do not know, nor do I know at present at whose expense he is to be maintained, but I see from the letter of Mr Thurban [sic] to Mr Maltass that the executors of the late Mr Salt consider it a charitable office.[9]

Considering Salt's careful preparation in his will for young Henry, this 'charitable office' seems strange. Of Salt's other child, Georgina Henrietta, neither the Salt family nor we have found anything.

In 1840 Dr Madden returned to Alexandria with the Montefiores and visited Salt's old house:

> I found with surprise the well-known house of my poor friend converted into an Armenian church. The principal saloon, in which I had spent so many pleasant and instructive days and evenings for the greater part of three years, was now a darkened room with gaudy paintings and glimmering lamps burning before an altar, with a profusion of tawdry ornaments and daubs of paintings of saints and angels, that certainly were like nothing in the heavens above or on the earth beneath.
> I sat down on a form at the opposite end of the room, where the divan

was formerly placed, and contemplated the change that had taken place since I had first known this pleasant house, and last left it with poor Salt, when I accompanied him up the Nile, and to which he returned no more in life.

This sanctum sanctorum, as he used to call the room in which he kept his books and papers, was now the vestry-room of the chapel. The spot over the door where the portrait of his beloved daughter used to hang, was occupied with some glaring picture; and on looking into the garden from the balcony — where he had spent so much time and money in beautifying those grounds — it was quite melancholy to see how everything had gone to ruin. I had spent many hours with him in this delightful garden that he took so much pride in, discoursing of Egypt and its ancient people, the antiquities he had collected, the progress he had made in knowledge of the ancient language, and availing myself of those stores of classic and antiquarian lore which Mr Salt was ever ready to communicate to those around him. The wells and reservoirs which he had constructed at so much cost, for the irrigation of the grounds, in which some vegetables were grown, I hardly thought it possible that 12 years could have brought so much to ruin, and effected so great a change.

In a corner of the garden, now walled in, and converted into a small cemetery, beside an ancient slab with a Greek inscription, which I well remember having assisted him to place at the summit of a hillock, on the left-hand corner of the garden, the remains of poor Salt were deposited.

Madden, having recorded the inscription on the cenotaph, completed the record of his visit with these words: "If I have conveyed in these letters any information of higher interest than this brief notice of the tomb of a British functionary, who upheld the interests of his country, who cultivated science and delighted in literary pursuits, I trust I shall be excused for gratifying my own feelings by ending these letters with this reminiscence of an old and valued friend."[10]

Notes and References

Certain books recur frequently and are referred to as follows:

d'Athanasi: *A Brief Account of the Researches and Discoveries in Upper Egypt made under the Direction of Henry Salt Esq., to which is added a detailed catalogue of Mr Salt's Collection of Egyptian Antiquities* (London, 1836)

Belzoni: *Narrative of the Operations and Recent Discoveries within the Pyramids, Temples, Tombs and Excavations in Egypt and Nubia; and of a Journey to the Coast of the Red Sea, in the search of the ancient Berenice; and another to the Oasis of Jupiter Ammon* (London, 1820)

Farington: *The Diary of Joseph Farington*, ed. Garlick and Macintyre (1978)

Finati: *Narrative of the Life and Adventures of Giovanni Finati, etc, dictated by himself and edited by Wm. John Bankes Esq.*, 2 vols (London, 1830)

Halls: *The Life and Correspondence of Henry Salt Esq. FRS*, 2 vols (London, 1834)

Irby and Mangles: *Travels in Egypt and Nubia, Syria and Asia Minor during the years 1817 and 1818* (privately published London, 1823)

Richardson: *Travels along the Mediterranean and parts adjacent in company with the Earl of Belmore 1816-18*, 2 vols. (London, 1822)

Salt: *Account of a Voyage to Abyssinia, and Travels into the Interior of that country in the years 1809 and 1810* (London, 1814)

Valentia: *Voyages and Travels to India, Ceylon, the Red Sea, Abyssinia and Egypt*, 3 vols (London, 1809)

PROLOGUE

1   Richard Burton, 'Giovanni Battista Belzoni', *Cornhill Magazine*, July 1880, 39

2   E. M. Forster, *Alexandria, a History and a Guide*, 156

1   A LICHFIELD MAN

1   Halls, II, 136

2   Halls, I, 1ff

3   John Glover (1767-1849) was a drawing master in Lichfield for some years. His large landscape oils were thought by contemporaries to rival those of J. M. W. Turner. President of the Society of Painters in Watercolours, 1807 and 1814-15, he was a founder member in 1824 of the Society of British Artists.

4   Joseph Farington (1747-1821) was a pupil of Richard Wilson. Elected to the

276

Royal Academy in 1785, he kept, between 1793 and 1821, a gossipy chronicle of his fellow artists. He was always sympathetic to the aspirations of younger artists.

5 Farington, III, various dates

6 Farington, IV, 1513-14, 5 March 1800

7 Ibid, 1129, 6 January 1799

8 Halls, I, 15. John James Halls (1776-1853) had been something of a prodigy, having a work accepted by the Royal Academy when he was only 15; he exhibited 108 portraits and history subjects at the Royal Academy between 1798 and 1828, including two portraits of Lord Valentia, in 1809 and 1811, which we have not been able to trace.

9 Ibid, 20

10 Farington, IV, 1280, 21 September 1799

11 Halls, I, 47

12 Ibid, II, 130. George Henry Hanson was baptised on 13 July 1821, at St James's, Westminster (International Genealogical Index)

13 Ibid, 56

14 Ibid, 58

15 John Hoppner (1758-1810), when a chorister in the Chapel Royal, was noticed by George III as "a Lad of genius" in drawing, sent to live with the Keeper of the King's drawings and given a royal allowance. He cannily never discouraged the rumour that he was the King's illegitimate son. Elected Royal Academician in 1795, he became principal portrait painter to the Prince of Wales (later George IV). Known for his skill in catching a likeness, after the retirement of Sir Joshua Reynolds he was considered the most important portrait artist in England. He was a close friend of Farington.

16 Halls, I, 27

17 Ibid, 34

18 Ibid, 40

19 Ibid, 61

20 Farington, V, 1770, 29 April 1802

2 VOYAGE TO THE EAST

1 Halls, I, 65

2 Valentia, too, left a family, two small sons, but was separated from his wife because of her adultery.

3 Halls, I, 70ff

4 Ibid, 76

5 Valentia, I, 235

6 Ibid, 66

7   Mildred Archer, 'A Forgotten Painter of the Picturesque — Henry Salt in India', *Country Life,* 19 November 1959, 891ff

8   Annesley, BL Add Mss, 19345, f7

9   Ibid, 19346, f91

10 Halls, I, 52: Salt's entry dated 7 November 1803

11 Annesley, BL Add Mss, 19345, f80

12 Valentia, I, 317

13 Ibid, Salt's journal, I, 435ff

14 *Dictionary of National Biography*

15 Charles Court, later Marine Surveyor-General of India, died 9 September 1821, at Bengal (*Gentleman's Magazine,* 1822, II, 479)

16 Pearce, *Life and Adventures of Nathaniel Pearce,* I, 1ff

17 Valentia, II, 235ff

18 Ibid, 316

19 Farington, VIII, 2895, 1 November 1806

3   THE RAS OF TIGRE AND THE PASHA OF EGYPT

1   Valentia, II, 449

2   Salt, 446

3   The Ark of the Covenant is reputed to be held at Axum, in Salt's time in the 17th-century church, now in a chapel built by Emperor Haile Selasse.

4   Valentia, III, 145

5   Ibid, 145

6   Annesley, BL Add Mss, 19347, f11-13

7   Hon. Sir Charles Murray, *A Short Memoir of Mohammed Ali,* 4

8   E. B. B. Barker, *Syria and Egypt under the last five Sultans of Turkey*, II, 48

9   Valentia, III, 368

10 As Robert Barker, who built rooms in Leicester Square to show panoramas, died in 1806, it may have been to his son that Salt sold the designs for a Panorama of Cairo.

11 Valentia, III, 378

12 Ibid, 389ff

13 Ibid, 432

14 Ibid, 454. The survey is annexed to Valentia's *Travels;* it is probably the only existing plan of the city at that time.

15 Farington, VIII, 2895, 1 November 1806. Thomas Salt married Sarah Morgan on 9 November 1805 — she may have been Sarah, née Frost, who was the mother of Bessy Salt's husband, Simon Morgan.

4   THE GOVERNMENT MISSION

1   *Gentleman's Magazine,* 1816, I, 41. More pointedly, a memoir of Valentia written in the 1830s ends: "With the exception of that portion written by Mr Salt, the account of his lordship's travels is fraught with little interest, and contains few facts of importance to geographical science" (Clarke, ed, *The Georgian Era: Memoirs of the Most Eminent Persons who have flourished in Great Britain,* III, 470). The comment is unjust, for Valentia's book is often fascinating to the ordinary reader, if not to the scientific geographer.

2   PRO FO1/1. f6ff

3   *Gentleman's Magazine,* 1816, I, 41

4   Halls, I, 144ff

5   Robin Hallett, ed., *Records of the African Association 1788-1831,* 226

6   Halls, I, 156

7   Valentia, III, 277

8   Salt, 7

9   Ibid, 19

10   Ibid, 34

11   Ibid, 175

12   Ibid, 108ff

13   Ibid, 142

14   Ibid, 152ff

15   Salt had formed a good opinion of Debib in 1806, when he was only about 16, and thought even better of him when he heard what a faithful friend he had proved to Pearce.

16   Annesley BL Add Mss, 19347, f69

17   Salt, 269

18   PRO FO1/1, f92

19   Halls, I, 161

5   THE 'LION' OF ABYSSINIA

1   PRO FO1/1, f182

2   Halls, I, 256

3   Salt, 505

4   PRO FO1/1, f191ff

5   Hallett, ed. *Records of the African Association,* 229

6   Salt, appendices I-IV. A specimen of the dik-dik, a very small species of antelope, given to the Royal College of Surgeons, who had "solicited me to make them a collection of Red Sea productions" (Annesley, BL Add Mss, 19347, f47,), in 1811, was passed to the Natural History Museum in 1946, and can be seen there to this day.

7   Hallett, ed., *Records of the African Association*, 229

8   Halls, I, 283ff

9   Salt, 343ff

10 Ibid, 338 and 341

11 Annesley, BL Add Mss, 19347, ff149 and 151

12 Captain George Peacock, who met Salt in the 1820s and greatly admired him, wrote that he had "rarely ever met with any gentleman who had a more exemplary regard for the truth, or who was less the victim of prejudice and vanity. That he may occasionally...have been inadvertently led by others into some mistakes, is certainly possible, but when he speaks from his own personal knowledge and experience, his warmest friends need be under no apprehension that time and investigation will tend to impeach the accuracy of his delineations or the veracity of his statements." *Handbook of Abyssinia*, 123

13 Halls, I, 267ff

14 Records of the Royal Society

15 Halls, I, 126ff

16 Salt, dedication

17 Francis Bickley ed., *The Diaries of Sylvester Douglas, Lord Glenbervie*, 1928 edition, II, 56

18 T. F. Dibdin, *The Library Companion*, 457

19 Halls, I, 391. Yorke wrote that he should preserve the drinking horn "in memory of your intrepid and successful peregrinations into a country scarcely known to modern Europe, as well as of your friend, the Ras...whose health, conjointly with your own, myself and friends here have not failed to drink out of it."

20 Ibid, 402. During his six weeks at Caledon Castle, Salt made many sketches. Halls had the sketchbook for many years, but eventually gave it to Valentia's son.

21 Ibid, 403ff

22 PRO FO24/6, f83

23 Ibid, f81

24 Halls, II, 171

25 PRO FO24/6, f53

26 Ibid, f66

27 Halls, I, 408

28 Ibid, 409

29 Annesley, BL Add Mss, 19347, f144

30 Halls, I, 418ff

6   MR CONSUL SALT AND THE PASHA OF EGYPT

1   Halls, I, 421ff

2   Ibid, 428

3   Ibid, 431 and 439ff

4   Ibid, 441

5   It is not for some years that Salt wrote of her again.

6   PRO FO 24/6, f34, 24.8.1815

7   Halls, I, 445

8   Valentia, III, attached plan

9   PRO FO 24/6, f109, 15.6.1816

10 Halls, I, 457. Tousson Pasha died of plague only a few months later on 29 September, 1816. Sir Charles Murray, Consul General from 1846 to 1853, was told by Abbas Pasha, Tousson's son, that it was "an undisputed fact" that his father had been poisoned by Mehemet Ali who had "grown jealous of Tousson's popularity with the army and considered his own safety thereby endangered". (Charles Murray, *A Short Memoir of Mohammed Ali,* 4)

11 Yousuf Boghos had the skills of a survivor. An Armenian merchant, in 1800 he came to Egypt in the suite of the Grand Vizier to join the British expedition sent to remove French occupation of Egypt. Boghos became interpreter to the English mission and then returned to Constantinople. He returned to Egypt as drago-man (interpreter) to the then Pasha. When this Pasha was driven out, Boghos joined Mehemet Ali's service and remained with him, "notwithstanding," remarked Count Forbin, "some affronts and menaces the situation may have been productive of". (Forbin, 23) He was, as chief interpreter and sometimes chief negotiator for Mehemet Ali, a significant person in Salt's work as Consul-General.

12 Valentia, III, 473

13 George Gliddon, *An Appeal to the Antiquaries of Europe on the Destruction of the Monuments of Egypt,* 1841

14 PRO FO 24/6, 15.6.1816

15 Edward Lane, Bodleian Mss English Miscellany, d. 234, ff73-4. E. W. Lane, *Description of Egypt,* fig. 14. Today, the whole area has been long re-developed. If one penetrates to the end of a side street off the market, past a small mosque — the only landmark left from Salt's days — and round a sharp corner, one reaches a cul-de-sac and a sad modern building where Salt's house once stood. Where the gardens lay is now rushing traffic. Lane's *Description of Egypt* was published for the first time in 2000.

16 John Carne, *Letters from the East,* I, 83

17 Halls, I, 467; BL Annesley papers, f169, 171, 181ff

18 Valentia, III, 474 and passim. When his book was published in 1809, Valentia wrote of how Sheik Suleiman of the Fayum had urged him to report the suffer-ings of the people on his return to England. As they parted, the Sheik, with tears in his eyes, had begged Valentia "to recommend him and his unfortunate coun-try to the protection of the English." The Beys, too, Valentia reported, had offered either to hold Egypt subject to the British or to place the whole trade of

the country in British hands. All this Missett was reporting to the Foreign Office while Valentia and Salt were in Egypt. The reply was only silence. (Valentia III, 475-6.)

19 R. R. Madden, *Egypt and Mohammed Ali*, 10, 27.

20 Murray, *A Short Memoir of Mohammed Ali*, 12

21 Ibid, 16

22 Madden, *Egypt and Mohammed Ali*, 4

23 Gally Knight's report was written to Stratford Canning, then a junior diplomat at Constantinople. Stanley Lane-Poole included it in his biography of Canning, who later became Ambassador to the Porte, and a correspondent of Salt.

24 Madden, *Egypt and Mohammed Ali*, 11

25 R. R. Richardson, *Travels along the Mediterranean*, I, 104

26 Moyle Sherer, *Scenes and Impressions in Egypt*, 173

27 Richardson, I, 108

28 Madden, *Egypt and Mohammed Ali*, 33

29 Halls, I, 468

30 Gliddon, 47 and 156

7   THE SHEIK AND THE GIANT

1   J. L. Burckhardt, *Travels in Nubia*, introduction by W. M. Leake, v

2   Renouard, BL Add Mss, 27620, f4

3   Dorset Record Office, Bankes, D/BKL, HJ1/132. The letter, dated Cairo, 1 June 1820, is signed 'Wm Thomson or Taylor'; both a William Thomson and a William Taylor were reported missing in the action at Rosetta, but that Osman was born Thomson, although he may have joined the army as Taylor, is proved by his will, which refers to his brother James Thomson.

4   James Silk Buckingham, *Autobiography*, II, 291

5   Alexander Kinglake, *Eothen*, 234 (1898 edition)

6   Katharine Sim, *Jean Louis Burckhardt*, 290

7   William Turner, *Journal of a Tour in the Levant*, II, 340

8   Colin Clair, *Strong Man Egyptologist*, 25

9   J. T. Smith, *A Book for a Rainy Day*, 173

10 Stanley Mayes, *The Great Belzoni*, 72

11 Turner, *Journal of a Tour in the Levant*, II, 357

12 *Quarterly Review*, October 1821, Vol. 24, 142

13 Ibid

14 Belzoni, 134

15 W. R. Hamilton, *Aegyptica*, 177

16 Belzoni, 22

17 Burckhardt, *Travels in Nubia*, lxvi, Cairo 18 April 1816, "I depart the day after tomorrow for Sinai"; and Dorset Record Office, Bankes, HJ1/51

18 d'Athanasi, 6ff

19 Halls, II, 44

20 Belzoni, 26ff

21 Ibid, 24ff

22 The British Museum, Department of Egyptology, Salt papers, Document 1

23 Halls, II, 3

24 Burckhardt, *Travels in Nubia*, I, lxix

25 *Monthly Review,* May-August 1821, 89

26 Belzoni, 112

27 Halls, II, 7. The drawing Burckhardt mentions (see *Description de l'Egypte*, III, Plate 48), may be the basis for the Comte de Forbin's claim that Napoleon's savants had already dug up these lion-headed statues; they had, indeed, found some, but in a different part of the Karnak temple complex.

28 Burckhardt, *Travels in Nubia* , I, lxxvi. Burckhardt was thankful, for the sake of preserving his alias, that, at Cairo, Salt's and Belzoni's names alone were attached to the enterprise.

29 Halls, II, 7. To be fair, Belzoni did not make this statement in his book; Salt must have heard of it from another source.

30 Halls, I, 498

31 The British Museum, Department of Egyptology, Salt papers, Document 3

32 T. R. Joliffe, *Letters from Palestine and Egypt*, II, 153ff

33 The British Museum Archives, Minutes of Trustees Meetings; General Meeting, 14 March 1818, 2691

34 Halls, II, 298

35 *Quarterly Review*, October 1821, Vol. 24/144

8   CAPTAIN CAVIGLIA AND THE PYRAMIDS OF GIZA

1   *Tait's Edinburgh Magazine,* August 1837, 20

2   Halls, II, 63

3   *Quarterly Review,* April 1818, pp. 395-409

4   Ibid

5   Halls, II, 66

6   Sherer, *Scenes and Impressions in Egypt and Italy*, 145-9

7   Belzoni, 138-9

8   Irby and Mangles, preface

9   *Quarterly Review,* April 1818

10 Halls, II, 86

11 *Quarterly Review*, April 1818. Howard Vyse in the preface to his *Operations carried out at the Pyramids*, volume 3, reproduced in full Salt's documentation of all that was found at the Sphinx. Although it would not satisfy a modern archaeologist, it is an amateur record of great quality. Vyse stated in his Preface that Salt's account and plans had been given to him by Lord Mountnorris. Salt told Halls that he was sending these drawings home, and it seems that eventually he sent them with Bankes. Halls never saw them. (Halls, I, 495)

12 Carne, *Letters from the East*, I, 100ff

13 *Quarterly Review*, April 1818

14 Irby and Mangles, 157ff

15 Described by the *Quarterly Review* as "the most dapper, best dressed gentleman in Paris — and the very dandy of the Museum," Count Forbin travelled with his brother, the Abbé Forbin, and various draughtsmen and assistants. Along the way he collected a 19-year-old midshipman, Linant de Bellefonds. Everywhere he went, Forbin's English critics say, "his vanity and self-sufficiency" were mortified by the popularity of the English. He certainly spoke of them most spitefully. (*Quarterly Review*, May 1820, 83)

16 *Journal des Voyageurs*, 1819, quoted in *Gentleman's Magazine*, April 1820

17 Dorset Record Office, Bankes, HJ 1/69. f5

9   DIGGING OUT THE TEMPLE

1   Burckhardt, *Travels in Nubia*, 90-1

2   d'Athanasi, 9

3   Belzoni, 164

4   These are all now in the British Museum.

5   Halls, II, 10ff and footnote

6   Dorset Record Office, Bankes, D/BKL, HJI/107

7   Hyde, BL Add Mss 42102, f196

8   Finati was born in about 1787. Conscripted into the French army in 1805, he deserted to the Turks in Egypt, was forced to become a Muslim, took the name of Mahomet, and in 1809 enlisted in the army of the Pasha. He was present at the massacre of the Mamelukes in 1811 (but, he says, posted where he had no part in the slaughter), and had campaigned against the Wahabi in Upper Egypt. In 1815, having left the army and visited Mecca, he was employed by William Bankes as interpreter. Bankes later edited and translated into English his account of his life.

9   Irby and Mangles, 3

10 Ibid, 13

11 Ibid, 25ff

12 Ibid, 28

13 Ibid, 38

14 Finati, II, 199

15 Ibid, 205

16 Irby and Mangles, 75

17 All are in the British Museum. The 'female' figure can now be identified as Pa-Set, governor of Nubia in the time of Rameses II.

18 Irby and Mangles, 106

10 LORD BELMORE AND THE LORDLY PARTY

This chapter draws on Dr R. R. Richardson's *Travels along the Mediterranean and parts adjacent*. The *Quarterly Review* of October 1822 was less than kind about Richardson: "The long series of ruins and rubble which strew the banks of the Nile from Alexandria to the Second Cataract — broken columns and broken pottery — temples, tombs and obelisks — sarcophagi and mummy-cases — hieroglyphs and mysteries which nobody understands, described in all the minutiae of dull detail (through some five hundred desperate pages)..." Richardson deserves better than this. Our access to the Castle Coole archive added a gloss to his account.

1   Joliffe, *Letters from Palestine and Egypt,* II, 256

2   Halls, II, 181

3   Ibid, 44

4   Richardson, I, 52

5   Anne Katherine Elwood, *Narrative of a Journey*, I, 144

6   Castle Coole archive, 25.8.1817

7   Richardson I, 55ff

8   Baroness Menu von Minutoli, *Recollections of Egypt*, 49

9   Richardson, I, 97

10 Ibid, 117

11 Halls, II, 39ff

12 Memoir by Henry Salt attached to Burckhardt's *Travels in Nubia*

13 Richardson, I, 169ff

14 Castle Coole archive, 21.10.1818

15 Belzoni, 227ff

16 Ibid, 230

17 Ibid, 232ff

18 Richardson I, 263

19 Halls, II, 5

20 Supplement to the 4th-6th edition of *Encyclopedia Britannica*, vol. IV. Egypt, 40ff

21 Halls, II, 14

22 Richardson, II, 307, 365

23 Ibid, 455, 535

24 Halls, II, 18

25 Belzoni, 250

26 Halls, II, 45

27 Belzoni, 457

28 Halls, II

29 Ibid

30 Comte de Forbin, *Travels in Egypt,* 50

31 Ibid, 46

32 Castle Coole archive, 28.10.1820. To his friend, William Gifford, editor of the *Quarterly Review,* Salt wrote that he was delighted by "the proper chastisement" which Forbin received from the journal's reviewer. There was, he said, "but one opinion throughout Egypt respecting his work, as being superficial, incorrect and full of malicious observations against those from whom he received the utmost civility and attention during his flying excursion through the country." Salt remarked one further insult. He had taken the trouble to show Forbin Seti's tomb "brilliantly lighted up with nearly a hundred candles", and yet Forbin remarks in his work of being "led through it by an Arab". (John Murray archive, 26.11.1820)

33 Frederic Cailliaud, 'Travels in the Oases', in Phillips *New Voyages and Travels*

34 Richardson, II, 112

35 Ibid, 93

36 Castle Coole archive

37 Richardson, II, 161

11 THE PYRAMIDICAL BRAIN

Both Giovanni Belzoni and Giovanni (Yanni) d'Athanasi reported, some time after the event, on how entry to the second pyramid — that of Chephren — was made. Their reports are contained in Belzoni's *Narrative* (Belzoni) and d'Athanasi's *Brief Account* (d'Athanasi)

1 Halls, II, 59

2 Sarah Belzoni's 'Trifling Account' in Belzoni's *Narrative,* 457

3 Belzoni, 252

4 d'Athanasi, 18

5 Belzoni, 260

6 Ibid, 264ff

7 Domenico Frediani (1783-1823) was a native of Milan. Sir Frederick Henniker met him in the Delta and travelled with him. He joined Ismael Pasha's expedition to Senaar in 1820, acting as tutor and dragoman to the Pasha. Edmonstone met him near the Second Cataract. Sadly, his mind gave way and he suffered delusions that he was a prince. He was sent back to Cairo, and died there. (M.

L. Bierbrier, *Who Was Who in Egyptology*, and Belzoni, 269.)

8   d'Athanasi, 20

9   Ibid, 21

10   Ibid, 12; Belzoni, 269

11   FitzClarence's version of events over the next few days is contained in his book *Journal of a Route across India through Egypt to England*, published in 1819, pp. 380-483.

12   FitzClarence's observations about Belzoni were published within the year and may well have influenced the huge man himself, when writing his own book, in his attitude to his arrangement with Salt. FitzClarence thought him "far too valuable a man for us to permit to labour for any other nation", and judged that fame, not money, was the object of which he was most anxious.

13   It was two of these black granite statues which Salt had given to Belzoni and he had sold to Count Forbin for the Louvre.

14   FitzClarence, 433ff

15   Belzoni reported taking FitzClarence to the pyramids (p. 282), but did not mention Salt's presence, except to say: "The Consul, Mr Salt, would have been kind enough to have paid all the expenses I had incurred in opening the pyramid, but this I actively refused, as I had thought it would not be fair and right that he should pay for what he had nothing to do with."

16   FitzClarence, 433ff

17   FitzClarence also noted that, under the carved name of the French writer and diplomat Chateaubriand, someone had engraved "Il n'etait pas ici", which FitzClarence was assured was really the fact. Finding that when he visited Egypt, he did not have time for the pyramids, Chateaubriand had requested another Frenchman to inscribe his name, "according to the custom of these prodigious tombs, for I like to fulfil all the little duties of a pious traveller."

18   FitzClarence, 466. Belzoni says he did not have time to write an account, but only made "a hasty sketch" for the "Antiquary Society" while Salt wrote the official account. He may be muddling two events.

19   The statue, or parts of it (that Beechey discovered at Karnak), still remain in Egypt. The head and the arm are in the British Museum.

20   This is the great pink granite sarcophagus cover which Belzoni presented to the Fitzwilliam Museum in Cambridge, and which is the central feature of one of the Egyptian rooms. The sarcophagus itself (that of Rameses III) was sold by Salt to the Louvre in 1826.

21   Halls, II, 27, and the British Museum Salt archive, Volume IV, No. 1490

22   Castle Coole archive, 18.4.1818

23   Halls, II, 53

12   COLLECTIONS AND AN EXPEDITION

1   Annesley, BL Add Mss 19347, f169. Riley, a former head gardener at the

Botanical Gardens in Malta, managed an indigo factory for the Pasha (Hyde, BL Add Mss 42102, f56)

2 Ibid, f193ff
3 Ibid, f244ff
4 Ibid, f169
5 Halls, II, 298ff
6 Frederick Norden, *Travels in Egypt and Nubia*, I, 97
7 Dorset Record Office, Bankes, D/BKL, HJI/ between 34 and 35
8 Ibid, between 66 and 67
9 Halls, I, 488
10 Halls, II, 124
11 Viola Bankes, *A Dorset Heritage*, 139
12 Ibid, 138
13 Halls, II, 23
14 Belzoni, 350
15 Mayes, *The Great Belzoni*, 228
16 Castle Coole archive
17 Belzoni, 351
18 Halls, II, 133ff
19 d'Athanasi, 39ff
20 Edouard de Montulé, *Travels in Egypt*, 100
21 d'Athanasi, 40
22 Finati II, 315
23 Wilson, BL Add Mss 22902. William Rae Wilson (1772-1849) was a lawyer. He published his travels in 1823.
24 Hyde, BL Add Mss 42102, f88. Hyde's journal is an invaluable chronological record of the travellers he met on the Nile. Between Cairo and Luxor he met Guido Sylvestre "from Rome"; "Mons Monlione, son of Count Monlione of Paris" (de Montulé?); W. Fisher and John Bowes Wright of Jesus College, Cambridge; Drovetti, who gave him some Greek and Roman coins. At Philae he spent time with Herbert Barrett Curteis (brother of Mrs Elwood) and Captain Ducane RN, also in Bowes Wright's party.
25 Ibid, f91
26 Ibid, f126ff
27 Halls, II, 106
28 Coffin, BL Add Mss 19421, f5ff
29 John Fuller, *Narrative of a Tour*, 150. An infection in his nose a few years before had forced Pearce to cut away the cartilage, causing this disfigurement.
30 Pearce, II, 334

13 "IF FRIENDS THUS TRADUCE ME"

1 Fuller, *Narrative of a Tour*, 248

2 Halls, II, 24

3 Ibid

4 Dorset Record Office, Bankes, HJI/98

5 Fuller, *Narrative of a Tour*, 249

6 Ibid, 248

7 Halls, II, 298ff

8 Ibid, 301

9 Ibid, 303

10 Ibid, 305

11 Ibid, 301

12 When Thomas Bruce, Earl of Elgin, was Ambassador to Constantinople in 1799, he had, at his own expense, brought to England from Greece, then under Turkish rule, a large collection of antiquities, including sculptures taken from the Parthenon in Athens. Elgin, who reckoned the collection had cost him £74,000, approached the Government in 1811, but rejected an offer of £30,000. In 1816 a parliamentary committee was set up to consider his renewed offer. After much deliberation, having questioned Elgin's right to have acquired the treasures for himself when he occupied an official post, and cast doubt on the value of statuary in such a "mutilated state", two detailed valuations were laid before the committee. William Richard Hamilton, who, as Elgin's secretary, had been involved in acquiring the collection, suggested £64,000; Richard Payne Knight, the Townley Trustee at the British Museum, recommended only £25,000. Faced with such a discrepancy, the committee accepted a "sort of conjectural estimate of the Whole, without entering into particulars", for £35,000, thrown out by another Museum Trustee, Lord Aberdeen. Aberdeen is known to have disapproved of Elgin taking the Parthenon sculptures, and, incidentally, is probably the Trustee who wished to offer a very low sum for Salt's collection. £35,000 is what Elgin received. Even so, with the country in considerable economic difficulties, and working people in want even of bread, that the Government should lay out a huge sum seemed to many unforgivable. (Based on the report of the Parliamentary Committee in *Gentleman's Magazine*, March and April 1816)

13 Halls, II, 315ff

14 Ibid, 311

15 Ibid, 305ff

16 Ibid, 308. It was a pity for Salt that he was unwilling to act the dealer and aim for the best price he could get. Since posterity has often sneered that he was one, he has, quite literally, received the kicks without the ha'pence.

17 Ibid, 314

18 Ibid

19 Annesley, BL Add Mss 19347, f251ff. Some account of Mountnorris's dissatisfaction must have reached the ear of one Sir William Gell in Naples, who acted
as a kind of clearing house for the news and gossip of the antiquarian world.
Ignorant of the true facts and mysteriously malevolent towards Salt, he wrote a
wittily sneering verse against him (see James Burton, Add Mss 25661, f32), of
which one couplet ran;

> Not a word of Mountnorris — that interest is past
> Sense of favours conferred is not likely to last.

This was patently untrue. Such differences as existed, though they pained Salt
deeply, never caused an actual breach in the long-standing friendship.

20 The British Museum, Department of Egyptology, Salt papers, Document 11

21 Ibid, Document 12

22 Halls, II, 317

23 Ibid, 320

24 Ibid, 137

25 Ibid, 144. Living in unaccustomed luxury, Pearce had put on a great deal of
weight.

14 ROMANCE AND DIPLOMACY

1 Halls, II, 126

2 Ibid, 127

3 Burton papers, University College London

4 BL Add Mss 19347 f.359

5 Bryn Davies, *Bulletin of Faculty of Arts,* Cairo II, 1/1934, 69

6 PRO Prob 8/1739, f227

7 Dorset Record Office, D/BKL HJi/132

8 Consular records 1851–, Family Records Centre

9 BL Add Mss 19347, f256

10 Halls, II, 147

11 Claude Terral, *Revue Archeologique*, series IV, vol. VII, 1906. In February 1820
Marcellus reached the island of Melos "at the very moment" when a newly discovered and very beautiful female marble statue was awaiting shipment. After
some problems, "this friend of the arts" succeeded in saving "this precious relic
of antiquity" for France. In the Louvre she still stands: the Venus de Milo. His
record shows that the Venus lay aboard Marcellus' ship all the time he was in
Egypt and up river in Cairo.

12 Martin de Tyrac, Comte Marcellus, *Souvenirs de l'Orient*, II, 230

13 Halls, II, 147

14 BL Add Mss 19347, 19.9.1819

15 Ibid

16 Ibid

17 Halls, II, 155

18 John Carne, *Recollections of the East*, 290

19 Halls, II, 162

20 Fuller, *Narrative of a Tour*, 154

21 Halls, II, 155

22 Ibid, 163

23 Ibid, 166

24 Ibid, 150

25 Ibid, 156ff

26 Fuller, *Narrative of a Tour*, 156

27 Halls, II, 159

28 Pearce, *The Life and Adventures of Nathaniel Pearce* (ed. J. J. Halls), Pearce's Will, II, 347-9, 31.7.1820

29 Whether with Jowett's help or Salt's alone, Cullum was on a boat from Alexandria to Cairo later that year. Baroness Minutoli, travelling on the same craft, was told she was heiress to Pearce's 'fortune' and related to the King of Abyssinia. Despite her 'high birth', she preferred to sleep on the deck on the sacks of corn which formed the cargo (Menu von Minutoli, 32). Still later, Coffin reported that Cullum was queening it happily around Abyssinia.

30 Martin de Tyrac, *Souvenirs de l'Orient*, II, 237ff.

31 Halls, II, 172

32 Robert Wilson papers, University of Aberdeen, ms notebook 415.

33 PRO FO 78/96, 1820

34 Ibid,

35 Rev. G. Waddington and Rev. B. Hanbury, *Journal of a visit to Some Parts of Ethiopia*

36 PRO FO 78/96, 1820

37 Halls, II, 177

38 Ibid, 199ff

39 Saulnier, M. Fils, *Notice sur le Voyage de M. Lelorrain en Egypte*, 1822

40 *Quarterly Review*, October 1822

41 Ibid

42 Halls, II, 189

43 Ibid, 193

15 NEGOTIATIONS

1 Annesley, BL Add Mss 19347, f288

2 *Gentleman's Magazine*, 1843, II, 211. Obituary of John Murray.

3   Redding, *Celebrities I Have Known*, 276

4   John Murray archives

5   Dorset Record Office, Bankes, HJI/159

6   Halls, II, 210

7   Ibid, 9 and 26

8   *Gentleman's Magazine,* 1821, I, 447

9   Halls, II, 333

10 Ibid, 328. "To this courteous letter, Mr Richards felt it unnecessary to reply, and contented himself by writing on the cover the following lines:

    'Picciol'anima fece monna natura
    in corpo di grandissima statura'"

    (A tiny spirit made mother nature/in a form of enormous stature.)

11 The British Museum, Department of Egyptology, Salt papers, Document 15

12 d'Athanasi, 81. Yanni does Belzoni an injustice; the Memnon head was moved to the Nile between 27 July and 12 August, and work had not been possible on some of these days.

13 Ibid, preface, ix

14 Halls, II, 335

15 Ibid, 337

16 Ibid, 324

17 Ibid, 342

18 Dorset Record Office, Bankes, HJI/196

19 Ibid, HJI/227

20 Ibid, HJI/169

21 Linant journal, Griffith Institute, Oxford

22 Dorset Record Office, Bankes HJI/169

23 Ibid, HJI/153

24 Ibid, HJI/153. The Reverends Barnard Hanbury (1793-1833) and George Waddington (1793-1869) were in Nubia in 1821, with James Curtin as their dragoman. Whatever advantage Linant's account might have had over theirs was lost to the public, for while Waddington published in 1822, Bankes, as usual, failed to do so.

25 Dorset Record Office, Bankes HJI/196

26 Ibid, HJI/227

27 Ibid, HJI/227

28 Halls, II, 323

29 Ibid, 352

30 The British Museum Archives, Minutes of the Trustees' Meetings, 2832. The sub-committee members were: Lord Aberdeen, President of the Society of

Antiquaries, an ardent philhellene, who had suggested only £35,000 be paid for the Elgin Marbles; Henry Bankes, who acted as the Trustees' voice in Parliament, known, for his desire not to lay out public money, as 'Saving Bankes', and perhaps acting in this capacity even on this occasion; Sir Charles Long, joint Paymaster General; George Booth Tyndale, joint Paymaster General; Sir John Singleton Copley, son of the eminent artist, Solicitor-General; Baron Colchester, at one time, as Speaker of the House of Commons, an ex-officio Trustee, but, since his resignation, a specially elected Trustee; Richard Payne Knight, the Townley Trustee.

31 Halls, II, 352ff

32 Ibid, 354ff

33 Dorset Record Office, Bankes HJI/227. Bankes was Tory Member of Parliament for Cambridge University, 1822-6.

34 Halls, II, 238

35 Ibid, 359

36 Ibid, 347ff

37 Ibid, 372

38 Ibid, 374ff

39 Dorset Record Office, Bankes HJI/262

16 SCHOLARS, TRAVELLERS AND TOURISTS

1 Sherer, *Scenes and Impressions in Egypt*, preface

2 Gliddon, *Ancient Egypt*

3 Sir William Gell was born in 1777, so he was 20 years older than the young intellectuals he encouraged. In his mid-20s he had written and illustrated a topographical work on Troy which earned him a wide reputation for scholarship, although it was considered descriptive rather than archaeological in intent. He was elected to the Society of Dilettanti in 1807, and four years later the Society sent him to Greece and Asia Minor. Byron, who knew him at Cambridge, wrote in *English Bards and Scots Reviewers* in 1809:

> Of Dardan tours, let dilettanti tell,
> I leave topography to Classic Gell.

Very flattering and often quoted. However, in the manuscript of the poem, Byron had written "Coxcomb Gell" and in the fifth edition changed the word to "Rapid Gell". In his own copy he wrote: "Rapid indeed! he topographized King Priam's dominions in three days — and I called him Classic before I saw the Troad but since have learned better than to tack to his name what don't belong to it." (*Complete Poetical Works*, I, 261)

4 G. Peacock, *Life of Sir Thomas Young*

5 Sir William Gell to J. G. Wilkinson, Naples, 10.8.1824, Wilkinson Mss, Bodleian Library

6 James Burton's diary, BL Add Mss 25624; Burton Papers, UCL, 35/1

7   Burton's diary, BL Add Mss 25624

8   Jason Thompson, *Sir Gardner Wilkinson and His Circle*, passim

9   Halls, II, 196

10 J. G. Wilkinson, *Materia Hieroglyphica*

11 Halls, II, 239

12 Joseph Wolff, *Life and Journals*

13 Halls, II, 196

14 J. G. Wilkinson, *On Colour and on the necessity for a general diffusion of taste among all classes*

15 Halls, II, 196

16 Burton papers, UCL, 35/2

17 Ibid, 35/4

18 PRO FO 78/126, 26.3.1824

19 *Quarterly Review*, 1824

20 Giuseppe Passalacqua (1797-1865) made a large and important collection at Thebes and other sites, much of the work carried out while he lived with or near d'Athanasi. His collection is published as *Catalogue raisonné et historique des antiquités découvertes en Egypt,* Paris, 1826. When the French government refused to buy his collection, it was sold, in 1827, to Friedrich William IV of Prussia for the Berlin Museum. The former 'horse-dealer' was installed as the Museum's Conservator of the Egyptian Collections in 1828. At his death in 1865, Richard Lepsius succeeded him. (Bierbrier, *Who Was Who in Egyptology*)

21 John Madox, *Excursions in the Holy Land etc*, I, 428ff

22 Westcar Diary, 123ff, Griffith Institute, Oxford

23 Madox, *Excursions in the Holy Land*, II, 48ff

24 Ibid, 16

25 The *Gentleman's Magazine* of July 1824 gave the date as 29 March. According to Baedeker's *Egypt* (1929), the huge Mehemet Ali Mosque, which is one of the landmarks of Cairo and where the Pasha's remains lie, was built "on the site of a palace that was blown up in 1824".

26 Halls, II, 237

17 THE YEARS OF CHANGE

1   Madox, *Excursions in the Holy Land*, II, 7ff

2   Halls, II, 235-7

3   Silvio Curto and Laura Donatelli, *Bernardino Drovetti Epistolario (1800-1851)*, 11.6.1824

4   Salt, *Egypt: a Poem*, introduction (Halls, II, 387)

5   Henry Dodwell, *The Founder of Modern Egypt*, 71ff

6   PRO FO 79/81, 6.6.1818

7   Henry Salt, *Essay on Dr Young's and M. Champollion's Phonetic System of Hieroglyphs,* introduction

8   *Letters to Thomas Young,* 130

9   John Leitch, ed., *Miscellaneous Works of the late Thomas Young,* Vol. III, 392

10 H. R. Hall, *Journal of Egyptology,* 2, 1915

11 *Edinburgh Review,* XLV, 1826, 110ff. The *Review*'s commentary in a long article on the study of the hieroglyphs was that earlier researchers had followed the belief that "hieroglyphic writing was solely composed of characters, each of which was representative of an idea...Then, imagination usurping the place of reason, and conjecture that of fact, the learned, who had addicted themselves to these inquiries, soon became involved in an inextricable labyrinth..." Salt, Young and Champollion took a new route.

12 J. F. Champollion, *Bulletin Universal des Sciences et de l'Industrie,* 1826

13 Hall, *Journal of Egyptology,* 2, 1915

14 Salt's *Essay on Dr Young's and M. Champollion's Phonetic System of Hieroglyphs*

15 Westcar Diary, Griffith Institute, Oxford, August 1824

16 Halls, II, 234

17 R. R. Madden, *Egypt and Mohammed Ali,* 57

18 R. R. Madden, *Travels,* I, 214ff, 239, 241

19 Information about Robert Hay is based on the Hay Diaries (BL Add Mss 31054) and Selwyn Tillett, passim. Robert Hay was born at Duns Castle, Berwickshire in 1799. Unexpectedly inheriting the family estates in 1820, on the death of his older brother James, he resigned his commission in the Navy, and decided to return to Egypt where he had been as a midshipman. Looking back over his life in a letter to a friend, Thomas Pettigrew, in 1842 he said that, when he returned to Egypt, he felt there was "nothing unknown, after the many learned and busy travellers who had preceded me, that I looked on everything more as a matter of wonder and instruction myself...." He soon discovered there was much still to learn.

20 Joseph Bonomi became, in 1862, the Curator of Sir John Soane's Museum in London's Lincoln's Inn Fields and thus, until his death in 1878, had charge of the marvellous alabaster sarcophagus that Soane had purchased from Salt's first collection.

21 BL Add Mss 25658, f7.9. Charles Sloane had come to Egypt to work with Mr Brine at the sugar refinery and took an interest in antiquities. Much later he served as Vice Consul in Alexandria. Selwyn Tillett in his biography of Robert Hay mistook the Mr S. referred to in Hay's diary to be Mr Salt (who was at that time in Alexandria), giving a very peculiar idea of the Consul-General.

22 PRO FO 78/147, f72

23 BL Add Mss 25658, f7.9

24 Much later Wilkinson gave others quite strong advice on this matter. In 1847

Murray published his *Handbook to Egypt*, for years the definitive guide. On the matter of dress, he said: "If a traveller inquires whether the Oriental dress be necessary, I answer, it is by no means so; and a person wearing it, who is ignorant of the language, becomes ridiculous."

25 Lord Bertram Ashburnham, Viscount St Asaph (1797-1878), would become the fourth Earl of Ashburnham in 1830. He was a keen collector of ancient coins and gems. The drawings they were shown may have been the sketches which have survived in the Salt family rather than finished work.

18 A FRIEND, THE LOUVRE AND GROWING DANGER

1 R. R. Madden, *Travels*, I, 189

2 Ibid, ii

3 Ibid, 192

4 Halls, II, 269

5 R. R. Madden, *Travels,* I, 209

6 PRO FO 78/147, 27.1.1826

7 R. R. Madden, *Travels*, I, 194

8 Ibid, 243

9 PRO FO 78/125, 15.9.1825

10 PRO FO 78/125, 24.10.1825

11 *Dictionary of National Biography*

12 PRO FO 78/135, f194, 1.11.1825

13 Stanley Lane-Poole, *Life of Edward William Lane*

14 PRO FO 78/147, 4.4.1826, and Halls, II, 261

15 PRO FO 78/147, 17.7.1826

16 This pensioner was almost certainly Mr Lenze, who was Vice Consul in Rosetta for many years.

17 Mrs Elwood wrote vivid and amusing, if romanticised, accounts of their journey to India and back around the Cape, under a long descriptive title, which can be abbreviated to *Narrative of a Journey Overland from England to India* (1830). Later she wrote a very personal and lively book of *Memoirs of the Literary Ladies of England*.

18 Elwood, *Narrative*, I, 123

19 Ibid, 173

20 Richard Hoppner, son of John Hoppner, the Consul at Venice.

21 Halls, II, 244

22 Ibid, 250

23 Ibid, 251-2

24 Ibid, 263

25 Ibid, 264

26 R. R. Madden, *Travels*, I, 292ff

27 Ibid, 336

28 Ibid, 334

29 R. R. Madden, *Travels*, II, 61

19 MR CONSUL-GENERAL SALT

Much of this chapter is guided by Henry Dodwell's classic history of the period, *The Founder of Modern Egypt: A study of Muhammed Ali,* and the Foreign Office files in the Public Record Office at Kew, particularly those classed as PRO FO 78 (Turkey).

1   Halls, II, 268

2   Lane-Poole, *Life of Sir Stratford Canning,* I, 394

3   PRO FO 78/147, 10.6.1826

4   Ibid, 31.8.1826

5   Ibid, 1.10 1826

6   Lane-Poole, *Life of Sir Stratford Canning,* I, 412

7   PRO FO 78/147, 12.8. 1826. Some Europeans, including Robert Hay and Edward Lane, rescued Greek girls from the slave market — by purchasing them and later marrying them. Mehemet Ali himself sometimes assisted with funds to retrieve these captives.

8   PRO FO 78/147, 1.10.1826

9   Ibid

10 PRO FO 78/149, 4.8.1826

11 *Literary Gazette,* August 1827. Sadly the giraffe lived just two years in the royal menagerie, but it was immortalized by the Swiss animal painter Jacques Laurent Agasse. In the painting, in the Queen's Collection, it stoops gracefully over its keeper, watched by the interpreter in crimson gown and the animal dealer, Mr Cross, as it is offered a basin of, presumably, milk. The two Egyptian milch cows are still quietly in attendance in the background.

12 Dorset Record Office BKL HJI/287

13 Edward Barker, *Syria and Egypt under the last five Sultans of Turkey*, 329. Later, Barker began to collect — as an investment — and his collection was sold at Sotheby's at much the same time as Salt's third collection.

14 Georges Douin, *Une Mission Militaire*, 21

15 PRO FO 78/152, 26.2.1827

16 PRO FO 1/2 24.4.1827

17 Halls, II, 270

18 Hay diary, May 1827

19 PRO FO 78/160, 11.6.1827

20 PRO FO 78/182 14.7.1827. In April 1827 the Prime Minister, Lord Liverpool,

had a stroke. After some hesitation, George Canning moved from the Foreign Office to become Prime Minister; Lord Dudley became Foreign Minister, under the close supervision of Canning. But only four months later, on 8 August 1827, Canning, too, was dead.

21 *Dictionary of National Biography*

22 PRO FO 78/160, 12.8. 1827

23 PRO FO 78/182, 21.8. 1827

24 PRO FO 78/153, Salt Memorandum, f252ff. To the agreement of secrecy Salt could not truly accede. He reported word for word this dialogue to both Cradock and Stratford Canning in a long document that is now filed at the Public Record Office as PRO FO 78/153, pages 252-7. However, Canning honoured Salt's word as far as he could. In January 1828 he reassured Cradock: "Consideration for the delicate position of the Vice Roy of Egypt prevailed with me to abstain from communication to the French Ambassador or the Russian Envoy more than the general result of your interviews with his Highness." (PRO FO 78/156, f313). The silence was so well kept that few people even today seem aware of the backdrop to the scenes at Navarino.

25 PRO FO 78/182, 21.8.1827

26 M. Loewe, *Diaries of Sir Moses Montefiore*, 37

27 PRO FO 78/182, f50

20 THE END

1 Halls, II, 276

2 Madden, *Travels*, II

3 Halls, II, 281

4 Clarke, *The Georgian Era*, Vol. III, Henry Salt

5 Halls, II, 284

6 Madden, 'Henry Salt', in *The Infirmities of Genius*

7 Ibid

8 Halls, II, 286

9 Loewe, *Diaries of Sir Moses Montefiore*, 149

10 Halls, II, 287. Sources differ as to the date of Salt's death, 29 and 30 October 1827 being variously given. This can happen when death occurs near midnight. In about 1932, when a new road, the Sharia Abd el Moneim, cut into the area, the cenotaph and coffin were removed to the British Cemetery at Chatby on the outskirts of Alexandria (*Bulletin de la Societé Archeologique d'Alexandria*, No. 16, from the archive of Mrs Neville Rolfe, with notation by her father). Recent searches have revealed no further evidence.

21 AFTERMATH

1 PRO FO 78/153, 1.9.1827

2   PRO FO 78/153, f177

3   PRO FO 78/182, f67

4   Ibid

5   Loewe, *Diaries of Sir Moses Montefiore*, 45

6   R. R. Madden, *Travels*, II, 397. The Anglican missionary who officiated at Henry Salt's funeral reported from Alexandria to Reverend William Jowett at the Church Missionary Society in Malta on 2 November 1827. "News has come from the Pasha's quarter that a Tartar had brought word from Constantinople that the Sultan had given strict orders to Ibrahim Pasha to attack the English, French and Russians with all his might, and to sink them all to the bottom of the sea." The next day (2 November) word came that the Turkish-Egyptian fleet was annihilated. On this eventful day "the constancy and faithfulness of the Pasha was put to the test, and it did not fail. We were as quiet as ever, and not a single instance of insult took place."

7   PRO FO 78/182 25.4.1828, ff71, 60, 80, 90

8   *Gentleman's Magazine*, 1835

9   Church Missionary Society archive, CM/095/8

10 R. R. Madden, *Egypt and Mohammed Ali*, 96

Bibliography

Annesley, George, Viscount Valentia, (later Earl of Mountnorris) *Voyages and Travels to India, Ceylon, the Red Sea, Abyssinia and Egypt*, 3 vols (London, 1809)

Archer, Mildred, 'A Forgotten Painter of the Picturesque — Henry Salt in India, 1802-4'. *Country Life*, 19 November 1959

d'Athanasi, Giovanni, *A Brief Account of the Researches and Discoveries in Upper Egypt made under the Direction of Henry Salt Esq., to which is added a detailed catalogue of Mr Salt's Collection of Egyptian Antiquities* (London, 1836)

Baedeker, Karl, *Egypt* (London, 1929)

Bankes, Viola, *A Dorset Heritage* (London, 1953)

Barker, Edward B. B., *Syria and Egypt under the last five Sultans of Turkey: experiences of Mr Consul-General Barker, chiefly from his letters and journals*, 2 vols (London, 1876)

Barry, Alfred, *The life and works of Sir Charles Barry* (London, 1821)

Belmore (see Richardson)

Belzoni Giovanni, *Narrative of the Operations and Recent Discoveries with in the Pyramids, Temples, Tombs and Excavations in Egypt and Nubia; and of a Journey to the Coast of the Red Sea, in the search of the ancient Berenice; and another to the Oasis of Jupiter Ammon* (London, 1820)

Description of the Egyptian Tomb discovered by Belzoni (London, 1821)

Plates illustrative of the researches and operations of G. Belzoni, with six new plates (London, 1820 and 1822)

Belzoni, Sarah, *Mrs Belzoni's Trifling account of the women of Egypt, Nubia and Syria* (within Belzoni's *Narrative*) (London, 1820)

Bickley, Francis, ed., *The Diaries of Sylvester Douglas, Lord Glenbervie*, 2 vols (London, 1928)

Bierbrier, M. L., 'The Salt Watercolours', *Gottinger Miszellan* 61, 1983

Who Was Who in Egyptology (Egypt Exploration Society, London, 3rd edition, 1995)

Bonomi, Joseph and Arundale, Francis, *Gallery of Antiquities selected from the British Museum* (London, 1842-3)

Bossi, S. and Cooper, Edward J., *Views in Egypt and Nubia from drawings taken of original drawings by Bossi with text by Cooper* (London, 1824)

Bosworth, C. E., 'Henry Salt, Consul in Egypt 1816-1827 and Pioneer Egyptologist'. *Bulletin of the John Reynolds University Library of Manchester*, 57, 1974

Bourchier, Lady, *Memoir of the Life of Admiral Sir Edward Codrington*, 2 vols (London, 1873)

Bruce, James, *Travels to Discover the Source of the Nile in the Years 1768-1773*, 5 vols (Edinburgh, 1790)

Buckingham, James Silk, *Autobiography* (London, 1855)

Burckhardt, John Lewis, *Travels in Nubia* (London, 1819)

Travels in Syria and the Holy Land (London, 1822)

Burton, James and Bonomi, J., *Excerpta Hieroglyphica* (Cairo, 1825-37)

Burton, Sir Richard, 'Giovanni Battista Belzoni'. *Cornhill Magazine* 42, July 1880

Cailliaud, Frederic, 'Travels in the Oasis of Thebes and other desert places to East and West of the Thebiade', in *New Voyages and Travels*, edited by Sir R. Phillips (London, 1822)

Carne, John, *Letters from the East*, 2 vols (London, 1826)

Recollections of the East (London, 1830)

Champollion, J. F., *Precis du systeme hieroglyphique des ancien Egyptiens*, 2 vols (Paris, 1824)

'Comments on Mr Salt's Essay on the Hieroglyphs', in *Bulletin Universal des Sciences et de l'Industrie*, (Paris, 1826)

Lettres écrites d' Egypte et Nubie en 1828-29 (Paris, 1833)

Clair, Colin, *Strong Man Egyptologist* (London, 1957)

Clarke, ed., *The Georgian Era: Memoirs of the Most Eminent Persons who have flourished in Great Britain*, vol. III (London, 1832-4)

Clay, Edith, *Sir William Gell in Italy* (London, 1976)

Clayton, Peter, *The Rediscovery of Ancient Egypt: Artists and Travellers in the 19th Century* (London, 1982)

Conder, John Josiah, *The Modern Traveller: A Popular Description of Egypt, Nubia, etc*, 2 vols (London, 1827)

Curto, Silvio, and Donatelli, Laura, *Bernardino Drovetti Epistolario (1800-1851)*, (Milan, 1985)

Davies, Bryn, 'Henry Salt', in *Bulletin of Faculty of Arts* (Cairo, 1934)

Denon, Vivant, *Travels in Upper and Lower Egypt*, translated by Arthur Aiken, 2 vols (London, 1803)

Dibdin, Rev. Thomas, *The Library Companion or the Young Man's Guide and Old Man's Comfort* (London, 1824)

Dictionary of National Biography (Oxford, 1901)

Disher, M. Wilson, *Pharaoh's Fool, a Life in Archaeology* (Belzoni) (London, 1957)

Dodwell, Henry, *The Founder of Modern Egypt: A study of Muhammed Ali* (Cambridge, 1931)

Douin, Georges, *Les Premieres Fregates de Mohammed Ali (1824-1827)* (Cairo, 1926)

Une Mission Militaire Français aupres de Mehemet Ali (correspondence of General Belliard and Boyer, 1824) (Cairo, 1923)

Navarin (6 July 1827-20 October 1827) (Cairo, 1927)

Elwood, Anne Katharine, *Narrative of a Journey Overland by the Continent of Europe, Egypt and the Red Sea from England to India*, 2 vols (London, 1830)

Encyclopedia Britannica, Supplement to 4th and 5th editions, 1819

Farington, Joseph, *The Diary of Joseph Farington*, ed. Garlick and Macintyre (1978ff)

Fiechter, J.-J. *Le Moisson des dieux* (Paris, 1994)

Finati, Giovanni, *Narrative of the Life and Adventures of Giovanni Finati, etc, dictated by himself and edited by Wm. John Bankes Esq.*, 2 vols (London, 1830)

FitzClarence, Lt Col., *Journal of a Route across India, through Egypt to England* (London, 1819)

Forbin, Comte de, *Travels in Egypt in 1817-1818 being a continuation of travels in the Holy Land* (London, 1819)

Forster, E. M., *Alexandria, a History and a Guide* (Alexandria, 1922; London, 1982)

Fuller, John, *Narrative of a Tour through some parts of the Turkish Empire* (London, 1829-30)

Gliddon, George R, *Ancient Egypt* (New York, 1843)

An Appeal to the Antiquaries of Europe on the Destruction of the Monuments of Egypt (London, 1844)

Hall, H. R., 'Letters to Sir William Gell from Henry Salt, JG Wilkinson, Baron von Bunsen'. *Journal of Egyptology*, 2, 1915

Hallett, Robin, ed., *Records of the African Association 1788-1881* (London, 1964)

Halls, J. J., *The Life and Correspondence of Henry Salt Esq. FRS*, 2 vols (London, 1834)

See also Pearce, Nathaniel

Hamilton, W. R., *Remarks on Several Parts of Turkey; Part 1, Aegyptica, and some account of the Ancient and Modern State of Egypt* (1801-2), (London, 1809)

Henniker, Frederick, *Notes during a Visit to Egypt, etc.*, (London, 1823)

Hilmi, Prince Ibrahim, *The Literature of Egypt and the Soudan from the earliest times to the year 1855*, 2 vols (London, 1886)

Irby, Hon. Charles and Mangles, James, *Travels in Egypt and Nubia, Syria and Asia Minor during the years 1817 and 1818*, privately published London, 1823 (Abridged edition 1844, 1852)

James, T. G. H., *Egypt Revealed* (London, 1998)

Jenkins, Ian, *Archaeologists & Aesthetes in the Sculpture Galleries of the British Museum, 1800-1809* (London, 1992)

Joliffe, Rev. T. R., *Letters from Palestine and Egypt* (London, 1822)

Jomard, Edmé François, ed., *La Description de l'Egypte*, 24 vols (Paris, 1809-13)

Collections Egyptiennes de Cailliaud (Paris, 1827)

Kinglake, Alexander, *Eothen* (London, 1844)

Lane, Edward, *An account of the Manners and Customs of the Modern Egyptians*, 2 vols (London, 1844)

Description of Egypt, ed. Jason Thompson (Cairo, 2000)

Lane Poole, Stanley, *The Life of Edward William Lane* (London, 1877)

The Life of Sir Stratford Canning, 2 vols (London, 1888)

Leitch, John, ed., *Miscellaneous Works of the late Thomas Young*, Vol. III (London, 1855)

Lewis, McNaught, 'Henry Salt: his contribution to the collection of Egyptian Sculpture in the British Museum'. *Apollo* 108, October 1978

Linant de Bellefonds, M. A., *Account of a Journey into the Oasis of Upper Egypt* (London, 1822)

Loewe, M., *Diaries of Sir Moses Montefiore* (London, 1850)

Madden, Dr R. R., *Travels in Turkey, Egypt, Nubia, and Palestine in 1824-27*, 2 vols (London, 1829)

The Infirmities of Genius, 2 vols (London, 1833)

Egypt and Mohammed Ali, illustrative of the condition of his slaves and subjects (London, 1840)

Shrines and Sepulchres of Old and New World, 2 vols (London, 1851-52)

Madden, Dr T. M., *The Memoirs of Dr Richard Robert Madden* (London, 1891)

Madox, John, *Excursions in the Holy Land, Egypt, Nubia and Syria*, 2 vols (London, 1826)

Malek, Jaromir and Smith, Mark, 'Henry Salt's copies of drawings'. *Gottingen misczellen* 64, 1983

Marcellus (*see* Martin du Tyrac)

Martin du Tyrac, *Souvenirs de L'Orient* (Paris, 1840)

Mayes, Stanley, *The Great Belzoni* (London, 1959)

Menu von Minutoli, Baroness Wolfradine, *Recollections of Egypt*, 1820-21 (London, 1827)

Montefiore, Lady J., *Notes from a private Journal, 1836* (London, 1844)

de Montulé, Edouard, *Travels in Egypt during 1818 and 1819* (London, 1823)

Murray, Hon. Sir Charles Augustus, *A Short Memoir of Mohammed Ali, Founder of the Vice-Royalty of Egypt* (London, 1898)

Norden, Frederick, *Travels in Egypt and Nubia*, 2 vols (London, 1758)

Peacock, George, *Life of Thomas Young* (London, 1855)

Peacock, Captain George, *Handbook of Abyssinia* (London, 1867)

Pearce, Nathaniel, *Life and Adventures of Nathaniel Pearce, written by himself*. 2 vols (Ed. J. J. Halls) (London, 1831)

Phillips, Sir R., *New Voyages and Travels* (includes travels of Cailliaud and Lelorrain), (London, 1822 onwards)

Redding, Cyrus, *Past Celebrities I have known*, Vol. II (London, 1866)

Richardson, Dr R. R., *Travels along the Mediterranean and parts adjacent in company with the Earl of Belmore 1816-18*, 2 vols (London, 1822)

Ridley, Ronald, *Napoleon's Pro-Consul in Egypt; the Life and Times of Bernardino Drovetti* (London, 1998)

Rifaud, J.-J., *Voyages en Egypte 1805-27* (Paris, 1830)

Russell, Rev. Michael, *View of Ancient and Modern Egypt* (Edinburgh, 1837)

St John, James Augustus, *Egypt and Mohammed Ali,* 2 vols (London, 1834)

Salt, Henry, *Account of a Voyage to Abyssinia, and Travels into the Interior of that country in the years 1809 and 1810* (London, 1814)

    A Geometrical Survey of the City of Alexandria (London, 1809)

    'Antiquities of Egypt', *Quarterly Review*, vol. 10 (1817), 391

    'Belzoni's Operations and Discoveries in Egypt', *Quarterly Review*, vol. 24 (1821), 391

    Egypt, reprinted from the Supplement to the Encyclopedia Britannica, vol. iv, p. 38, with 5 illustrations (Edinburgh, 1819)

    Egypt, a descriptive poem with notes (Alexandria, 1824)

    Essay on Dr Young's and M. Champollion's Phonetic System of Hieroglyphs (London, 1825)

    'Greek Inscriptions copied by Mr Hyde in the Oasis', *Classical Journal,* xxiii, 1821, 156

    'Light's Travels in Egypt', *Quarterly Review,* vol. 19 (1819), 178

    Twenty-four Views taken in St Helena, the Cape, India, Ceylon, Abyssinia and Egypt, and Letterpress text to the Views (London, 1809 and 1822)

    Essai sur le Systeme des Hieroglyphes Phonetique du Dr Young et de M. Champollion le jeune, trans. L. Devere (Paris, 1827)

Saulnier, M. Fils, *Notice sur le Voyages de M. Lelorrain en Egypte, et Observations sur le Zodiaque Circulaire de Denderah* (Paris, 1822)

Sherer, Moyle, *Scenes and Impressions in Egypt and Italy* (London, 1824)

Sim, Katharine, *Jean Louis Burckhardt: a biography* (London, 1981)

Smith, J. T., *A Book for a Rainy Day* (London, 1845)

Thompson, Jason, *Sir Gardner Wilkinson and his circle* (Austin, Texas, 1992)

Tillet, Selwyn, *Egypt Itself: The Career of Robert Hay* (London, 1984)

Turner, William, *Journal of a Tour of the Levant,* 2 vols (London, 1820)

Valentia, George, *see* Annesley

Vyse, Howard W. H., *Operations carried on at the Pyramids of Gizeh in 1837 with an account of a voyage to Upper Egypt, etc.* (Appendices on Belzoni, Caviglia and Salt), London, 1840)

Waddington, Rev. G. and Hanbury, Rev. B., *Journal of a visit to some parts of Ethiopia* (London, 1822)

Walpole, Robert, *Works on Eastern travel* (London, 1817-20)

Webster, James, *Travels through the Crimea, Turkey and Egypt 1825-28*, 2 vols (London, 1830)

Wilkinson, John Gardner, *Materia Hieroglyphica* (privately printed, Malta, 1824-30)

Manners and Customs of the Ancient Egyptians, 3 vols (London, 1837)

A Handbook for Egypt (London, 1847)

On Colour and on the necessity for a general diffusion of taste among all classes (London, 1858)

Williamson, David (ed.), *Burke's Royal Families of the World*, Volume II, Africa and the Middle East (London, 1980)

Wilson, William Rae, *Travels in the Holy Land* (London, 1823)

Wolff, Rev. Joseph, *Life and Journals* (London, 1827)

Wood, Alfred C., *A History of the Levant Company* (Oxford, 1935)

Yates, William Holt, *The Modern History and Condition of Egypt,* 2 vols. (London, 1843)

Young, Dr Thomas, *An Account of some recent discoveries* (London, 1823)

JOURNALS

Bulletin of Faculty of Arts, Cairo, II, 1/1934

Bulletin de la Societé Archaeologique d'Alexadria, No. 16

Cornhill Magazine, June-December 1880, p. 39

Edinburgh Review, various volumes, and December 1826

European Magazine: 1796, Valentia; 1822, Belzoni

Fraser's Magazine IX, 1830, p. 629

Gentleman's Magazine, 1816, 1820, 1821, 1822, 1824, 1835, 1843

Literary Gazette, 1827

Malta Government Gazette, (1820-27)

Modern Review, 154, p. 329

Monthly Review, May-August 1821

Quarterly Review, 1818, 1821, 1822, 1824

Revue Archaeologique, series IV, vol. VII, 1906

Tait's Edinburgh Magazine, New series 5 p. 695

MANUSCRIPT SOURCES

Alnwick Castle: archives of the Dukes of Northumberland (Diary of Algernon Percy, Lord Prudhoe)

Bodleian Library, University of Oxford: Edward Lane, Correspondence with Robert Hay; J. G. Wilkinson archive

Bristol City Museum and Art Gallery: Sarah Belzoni papers; drawings of Tomb of Seti I, mainly by Alessandro Ricci

The British Library: Add Mss: G. Annesley; J. L. Burckhardt; W. Coffin; T. Galloway; R. Hay; J. Hyde; E. W. Lane; J. Madox; Renouard; H. Westcar

The British Museum: the Salt papers in the archives of the Department of Egyptian Antiquities; Central Archives holding Minutes of Trustees' General Meetings, and Trustees' Standing Committee Minutes

Cambridge University Library: J. L. Burckhardt papers

Castle Coole archive, County Fermanagh: correspondence about Lord Belmore's travels

Church Missionary Society archive, Birmingham University Library

Dorset Record Office, Dorchester: Correspondence of W. J. Bankes and H. Bankes

Family Record Centre, London: Consular records

Griffith Institute, Oxford: transcripts of diaries of Bonomi, Linant, Westcar

John Murray archive, London

Public Record Office: Much of the material related to Henry Salt's mission to Abyssinia and his political activities as Consul-General in Egypt is based on Foreign Office records under a number of files. We have mainly referred to: FO 1/1 (Abyssinia), FO 24 and FO 78 (Turkey)

Royal Society: certificates of election

University of Aberdeen: Robert Wilson papers

University College London: James Burton papers

Index

Straton, General Joseph, 137–8
Stuart, Richard, 53, 56
Subagadis, 28, 29, 169, 193, 256
Sublime Porte, 34, 38, 190–1, 193, 220,
    226, 239, 241, 250, 255, 260
Suleiman Pasha (see Seve)
Suez, 17, 20, 21, 25, 33, 34, 169

Taranta, mountain and pass of, 28, 48
Thebes, 83, 87, 90, 92, 95, 96, 110, 111,
    158, 159, 160, 163, 164, 165, 167, 173,
    200, 202, 216
Thomson, William, see Osman
Thurburn, Robert, 69, 230, 236, 267, 268,
    274
Tousso(u)n Pasha, 70, 251, 281
Townley Gallery, 99, 175
Turin Royal Museum, 244
Turner, William, 86
Tyndale, George Booth, 293
Tyrac, Martin de, see Marcellus

Valentia, Viscount (later Earl of
    Mountnorris), xii, xiii, 7–25, 26, 28, 29,
    32–41, 43, 46, 56, 57, 60–6, 154, 155,
    198, 277, 279, 281–2
Valentia Island, 19, 25
Valley of the Kings (Biban el Malook), 96,
    123, 133, 134, 153, 163, 165, 231

Venus de Milo, 290
Vyse, Col. Howard, 107, 284

Waddington, Rev. George, 81, 205, 292
Wadi Halfa, 94, 167, 168, 172
Wahabi, Wahabee, 20, 41, 72, 73, 84, 139
Walmas(s), Francis, 146, 181, 265–6
Weatherhead, Captain, 43, 54
Webster, James, 243–4
Welled Selasse see Ras
Wellesley, Marquess of, 13–16, 19, 21, 55,
    56
Wellington, Duke of, 67, 220
Westcar, Henry, 219, 221, 224, 229
Westmacott, Richard 206
Wiggett, James Samuel, 216
Wilkinson, John Gardner, 213, 215, 216–17,
    224, 227–8, 229, 231, 233, 234, 295
Wilson, Robert, 190
Wilson, William Rae, 167, 288
Wolff, Joseph, 218
Wyse, Thomas, 165, 167

Yanni, see d'Athanasi
Yorke, Hon. Charles, 42, 56, 62, 63, 64,
    177, 178, 180, 186, 187, 199, 207, 208,
    280
Young, Thomas, 65, 70, 106, 134, 214, 217,
    227, 295